# JOSH WHITE
## SOCIETY BLUES

# JOSH
# WHITE
# SOCIETY
# BLUES

. . . . . . . . . . . . . . . . . . . . . . . .

## ELIJAH WALD

University of

Massachusetts

Press

Amherst

Copyright © 2000 by Elijah Wald
All rights reserved
Printed in the United States of America
LC 00-055211
ISBN 1-55849-269-0
Designed by Richard Hendel
Set in New Baskerville & Smokler by
    Keystone Typesetting, Inc.
Printed and bound by Thomson-Shorc, Inc.

Library of Congress
Cataloging-in-Publication Data
Wald, Elijah.
Josh White : society blues / Elijah Wald.
    p. cm.
Includes bibliographical references and index.
ISBN 1-55849-269-0 (cloth : alk. paper)
1. White, Josh.    2. Blues musicians — United
States — Biography    I. Title.
ML420.W48 W35 2000
782.421643'092 — dc21        00-055211
[B]
British Library Cataloguing in Publication
data are available.

This book is published with the support and
cooperation of the University of Massachusetts
Boston.

*Frontispiece:* Josh White, c. 1944.
Courtesy of the White family.

*To*

JACK  LANDRON

*who made this work possible*

*and to the memory of*

CAROL  WHITE

*who made it a pleasure*

# CONTENTS

*Photographs follow page 140.*

# PREFACE

Josh White was one of my first heroes, but the Josh I knew when I started this book was only a shadow of the man. He died in 1969, when I was ten years old, and I never saw him stride onto the stage at Cafe Society or a packed concert hall. I had only the records, and good as they are, they were never his greatest work. Josh was first and foremost a live performer. He was a fine singer and a versatile and unique guitarist, but that was not what made him a star. He was, rather, a personality, a great entertainer, a self-directed theatrical creation. When he entered a room, every eye was on him. He had what would come to be called charisma, on- or offstage, and people who saw him in his heyday describe a magnetism and magic that will forever be elusive to those of us who know him only from the records, some photographs, and a few minutes of film.

Josh reinvented himself over and over, drastically at first, then subtly, keeping pace with the world around him as he grew from a poor boy leading blind street singers through the South into an international star, darling of the nightclubs and guest of presidents. He was a rich blend of contradictions: "the Singing Christian" and a sly blues singer, an unschooled folk artist and a slick cabaret performer, a powerful voice for social justice and the first black man to base his stage appeal on the seduction of white women.

I fell in love with Josh's music at an early age and was quickly made aware of the contradictory power of his persona. Every time I put on a Josh White record, my parents would get in an argument. They had seen him only once, in the 1950s, performing at the Boston Museum of Fine Arts. As soon as Josh's guitar introduction came out of our living room speakers, my father, who could not recognize any other instrumentalist, would say "Hey, that's Josh White!"

He would sit down to listen, revisiting a favorite experience, but would quickly become disappointed. "That sounds too slick," he would say. "Josh didn't sound like that when we heard him. Josh was a real blues singer. I remember him singing a chain-gang song, with the sweat pouring down his face."

At this point, my mother would chime in: "What are you talking about? He changed his silk shirt twice in the course of that show. And they were very fancy silk shirts."

"Oh, you're crazy," my father would say.

This argument, emblematic of Josh's success, must have been repeated in households across America and, later, around the world. Men would talk about him in the same breath with Leadbelly as a black folk archetype. Women would remember him as smooth and seductive, the sophisticated star who became the model for Harry Belafonte.

Although I never saw Josh perform, I have lived with his records all my life. My grandparents had his 78 albums, and I played them over and over, along with the Almanac Singers, Paul Robeson, and the Spanish Civil War songs of the International Brigades. Later, like other folk and blues fans of my generation, I gravitated toward more obscure figures: Skip James, Lightnin' Hopkins, the Reverend Gary Davis, and Mississippi John Hurt. They were, we all agreed, the real thing, whereas Josh was a smooth popularizer. I would still listen to his records on occasion, looking for songs I might use in my own performances, and I never ceased to admire his gorgeous guitar tone and the wit and humor of his vocals. But I thought of his work as blues for the white folks — pleasant, but not serious art.

My interest in Josh, and the germ of this book, began to grow when I made a trip south to interview and play music with older traditional singers. I was staying with Turner Foddrell, a blues singer who lived on the Virginia–North Carolina border, and I happened to ask whom he had listened to when he was growing up. Without hesitation, he answered, "Blind Boy Fuller and Josh White — they were the big stars around here."

I had known of Josh's first career, as a recording artist for the African American "race record" market of the 1930s, but these early sides rarely show up on reissue albums, and he is barely mentioned in most histories of the genre. It would never have occurred to me, or to any blues fan I knew, to mention him in the same breath with Blind Boy Fuller, a major star and key figure in later ragtime-blues. Yet a couple of months later, the same thing happened again. I was writing a piece on John Jackson, the best living performer in the old Piedmont style, and was transcribing two of his trademark songs. The first I knew to be a Fuller piece. The second, "Blood Red River," had become a blues standard, but I wondered where he had first heard it. His answer was Josh White.

As I looked into the history, I found that Josh had been a star in the southeastern race market before Fuller began recording, and Fuller had even copied a couple of Josh's records. I began hunting down the few reissues of Josh's work from the 1930s and was startled by their swinging energy. I was irritated, though, by the tone in which these records were discussed by most blues experts. Josh's first recordings are entertaining, with fast, bright guitar work and an engagingly youthful vocal style, and I could easily see how they would have captured the audience of their time, the teenage Turner Foddrells and John Jacksons. According to the blues books, though, they are to be celebrated for having a soul and energy that Josh lost later on, when he came to New York and started playing for white audiences.

To my ears, this is ridiculous. Josh reached his artistic peak in the 1940s, exactly the time when he was at the height of his career as a cabaret star. This music has a variety, a depth, and a uniqueness that were missing in his earlier work. It shows an artist with a mature style, whereas the Josh of the race records had been a callow, though engaging, youngster. It also shows a man who was carrying blues beyond previous boundaries, giving it a new social consciousness, mixing it with other styles, and bringing it to a new audience — blazing the trail for the blues and folk revivals of the 1960s. So why has his contribution been universally underplayed and his work consistently misjudged?

I became fascinated with that question, and with the larger story of Josh White and his times. Not a simple story, it can be seen in several ways. In one view, Josh is primarily a musician, the one artist who can be found at every stage of the evolution of traditional or folk blues as a professional style: a southern street performer when the streets were the only venue for the music, one of the early recording stars when records began to be marketed nationally to an African American market, a star of urban jazz clubs when blues was recognized as the roots of that genre, and a folk star in the boom years of the 1960s.

In another scenario, Josh was a key figure in the new wave of black artists, regardless of genre, who refused the stereotyped roles of earlier days. Where previous black performers, if they wanted to reach a wider public, had been forced to choose the character of grinning clown, quaint "plantation darky," brutish villain, or antiseptically dignified spiritual singer, Josh exemplified a new persona: the proud, suave, sexy, smart black man of the future. As a cabaret artist, an actor on Broadway and in Hollywood, and simply what is now called a celebrity, he blazed the trail for Harry Belafonte, Sidney Poitier, Nat "King" Cole, and Sam Cooke—not to mention modern figures such as Will "the Fresh Prince" Smith, who continue to present variations on Josh's distinctive blend of black cultural credibility with a smooth, white audience–friendly presentation.

Outside of show business, Josh's life was emblematic of a generation of African Americans who emigrated en masse from the South to the North and sought to assimilate into a culture that previously had had no place for them. It was a generation not only of black artists, poets, and intellectuals but also of doctors, lawyers, and small businessmen. They came first to Harlem or other urban black centers and then, with the victories of the civil rights movement, spread out into previously all-white suburbs. Like other immigrants, they sought to lose their accents and customs, sent their children to white private schools, and dreamed of an imminent future of complete equality.

There is also the story of the American Left in its golden age, with which Josh was intimately linked before abandoning it and in turn being abandoned by it during the bleakly polarized period of the Cold War. For ten years it was possible to be equally associated with Communist leaders and mainstream liberals, and Josh was courted and embraced by both, then saw his career collapse in the McCarthy era, never to recover completely. To some observers, this is just a pitiful, ugly detour; to others it is the stuff of high tragedy and the most compelling moment in his life.

A biography, if honestly written, cannot have the clean narrative flow of a novel. I had originally imagined Josh's story as moving through four distinct acts: his early days in the blues world, his period of stardom, the tragedy of the blacklist, and the redemptive era of the 1960s folk revival. To some extent it does fall into that pattern, but never as simply as I might have liked. There were ups and downs within each period, human foibles, and the accidents of surviving sources: what was captured on records, what was written down, which people were alive and willing to speak with me, and what they chose to say. Some viewpoints are unavoidably underrepresented; the high mortality rate of black males in this country is dismayingly evident when one tries to find witnesses to a black man's life, and few of Josh's buddies from outside the entertainment world were still around to be interviewed. Given what information I was able to accumulate over five years of searching — talking with everyone I could find who knew him, listening to his recordings and those of his contemporaries, hunting down film and television footage, reading through books, newspapers, and microfilm archives, and traveling around the United States and Britain — I have tried to shape as cohesive and readable a narrative as possible. But I have avoided the procrustean stretchings and choppings, the imaginative jumps and elisions that would have been necessary to make Josh the great fictional creation of my — and, I believe, his — dreams.

Even more than most performers, Josh was almost always "on." What happened onstage was only the teaser for the great performance that was his public life. Robert Shelton, his original biographer, wrote me that Josh had said at the outset of their collaboration not to trust his remembrances too closely, as he would often rather tell a good story than dry facts — and not only when he was speaking for publication. Josh would open up and talk with surprising frankness to people he had just met, giving his listener the sense that they shared a special bond. He had a gift for establishing a feeling of intimacy, whether onstage or talking one to one, and of exciting fierce loyalty even when a friendship was quite brief or casual.

Consequently, as I interviewed his friends and associates, I found that almost everyone remembers the Josh White they wanted. White men, even if they spent a great deal of time with him, saw him much as the white men in his audiences did: he was a hero, larger than life, surrounded by beautiful women and drinking whiskey (or was it vodka?) like water. Women remember him as devilishly charming and handsome but with a boyish vulnerability. Among the different stories that overlap and diverge, I have done my best to sort out the facts from the myths, but I have also included the myths, which are in their way at least equally illuminating.

Jack Landron (better known on the folk scene as Jackie Washington), whose enthusiasm for this project is the only reason it ever got off the ground, insists that the story of Josh the musician is almost incidental to the story of Josh the personality and the legend. "He was a great actor, and he kept finding new values in the one part that he played.

Josh's music had style, but that was secondary to the fact that the very fabric of his life, and every thread in that fabric, had been given serious consideration. He was a creation from start to finish. Even ordering breakfast: 'I'll have a half a dozen eggs, please [pause] . . . scrambled, I guess [pause] . . . and half a pound of bacon,' Just saying that, the way he did—every single thing had been thought out, and every single thing was a creation that was designed to do something. His walk, his clothes, that look of exasperation on his face when that guitar string would break, and then the laugh, with his head down, and then raising it as the laugh built. Every fucking minute of this man's life was a work of art. And there aren't too many living, breathing works of art. Josh was his own greatest work."

I hope some of that comes through in these pages, along with some glimpses behind the public mask. Josh had his weaknesses as well as strengths, and he was not always the grand creation that Landron remembers. Nonetheless, everyone who was close to him continues to speak of him with admiration, and frequently with love. This seems to me an extraordinary legacy for such a complex and unusual man, and an equally important part of his story.

For me, having come to Josh first as a fan of his music, his records give even more pleasure now that I know them so well, but they are only one part of what has become a much bigger picture. He was a fascinating figure whose life intersected several key periods of this century's history, and his influence can be traced not only in our modern perception of folk and blues music but in the generations of performers, both black and white, musical and nonmusical, who followed him. He was not an easy man to know or to love, but after five years of research I admire him more than ever and am convinced that my time could not have been better spent.

Perhaps the greatest pleasure of this project has been all the people I got to meet and speak with over the years of research, especially those who were close to Josh. First and foremost was Carol White, who welcomed me into her home many times with a graciousness and warmth that made every visit a joy, and who spoke with extraordinary openness and candor. It is impossible for me to imagine what this book could have been without her, and it is one of my great regrets that she is not here to see it. As the book was almost finished at the time of her death in 1998, it refers to her in the present tense throughout, and I have chosen not to change that. Josh White Jr. was equally welcoming and open, and I like to think that what began as a shared interest in this project has become a friendship. Beverly and Bunny White both invited me into their homes and shared their time unstintingly. Fern and Judith I met more rarely, but they were always ready to take my phone calls and answer prying questions, and I am eternally grateful. Every biographer's dream is a family that is open and helpful but never tries to exercise control over the finished book. I was extremely fortunate that the Whites chose to treat me with this degree of trust, and I hope they feel that I have respected and rewarded it.

I also received immeasurable assistance from Doug Yeager, who has for years acted not only as Josh Jr.'s manager but as guardian and helper to Josh's family and legacy. He was a constant source of encouragement and information, never too busy to answer yet another question or help in tracking down a source. Many other people opened their doors at the mention of Josh's name; his friends have long felt that he was unfairly overlooked, and the zeal with which they came to my assistance was a constant aid and pleasure. I owe special thanks to Rene Dannen Gordon, whose collection of letters from Josh made me feel, for the first time, as if I really had some idea of what he was like offstage. Both she and Devon McGovern Brenner treated me as a friend and answered my questions with often astonishing directness, despite the obvious invasion of their privacy, and I hope they are comfortable with the use I have made of their confidences. I had long and pleasant visits with Larry Adler, Oscar Brand, Lila Mae Brock, Beverly Chase, Charles Chilton, Liam and Paddy Clancy, Leonard de Paur, Marty Erlichman, Jack Fallon, Perry Fuller, Tom Glaser, Jon Hendricks, Bill Lee, Don and Sandra Luck, Ivor Mairants, Brownie McGhee, Josephine Premice, Chuck and Diane Ramsey, Susan Reed, Len Rosenfeld, Pete Seeger, and Stan Wilson. Given my limited budget, I could speak with many others only on the telephone, but I am equally grateful for the time and trouble they took, often again and again, to respond to my calls. I am particularly indebted to Katie Lee, who not only spoke with me at length but also provided invaluable tapes of Josh. Further thanks are due to Bernie Asbell, Enrico Banducci, Leon Bibb, Les Brown, Oscar Brown Jr., Jay Chase, Irwin Corey, Gideon Craig, Karl Dallas, Ray Flerlage, Sam Fuller, Milt Gabler, Bob Gibson, Manny Greenhill, Bess Lomax Hawes, Jac Holzman, Bill Kaman, Millard Lampell, Jo Mapes, Kelsey Marechal, Don McLean, Ed McCurdy, Michael Merepol, Vivienne Muhling, Bengt Olsen, Bob Shane, Richard Southern, Creed Taylor, Dave Van Ronk, and Jerry Waitz. Some of these people are no longer alive, but I have no inclination to find out which ones, so I thank them all and hope that they are well.

On any such project, one must be indebted to the work of dozens of previous researchers. I cannot cite all the writers whose work aided me here but must mention those who also gave personal assistance. First, of course, comes Robert Shelton, whose excellent biographical section in *The Josh White Song Book* provided the foundation for this work, whose lengthy interviews with Josh must be the basic source for anyone interested in Josh's life, and whose encouragement at the beginning of this project was very welcome. It is a rare writer who not only cheers on his followers but warns them of the problems in his own work, and Shelton's advice that I take Josh's quotations with a grain of salt was a wise word at the right time. Dorothy Siegel's research for her book, *The Glory Road,* was also helpful, and her willingness to respond to my further queries is appreciated. Ronald Cohen gave much valuable advice, provided firsthand source materials, did invaluable fact-checking, and put me in contact with many of the people whose reminiscences brought Josh to life for me. Israel Young's efforts to fill out the Swedish portion of Josh's life — finding news clippings and people who knew Josh, and translating page after page of material — were above and beyond the call of duty. Among other people whose help was invaluable are Mary Katherine Aldin, Alan Balfour, Scott Barretta, Matthew Barton, Ray Funk, James Gavin, Kip Lornell, Richard Markow, Stephan Michelson, Jeff Place, Dave Samuelson, and Mike Seeger.

Then there were all the institutions that provided research materials, and the employees who helped me make use of them. I spent weeks in the Harvard University libraries, the Boston Public Library, the Schomburg Center for Research in Black Culture, the Lincoln Center Library in New York, and the British Newspaper Library in London. I also found valuable material in the clippings files of the *Boston Globe* and the *San Francisco Chronicle*; in the Rutgers University Jazz Archive; in the Greenville, South Carolina, Public Library; and in recorded materials in the Schomburg Center, the Museum of Television and Radio in New York, and the BBC Archives in London.

Among those who helped me get a book written and published, I must first thank Jack Landron, who convinced me that this project was worth doing and introduced me to the White family, and whose comments throughout the process made the book what it is (whatever he may think of that). Peter Guralnick gave encouragement and introduced me to Richard P. McDonough, a marvelous agent who signed on to this project despite my relative lack of a track record and who stuck with it unwaveringly. Had he had less confidence, this book would not be here today. Michael Rockliffe was a strong advocate for the manuscript, and his encouragement was much appreciated. Ruth Hubbard, Peter Keane, and Jeff McLaughlin all were excellent readers, providing sharp criticism mixed with enough encouragement to keep me happy. I would like to thank everyone at the University of Massachusetts Press involved in seeing this project through to completion, including Paul Wright, Carol Betsch, and Bruce Wilcox, as well as Patricia Sterling, whose copyediting prevented much embarrassment.

ELIJAH WALD

*Somerville, Massachusetts*

# JOSH WHITE
## SOCIETY BLUES

**1**

■ ■ ■ ■ ■ ■ ■ ■ ■ ■ ■ ■ ■ ■ ■ ■ ■ ■ ■ ■ ■ ■

It is a long walk from the bright, tree-lined business district of Greenville, South Carolina, to the narrow lanes by the railroad track on the south side, and it feels like a trip to another world and time. While the downtown has blossomed and modernized, this neighborhood has remained unchanged, except for the inevitable wear and tear on the small wooden houses. Just as at the turn of the century, everyone living here is black, and a white stranger is regarded suspiciously by the inhabitants, who assume he can only be bringing trouble.

None of the people living on what is now called Dean Street remember Josh White, but it was here that he was born and spent his early years. In 1920 a federal census taker recorded him, age five, living with his mother, Lizzie White, four siblings, and two young cousins, Marie and Belmont Huff, in the house of his maternal grandparents, Boshel and Louise Humphrey. The Humphrey place, then number 302 Douglass Street, is much like other houses on the block. A few steps lead up to a front porch with room for a couple of chairs. The building is small, a decent home for a couple but cramped quarters for an extended family of ten.

Boshel Thomas Humphrey, was born around 1855, a slave of the Mauldins, a prominent Greenville family, and he and his wife had stayed on as servants in the Mauldin household. The Humphreys referred to the Mauldins as "their" white people, and the Mauldins supplied them not only with work but with a succession of houses. From Douglass they moved to a place on the corner of Jenkins and Batson Streets, in a nicer neighborhood near the "colored" high school, then to the two-story house next door on Batson. That is the house which Josh's surviving friends and family members recall and where much of the family lived until Boshel Humphrey's death in 1937.

"As long as grandpere lived, they didn't have to pay for nothing," says Josh's cousin Perry Fuller. "They didn't have to pay no rent and the Mauldins would bring them food. We'd go there and get just big bags of pecans and peanuts, 50 and 100 lb. bags, 'cause they had pecan groves and all that stuff. As long as the Mauldins lived and my granddaddy lived, they lived good."

Fuller's mother, another Humphrey daughter, had married and moved thirty miles down the road to Anderson, near the Georgia border. The Fullers would come in to visit the Humphreys every other weekend, and both Perry and his older brother Sam remember their grandfather with affection. Perry recalls that they all called him "Bobo" and that "he was considered the strongest man in Greenville County. He could pick me up just like dust." Sam spent hours listening to the old man's stories. "He was quite a colorful character. He was nine years old when Lincoln wrote the proclamation for the slaves, and he was like a houseboy for Mauldin there. He would tell me all about stump speakers, and about how when he was selling mules they would feed them soda and let them drink water to plump them out."

The Fullers also recall their Aunt Lizzie, known formally as Daisy Elizabeth, and her husband Dennis White. Sam describes him as a handsome, light-skinned man, nearly six feet tall, and recalls that he worked as a tailor. According to the Greenville City Directory, he was proprietor of the Peoples Pressing Club and had two brothers in the same business. It is not clear where they came from, but by 1907, when they are first listed, Dennis and Lizzie were already married, and the 1910 census found them living next door to the Humphreys at an earlier address on Dugan's Alley, with their first two children, Daniel and Le Roy.

A daughter, Minnie, was born later that year. Then, on February 11, 1914, came another son, who was baptized Joshua Daniel. Josh would later tell interviewers that his parents had named him after two biblical heroes, hoping that he would accomplish great things, but his middle name was probably at least in part a remembrance of a recently deceased brother, since Daniel White is never mentioned after the 1910 census listing. Josh was followed by three further siblings: Deborah in 1917, William in 1918, and a few years later the baby of the family, Boshel, known to everyone as B.P.

In the many interviews he gave after becoming a star, Josh rarely said much about his parents or his early childhood. When he did, his father's day-to-day profession was forgotten. If Dennis White made his living as a tailor, his avocation was preaching: he served as a Methodist minister at the nearby Allen Temple. Perry Fuller remembers him as a wonderful speaker, and Josh enjoyed telling of the power of his father's voice in the pulpit. In general, though, Josh's memories of his parents' religion tended to focus on its strictness. In the White household virtually all public entertainments were forbidden. Josh could go to the occasional ballgame, but movies and dances were out. The only acceptable drinks were buttermilk, milk, and water; the only acceptable music was spirituals; and the only acceptable social gathering was church. "We couldn't do anything at home for fear of the Lord," Josh recalled to his first biographer, Robert Shelton. "We weren't allowed to drink soda water, like orange soda, cherry, root beer. . . . At meal time — that was breakfast, dinner, and supper — there was a long prayer, everyone got on their knees, and my daddy would pray ten, fifteen minutes. Then you'd get up and read a Bible verse. You couldn't repeat a verse . . . you had to know your Bible.

"I remember the worst whipping I ever got in my life was coming home from school and I was in the sixth grade — that's as high as I went in school — we were shooting marbles. Like you stand and shoot your marble out and the guy next to you would shoot and try to hit your marble. . . . My mother saw us and told my daddy and Papa stripped me and gave me one of the worst whippings I've had, because that was sinful.

"The first time I ever took a puff of a cigarette (and got caught) my mama saw it again and slapped my face in front of my friends. My mother was a big woman and those slaps were not like slaps that you give your kids."

"I think you can be too religious," Josh added. "I know you can be too sinful, but at times you have to have some recreation." And he cited an old maxim: "Enough is enough, and too much stinks."

Still, despite the harsh discipline, there were also good memories. All the Whites sang, and Mrs. White would accompany them on the autoharp. This was not only for household amusement but included church performances and, on Christmas, an ambulatory concert through the streets. On a broadcast for the BBC, Josh told how Dennis White, along with the preaching and tailoring, did some light hauling with a wagon and a big steel-gray workhorse. On Christmas morning he would hitch up the horse, load the family into the wagon, and drive them around town to sing carols. "The first indication to most people in Greenville that Christmas had come was the sound of the whole White family singing their heads off beneath their windows," Josh said. "To my father, the serenading was just as important as the church services he held later. . . .

"We went from house to house and sometimes other families would join us and we'd end up with a whole choir. Our voices carried a long way in the clear, frosty night air and I guess it must have sounded pretty good, for some of the people we visited offered us gifts. Neither my father nor my mother would take them, but we children didn't mind, and by the time we got back home, we had quite a collection of chickens, cakes, hams, and turkeys. We didn't keep them long, though. My father saw to it that most of them were redistributed among the poorer families of Greenville."

It was a respectable and even, by the standards of the neighborhood, a rather middle-class upbringing. Although it is not clear how profitable the Pressing Club was, to have one's own business was a mark of distinction for a black man in Greenville. The Humphreys, as well, were part of the better set among the older black community, which, to a large extent, still maintained a hierarchy based on the slavery-time distinction between house and field workers. Josh would later describe his family as poor, but that was in retrospect. At the time, though far from wealthy, the Whites were doing nicely, with the children in school and hopes of a bright future for them.

It was a dangerous time, though, to be an upwardly mobile African American in western South Carolina. Like Mississippi, South Carolina had a black-majority population, and the white minority was ready to go to any lengths to keep it under tight control. This was especially true in the western part of the state. The old southern aristocracy centered in coastal Charleston, locked in a bitter political rivalry with the new industrialists who had opened tobacco- and cotton-processing plants to the west, had tried to cement their traditional power by reaching out to the small but potentially significant group of blacks who had passed the intentionally slanted voter registration requirements. The western magnates countered by stirring up poor whites, who were becoming ever more dependent on segregated factory jobs.

Western politicians pointed out the dangers of blacks moving into the factories, but their invective was by no means limited to bread-and-butter issues. They were out to stir up strong emotions, and their most inflammatory speeches centered on the defense of white homes, social structures, and family. The apex of demagoguery was reached by Coleman Livingston Blease, who was elected governor in 1910 and 1912 and U.S. senator in 1925. Blease fought to extend segregation, to defund black schools, to outlaw black social lodges, and to make miscegenation a federal crime, but he was most famous for his position on lynching, which he referred to as "the divine right of the Caucasian race to dispose of the offending blackamoor without benefit of jury." During his tenure as governor, Blease was asked at a southern governor's conference, not a notably radical setting, to moderate his views. His ringing reply was, "Whenever the Constitution of my State steps between me and the virtue of the white women of my state . . . then I say, to hell with the Constitution."

Blease was considered an extremist by many of his contemporaries, but his views were by no means unique. Benjamin "Pitchfork Ben" Tillman, a more moderate politician who was considered the grand old man of South Carolina populism, would speak of "black brutes . . . pulsating with desire to sate their passions upon white maidens and wives." This virulently racist style was probably most popular in rural areas, but Greenville was the capital of the western region and a leader in the institutionalized separation of the races. (It was among the first towns in the United States to pass a statute segregating residential districts, in 1912.) Josh would often tell of a "walking tax" that was levied on the town's black citizens simply for the right to walk through the streets. All in all, those years were probably the bleakest period for South Carolina blacks since the end of slavery. As the Reverend Gary Davis, a master guitarist who led a Greenville string band during the 1910s and early 1920s, once put it, "In South Carolina they hung colored people when they felt like it. In Georgia they staked them [i.e., burned them at the stake]."

The period after World War I brought further societal upheaval throughout the South. The war had exposed poor rural southerners, both black and white, to the outside world, but the refrain of "How Can You Keep Them Down on the Farm (After They've Seen Paree)?" had rather special meaning when applied to returning black soldiers. Times were changing, and poor whites felt their way of life threatened as old customs and agricultural systems were replaced by new ways and technologies. Meanwhile, their black neighbors were feeling a new sense of optimism as emerging leaders preached of a coming age of equality. The result was to escalate the intimidation designed to "keep them in their place."

The Whites and Humphreys were by no means agitators; indeed, their lives pretty much typified the behavior commended by the white conservatives. They were respectable servants living under the traditional mantle of white patronage. Nonetheless, it only took one wrong step to put Dennis White over the line of acceptability and to bring the comfortable life of the White family crashing down. Ironically, it was Dennis White's very respectability that led to his downfall. "My daddy was a learned man, educated, and I have never seen my father come to the table other than in a tie and collar," Josh recalled. "I never heard my mother address my father other than 'Mr. White,' or Papa address Mama other than 'Mrs. White.' And when people came into the house, men especially, they removed their hat—you respect the family."

One day, a white bill collector came to the Whites' house. "The man had his hat on, and Papa said to him: 'Would you please respect my house—remove your hat.' Well, the man had heard but he acted like he didn't hear. He had a wad of snuff in his mouth. We had no rug on the floor, but it was clean. Papa said: 'Would you respect my wife and children and remove your hat, please?' The man still didn't acknowledge it, and he spit. We had a fireplace in the living room to keep the place warm and he spit and he was standing on one side of the room—it was a small room—and he didn't quite make the fireplace and this wad of spit plopped on the floor. My daddy got the man—he was about six-foot-two, I would think—by the scruff of the neck and put him out the door."

In the context of the time and place, this was a step away from revolution. Although Dennis White had not gone so far as to strike the bill collector, by physically ejecting him he had committed an act that could not be allowed to stand as an example to other "uppity" blacks.

The collector went away furious, and a day or so later four policemen drove up and took Dennis White to jail.

There was no trial, very likely not even a charge, but the punishment was swift and brutal. "This matron comes down to my mama and says: 'If you want to see your rooster, you'd better come up to the jail and see him now, because he is crazy and he is going to be sent to the asylum,'" Josh remembered. "My mother and I went to the jail. We went in the door, which was gated, and there was a long corridor with cells in the back which you couldn't see. The chief of police was called Big Chief Noe. He was about 280 [pounds]. My mother and I couldn't get in the gate. The chief and another policeman hit my daddy back there, and my daddy, in going down, grabbed Noe and I saw my daddy beaten to a pulp."

The authorities made good their threat and sent Dennis White to an insane asylum, though Josh remembers his escaping at some point and coming to live with the family on Batson Street. "He never bothered anybody, but they thought my daddy was crazy so they came back and caught him and sent him back to the asylum," he recalled. Dennis White shows up twice more in the city directories, once living with Lizzie and the Humphreys on Wilkins Alley in 1926, then alone on Hammett Street in 1930, but there is no mention of him in the intervening or subsequent years, and one may assume he spent them in the asylum. Josh said that he finally died there. "I can remember the funeral parlor, brushing his hair, fixing his mustache just right and fixing his tie."

For Josh, the loss of his father was made even worse by the stigma of mental illness. His daughter Bunny says that she did not learn that Dennis White had been sent to an asylum until the late 1950s, and Josh never told the full story of his father's beating and incarceration until he spoke to Robert Shelton in the 1960s. (Even then, he introduced the tale by saying, "There might be repercussions, so I'd better swing around and tell you a bit of the story and not really tell you," though he gave no hint as to what this might mean.) In 1945 he had described his father as suffering from a heart condition that eventually led to hospitalization and gave this as the reason for Dennis White's disappearance from his home. The story of heart trouble may well have been true — it is supported by Josh's own medical history — but it also provided an acceptable cover story for a more complex and disturbing reality.

With her husband gone, Elizabeth White did her best to hold the family together. It was a formidable task. Le Roy, the oldest living son, was mildly retarded, though he would later hold down a job as a city employee. The other children, not yet even in their teens, were still attending school. Elizabeth White moved in with her parents, but even with the patronage of the Mauldin family it cannot have been easy for the Humphreys — both by then in their mid-sixties and already saddled with two of Josh's young cousins — to feed a grown daughter and seven grandchildren. Elizabeth White seems to have picked up some income by taking in laundry, but that can have made only a small difference in the family fortunes. Especially in comparison with their previous life, times were tough.

Fortunately, Elizabeth White was a strong and forceful woman. She worked hard, and prayed harder still. Even before her husband's incarceration she had shifted her allegiance from the old-line Methodist worship of Allen Temple to a "sanctified" or "holiness" denomination. The Methodist church "was hoity-toity," Josh said, explaining her move, "and that wasn't my mama."

The holiness churches, which had proliferated throughout the South since the turn of the century, tended to share a more democratic structure, a more local character, and more passionate and demonstrative forms of worship than the older, European-rooted churches. For Josh, the change brought a kind of liberation; his mother's religion remained as strict as it had always been regarding secular matters, but the sanctified worship allowed a degree of emotional expression that immediately appealed to him. "We got a different kind of feeling from your Methodist church," Josh said. "The difference in the singing — I liked the spirited quality of the sanctified church."

Mrs. White's denomination, which Josh remembered as the Church of God and the Saints of Christ, allowed a far wider range of music than the old-line churches. In traditional congregations, instruments were often banned or limited to the sedately European church stalwarts, the piano and organ. By contrast, many holiness denominations, both black and white, took seriously the biblical injunction to "make a joyful noise unto the Lord," and to "praise Him with the sound of the trumpet . . . with psaltery and harp . . . with stringed instruments and organs." It was not only a question of instrumentation; sanctified singers and musicians often mixed in elements of blues phrasing, ragtime piano, and hot guitar and horn parts, and adapted secular melodies. After all, the preachers would rhetorically ask, why should the devil have all the good tunes?

The holiness churches never accounted for more than a small percentage of black churchgoers, but their style of worship, and especially the rhythmic exuberance of their music, had a wide-ranging effect on African American religious culture. In the late 1920s, largely through the influence of Thomas A. Dorsey — a blues singer and pianist turned religious songwriter — their blend of secular and sacred music gave rise to a new form known as "gospel," which would become the defining style of the black church in the twentieth century.

The White family, with its singing tradition, was ready for this change. Perry Fuller, whose mother had joined what he remembers as the Church of God Holiness at about the same time as Lizzie White, says that a few years later, after Josh had learned to play guitar, the White children formed a singing quartet of Josh, Minnie, Deborah, and Bill: "We would go to visit their church, and they would come to our church over in Anderson, and they'd pit each [church's] quartet against the other and oh, what wonderful times we would have."

Fuller also provides a vignette that shows how closely secular and sanctified music could overlap, at least among the younger members of the family. He remembers the kids gathering around the piano while Marie Huff, who was seven years Josh's senior, pounded out ragtime dance tunes: "She would be playing that song about 'Coonjine, baby, coonjine / Coonjine, baby, coonjine / Mama don't 'low you to coonjine, papa don't 'low you to try / Get up in the morning, coonjine on the sly.' " Fuller sings quietly, bobbing his head in time to the bouncy melody. "And then Aunt Lizzie started coming in the room and they'd change around, start to singing [to the same tune]: 'Jesus loves me, this I know, 'cause the Bible tells me so.' "

With all the music around his home, it was natural for Josh to be interested when he saw a blind man with a guitar walking through the neighborhood. John Henry "Big Man" Arnold lived a few blocks west of the Humphreys' house, on Barnwell Street. In the Greenville directory for 1919 he is listed as a grocer, living with his daughter Willie Mae, a laundress, but by the following year the census found him unemployed. In fact, he had taken up a less formal trade: he had become a street musician, playing guitar and singing religious songs for whatever coins the local populace would throw him.

Josh was seven or eight years old when he met Arnold. "I was coming home from school, and there was a blind man trying to cross the street," he remembered. "So, I led him across. He had a guitar on his back. He asked me what my name was, I told him Joshua, so he says, 'I'd like to sing a song for you.' So he sang a song called 'Joshua Fought the Battle of Jericho and the Walls Came Tumbling Down.' He asked would I like to lead him after school, and I said to ask my mother. So we went down by the house and asked Mama, and Mama says 'I'll have to sleep over it.' So for about three days and three nights she slept over it and decided yes. So, after school, I would lead this man, . . . John Henry Arnold. He was about 265 pounds, and he was a *man,* too. He could take two bushels of grained corn and throw them over his shoulder either way. [He paid me] four dollars a week, and four dollars a week in those days was good money. That's how I started out playing — I wasn't playing guitar, I was beating a tambourine."

# HOMELESS AND HUNGRY BLUES
## 1921-1930

■ ■ ■ ■ ■ ■ ■ ■ ■ ■ ■ ■ ■ ■ ■ ■ ■ ■ ■ ■ ■ ■

Josh worked as lead boy for John Henry Arnold and other blind Greenville singers for most of the 1920s. Older members of the town's black community still remember him, a barefoot boy with a tambourine, standing on a downtown street corner and keeping time as the men sang gospel songs in their loud, rough voices. Already a show-off, he became something of an acrobat with his simple instrument. Perry Fuller remembers that "Josh could beat it all on his knee, on his elbow, or his head, and it was quite a show." Indeed, Fuller was so impressed that for a month or so he got himself a job with a blind singer in Anderson and tried to work up his own tambourine routine in emulation of his adventurous cousin.

The money Josh made was a great help to his family. Four dollars a week was more than many full-grown farm laborers were making. Though Elizabeth White said that she approved his employment because he was doing God's work, helping the blind and afflicted, and that she hoped it would prepare him for a future as a preacher, he also was now the family's main wage earner. Religious as she was, one cannot help thinking that it was the money more than her sense of charity that led her to consent when Arnold said that he wanted to take Josh with him on an extended road trip, traveling down to Florida to play for the wintering tourists.

He promised to send the boy's wages home regularly, and Josh was eager to go, but even if she had complete faith in Arnold's honesty and experience, she must have realized that it would not be an easy life for a child not yet in his teens.

Josh had no such worries. He was full of fantasies of escaping Greenville and seeing the world. "To a kid—well, it promised fun, adventure and no regular school, day in and day out," he remembered. "And I believed I'd soon be playing the guitar." Once on the way to Florida, however, he found that the reality was very different. "This fellow, so kind and soft-spoken in Greenville, was a hard taskmaster on the road. He had hired me to lead him, not to teach me any guitar-playing. Also, I had to go through the crowd as he sang, passing a tin cup. I hated that. I've always felt ashamed, even as a small boy, to see anyone in a position where he has to beg."

Along with the day-to-day grind of life on the road, and the loneliness of being far from home and family, there were more brutal lessons to be learned. Greenville had already taught Josh plenty about southern racism, but his travels with Arnold brought him into frequent, direct contact with the worst excesses of the society and supplied him with memories that stayed with him until he died. A small black boy traveling with a blind man was painfully vulnerable, and the world he had dreamed of seeing was often far from welcoming.

His most vivid and horrifying memory came from that first trip south and provided a story that he would tell over and over in later years. "In those days on highways there were no lights. Unless there were cars coming or you were near a city, it was black out. When it got to be dark, I'd lead Mr. Arnold over and we'd lie down, if it was dry in the fields, and go to sleep. If it was wet, we'd try to find a place under trees or keep on walking. This particular time, I saw something which I was never to forget in my life.

"I led Mr. Arnold over and we went to sleep, and I was awakened by a hand put over my mouth. It was like being smothered, but then I heard a voice in my ear. 'Joshua, what is it? Don't be afraid, this is Mr. Arnold.' Then he stopped holding my mouth. My ears became adjusted first and I heard sounds, and then my eyes got adjusted to what was around me and I saw where the noise was coming from. It might have been like across the street, there was a crowd of people stirring about and they had a bonfire.

"There were kids and adults. Drinking, a lot of drinking. Cider and white lightning. Then I saw this — there were two figures. They were stripped other than their shirts. Like on tiptoe. I don't think I could see them dangling, but what I could see and what I can't get out of my eyes: I saw kids, ten, twelve years old, girls and boys my age, mothers, fathers, aunts, adults. The kids had pokers and they'd get them red hot and jab them into the bodies' testicles . . . it was a hell of a thing to see. I came close to screaming but Mr. Arnold could sense, as I was telling him what was happening, when I might scream and he would put his hand over my mouth. It wasn't torture, it was just mutilation; they must have been dead. The people were laughing. . . .

"We were afraid to leave until they left. It was not quite dawn. They wouldn't wait till it got light for anyone to see what was happening. They vanished. It was a few miles from Waycross, Georgia. We were going there, but we turned back in the direction from which we came."

For Josh, the double lynching was a key event in his life, and he would often cite it as a source of the powerful anger that fueled both his singing and his attacks on American racism. Horrifying as it was, moreover, it was only one of several racist episodes that he would remember from his travels with Arnold.

In Jacksonville, Florida, he was arrested and thrown in jail. Like many of Josh's reminiscences, this story changed slightly with each telling: In one version, he and Arnold were both arrested for vagrancy; in another, he alone was held as a suspected runaway; in a third, he was walking past an orange stand and could not resist the temptation to reach out and take a piece of fruit. However it happened, the arrest itself was less traumatic than what went with it.

"As I went into the jail, a sergeant or captain or whatever, he was up three stair steps, with a little swinging door, and he said, 'Hey, nigger boy, come here,' " Josh remembered. "I'll tell you something: the majority of Negroes in the South were afraid of anybody in a blue suit or a uniform or with brass buttons. This man was in a uniform and he was white, anyhow, so I had to comply. So I went up the stair on my tiptoes, and I said, 'Yes, Sir.'

"He said, 'What the hell do you mean coming up here?'

" 'But you called me.'

"He had a wooden blackjack and he shoved it into my gut and I started puking, and he said, 'Nigger, clean it up.' I didn't have a handkerchief and I was trying to clean it up with my hands. The guy behind me tore off my shirt to clean it up with. So they threw me in jail for four days till they heard from my mother. . . . I was eight years old, and you think this doesn't hurt?

"Going further, I don't ever wear a hat and here's the reason: The same place, Jacksonville. We used to wear a thing called a skull cap, like a man's hat, only with the brim cut off. I was sent to the store by a woman who asked Mr. Arnold and he said yes. She wanted chewing tobacco and snuff. I know it is my place, as a Negro, you must go into the back of the store and say please — right? I go in and said, 'May I please have fifteen cents worth of chewing tobacco and some Blue Ribbon snuff?' All of a sudden I was hit on the back of the head and my cap went sailing, and, as I stepped to pick it up — you know what a drop kick is — that's how I was used. . . . I don't know how long I was unconscious. They did this because I didn't say 'Please, *sir,*' and I didn't take off my hat. My balls were swollen for four weeks from this thing. I hobbled back to the house. You couldn't tell adults anything in those days about your privates, this is taboo, so I'm going around swollen like a balloon, leading the blind man with one hand holding, and beating the tambourine."

These incidents that stood out in Josh's memory were only the worst moments of a life filled with lesser slights and indignities. Indeed, Josh would have few pleasant memories of his days on the road with Arnold or the other blind musicians with whom he traveled. "I never had the childhood I wanted," he would say. "Like having skates or a sled or what kids would have in those days. I never had a toy because I've worked all my life."

As for schooling, Josh got little more than what he could pick up on the road. "While we were in a city making money I would go to school until it slacked off, and then we'd move to another city. One, maybe two months. But every time you'd go to another city, you'd go back a grade until they found out what you knew, but by that time we'd be off again. That's why I had no schooling; sixth grade is nothing."

The blind men were generally fair to him, but they gave him no affection. Their lives were a steady grind of playing, making some money, and moving on to the next town, and they regarded him simply as a tool of their trade. At worst, they beat him; at best, they treated him with guarded decency. He would say that Arnold, at least, kept him fed and clothed, and on rare occasions even gave him a nickel for himself, but when he spoke of his days as a lead boy the word "mean" came up again and again. "All blind people are [hard]," he later explained, summing up his experiences. "That is, I haven't found one yet that wasn't. They can't see and they don't want to be taken advantage of, so they are inclined to be sensitive and a bit suspicious."

At eight or nine years old, Josh was entirely at the mercy of his employers, and they resented even the slightest deviation from the serious business of bringing in the tips. "It's hot and people see a kid walking with the blind men and they would say, 'Let me buy you an ice cream cone,'" he recalled. "[But] if I had had an ice cream cone, I'd have to suck it. The blind man would have his hand on your shoulder, and he could have felt it, and hit you 'cause you were stealing — if the man didn't buy you a cone he would have given you the money for the blind man."

The blind men's dependence on Josh made them vulnerable, and they monitored his every move. Arnold, in particular, had an uncanny ability to keep track of what was being thrown into the tambourine, judging the size of the coins by the sound they made as they hit. When he teamed up with other blind singers, this could lead to complicated and often crooked accounting. Arnold had no compunctions about taking advantage of his blind peers and would insist, when it came time to divide the day's takings, that Josh slip an extra share of coins off the top. "Wherever we stayed at night, John Henry would count his share of the money, and compare it to the amount from my pocket. If it added up to more than he had, as he took it from me, that was okay. But, if as much as a penny was missing he'd fly into a temper and beat me."

Some people might wonder why Josh put up with this treatment, not just on that first trip with Arnold but on dozens of subsequent journeys, but the answers are plain enough. "Why didn't I run away ever?" he asked rhetorically. "I didn't dare, then. I was little, and a long way from home. Besides, [my employer] did keep his word and each week sent my mother the money he'd promised her. I'd always known what it was to be poor, and even then I understood how badly money was needed with a sick father and other children to be cared for. My mother took in washing — but you don't get much for that kind of work, ever."

By contrast, Arnold made more money than Josh had dreamed possible. "People seemed to come out of the earth to hear him," Josh said. "A human magnet, that voice and guitar of his — neither very special — pried about $500 each week from fascinated audiences. I know, because I used to lead him to various banks where he kept his savings accounts."

It is extremely unlikely that Arnold earned anything like that much money on a regular basis, but he may have done so during an occasional lucky week. Florida, in particular, seems to have been good pickings, and Josh would recall wealthy patrons tossing astonishing contributions into his tambourine. Josh also remembered Arnold as owning two racehorses back in Greenville: "Dan Patch II, a pacer that made a mile in 2:51 — in those days that was running — [and] Willibelle, named after Willie Mae, his daughter, a trotter. Those two horses made money. While he was traveling his daughter ran the horses. This cat made a lot of loot." All in all, even allowing for exaggeration, Arnold's takings certainly exceeded the earnings of the respectable people Josh had known back home.

It is not clear just how much time Josh spent on the road, how many different singers he worked for, or how far he traveled. The names and dates ran together over the years as he told and retold his stories, and an incident ascribed to his time with Arnold might, in another telling, be attached to Joe Taggart, his other regular employer. At times he spoke of going as far west as Mississippi or mentioned passing through Kentucky and Tennessee, but with the exception of the lynching in Waycross and the arrest in Jacksonville, he was rarely specific as to his whereabouts. The one place distinctive enough to make an impression was Chicago, which he sometimes reported visiting as early as 1924. It was the first big city he had seen, and he naturally found it exciting, but he also discovered that the northern climate could be punishing for a street performer. "It was so cold," he would recall. "I'm beating the tambourine, knuckles were twice the size and they would crack and not bleed. The men wouldn't buy you stockings. I had to wrap my feet in newspapers, [inside] fireman's boots, hip boots. I couldn't wear gloves beating the tambourine. Sometimes I'd get the spirit and I'd beat so hard I'd break the head and have to beat the rim."

It was a hard life, but it provided Josh with a unique education, a wealth of experiences and knowledge he could never have picked up back home. The blind singers spent most of their time playing on city sidewalks, or picking up traveling money on the dirt streets of country towns, but they would take whatever opportunities came their way, and he got to see a wide range of humanity in the raw. Along with the religious numbers, many of his employers had a repertoire of secular tunes, the old reels and ragtime dances or the new blues, and they might get offered a few dollars to play at a dance or a house party. There were few formal establishments for black people in the rural South, but in every area there was someone who would pick up extra money by holding a party on Saturday night, hiring a musician, and selling homemade whiskey and barbecue. A traveling guitarist might also stop by the local barber shop, where men would gather to talk and play cards or dominoes, and pick up a few coins playing for them. Sometimes there was even a job playing for white patrons at a country supper or picnic, and the best musicians vied for this work and the better pay that came with it.

Mostly, though, the blind men played outside for whatever tips got thrown to them. "We called it canvassing," Josh said. "We'd go into a town like Chicago, and as long as the money was plentiful we'd stay around, and when it wasn't we'd branch off to, like, South Bend."

Josh often described the loneliness and deprivation of his life as a lead boy, but it was during this time that he learned the trade that would carry him around the world. "It was a life that no child should know," he would say. "Roaming the roads, never certain where I'd sleep, and almost always hungry. I heard plenty of bad talk, too, and at first I was too young to understand it. But the music — the songs and the guitar, somehow they made up for everything."

From a musical point of view, Josh could hardly have found himself in a more exciting place or time. The 1920s were a golden age for American music, and especially for the vernacular styles of the South. The region had always been a musical melting pot in which African rhythms, instruments, and vocal styles fused with those of Anglo-Irish immigrants. Now, the process was heated up by the new phonograph records that were being sold door to door. By the 1920s the recording boom had moved beyond the classical and New York pop fare that had largely monopolized its first decade, and records were being pressed for ethnic and niche markets. Of these, the African American or "race" market was the largest and by far the most influential. The commercial jazz-blues style, which had swept the nation in the 1910s with W. C. Handy's compositions, took off in the hands of the "blues queens," first uptown vaudevillians such as Mamie Smith and Alberta Hunter, then southern "tent show" singers such as Ma Rainey and Bessie Smith. By mid-decade they were joined by a host of male, largely rural performers, both "street-corner evangelists" in the style of Arnold and

Taggart and the secular guitarists, pianists, jug bands, and singers whose range of styles would all tend to be grouped under the loose rubric of blues.

Because of the debates about folk versus commercial music that came up in Josh's later career, it is worth pointing out that these were by no means pure folk artists in the sense of being carriers of an anonymous, nonprofessional tradition. Their music was the popular style of their time and place, and most of them were canny and blatantly commercial performers, carefully tailoring their acts to the tastes of their listeners. Their repertoire could range from older church hymns to gospel shouts, from ballads to minstrel ditties, blues, and the products of Tin Pan Alley. Songs could be as old as the early settlers and as new as the latest hit records.

For the street singers in particular, the blossoming of new styles can also be partly attributed to the arrival of cheap guitars, which had become available shortly before the turn of the century through mail-order catalogues. Light and portable, they provided more versatile accompaniment for a singer than the fiddles and banjos that had previously dominated southern rural music. By the time the first recordings were made of black country players, in the 1920s, several virtuoso guitar styles had developed. Players in Mississippi and Texas had learned to produce a voicelike sound by sliding a metal tube or glass bottleneck along the strings. Meanwhile, in the eastern states, the light classical techniques of white, middle-class "parlor" guitarists had been wedded to the complex rhythms of piano ragtime. The majority of street-corner players still tended just to strum chords behind their songs, but every region produced a few masters, and no other place could boast a higher level of guitar virtuosity than the area around Greenville.

These Greenville players were Josh's main instrumental influences. He told of leading anything from thirty to four dozen different musicians in his ten years in that trade, and of picking up new employers here and there during his travels or being hired out by Arnold to other singers, but he cited only eight by name, and all but two of these were based in Greenville. His main employer after Arnold was Joe Taggart, who in 1926 became the first street-corner evangelist to record. Both Arnold and Taggart, however, were quite rudimentary musicians and can have provided only the most basic foundation of Josh's style. Like many older singers they just "frammed," or strummed, rather than doing any picking. "Arnold had a powerful voice and you believed what he was singing, but he couldn't play worth a damn," Josh said. "He played about four chords and an open key. I think I learned the open key tuning from him, that's about it." As for Taggart, he had a strong and consistent rhythmic sense, but his records show him to have been among the least accomplished guitarists to find their way into a studio during that early era.

Other blind players around Greenville, though, were anything but frammers. Chief among them were the Walker brothers, Joe and Willie. Willie Walker was the region's outstanding guitarist and one of the greatest players of the era. He made only one record, but the two songs on it are among the gems of the southeastern, or Piedmont, ragtime-blues style. One is "Dupree Blues"—a traditional blues ballad with a smoothly loping approach—which Josh would adopt as a staple of his own repertoire, calling it "Betty and Dupree." The other, "South Carolina Rag," is among the crowning masterpieces of ragtime-blues guitar playing, with a swinging rhythm and the fastest, cleanest, single-string runs ever recorded in the genre. Good as these recordings are, by all reports they give only a hint of Walker's abilities. Gary Davis, whose ragtime guitar instrumentals were of a complexity unequaled by any other recorded player, attributed several of his best numbers to Walker, with whom he played in a Greenville string band around 1910. As for Josh, he considered Walker the greatest guitarist he had ever heard, "even better than Blind Blake" (the most popular blues guitarist in the Southeast), he told an English interviewer. "Blake was fast but Walker was like Art Tatum. They didn't teach that kind of guitar. I don't know where he got it from—he was born blind in the first place—but this man played so much guitar it wasn't even funny."

Josh mentioned only two other local artists by name: Columbus Williams, whom he remembered as a rather nondescript performer, and Archie Jackson, who doubled on fiddle but stood out in Josh's memory for his habit of playing guitar with metal finger picks he made from sardine cans. Josh seems to have led all of these Greenville-based performers regularly, though intermittently, through the years, getting to know them well. His other employers were men he briefly took up with on the road, and he forgot them as soon as they moved on unless, like Blind Blake or Blind Lemon Jefferson, they were famous stars.

Although he took these employers as his musical models, Josh said that they almost never gave him any direct instruction. In fact, most of them refused even to let him experiment with their instruments, for fear that, once he could play his own music, he would go off and leave them. As a result, he worked out his guitar style largely on his own. He would watch them play, then sneak off with a guitar after they had gone to sleep and try to duplicate what he had seen and heard. At first, as he laughingly explained, he learned it all wrong. He would hold the guitar at a slant and bring his left hand over the top of the neck, rather than reaching around and fretting the strings in a normal fashion. It was a clumsy technique, but having started out by making things difficult for himself, he said, his playing was all the stronger once he learned to hold the instrument correctly.

As usual with Josh's stories, this one is probably a bit of an improvement on what actually happened. It seems strange that a boy who was spending all his time surrounded by guitarists would not know how to hold a guitar, even if he did not yet know how to play one. Still, it is true that it can be awkward for a small child to hold a full-size guitar normally, and more comfortable to rest it flat and try to finger it overhand. It is also quite possible that he had seen lap-style "Hawaiian" slide players, who hold the guitar more or less as he described, and was trying to imitate them. Either way, it was a good story, and at parties Josh would sometimes back it up with a demonstration of the overhand technique, tuning his guitar to an open D chord (in what is often called "sebastopol" tuning) and playing his arrangement of "Careless Love" in this unorthodox style.

In another, even more doubtful story about his early training, Josh regularly claimed that although he picked up most of his guitar technique on his own (with a little help from Archie Jackson), the man who served as his mentor and who became his greatest early influence was Blind Lemon Jefferson. Some blues historians, including Robert Shelton, doubt whether Josh even met Jefferson, and his descriptions of their meeting certainly have a disconcerting way of shifting both time and place. Nonetheless, it would be surprising if they had not run into each other, though probably not until Josh was already quite an adept guitarist and had begun to strike out on his own. In the fall of 1928, Josh and Jefferson were both in Chicago, working for Paramount Records, and a year later both were in the Richmond, Indiana, studio of Gennett Records during the month of September, though their sessions were some three weeks apart.

Jefferson was the biggest male star in the blues world, the only rural guitarist who rivaled the blues queens, and it is easy to see why Josh might have exaggerated a relatively brief acquaintance with him into a long-term teacher-student relationship. He often talked of the hypnotic power of Jefferson's music: "He would sit all night long feeling bad and just continue singing and playing, improvising one song after another, and tears would stream from his eyes. And he'd get other people crying. Then sometimes he would be on another kick, you know, love . . . he'd just love women. Listening to him he'd make you think you were, well . . . this can't be written down but you know what I mean. That is, you couldn't understand what the hell he was singing but you didn't have to. . . .

"As far as a lot of guitar playing goes, Lemon did not play a hell of a lot of guitar. He'd take a note and make it do things, but for actual chord work, he didn't do it that way. He did more with rhythmic and single note patterns, as you can hear if you listen to his records. But it fitted well with his singing, and that was powerful."

Josh was clearly familiar with Jefferson's work, but however much time they spent together, the musical evidence suggests that he learned little if any guitar technique from the Texas master. His early playing was squarely in the mainstream Carolina style, a smooth, ragtime-oriented approach utterly unlike Jefferson's eerie moans and quirkily idiosyncratic rhythms. Josh's work resembles the blues recordings of Gary Davis and Pink Anderson, both of whom came from the region, and of Carl Martin, who grew up in Knoxville, Tennessee, but whose family had had a string band in nearby Spartanburg, South Carolina, and often played in Greenville. Although there is little reason to doubt that Josh met both Jefferson and Blind Blake, whom he also recalled leading, he unquestionably picked up most of his style back home.

However he acquired his skills, by age fourteen Josh had become an accomplished player. He was good enough that, when he traveled to Chicago in 1928 as lead boy to Joe Taggart, Taggart chose to use him as an accompanist on a recording date. The tightness of their recorded duets suggests that the two had been playing together for some time and Josh said that his employer willingly deferred to his superior abilities. "I managed to get on those recordings because I could play better guitar than Joe Taggart," he explained. "I'd been playing guitar then and he wanted me on his recording. I wanted to be in on the session too. And he didn't have to pay me anything, so that helped."

It is thanks to his partnership with Taggart that we have a record of Josh's formative years as a musician. The guitar evangelist (whose name is sometimes given as Joel rather than Joe) is first listed in the Greenville City Directory in 1923, and he may well have met Josh then. At that time, though, he was living with a wife, Annie, and his first record sessions, in 1926, have him accompanied by Emma or James Taggart, suggesting that he would not yet have needed to hire a lead boy from outside the family. It is not clear when he and Josh hooked up on a regular basis, but Josh would later describe him as an even worse boss than Arnold. Arnold, he said, was "mean, but honest mean," whereas Taggart was "lowdown, nasty mean." Unlike Arnold, who was totally blind, Taggart suffered from cataracts, which prevented him from seeing what was in front of his eyes but left him some peripheral vision — a fact Josh discovered when he found his employer rewriting one of his letters home, removing all complaints of ill-treatment.

Josh first recorded with Taggart in October 1928, cutting four sides that were released on the Paramount and Herwin labels. Three of the songs were old-fashioned spiritual numbers, with Taggart singing a strong, rather heavy lead and Josh's voice adding a more modern note as he chimed in on the repeated lines, his harmonies already more adventurous than Taggart's and his voice lighter and more supple. His guitar work sounds completely different from the older man's, following the vocal line rather than providing rhythmic backing.

It is on the fourth song, though, that Josh proves his mettle, taking the lead on both vocal and guitar for a bright, upbeat reading of the popular "Scandalous and a Shame." Though the record, when it was released, was credited to "Blind Joe Taggart and Joshua White," Taggart did little more than add a brief vocal response on the song's chorus; it is Josh's performance that makes it the standout recording of their partnership. His guitar, in the sebastopol tuning that he would continue to use for almost all his gospel work, rings out clear and smooth, and he sings with a grace and humor that Taggart lacked. This approach is perfectly suited to the song. Recorded the previous year by a Georgia preacher, the Reverend W. M. Mosely, as "Drinking Shine," it is a wry attack on "backsliding" church members. By extension, it is also a critique of the old-line denominations, which were lampooned as putting their religious efforts into churchly formalities rather than imbuing their congregations with the holy spirit. Josh sang the verses with obvious relish:

Well, the deacon's sitting in the deacon's chair, drinking all the
    whiskey and beer
And if you get at the deacon about it, well the deacon says he don't
    care

Do you call that religion? (Taggart replies: No, no)
Do you call that religion? (Josh and Taggart together cry: No, no)
Do you call that religion? (No, no)
It's scandalous and a shame . . .

You hear that preacher's preaching, he seem to preach mighty
    sweet
But the reason he don't believe in holiness, he want to court every
    woman he meet.

(Chorus as before)

Unlike most religious songs, "Scandalous and a Shame" has as much
comedy as admonition, and Josh sang it with his tongue at least partly
planted in his cheek. Indeed, the song's widespread popularity may
be ascribed to the fact that nonchurchgoers could join their sanctified counterparts in relishing its acid humor. Certainly, Josh would not
prove averse to drink and female companionship, and Taggart was
apparently no puritan either. Though he was best known as a religious
singer, Josh remembers him "mixing it up" and singing blues at house
parties, and he recorded at least one popular title under the pseudonym Blind Joe Amos.

"Scandalous and a Shame" seems to give Josh the distinction of
being the youngest recorded soloist in pre–World War II race music. It
also signaled the beginning of a new freedom for him. He had become
a better than average performer in his own right, and though he remained with Taggart for a while longer, his situation was no longer one
of complete servitude. His independence was further encouraged by
people at the record company. An unnamed Paramount employee
later recalled both Taggart and his young charge, who he said had been
brought to the company by the influential black talent scout and producer Mayo Williams. The Paramount man, who took an immediate
liking to Josh, was bothered by the fact that Taggart was not paying the
boy for the recording work and "horrified" to find that Josh had not
been able to attend school and seemed trapped in the life of a street-
corner vagabond.

"Josh loathed the idea of being forced to appear in clothing that was literally rags in order to get the sympathy of the public," he remembered. "I told Taggart to either let Josh go to school or send him back home, or I would report him to the authorities." Taggart promised to send Josh to school in the future, but the Paramount man felt that it was high time Josh got himself another guardian. He had little faith in Taggart, and was struck by Josh's pleasant demeanor. "As a young boy, Josh had impeccable manners," he said. "He was considerate at all times, and seemed to be congenitally nice and decent."

The Paramount man claimed to have encouraged Josh to leave Taggart's charge and even recalled arranging for the boy to stay at his mother's house, sharing a room with Blind Blake. If so, this living arrangement must have been very brief, for despite Blake's reputation and Josh's open admiration for his playing, Josh never mentioned the incident. In his recollection he was taken in by his cousin Marie Huff, who had married a man named Miles and moved to Chicago some time previously. She came upon him while he was playing with Taggart that winter and, after hearing how badly he was being treated, took him away from the blind man and gave him a place to live for the next few months.

By then, Josh had proved his abilities, and leaving Taggart did not mean that he was out of the music business. The Paramount man recalled that he became something of a regular around the company and "recorded frequently, with just about everybody." Just how much accompanying work Josh actually did is hard to say, but he was almost certainly the guitarist on a 1929 recording session in Richmond, Indiana, by the pianist and singer Charlie Spand. If so, he had attained an astonishing level of speed and technical mastery for a fifteen-year-old, but speed is often the hallmark of young players, and he performed a song from the Spand session, "Good Gal," on one of his first solo recordings three years later.

Josh's only fully identified appearance from this period was a month after the Spand date, when he was back in Richmond playing lead guitar on "Wang Wang Harmonica Blues" with a white hillbilly band called the Carver Boys. In light of his later career, it is interesting to note that this was one of only a handful of recorded collaborations between black and white country musicians in the 1920s and 1930s. Although such partnerships seem to have been more common in live performance (Mississippi John Hurt frequently backed the white fiddler W. T. Narmour at country dances, and there are many stories of older black artists, particularly fiddlers, sitting in with white bands at similar functions), the only other surviving recordings are of a couple of mixed string bands and occasional guest appearances by black players on the records of white blues singers such as Jimmie Rodgers and Jimmie Davis.

It is easy to see why the Carvers wanted Josh on their record. The other piece they recorded in Richmond, "Sisco Harmonica Blues," has a fine harmonica lead, but the guitar backing is pedestrian rhythm work. On "Wang Wang," by contrast, Josh provides tasteful bass runs and subtle riffs behind the harmonica, then demonstrates his bright, clean articulation on a carefully worked-out solo, which he plays twice in the course of the record. The playing is not typical of Josh's later work, but this was still three years before he would record a substantial solo repertoire, and it is not surprising that at fifteen he would have been experimenting with different styles.

Along with these side jobs, Josh continued to perform with Taggart and seems to have added harmony vocals on Taggart's records through late 1929. By then, though, Josh had proved that he could make it on his own, and he could congratulate himself that his days as a lead boy were over. "At the end of the summer he came to the Paramount office in a new suit," the Paramount man recalled. "He told me he had saved some money and was going home to his mother."

# 3

## THINGS ABOUT
## COMING MY WAY
## 1930-1936

■ ■ ■ ■ ■ ■ ■ ■ ■ ■ ■ ■ ■ ■ ■ ■ ■ ■ ■ ■ ■

Josh had finished his musical apprenticeship and was ready
to embark on a solo career, but he was still only in his mid-
teens and for the moment chose to return to Greenville. For
the first time, he relaxed into the more or less normal life of
a small-town teenager. He enrolled at Sterling High School,
a block from the Humphreys' house, though apparently his
classes were only at a sixth-grade level (Sterling seems to
have been the school for all older black students, regardless
of scholastic grade). He did not stay long enough to graduate, but several of the remaining black Greenville residents
in his age group remember him. His years on the road,
though they had interfered with his academic achievement,
had given him a degree of worldliness that was exotic and
impressive to kids whose own experience did not reach beyond the surrounding farms, and his musical abilities further increased his popularity.

Lila Mae Brock, who was a friend of Josh's at Sterling, says
that he was regarded by his schoolmates as a dashing and
romantic figure: "He told us, 'When you sit around right in
one spot in a place like Greenville, you don't know what's
really happening, until you start traveling and see so many
different things and different peoples. You'd be surprised
what all goes on in the world.' " Brock recalls that the best
stories were saved for when the girls were not around. "He

didn't tell too much to us ladies," she says. "I think he told more of that to the boys. You could always tell when he was telling something fascinating, because they would all be right around him and, boy, they would just be having a time. We'd know he must have been telling them some wild stories, but he wouldn't include us."

When it came to music, though, Josh welcomed attention from both sexes. Brock says that he played in all the church programs and at parties put on by the BTU, the Baptist Training Union. "We didn't have all these bars and things," she explains. "We hung out at the church, and that's the only way the boys and girls got to get themselves together. They had refreshments and they learned to dance and different things like that."

Josh would perform at the programs but was just as happy to play his guitar for a group of friends on a front porch. "He wasn't doing that blues and all," Brock says. "He was doing religious songs and love songs, soft stuff like 'Carolina Moon' and 'I Wish You Could.' We used to laugh and say we felt like he was singing it to us, and he said, 'If it make you feel good, I *am* singing it to you.' "

Of course, like any teenager, Josh involved himself in plenty of other things besides music. He was an avid football player, and Perry Fuller remembers that he briefly ended up in jail in Anderson because of a scuffle following a game between Sterling and Anderson's Reed Street High School. Sometime during his second year back home, he broke his right leg at the ankle and knee while playing football and ended up in the hospital. The leg was improperly set and had to be rebroken, and Josh was in bed or a wheelchair for several months. The experience had its amusing side, at least in retrospect. Josh's comment to Shelton on the hospital stay was, "The nurses took a liking to me at the time; I was big enough."

It was while he was laid up with the broken leg that opportunity knocked. Edward Arthur "Art" Satherley was one of the foremost A&R men for race and hillbilly music. An A&R, or Artists and Repertory, man was a bit like the modern producer. He would search out artists, put them together with material, and supervise the recording sessions. Many A&R men were in it just for the money, but Satherley, an Englishman, showed a sincere interest in the music he recorded. Decades later he was able to provide blues collectors with masters of unissued recordings he had preserved of such performers as the Atlanta bluesman Blind Willie McTell. Satherley had been employed by Paramount in the

1920s, working with Mayo Williams, and may have met Josh at that time. He left the company in 1929, however, and went to work for the Plaza Music Company, which almost immediately merged with two other small companies, the Cameo Record Corporation and the Pathé Phonograph and Radio Corporation, to form the American Record Corporation (ARC).

In October 1929 the stock market crashed, ushering in the Depression, and the economic hard times brought an end to the adventurous spirit of the early record business. Record companies could no longer afford to have scouts combing the South for new talent, and even major stars such as Bessie Smith saw their recording careers virtually disappear and were forced to scale down their big touring shows in favor of small-town vaudeville appearances. All the major blues labels drastically cut back production, and several, including Paramount, disappeared. ARC was the exception. A cut-rate company that sold its records in department stores for twenty-five cents each — one-third the price asked by the major labels — it had entered the field at just the right moment. It contracted with the dime-store chains to issue its product on house labels for each store: the same record would appear at S. H. Kress stores on the Romeo label, at McCrory stores on Oriole, and at other stores on Banner, Melotone, or Perfect.

ARC featured relatively slick, contemporary artists in a small-combo, pop-blues vein. This was a style that had swept the blues world in 1928, paralleling the rise of "crooners" on the white pop scene. Largely piano-based, it came halfway between the theatrical jazz-band approach of the blues queens and the stripped-down country sound of the street-corner guitarists. Thomas A. Dorsey, who was later known as the father of gospel music but at this time had a blues career as Georgia Tom, would ascribe the change to the fact that more African Americans were moving to the cities and holding parties in apartment buildings, and they needed a quieter blues style that would not disturb the neighbors. The new singers approximated a normal speaking voice, and favored clever lyrics set to simple, repetitive melodies over a regular piano rhythm fleshed out with guitar and the occasional harmonica or kazoo. The stars were Leroy Carr, king of the sophisticated blues ballad, and rowdy, double-entendre "hokum" singers like Tampa Red and Georgia Tom. The quirky, regional styles of the earlier guitarists and singers were replaced by a homogenized, urban sound, exemplified by the

Chicago studio musicians, including Tampa Red, Memphis Minnie, and Big Bill Broonzy, who became a virtual assembly line for blues hits.

For the record companies, this trend was a case of better safe than sorry. By relying on a few regular studio players and tried-and-true musical formulas, they could expect consistent, if generally unspectacular, sales. ARC was soon the top player in the field. In October 1930 it was bought by Consolidated Film Industries, which, in December 1931, added the Brunswick Record Corporation to its fold. Its stable of artists was unmatched, with the top-line Vocalion label releasing such stars as Carr and Tampa Red, and the dime-store brands producing cheaper substitutes by reliable journeymen like Broonzy.

The companies had cut back on their southern scouting trips, but Satherley and his partner, W. R. Calaway, alternated between New York and regular visits to Georgia, and it was probably on a journey between these points that they stopped over in Greenville. According to Josh, Calaway had recorded him in Chicago and had brought Satherley to Greenville to find him. It was late 1930 or early 1931, not a time when companies were inclined to take chances on new artists, but Josh was young, handsome, and talented and had been something of a favorite around Paramount's Chicago offices.

As Satherley remembered the meeting, "Josh was . . . very weak and thin. He was in this little wooden unpainted house by the side of the road. In the little fireplace were a few smoldering embers giving off very little heat. There was no spare wood. Josh was covered with a blanket and sitting in a chair. At that time he insisted that if he could record for American he would follow the advice of his mama and daddy and sing 'Christian' songs only. I asked Mr. Calaway to go to the store and get anything that Josh needed."

According to Josh, his mother's admonition to sing only religious songs was more than just advice. He had got out from under the thumbs of the blind men, but at home his mother was still the boss. Now, just as when he had met John Henry Arnold, she had the final say over his career decisions, and once again she consulted the Lord: "She prayed over it and the answer from upstairs said yes, but there was a clause in the answer that said 'providing he does nothing but spirituals.' "

The agreement was made, and a few months later ARC sent for Josh to come to New York. He went into the studio in April 1932 and recorded twenty songs in four sessions (he recalled recording twenty-eight songs, but that number seems to have included alternate takes), for which he remembered that his mother was paid $100. It was a lot of money and may have made up for her disappointment at finding her son less than obedient—for although Satherley would later say that the first songs were "Christian" numbers per Mrs. White's instructions, that was by no means the case. If the blues record business had been hurt by the Depression, recordings of guitar evangelists were doing even worse, and all twenty of Josh's first titles were in the blues vein. It has often been written that these first records were released under a pseudonym to keep his mother from finding out that he was singing secular music, but in fact Mrs. White did not have even that consolation. Later recordings would be made pseudonymously, but Josh's first seven releases all bore the name Joshua White.

If the descent into profane music was troubling to Josh, his recordings certainly do not give any hint of the fact. On his first solo sessions he sounds young, energetic, and supremely confident. At eighteen he was already a veteran performer, and his state of mind is evident in the lyrics to "Greenville Sheik," a bright and boastful ragtime-blues.

> The Greenville Kid's my name, folks I'm trying to introduce myself
>     to you (repeat)
> Says I'm all hot and bothered, I don't know what to do
>
> Say the Kid's not so hot and the Greenville Kid's not so cold
>     (repeat)
> He's caused so many girls to worry 'bout him deep down in their
>     soul
>
> I'm a young healthy kid, but it's my girl what's worrying me so
>     (repeat)
> I wouldn't be feeling so lowdown, but I can't see my girl no more
>
> Here I am in this big city and I'm doing the level best I can (repeat)
> If I keep on worrying about her, [I'll] act a fool, go back home
>     again

Presumably the song was written by Josh (the ARC recording card lists no author but assigns publishing credit to his co-mentor, W. R. Calaway), and he calls himself "the Greenville Kid" with the joking bravado of a western gunfighter. Other songs from the session reveal the same cocky sensibility. For example, "Little Brother Blues" is about his trusty knife and the mayhem he will wreak with it if anyone tries to mess with him or his woman ("Since I've sharpened Little Brother, got Little Brother by my side / When I find that thievin' rascal, Lord, I swear I'm gonna cut his lowdown hide"). Josh sings with a smooth, easy feel and often tosses in little vocal tricks. On the repeat line of his verses he sometimes replaces the last phrase with a soaring, falsetto yodel, and on a couple of tunes he scats over his instrumental part in a gruff, Louis Armstrong growl — probably a relic of his Chicago days, which coincided with Armstrong's first great triumphs as a bandleader and vocalist. Armstrong was the city's hottest black star, and one can imagine that imitations of his style would have been a big hit on street corners, especially coming from a perky teenager.

From ARC's point of view, the things that set Josh's style apart seem to have been less important than his willingness to submerge his own taste and go along with the company's program. As an eager young man just starting out on his own, he was ready to record whatever his producers wanted, and they used him at first as what we would now call a cover artist: his first two releases were versions of recent hits on Vocalion, ARC's more upscale race label. "Howling Wolf Blues," which came out with "Bad Depression Blues" on its flip side, had been recorded in 1930 by J. T. "Funny Paper" Smith (the Howling Wolf), while "Things About Coming My Way," which was backed by "So Sweet, So Sweet," had been recorded in 1931 by Tampa Red. Presumably, Josh's records, released on ARC's full range of dime-store labels, were a way of reaching customers who wanted the Vocalion hits but were not prepared to pay the full price.

Although the idea of producing covers runs counter to the stereotype of blues as a music of personal expression, such records were as common in the 1930s blues scene as in later pop and rock. The recording industry milked any hit for all it was worth, cutting sequels, imitations, and whatever else might be an effective spin-off. In Josh's case, the covers were clearly learned to order and possibly even sung from written lead sheets handed him in the studio. Unlike the songs he originated, which tended to have their own trademark guitar arrangements, the covers were played over what could be called his "default" blues guitar chart, a basic arrangement in the key of A. He used this for more than half the songs issued from his first sessions, and these seem to have been the so-called A sides of the records, the ones aimed at attracting buyers. Their flip sides, presumably drawn from Josh's regular repertoire, are far more interesting, their guitar parts more fully developed and generally set in the open, sebastopol tuning he favored.

Even taking these songs into consideration, though, the material recorded at Josh's first sessions probably reveals more about the contemporary blues market than about his own tastes and musicianship. Whereas five years earlier the record companies had been searching out and recording unique stylists such as Lemon Jefferson and Willie McTell, they now wanted more Leroy Carrs and Tampa Reds. Following a formulaic, pop approach that would maximize profits, they squeezed all their artists into a narrow, twelve-bar framework and discouraged any wider experimentation. Consequently, the recordings of blues artists of this period give only a very limited idea of what they would have been playing at live appearances. By 1932, Josh had a large religious repertoire, knew standard Greenville-area songs such as "Betty and Dupree," and probably had a sizable stock of pop and jazz numbers — including the "soft love songs" that Lila Mae Brock remembers, but none of these show up on his first records.

What does show up clearly is Josh's youthful energy. Almost twenty years younger than Big Bill Broonzy or "Funny Paper" Smith, eleven years younger than Tampa Red, he lacked the depth and solidity that they brought to their performances, but his bright, fluid sound with its yodels and growls has a good-natured excitement that is still infectious almost seventy years later. His singing is very much in the pop style of his day, showing Carr's strong influence, while his guitar lines are extremely fast and smooth, with single-string runs that recall the work of Willie Walker. His preference for sebastopol tuning, however, makes him unique among nonslide players. Blind Blake played occasional ragtime blues in that tuning, as would Blind Boy Fuller (though Fuller may have got the idea from Josh), but no other guitarist used it with anything like the frequency that Josh did, nor did they find in it anything like his range of styles and sounds.

One possible explanation is that Josh had spent his early years traveling with guitarists who used the tuning because it was easy or because they were playing slide, and he developed his style while trying to play more complicated licks on their guitars. The Texas player Blind Willie Johnson, the most famous and imitated of the guitar evangelists, played the majority of his numbers in sebastopol. If it is true that Josh first learned to play by bringing his left hand up over the neck of the guitar, he may have done so in emulation of slide players, and this would also explain the clean, slidelike vibrato that was to remain the most notable hallmark of his playing.

Be that as it may, Josh's style was both interesting enough to set him apart from the era's lesser artists and mainstream enough to support a career through the dark days of blues recording. Four records were released in 1932 and another six in 1933, not counting a couple of duplicate titles that were issued on Vocalion and Paramount under the pseudonyms Tippy Barton and Jimmy Walker. It is hard to say how well they did, as no regular tabulations of race record sales have been kept, but the fact that ARC consistently released more of his records each year for four years suggests that they were reliable sellers. For Josh's own financial affairs, the fact that he kept being invited back into the studio would have been more important than the record sales. Like most race artists, he recorded for a flat fee and received no royalties, except possibly on the handful of sides for which he received author credit (on most of his records no author is given, and all royalties presumably went to the publisher, usually W. R. Calaway).

Even without sales figures, the popularity of Josh's recordings is reflected in their effect on other players. Bruce Bastin, in *Red River Blues*, his landmark book on southeastern blues styles, cites their influence on Buddy Moss and Blind Boy Fuller, who were, along with Josh, the region's most popular recording stars of the 1930s. Bastin writes that another guitarist from Fuller's hometown of Durham, North Carolina, remembered Fuller sitting by the phonograph, playing Josh's "Low Cotton" over and over until he had learned it by heart. Fuller also recorded a nearly exact cover of Josh's "So Sweet, So Sweet," and he was by no means Josh's only imitator. Forty years later the Virginia bluesman John Jackson would record "Blood Red River" in a version so close to Josh's recording (the flip side of "Low Cotton") that he even duplicated Josh's mistakes.

Josh recorded both "Low Cotton" and "Blood Red River" (a song he apparently learned from Joe Walker) at his first sessions, but ARC rejected those versions; the issued recordings were done at his next studio date, in August 1933. This session was also notable for including Josh's first religious pairing, "Jesus Gonna Make Up My Dying Bed" and "Motherless Children," both drawn from Blind Willie Johnson's repertoire. Apparently, this first religious release sold well, for when Josh returned to the studio in November he recorded eight religious songs, and his next two releases were gospel pairings.

In the light of Josh's later career on the folk scene, these first religious recordings are even more interesting than their blues counterparts. With only a handful of exceptions he dropped his early blues hits from his "folk" repertoire, but many of the gospel numbers remained staples of his stage act until his death. From an older and deeper tradition, they had an enduring quality that the trendy pop-blues songs lacked. More important, it was in his gospel work that he formed the basis of what would come to be his trademark guitar style. He generally sang his blues pieces over solid but relatively unimaginative arrangements, but on his religious pieces he used the guitar to parallel and answer his vocal lines, giving full rein to the vibrato and warm, singing tone that made his playing unique.

Josh was by no means the only player who found sacred material a spur to his musical creativity. Whereas the blues form was harmonically and melodically limited and repetitive (albeit capable of infinite, subtle variations), African American religious music had adapted the more complex harmonies and song forms of the European church tradition and was beginning to receive further input from the mainstream pop world. It is no accident that Blind Willie Johnson became the most harmonically advanced slide player of his era, far outdistancing his blues counterparts, or that the Reverend Gary Davis regularly introduced chords and harmonies into his music that would have been outside the reach of even such a technically adept contemporary as Blind Blake. The church music, developed for group singing and keyboard accompaniment, simply made greater musical demands and, in Josh's case, provided an education that would in later years help him adapt his style to jazz, pop, and European folk melodies.

That was all in the future, though. For the time being, Josh was getting used to a new life. He had established himself as a reliable record-seller, becoming the only artist in the race market to maintain equally strong careers in both blues and gospel. He had also found a new home, for although his records were sold mostly in the Carolinas and neighboring states, he would never again return to the South for anything but fleeting visits. Josh had seen enough of rural poverty and racist abuse. New York was fast establishing itself as the center of black America, and he was ready to take advantage of all it had to offer.

Josh was far from alone in his migration. Since World War I, black southerners had been moving north in unprecedented numbers. In the 1920s, black South Carolinians had still tended to relocate to other southern states when they first left home, but by the 1930s they were heading to northern industrial centers. Washington, D.C., and Philadelphia were both popular, but New York was the destination of choice. Just as African Americans from Mississippi and Louisiana gravitated to Chicago and Detroit, those in the Carolinas set their sights on Harlem. They were looking for work but also, and more important, for freedom from Jim Crow laws, lynchings, and the constant pressures of the southern caste system.

New York was no paradise. Although cultural historians often praise the artistic flowering of the 1920s Harlem Renaissance, Langston Hughes pointed out that most blacks, even in New York, had not heard of the movement, "and if they had, it hadn't raised their wages any." By the time Josh arrived, the Depression had hit hard, making life still more difficult. In 1933, a WPA study found that nearly half the black families in Harlem were on the meager federal relief assistance, crowded together in tenements and living in dire poverty.

Still, for a young, single black man, New York was full of promise. It was a place where blacks could vote, sit on juries, and hope for some measure of justice even in disputes with whites. It was also a place where a successful African American was not just a former house servant living on white patronage, or the proprietor of a hand laundry. Harlem had black businesspeople, doctors, lawyers, and a thriving community of successful entertainers. Even had Josh not been a musician, he would have been likely to end up there. His journey was typical of his generation — most of his Greenville siblings and cousins joined the migration north in search of a better life — and his music reflected the aspirations and interests of his peers. In New York he could provide a taste of home for the large population of relocated southerners and, at the same time, expand his musical horizons by listening to the hundreds of sophisticated musicians who packed the Harlem clubs and house parties.

Indeed, black New York in the 1930s was uniquely hospitable for musicians. With a recording company providing him prestige and frequent, if somewhat irregular, employment, Josh was in just the right place and time. The Depression, devastating as it was, had only sharpened the community's need for entertainment, and the high rents (often amounting to half a family's monthly income) led to thousands of unofficial "rent parties." Sometimes more elegantly denominated "parlor socials," these parties provided work for a generation of pianists, guitarists, and singers, both jazzmen like the "Harlem stride" piano masters Willie "the Lion" Smith and James P. Johnson and the newly arrived southern blues artists. Roi Ottley, the black social historian whose *New World A-Coming* helped define a new African American sensibility in the early 1940s, describes the parties with obvious nostalgia:

> Usually admission . . . was fifteen cents. What was spent once inside was another matter. A small bare room with a red glow for light served as the "ball-room," where the strenuous business of rug-cuttin' was performed. The only furniture was a piano from which a "box-beater" extracted close harmonies and "jump rhythms," or "gut-bucket," which is now called boogie-woogie. In the kitchen pots of chitterlings and pigs' feet stood ready for the hungry revelers. A jug of corn was a staple for such affairs, sold at a makeshift bar in the hallway in half-of-a-half-pint portions—called "shorties." Then there would be goings-on until daybreak, and rent next day for the landlord.

Josh, with his bright energy and humor, was a natural for this circuit. His recordings would make him something of a special draw, and soon a stroke of luck further increased his reputation. At one of his recording sessions he happened to catch the ear of Julian Street Jr., a white, well-to-do music fan who served as a talent scout for NBC radio and had come to hear another group. Through Street, he got a regular job appearing on *Harlem Fantasy,* an all-black radio show featuring a popular New Jersey singing group, the Southernaires. Josh both sang his own songs and acted as the group's guitarist. The show was broadcast every Saturday on WEAF, one of NBC's two local stations, and Josh was on it for some nine weeks, getting a weekly salary of $84 (another account says nine months at $40 a show). He also played for weekend parties at Street's home. "He'd entertain us after dinner," Street later said. "Y'know, he had some *marvelous* songs that he'd made. He was so prolific, so creative, so gifted . . . One night he sang a song that he'd written for his grandfather's funeral . . . one of the most moving things I've ever heard . . . and he was *always* composing new songs."

Since the only grandfather Josh seems to have known was Boshel Humphrey, who lived until 1937, it is probable that Street was misremembering; the song was more likely written for Josh's father's funeral. The last evidence that Dennis White was alive is an entry in the

Greenville City Directory for 1930 and if Josh went south for the funeral, as he said, it must have been around this time. Either way, Josh had found in Street a useful patron, and he had begun to make inroads both into the New York entertainment world and into the white, liberal society that would provide his most faithful and appreciative audience in later years.

Only one more thing was needed to complete Josh's assimilation as a New Yorker. In 1933 he made the acquaintance of a young woman named Carol Carr. Carol's parents had moved to New York from Charlottesville, Virginia, but she had been born and raised in the city and carried no trace of the South in her speech or attitude. The Carrs lived on East 136th Street, in the Mott Haven area of the Bronx, and Carol's mother was friends with a woman named Mrs. Payton. The Paytons were from Greenville and had a son named Walter, who was a friend of Carol's. When Mrs. Payton took to speaking of another young man as her "son" as well, Carol assumed that he was just that, though she had never happened to encounter him.

As Carol tells the story, the fateful meeting happened after Mrs. Payton asked her mother if Carol could sing at a church affair. "My mother said yes. Then [Mrs. Payton] and Josh come over to visit. I had come downstairs to go to the store, and I saw her son and Josh standing across the street. Her son called me, and I walked over there and Josh said, 'Oh, is this the little chick you were telling me about?'

"Well, I was very insulted. How dare he refer to me as a chick? So right off the bat I didn't like him. Also, I realized that he was terribly handsome, and handsome men can be very dangerous. However, I knew how to be nice. I was on my way to the store, and he just stood there and I knew that he never took his eyes off me. You know how you know someone's looking at you? So when I came back, I said to my mother, 'I just saw this lady's son downstairs and he was with some fella, very good-looking. It's probably the one that Mrs. Payton was telling us about.'

"I believe it must have been the next night, on the weekend, they were going to have this affair at this lady's church in Harlem. We went and Josh sang; I think the song was 'Well, Well, Well [Jesus Gonna Make Up My Dying Bed].' Of course, at the time you were always told, 'Now, be careful of boys.' This was the 'be careful of boys' era, and if I had not been in church and if he had not been in church, it would have been all over. I would not have known him at all. He sang, and my mother said, 'What a lovely boy — such a clean-cut, lovely young man.' And I said 'Uh-ohhh.'

"So he later asked my mother could he come to visit. Now really, I thought he had some nerve. I didn't want to know him. I *thought*. And [Mrs. Payton] was great. She felt very badly, because she said to my mother, 'Don't let him come to your house, don't ever . . .' Now, up to this point, oh God, she bragged about Josh like you would talk about Princess Di, but then after once she heard my mother say, 'Why yes, you can come over,' she said, 'Oh, no, don't let him come.' However, my mother thought, 'How wrong can it be? Here's a nice young man in the church. He's got to be all right.' So he began to come over, and the rest is history."

Carol had good reason to worry. Josh was bright, handsome, and in a business that gave him plenty of opportunities to meet pretty women. According to her recollection, W. R. Calaway was working not only as Josh's producer but also as his agent, and Josh was playing at parties for "lots of very big people." The sex appeal that would become legendary in later years was already in full force, and as she got to know him better, she found that he was leading a complex romantic life. "He apparently was going with a very beautiful young girl and at the same time, I think, an older woman. Then there was a very high official of CBS, he had a home somewhere in Jersey, and he wanted Josh to come there. He had a daughter that also was looking at Josh."

Carol was smitten, but she had no interest in becoming one more addition to Josh's unofficial harem. She decided to put him to the test and see whether their budding relationship was going to be something more serious than his previous affairs. Her opportunity came when he said that the CBS official had asked him to come and play at a dinner party. With the daughter in mind, she decided to put her foot down and make a stand. "I said 'Well, if you go, don't come back here anymore.' Just sort of exercising to see if I had that much authority. And when he did not go, I thought 'OK, Carol, you are in trouble now.'"

Josh might have been young and wild, but he clearly knew the real thing when he found it. Carol was someone who would stick with him through thick and thin, who loved him deeply but was also prepared to understand the complexities of being a musician's wife. A native New Yorker with a warm, supportive family, she could provide him with a solid foundation in the urban world in which he was making his new life, and a stability he had not known since his father's arrest. Also, though he was just turning twenty, Josh had been on his own long enough to consider himself a worldly and experienced adult, ready to have a family of his own. Soon the arrangements were made, and Josh and Carol were married by the Reverend George A. Taylor on her birthday, December 23, 1934, at Epworth Methodist Episcopal Church in the Bronx.

The marriage tied Josh even more closely to New York. During his first years in the city he had continued to travel quite a bit, following the routes he had learned in his days with the blind men. Jon Hendricks, later to become a well-known jazz songwriter and singer, remembers that when he was growing up in Kenton, Ohio, in the early 1930s, Josh had somehow become friends with his parents and used to come by occasionally, hoboing on the freight trains, and stay a few days with them. Hendricks says that, as far as he knew, Josh did not play professionally in Kenton, and no one seems to have a clear idea of just where or how he was performing. He was probably picking up odd gigs wherever they presented themselves, "pulling doors" in neighborhood taverns, entertaining at rent parties, and playing on the street when nothing else turned up.

Josh's travels occasionally took him to Greenville, but a visit he made shortly after meeting Carol reminded him of why he had left. As he told the story, he had been called home to attend the funeral of an aunt and took a train down from New York. Almost immediately upon arrival he was pulled in by the police for failure to present a certificate proving that he had paid the so-called walking tax. Josh paid the tax, but that was only the beginning of his problems. On the weekend he got in a fight at a football game, during which he hit a plainclothes policeman. The police, noting that his hands were soft and uncalloused, concluded that he was an undesirable and threw him in a jail cell with three murderers.

Fortunately, Josh's cellmates turned out to be fans of his records. Old hands at local prison procedure, they warned him that the police would soon be back to rough him up and told him to climb into the upper bunk. A few minutes later, when three guards appeared carrying rubber hoses, the convicts lined up in front of the beds and announced: "We're going to die anyway. You're not going to touch the Singing Christian." Meanwhile, Josh's family had contacted "their white people," the Mauldins, who promptly saw to it that he was released.

If there had been any doubt in Josh's mind, this incident affirmed his decision that home was now New York. His marriage came as the culmination of a year in which his professional life had gone exceptionally well. ARC had released nine of his records, and he was shaking off the last of his remaining "country" mannerisms. A religious number recorded in March, "You Sinner You," put his Louis Armstrong impression to extended and surprising use, adapting the jazzman's "You Rascal You" to the gospel market while keeping its wry humor and hip phrasing. At the same session he did his first work in the popular piano-guitar duet format, recording "Welfare Blues" accompanied by his cousin Marie Huff Miles. While Josh's guitar part still relied on his basic A licks, the piano freed him up to do some more adventurous soloing and brought him closer to the sound to which he had long aspired, the streamlined, modern style of Leroy Carr and Scrapper Blackwell.

Carr, born in 1905, played piano and had become the defining blues crooner. Blackwell, two years his senior, was the blues lead guitarist par excellence (rivaled only by the New Orleans jazzman Lonnie Johnson). The two had teamed up in Indianapolis, and starting with their first record, 1928's "How Long—How Long Blues," they pioneered a new approach to blues: they were more understated and quiet than the blues queens and more smooth and professional than the rural players. Carr wrote intelligent, carefully crafted songs and delivered them with a clear, precise diction and cool, almost conversational phrasing that would remain the mainstream blues vocal style for the next two decades.

Like most male singers of his generation, Josh had taken Carr as a model, and in 1934 he made the acquaintance of the duo while they were on a recording trip to New York. He apparently met them through Clarence Williams, a jazz pianist, songwriter, and entrepreneur who was one of New York's few black A&R men. Williams worked with everyone from country blues singers to Louis Armstrong and Bessie Smith and was known as a brilliant hustler with his finger in multiple pies—among them the *Harlem Fantasy* radio show. Early in 1934 he seems to have taken over as Josh's manager for about a year, as Calaway temporarily disappears from Josh's ARC recording logs; on almost all the songs Josh recorded then, Williams is listed as either composer or publisher.

Williams was also working with Carr and Blackwell, and it was undoubtedly due to his influence that they let Josh sit in and show his stuff at their studio session on August 13, 1934. Josh sang four numbers with

Carr on piano and either himself or Blackwell on guitar (the aural evidence suggests that they alternated). Two were Carr's compositions, two Josh's, and although Josh's voice did not have the depth and control of Carr's, they are all creditable examples of the blues ballad style. To have the two stars backing him must have been quite a thrill, and Josh's guitar work suggests that hanging around with Blackwell was doing him a lot of good. Carr and Blackwell also seem to have enjoyed the session, for they brought Josh back into the studio in December to play second guitar on a dozen of their songs, the only time they ever used an additional guitarist on their records.

In a twist that would confuse some fans, Josh's records with Carr and Blackwell were released as by "Pinewood Tom and his Blues Hounds." The Pinewood Tom pseudonym had been adopted for Josh's first releases of 1934, and he continued to use it for all his blues performances until he stopped working for ARC two years later. It is unusual for an artist to change his name in midcareer, and Josh's usual explanation that he did it to protect his mother from the knowledge that he was singing "reels" makes little sense, since he had already released seven blues records under his own name and could hardly have kept them secret. The real explanation seems to be that he now had two careers, and they had to be kept separate. His last three records of 1933 had all been religious pairings released under the name Joshua White (the Singing Christian) and advertising him as "the Sensation of the South," who "sings Christian songs for the colored people." These sold quite well, making the name change necessary to avoid uncomfortable mixups: imagine the distress of a sanctified churchgoer who ordered the new Joshua White record and got "High Brown Cheater," backed with "Baby Won't You Doodle-Doo-Doo."

The change had no effect on Josh's popularity as a blues artist. Of the dozen records he released in 1935, all but two were blues pairings. The first, with Clarence Williams on piano, was a two-sided cover of recent hits, "Black Gal" and "Milk Cow Blues." (According to White family legend, this record caused a minor racial uproar when African American workers at the shipping plant refused to handle it, objecting to the use of the then derogatory term "black.") "Milk Cow" was the debut hit by Kokomo Arnold, who would become one of the era's top stars. Despite his nickname, Arnold was from Georgia and had a rougher, more countrified sound than most 1930s bluesmen. He was a dazzling slide guitarist, and his singing was marked by a distinctive falsetto howl that was instantly copied by younger singers, including Josh and his Mississippi contemporary Robert Johnson. "Milk Cow Blues" was Arnold's most popular song (twenty years later Elvis Presley would cover it as his third single), and he recorded four sequels; Josh joined in the gold rush with both a straight cover and, a month later, a "New Milk Cow Blues." (Blues record companies of the 1930s ground out sequels with a zeal comparable to that of modern Hollywood. Josh would also follow up his cover of Carr's "Mean Mistreater Mama" with "New Mean Mistreater," and the latter record's flip side, "D.B.A. Blues," with "New D.B.A. Blues.")

By this time, Josh had become a fixture at ARC, and March 1935 found him practically living in the studio. He had formed a partnership with a pianist and singer named Walter Roland, and they traded off playing on each other's sessions as well as accompanying Lucille Bogan, a female blues star whose recording career reached back to 1923 and who was then working under the pseudonym Bessie Jackson. Josh recorded fourteen vocal sides that month, of which the most interesting was another Kokomo Arnold song, "Sissy Man Blues." This was an adaptation of "I Believe I'll Make a Change," which both Josh and Leroy Carr had recorded seven months earlier, but Arnold had added a distinctive verse in which the singer wakes from a wet dream and prays, "Lord, if you can't send me no woman, please send me some sissy man." Startling as this lyric is, the song seems to have been a big hit with blues fans; it was covered not only by Josh but also by Robert Johnson, who used it as the model for his classic "Dust My Broom."

The burst of recording may in part have reflected a new financial responsibility. Carol was pregnant with their first child and on May 23 gave birth to a daughter, Blondelle. The most effusive of the White children, she still howls with laughter as she tells the story of her birth. "About a year before, or maybe two, there was a problem with two mothers who had inadvertently been given the wrong children [at the hospital] and my mom said 'Not my baby.' So it was planned that I be born at home, in my godmother's bed, my Aunt Carrie's.

"Doctor Henry delivered me. He was a family practitioner — your kid got sick with a fever at two o'clock in the morning, Doctor Henry was there at your house. My mother had had rheumatic fever and been laying prone for like a year, and when she met my dad she had only been walking for a year. Well, it was a difficult labor, but Doctor Henry had cared for my mother when she was ill and he wouldn't leave her.

Not only did Doctor Henry not leave my mother; all my mother's sisters, everybody stayed with her. She started labor on a Monday and I said 'piss on her' till Friday. Doctor Henry had her doing push-ups and everything. Meanwhile, he was having a difficult problem with his wife and, when he called and said that he wasn't leaving my mother, she accused him of whatever. So I broke up a marriage being born. Then, when I was finally born on Friday, my father passed out. When he saw the [umbilical] cord, he thought I was a boy and he passed right out, he was so excited. I was named Blondelle Deborah White, but Doctor Henry said 'You can't give all that to the child,' and he nicknamed me Bunny."

Josh stayed out of the studio for the next three months, but he returned with a vengeance in August. This time, he was working in partnership with Buddy Moss, one of his strongest competitors for the southeastern blues market. Moss was an exact contemporary, having been born two weeks before Josh in a small town just across the Georgia border. Like Josh, Moss had first recorded as a sideman while still in his teens, and he began as a solo artist for ARC eight months after Josh's debut. He had been in and out of the ARC studios a year earlier, when Josh was recording with Roland and Carr, and they may well have met at that time. As their musical approaches were quite similar and both were favorites of Art Satherley, it is not surprising that they were matched up as a duo.

At their first two sessions Josh acted as Moss's accompanist, and the pair jelled perfectly. Moss would hit a high, steady riff while Josh played boogie-woogie figures on the bass strings, then break into a melodic figure as Josh fell in behind him in perfect synchrony. The songs were a typical collection of pop-blues numbers, but one, "Oh Lordy Mama No.2," had a shouted tag line, "Oh, Lordy Mama, great God-amighty," which Josh would later take as one of his trademarks.

Josh took the lead for their third session, but the results were far less satisfying. Rather than straight-ahead blues numbers that they could just jam on, Josh was singing gospel and playing mostly on the bass strings, leaving Moss with nothing to do but attempt treble leads that kept getting in the way of the vocal. Clearly, some practice was needed, and another session two days later showed that the duo had been rehearsing in the interim. They had worked out beautifully complementary guitar parts, and Moss had come up with vocal responses as well. They recorded two more gospel numbers, both from the pen of

Thomas A. Dorsey, but the most interesting song from that session is an old prison song, "Talking about My Time" (usually known as "Cornbread, Meat and Molasses").

This was a departure for Josh, the first secular record he had made that was not in a mainstream pop-blues style. As it is exactly the sort of material with which he would later make his name on the folk music scene, its appearance at this point is significant, especially since it was almost certainly inspired by the publicity surrounding a man who would strongly influence his later career. Huddie Ledbetter, better known as Leadbelly, had been "discovered" in the summer of 1933, while incarcerated in the Louisiana State Penitentiary in Angola, by the father-and-son folklorist team of John and Alan Lomax. When he was released the following year, he wrote to John Lomax in search of a job. The Lomaxes took him on a song-collecting tour of other southern penitentiaries, then brought him to New York, where he gave his first concert on New Year's Day, 1935.

The next week, Leadbelly was signed by Art Satherley to an ARC recording contract. Josh would later say that he first met Leadbelly at that time, and it was probably the publicity surrounding Leadbelly's arrival that inspired him to record a prison number. The "Singing Convict" had become something of a media celebrity, with garish newspaper coverage, a *March of Time* newsreel, and even a poem by William Rose Benet in the *New Yorker* all emphasizing his violent past and prison background. (One can get an idea of the way the press treated this story from the title of a *Life* magazine piece: "Bad Nigger Makes Good Minstrel.") ARC responded to this publicity rather ineptly, released records of Leadbelly singing straight blues rather than prison songs, and marketing them to a black audience that found them archaic. But the fact that Josh should choose this moment to diverge from his normal repertoire and record a prison song can hardly be a coincidence. It suggests that although he had been recording purely for the mainstream blues and gospel markets, he was keeping his ears open to other possibilities.

There is no reason to think that "Talking about My Time" attracted particular attention when it was released, but it provides an interesting pointer toward Josh's later work and was shortly followed by a pair of songs that are even more in the vein he would soon mine so successfully. Though his next trip to the studio, in September 1935, produced only a cover of a recent Carr and Blackwell hit, "When the Sun Goes

Down," his first session of 1936 featured the pairing of "No More Ball and Chain" and "Silicosis Blues." Whereas "Talking about My Time" had been a traditional chain-gang work song, these new songs were contemporary protest pieces. The first was a blues ballad about a group of prisoners who died in a jailhouse fire, the second the lament of a miner stricken with silicosis, or "black lung."

Both songs were written by Bob Miller, a country songwriter who had been the production supervisor for Columbia Records' hillbilly series since the late 1920s. Miller had made a name in populist and progressive circles with such compositions as "Eleven Cent Cotton, Forty Cent Meat" and through his work with such artists as Aunt Molly Jackson, a Kentucky coal miner's wife who was one of the primary inspirations for leftist composers in search of a new "people's music." (The folk expert Dave Samuelson has hypothesized that Jackson's experiences inspired Miller to write "Silicosis Blues.") By the mid-1930s he was functioning as writer, publisher, and producer for country artists such as Patsy Montana and Red River Dave McEnery, and by the end of the decade he would be associated with left-wing musicians, including Earl Robinson and the Almanac Singers, both significant names in Josh's later career.

Considering the role that protest music would play in Josh's life, it is tempting to see this record as a significant step, but unfortunately there is no evidence beyond the record itself. No one remembers how Josh became involved with Miller, why he chose to make a protest record at this time, or what importance he may have attached to it. The songs were certainly not of the sort he would have been playing at Harlem rent parties, but it may be that the whole project was Miller's idea and that Josh was just a hired performer. Nonetheless, no other major race artist recorded anything comparable, and the fact that Josh did so provides a tantalizing suggestion that he was already in some sort of contact with the progressive musical world and out to capture a whole new audience. It is no more than a suggestion, though, as his career was about to be brought to an abrupt halt.

# JOHN HENRY
## 1936-1939

■ ■ ■ ■ ■ ■ ■ ■ ■ ■ ■ ■ ■ ■ ■ ■ ■ ■ ■ ■ ■ ■

There are two stories about the injury that ended Josh's run as a commercial blues star. The story he told to interviewers, which Carol backed up, was that he suffered a freak accident. "I'm funny," he told one reporter. "I'm one of those people who happen to like buttermilk. One day . . . I went shopping. It was icy and bad going — and I wear steel taps on my heels. Well, I lost my footing on the ice, skidded and went down, the groceries flying every way. I landed on a broken milk bottle and cut my right hand, including the tendon."

There is another story, though, which he sometimes told in private and which his friends find a good deal more credible. Richard Southern, a longtime admirer who met him in the early 1960s, heard it after a gig in Texas: his father had suffered a similar injury in a car accident, and Southern remarked that "my dad had to totally destroy a '51 Ford to maim himself, and you did it on a 25 cent milk bottle." Southern says that Josh looked down at the floor for a few seconds and then said, "That's not really the way it happened. It's the story we tell to keep from sounding like the stereotype of the hard-drinking, worthless black musician. The truth is it was because of a woman. I was quite a lady's man in those days and another man and I were seeing the same woman. He said some things about me, and one night I ran across him on the street and took out after him. He ran into a building and held the door shut, and I just went right through the glass with my fist. The milk bottle story is just for public relations."

Whether on a bottle or a door, Josh was so badly cut that when he was rushed to the nearest hospital, the doctors told him they would have to amputate two or three fingers if he did not want his hand to become permanently paralyzed. Josh rejected this prognosis and insisted that they patch him up the best they could: "I made them sew it up, and I didn't take any gas. I didn't want to wake up and find myself without a hand." By one report he required three separate operations, but the result was that he kept the fingers. Nonetheless, for several years they were so stiff and clumsy that his guitar playing was reduced to the most rudimentary strumming. Josh's guitar had been like a second voice to him, and it "felt as if I had been struck dumb."

The accident could not have come at a worse time. Recently married, and with a baby not yet a year old, Josh was now without a trade. These were still the Depression years, and jobs were scarce, especially for African Americans. Still, Josh was young and resourceful, and he found ways to get by. "I was a stevedore, a longshoreman, elevator operator and bell hop," he recalled. Finally, a friend found him a job as superintendent in an apartment building at 565 West 124th Street. The family was joined there by Josh's younger brother Bill, freshly up from Greenville, and by Carol's mother. All were employed in the building, the men each earning $45 a month and the women $25, and Carol remembers it as quite a happy time. The tenants were mostly teachers and students from Columbia and Yeshiva Universities, and they were great fans of Josh's singing, often coming down to visit him or inviting him up to their apartments. "Our house was always full, no matter where we lived," Carol remembers. "[After the accident] he still always tried to play, because he realized the stiffness would not be good. He couldn't play professionally, but he always had his guitar with him, and he played as much as he could. Sometimes he couldn't, because of the pain."

Gradually, though, Josh's hand improved. He told Southern that his mother sent him creek or riverbed mud from South Carolina, and each evening he and Carol would mix it with water, pack it around his injured hand and dry it over low heat in the oven. He would sit by the oven with his hand inside until the mud dried, and then he would go to bed; the next morning they would crack the mud off, and he would go to work. He referred to this as heat therapy, but it would equally well have served as a sort of cast to keep him from holding his hand in a harmful position while he slept.

Josh was relatively comfortable with the superintendent's job, but it got derailed through some complex machinations between the management and a new janitors' union. Both he and Bill joined the union, and its contract required that members be paid $65 a month for men and $45 for women. As Josh told the story, the management balked at the higher wages and insisted that although they would pay the new scale, the White family would have to kick back twenty dollars apiece, bringing their actual wages down to the previous rate. Josh would not accept this deal, and he lost the job. "They fired me because I was the shop steward and I was the one who wouldn't kick back, and I told what happened," he said.

To make matters worse, the union gave the Whites no support, and Josh bitterly concluded that union officials were being paid off by the management: "They must have been getting something out of it if they wouldn't fight for us. They told me to go in and accept the kickback, just cash my check . . . But I didn't do it. The reaction was this: They tried to shut me up and I wouldn't be shut up and there was a meeting and they wanted to hear what I had to say, but some people didn't want to hear it, so I'm being kicked out and they get word to me that if I don't shut my mouth I'd be found floating in the Hudson River. This was from the union."

When Josh lost his job, and with it his home, the Whites moved farther uptown, renting a single room in the apartment of a singer friend, Jean Cutler, at 400 West 148th Street, in the heart of the neighborhood known as Sugar Hill. The quarters were cramped, but the Hill was considered by many people to be the best neighborhood in Harlem. Roi Ottley called it "perhaps the most modern and beautiful residential area for Negroes in Black America." Though not as tony as the block of mansions a half-mile south, which had been dubbed Strivers Row, Sugar Hill was home to the city's intellectual and artistic elite. These were the days of residential segregation, in the North as well as the South, and even successful African Americans still made their homes in Harlem apartments; not until the late 1950s and early 1960s did they make a mass exodus to the suburbs. Langston Hughes lived in Sugar Hill, as did, over the years, W.E.B. Du Bois, Duke Ellington, Ralph Ellison, Canada Lee, Thurgood Marshall, and most of the other movers and shakers of Du Bois's fabled "talented tenth."

In 1938, though, the quality of their neighbors can have given the Whites only the most limited satisfaction. Unable to play music, Josh began a frustrating search for work. Meanwhile, his hand, which had been getting better, got slammed in a door, and he had to start the healing process all over again. Carol was working, but she was pregnant with their second child. For the Whites, these were the worst of hard times. Jobs were few and far between, and Josh had multiple handicaps: he was a black man with an injury and no specialized skills, his previous employers refused to give him a reference, and he had an ambiguous standing in the union. He eventually found work as an elevator operator in the Grand Hotel, but he said he never really got the hang of the work and was eventually fired from that position as well.

All in all, the situation was dire. "Carol worked in walk-up flats until she was better than seven months pregnant, carrying laundry. I couldn't work, so I wanted to help her, at least carry the clothes, but they wouldn't allow that to happen. So what I would do then was try to go around and find house parties. I couldn't really play, but I could fram and make a couple of dollars, so that would help. Carol was making about $45 a month, and the rent was $50. So what were we living on?"

"It was a sad time," Carol recalls, but she is quick to add that it was only because they had been forced to move that they were in the right place when opportunity came knocking. "Truly, it was a blessing in disguise," she says. "Because had we not left the old place, we wouldn't have been around the corner from Leonard."

Leonard de Paur was a rising young choral director in a line of educated black musicians who had chosen to explore the African American folk tradition. Originally from Summit, New Jersey, he had gone to school in Bordentown, where the glee club was overseen by a relative of John Wesley Work, the director of the Fisk Jubilee Singers and one of the most important collectors and arrangers of traditional Negro spirituals. De Paur went on to the University of Colorado, then studied at Juilliard before becoming associate director of the Hall Johnson Choir. Johnson was the pioneer of black choral ensembles, leading large groups that specialized in the spiritual repertoire, and had been musical director for the most popular all-black play to hit Broadway, *Green Pastures*. In the mid-1930s Johnson moved to Los Angeles to work on the film version of this play, and when Roark Bradford, from whose book it had been adapted, decided to try his own hand at Broadway success, he turned to de Paur to direct the chorus.

In 1931 Bradford had written a book called *John Henry*, transmuting the title character from the mythical "steel driving man" of southern railroad legend to a roustabout on the Mississippi River. He expanded it into a musical with the help of Jacques Wolfe, a Brooklyn songwriter who specialized in songs adapted from or imitative of black folk material (his biggest success was "Shortnin' Bread"), and they found a producer named Sam Byrd, an ex-actor from Charleston, South Carolina. By the end of 1938 they were looking around for a suitable cast. They had signed Paul Robeson, then the most celebrated black actor and singer in the world, to play the title character but were having difficulty finding someone to play the key role of Blind Lemon, a wandering blues guitarist who served as a sort of Greek chorus, opening the show and providing continuity with a string of blues and gospel numbers. That was the situation when Jean Cutler, who was a member of de Paur's chorus in a production of *Androcles and the Lion* at the Federal Theater Project, invited him to come by her house for a New Year's Eve party.

De Paur lived diagonally across the street from Cutler, and on New Year's Eve he was out walking his dog and decided to drop in for a minute. "Me and my little Boston Terrier, we went over and rang the bell and went up," he remembers. "There was a good size party going on, a big group of people doing various things: drinking, dancing, joking. But the thing that caught my eye was a whist game, a four-handed card game similar to bridge. Nothing unusual about a whist game, but the thing that *was* unusual was one of the players, who for some reason or another smoked a cigarette and parked it behind his ear. Instead of in an ashtray, you know, he'd put it in his mouth, drag, and put it behind his ear. I said, 'Damn, boy, I hope he hasn't got too much pomade on his hair; he could be a conflagration any minute.'

"I didn't know who the hell it was, and it struck me as an odd way to use a cigarette. On top of that, between every hand, he'd pick up a guitar from by his seat and strum a few chords and sing. He would improvise — and this was the fascinating part — he would improvise about the hand they had just played; it would be a commentary about the game. 'Well, you trumped my ace, and I don't like your face,' that sort of thing. I said 'This is really interesting.' I'm into folklore and this was basic folklore, at least the technique.

"After a while I took my little dog, and we went on back home and that was that, but a couple of days later at the theater, I spoke to Miss

Cutler, and said, 'Jean, there was an interesting guy over there playing cards with a guitar and a cigarette in his ear.' She said, 'Oh yeah, that was Mr. White. He and his brother and his wife and their child are all rooming with me there.' So I said 'Oh, I'd like to meet this Mr. White sometime.' She says, 'OK. Come by and I'll see that you meet him.' So eventually I did go over, and I met him. I found out he was from South Carolina and had been a singer, and he told me he'd made a couple of records, which I'd never heard."

Although de Paur was unaware of Josh's earlier career, *John Henry*'s producers had fallen in love with the voice and guitar of "the Singing Christian," a performer they knew only from recordings. With his mix of clear diction and blues-flavored delivery, they thought he would be perfect for the role of Blind Lemon, but they had no idea how to go about finding him. De Paur says that they had even contacted the recording company, "but all they could find out was that this guy who did the record was from somewhere down in South Carolina." When Josh said he was from South Carolina, "something clicked. After thinking about it a few days, I said 'Well, maybe this is the guy.' So I got in touch with him again and I said 'Look, what was the record you made?' You know, I tried to pin down the facts. Soon I was satisfied that this was the guy on the record, and this was the guy they were looking for to be Blind Lemon in the show."

De Paur realized he had an ace in the hole, something that could cement his position as musical director for the whole *John Henry* production. "I said to myself, 'If I can come up with the guy to play Blind Lemon for them, I further entrench myself in their affections, and they wouldn't dare attempt to produce this damn show without me.' So, a couple of days later, with Josh White in tow, I went down to the Ansonia, where Jacques was living.

"I made a big production of this—when you've got something good, play it to the most. There was Sam Byrd and Jacques Wolfe in the house. I said, 'You know, I think I found somebody you guys are interested in.' (Nothing to it, you know, I find people all the time.) So I built it up as much as I could, and finally I bring in Josh."

Josh had been a bit suspicious of the whole business, thinking it too good to be true, but he rose to the occasion. "Mrs. Bradford asked me if I was the Singing Christian, and I said yes, the only one I knew of on records. . . . She said, 'I know how we can prove it. Will you sing a song? The one song that made me want this particular man in the show . . . is

"I Can't Help from Crying Sometimes." ' Well, when I made the record I played a lot better guitar, so I said, 'I couldn't do it the way you heard it on the record,' and I showed her my scars on my hand, 'but I think I can convince you who I am.' So I did a bit of it, and they stopped me and said, 'Enough said.' "

The most amazing thing, de Paur adds, was that "when they told him what the role was, he said, 'Blind Lemon? I knew Blind Lemon.' He said 'That's where I learned these songs. I was the boy who led Blind Lemon.' "

This story has a mythical quality to it but seems basically true, if somewhat improved in the retelling. Both de Paur and Josh would vary their versions a bit over the years, adding dramatic flourishes. In one telling, Roark Bradford and his wife had been insisting that the only man for the part was Joshua White, the Singing Christian, while de Paur was arguing that a better choice would be a bluesman named Pinewood Tom, and they were amazed to find that these were one person. In another interview, Josh had Bradford himself wandering up to that Harlem whist game and, sparked by Josh's singing, remarking "I wish I could find the Singing Christian," only to be startled by Josh's reply: "You're looking at him." De Paur would sometimes draw out the story, adding several days of detective work and game playing between himself and the producers. Whatever the details, it was a serendipitous meeting for all concerned. (It is also the probable source of Josh's exaggerations of his relationship with Blind Lemon Jefferson. It is easy to imagine him, told that he was being considered for the role of Blind Lemon, saying, "Blind Lemon? Sure I can play Blind Lemon. He taught me how to play guitar.")

Lucky as it was, this was a break that Josh was perfectly equipped for. Younger and more adaptable than most prewar blues and gospel artists, he had a smooth voice and clear diction that made his singing easily accessible to white, northern listeners, as he had proved at Julian Street's parties. His marriage to Carol had aided a natural process of assimilation into the modern world of New York, and he mixed easily with the theatrical crowd. Meanwhile, his background gave credibility to his performance as a traveling blues minstrel and added a romantic aura that would enthrall the urban, liberal audience.

For the White family, de Paur had not arrived a moment too soon. In may 1939 Carol gave birth to a second daughter. She was named Juli-anne Beverly, though Beverly was the name by which she would always be known (Julianne was a momentary addition, given because it was the name of *John Henry's* heroine). The family, already too big for one room in Jean Cutler's apartment, desperately needed more space and now moved into their own place, three blocks north at 466 West 151st Street, where they would remain for the next half-dozen years.

Grateful as he was for the chance to get back into music, Josh would later explain that he had a few changes he wanted to make in the Blind Lemon role. Though young, he had been in show business as long as anyone involved in the *John Henry* production, and he provided his own musical arrangements as well as recycling some of his older numbers, such as "My Soul Is Gonna Live with God," which was added to the play's final scene. He also did his best to ameliorate the more blatantly patronizing portions of Bradford and Wolfe's script. *Green Pastures,* though a big hit, had excited a lot of resentment in New York's black community with its picture of happy, childlike Negroes singing and fooling around at fish fries. As Josh would stress in interviews, he wanted to make sure that this show would not shame its cast members. "I told [Bradford], in the first place, 'I know good and well I will not be in a show with all that dialect and all that "nigger" stuff.' It was something I never bought and never liked. . . . Well, the changes were made in the show. There was a song about a character called 'A Nigger Named Sam.' That came out, and he was called 'The Man Named Sam.' There was a song called 'Mules Cost a Hundred Dollars and Niggers a Dime a Day.' That was changed to 'Bullies a Dime a Day.' All of these kind of things were changed."

Josh added that some of the older actors were already inured to the popular stereotyped and did not share his feelings. "I will admit that some of the people hadn't gotten around to the idea of just talking naturally, so they would use 'dem,' 'dose,' 'dat.' But you weren't compelled to do this and that I never have done. And Paul didn't do it."

"Paul," of course, was Paul Robeson. Robeson was one of Josh's heroes, and he would become something of a friend and mentor, as he was to many young, black artists (among other things, he acted as Beverly's godfather). By the late 1930s, Robeson had become a larger-than-life figure: a champion athlete, law school graduate, singer, actor, and spokesman for black pride and social justice. Like Joe Louis, he was regarded as almost superhuman, more of a legend than John Henry himself. Robeson rejected many theatrical roles, doing his best to choose parts that would increase the stature of black artists in general and carrying them off with majestic charisma. Starting in the early 1920s he had starred in Eugene O'Neill's *All God's Chillun Got Wings* and *The Emperor Jones*. He dominated *Showboat* with his rendition of "Ol' Man River," then went on to star in acclaimed productions of *Othello*, first in London and later on Broadway. He was also among the most popular singers of Negro spirituals, his huge bass voice combining operatic grandeur with a simplicity of phrasing that made him the perfect interpreter of this repertoire for a mainstream concert audience.

While in Europe in the late 1930s, Robeson had become strongly politicized. His previous concern for the cause of black Americans became blended with a passionate interest in the Spanish Civil War and other fights against international oppression and fascism. He became closely allied with the Communist Party, and when he returned to the United States from England in 1939, he threw himself into the growing antifascist movement, giving concerts that mixed the spirituals with "people's songs" from around the world. Just three weeks before he started rehearsing *John Henry*, Robeson had heralded his return to the American scene with one of his greatest triumphs: a stirring radio performance of Earl Robinson and John LaTouche's populist patriotic cantata "Ballad for Americans," which, issued as an album, became ubiquitous in progressive households.

It was undoubtedly Robeson's influence more than Josh's that led to the cleaning up of the *John Henry* script, and his involvement guaranteed that the play would attract the interest of the New York left, still in the early throes of its love affair with American folk music. For Josh, this interest proved more important than the production itself—which, as it turned out, was fortunate. After December tryouts in Boston and Philadelphia and some substantial rewriting, *John Henry* opened at New York's 44th Street Theater on January 10, 1940, to universally mediocre reviews. Robeson was hailed as "awesome" and "heroic"; the cast was generally praised; and Josh was singled out for special mention (though a couple of reviewers, apparently still stuck in the minstrel era, described him as playing the banjo). But the script and staging were dismissed as wooden and uninteresting, and the show closed after a week.

According to de Paur, the play might have run much longer had its structural problems not been exacerbated by external factors. "At that point in time people were so enamored of Robeson they would pay to just watch him walk on stage, regardless of what he did after he got there," he says. "But the guy who owned the theater and the guy who owned the star — Robeson's attorney, [Robert] Rockmore — had bad blood between them of long standing. Byrd, in his desperation to raise money, had gone to the guy who operated the theater before we came back to town, for some additional money. So [the theater owner] had two prongs into Byrd, and Rockmore had the star of the show. You had a classic standoff, which, coupled with the show's inadequacies, which were considerable, resulted in the thing closing."

# 5

## RAISE A
## RUCKUS
## (1940)

∎ ∎ ∎ ∎ ∎ ∎ ∎ ∎ ∎ ∎ ∎ ∎ ∎ ∎ ∎ ∎ ∎ ∎ ∎ ∎ ∎ ∎

*John Henry* was finished, but it had provided a springboard for the future, and Josh was well equipped for the next leap. "He had a pretty good sense of where he wanted to go," de Paur remembers. "He was serious about it, which was all you could ask of a person trying to be a professional without any professional background. His background was plowing around the streets with a blind man holding him on the shoulder. He had no idea what 'professional' life was like until he landed up here and landed the show with people like Robeson on the stage, and that was a whole new world for him to encounter."

De Paur's assessment includes a degree of romanticism and misinformation. By the time he appeared in *John Henry,* Josh had been in New York for almost a decade and in Chicago before that. His records had been astutely recorded and marketed for what was essentially a pop audience, albeit one that was almost exclusively poor, black, and based in the South. He had consorted with polished professionals such as Leroy Carr and, as far back as 1933, had been playing at parties for wealthy white people. Even in his teens, he was remembered as singing soft pop ballads, not rural folk music.

Nonetheless, *John Henry* had certainly introduced him to a new audience, and if that audience wanted to think of him as a romantic folk artist, fresh from the southern streets,

Josh was willing to oblige. He had always been a versatile entertainer, and over the next couple of years he would shape his image and his music to fit the educated New York crowd. In so doing, he would develop a performance style that set the pattern for the rest of his career and influenced two generations of city folksingers. His appearance with Robeson had attracted the attention of the left-wing intellectuals, as well as the white urban fans who were beginning to recognize and celebrate the artistic contributions of African American vernacular musicians. These two overlapping but not identical groups would form the core of his new audience.

Soon after *John Henry* closed, Josh began to make his first forays into the white entertainment world. Pete Seeger remembers that he appeared on March 3, 1940, at a "Grapes of Wrath Evening," arranged by the actor Will Geer as a benefit for California migrant workers. The advertised performers included Leadbelly, the Golden Gate Quartet, Alan Lomax and his sister Bess, Aunt Molly Jackson, and a brand new arrival from the West Coast, Woody Guthrie. Josh was an unadvertised guest, as was Seeger himself, who was twenty years old and making his concert debut. Alan Lomax later described that evening as the beginning of the American folksong revival, and although that may be somewhat overstating the case, it was certainly a moment when a lot of pieces fell together. It is not clear who invited Josh, but the evening introduced him to many of the people who would influence and interact with him over the next few years and marked his entry into the burgeoning folk world.

His new career was beginning to get under way, and four days after the concert Josh went into the studio for the first time since before his accident. He recorded eight sides for two different labels, and they show the potential breadth of audience that lay before him. The first two songs, released as a single by the two-year-old Blue Note label, aimed at the new crop of white jazz fans, educated listeners who were prepared to treat the music as a serious artistic endeavor rather than simply the accompaniment for a hot night of dancing. For these, Josh was joined by bass player Wilson Myers and the New Orleans clarinetist Sidney Bechet. Bechet had been among the first jazz musicians to be lionized by a white audience: He was hailed by classical music critics in Europe, and New Orleans jazz fans place him on a par with Louis Armstrong as the style's other great soloist. In some ways, he was a rather surprising choice to accompany Josh, but the records worked out fine.

Bechet provided sensitive background for the vocals and turned in fine, warm solos that meshed neatly with the guitar leads. The first tune, "Careless Love," finds him staying rather carefully in the background, but he comes in stronger on "Milk Cow Blues," blowing full-throated melodies over Myers's bowed bass.

The session's remaining six sides made up Josh's first album, *Harlem Blues,* released on the Musicraft label. Unlike Blue Note, which was single-mindedly devoted to jazz (and remains a respected jazz label today), Musicraft provided an eclectic selection of records aimed at serious music listeners. Established five years earlier to record baroque and early music, in 1939 it had branched out with a Leadbelly album and gone on to record folksongs and classical pieces from India and China. As the company's owner, Samuel Pruner, recalled for Leadbelly's biographers, "We did a number of things that other record companies simply were not doing. We weren't making any money at it, but we were doing it for love, I suppose. We were deeply involved in liberal causes. The plight of the black men and women in this country was a heck of a lot worse than it is today. We even wanted to get Paul Robeson, but Victor had him under contract."

The arrival on the scene of small labels such as Blue Note and Musicraft was key to the development of a new jazz and folk aesthetic. Previously, when genuine folk music or deeply personal jazz performances were captured on record, that was largely by chance; the record companies were in search of immediate sales, not enduring artistic quality or ethnomusicological importance. In the late 1930s, however, labels began to appear that were run by people who considered themselves music lovers rather than businessmen. They did not expect huge sales, and rarely got them, but were able to maximize profits by marketing albums of three or four records rather than selling single discs, and they found a small but devoted audience of white, educated enthusiasts who were just discovering the rural, black vernacular styles that were already considered archaic by most African Americans.

White New Yorkers had been primed for a deeper exploration of African American music by 1939's "Spirituals to Swing" concert at Carnegie Hall. This event had been put together by the record producer John Hammond (who had produced Bessie Smith's last sessions, discovered Billie Holiday, and worked with the Count Basie and Benny Goodman bands) and was sponsored, despite some misgivings on Hammond's part, by the Communist-oriented magazine *New Masses.*

The program attempted to show the evolution of African American music, mixing swing and New Orleans jazz bands with the gospel singers Sister Rosetta Tharpe and Mitchell's Christian Singers, the blues artists Big Bill Broonzy and Sonny Terry, and the boogie-woogie masters Albert Ammons, Meade Lux Lewis, and Pete Johnson. The concert was a huge success and is often cited as a turning-point in the history of jazz. Before, the typical white jazz fans had been young dancers out for a good time. Afterward, in the culmination of a process begun with the Harlem Renaissance, white critics began to consider the music as serious art and as part of an African American folk continuum that was hailed by many as America's richest cultural resource.

In these years there could be a good deal of overlap between the folk and jazz audience, especially where black artists were concerned. White urbanites were fascinated by the "primitive" sound of the older styles, and blues was hailed, with questionable accuracy, as both a pure folk expression and the root of jazz. Pruner was imbued with this new aesthetic; whereas ARC had opted to record Leadbelly's most contemporary-sounding blues songs, Musicraft tried to capture the singer's prison and field-holler material, along with leftist topical compositions such as "Bourgeois Blues." In Josh's case, the six *Harlem Blues* sides were largely drawn from his previously recorded repertoire but carefully selected to attract a folk audience (although, interestingly, the album was released in Musicraft's "Night Life In New York" series rather than the regular series devoted to classical and folk albums). "Things About Coming My Way," Tampa Red's ten-year-old hit, was retitled "Hard Time Blues" and reworked to emphasize the hoboing character of the singer. A two-sided version of "Motherless Children" made a bow to the spiritual tradition. "Careless Love" (which had the same tune and guitar arrangement as Josh's early gospel recording "Lay Some Flowers on My Grave") was recut in a more countrified style, without Bechet's clarinet. Finally, there were two prison songs: a blues called "Prison Bound" and a traditional work song titled "Monday, Tuesday, Wednesday," with Josh's brother Bill on second vocal.

According to a later interview, Josh was less than happy with these recordings. "We started [that session] at 2:00 A.M. and kept it up till 2:00 P.M. the next afternoon," he remembered. "We okayed several recordings and the rest were to be destroyed. Blue Note got new owners and they were sold and came out as my *Harlem Blues* album. And I'm not proud of it."

In fact, they are not too bad. Josh's hand was still stiff, and some of the playing is a bit clumsy, but he was singing well and had learned how to work around his handicap. Even after his hand had healed completely, the injury left a permanent impact on his playing style, and he would never again have the lightning speed that marked his first recordings. He was more than willing to grant this fact. "I massaged that hand all the time, and tried to practice" he said in a 1952 interview, recalling the period after his accident. "Gradually it came back, [but] it's not perfect yet. And I have to play in an unorthodox way."

Unlike other blues fingerpickers, who tend to anchor their last two fingers on the face of the guitar and pick with the thumb, index, and sometimes middle fingers, Josh held his right hand in a perfect classical position, the thumb curving forward and all four fingers poised over the strings. His earliest photographs, taken before the accident, show him already in this posture, but it became a necessity rather than a choice when his fingers stiffened and he was forced to move them in a clump. He went on to turn what must have seemed a severe handicap into a virtue, abandoning the facile picking patterns of his youth in favor of full-handed chords that gave his playing exceptional body and power.

The other effect of Josh's injury was to emphasize his left-hand technique. While his religious tunes had, from the first, been marked by a crystalline, steel guitar–like vibrato, his blues work had often relied on right-hand speed, a dazzling but far less distinctive style. When he lost that right-hand facility, he was forced to form a cleaner, less busy approach. His gospel arrangements provided an obvious model, which he adapted to fit the rest of his repertoire. Thereafter, instead of speed, his work was marked by superb tonal control and a tasteful spareness that would perfectly suit his expanding non-blues repertoire.

It may have been that Josh still felt insecure about his playing, or perhaps he was simply looking for something that would be sure to please his new audience. In any case, even as he was recording these first new solo sides, he was also rehearsing a singing group. Called the Carolinians, it included his brother Bill and three members of the *John Henry* chorus: tenor Bayard Rustin, soon to become one of America's foremost civil rights leaders; another young tenor named Carrington Lewis; and the rumbling bass, Sam Gary, who would remain Josh's frequent partner and closest friend.

To pull the group together and provide musical arrangements, Josh naturally turned to Leonard de Paur. "He asked me if I would help," de Paur remembers. "I said, 'Well, what can I do for you?' He said, 'You can tell us what to do.' I said, 'You sing.' " De Paur laughs at the recollection. "He said 'We need some coaching. We need some parts.' I said, 'You mean arrangements?' He wasn't sure that was what he meant, but if they would make him sound like what he thought a quartet should sound, that would be it. So I said 'Fine, I'll do it. Be glad to.'

"We had a rehearsal scheme that you wouldn't believe: two mornings a week around seven o'clock and three nights a week around midnight. Josh had a split-shift job on the elevator, and one of the other guys had some sort of temporary job of questionable nature, and that's when they could get together. They would come to my apartment there on St. Nicholas Avenue, seven o'clock in the morning. We'd be plunking away and rehearsing, and the thing about singing is that when you sing, particularly small-group fashion, you pat your foot. So there'd be these five guys patting their feet and singing and playing a guitar, and the old lady in the apartment adjoining right through the wall, she was getting a sunrise concert. She thought we were crazy. Then the rest of the week would be midnight and past, and we'd still be up there doing it; people would be trying to go to sleep in the various apartments and there we were plunking away.

"It was weird, but it wasn't too weird for the times. It was a time when you did what you had to do to pay the bills and eat. It was no hardship for me to be visited at midnight and seven o'clock in the morning. All I had to do was be there when they got there and rehearse them, prepare the material for them, coach them in it. I didn't particularly like getting up at six o'clock to rehearse somebody, but what the hell, it promised a buck. Then we had to find a name for this quartet and Josh was from Carolina, so why not Carolinians? And that's how that happened."

John Hammond, who according to some reports had first met Josh during the ARC days, heard the Carolinians and immediately became their biggest booster. They could not have had a better-connected fan. On his recommendation they were signed by Goddard Lieberson to Columbia Records, one of the most powerful and prestigious labels in the country. Columbia was the big time, and the Carolinians were an unknown group, but they came up with a concept that was perfectly suited to the new folk-jazz audience. In the late 1930s, Leadbelly's story had excited an interest in the music of black chain-gang convicts, which was reinforced by the publication in 1939 of a collection of convicts' songs titled *Me and My Captain (Chain Gangs)*. This was compiled by a Hungarian emigré named Lawrence Gellert, who had strong connections in New York's left-wing and artistic circles through the popularity of his brother Hugo, a well-known progressive artist. Gellert had done most of his collecting in the Carolinas and Georgia, and his work had created a ready-made audience for an album of chain-gang songs sungs by a group of men who claimed genuine roots in the culture.

Gellert's influence would later be a sore point for both Josh and de Paur, especially after he brought suit for composer royalties. He had been quoted as a blues authority in the notes to Josh's *Harlem Blues* album, but de Paur describes him as "a phony if there ever was one. He did some good work, but if he'd heard something down south and heard you doing it, he would want to claim it as his because he had it on a field recording. The world was full of people then who were great at telling you that they owned your folk music. We said 'The hell with you.'" Josh was similarly contemptuous of Gellert's claims. Introducing one of the chain-gang songs in later years, he would say: "I've been beaten twice by the Ku Klux Klan—with my mother, once, and my brother. I saw two lynchings in my life at the age of going on eight years old. But he was my inspiration to sing this song? Never happened." He would also point out that he had been familiar with chain gangs and their traditional work songs ever since his early days of walking the roads and hitchhiking with his blind employers.

Nevertheless, Gellert's book certainly provided a key inspiration for the Carolinians' album, which was titled *Chain Gang*. Six of the seven songs were taken from it, and the seventh had been printed in Gellert's 1936 collection, *Negro Folk Songs of Protest*. De Paur's and Josh's dismissal of his work was thus disingenuous at best—though ownership of folk-songs is a questionable business, and it is ironic that an outside researcher should sue someone who grew up in a given culture for singing that culture's folk songs.

In later years Josh would often talk about his early experience of listening to convict road gangs and cite it as a defining influence in his work. "[They had] whiskey voices, and they would sing [one] song all day long and never repeat a verse," he said. "It sort of gave you goose pimples listening." His interest in prison songs certainly predated Gellert's work, since he had recorded one back in 1935. Moreover, though they took Gellert's collection as a starting point, he and de Paur adapted, expanded, and rewrote the songs as they saw fit. "Trouble," for example, a powerful attack on racial injustice which would remain a staple of Josh's repertoire, shared only a few lines in common with the version Gellert had printed, and none of the melodies bore much resemblance to those in the book.

It must be noted that they bore still less resemblance to the singing of southern convicts. De Paur says that he "tried to be as traditionally accurate and authentic" as he could, but his experience of black southern folklore was almost as academic and removed from its source as that of his white contemporaries. Like his mentor Hall Johnson, he was trained in a style pioneered by the Fisk Jubilee Singers, who created sophisticated, concert-hall arrangements of traditional pieces, keeping some of the original words and melody but few of the folk harmonies and nothing of the rough, "whiskey-voiced" singing style.

If the Carolinians did not sound like a southern work gang, though, their approach was exactly what was needed to bring the material to a wide audience. It was analogous to the way Burl Ives and Richard Dyer-Bennet were polishing songs from the white rural tradition. The lyrics drew on folk sources and provided a strong evocation of the convicts' sufferings, but they were performed in a way that would be immediately accessible to white, urban listeners. Hammond produced the sessions himself in June 1940, and Columbia brought out the album with a striking cover: a chain breaking in a splash of bloody red over a background of black and gray prison stripes, with the words "Chain Gang" stenciled in harsh white type.

Smooth as the arrangements were musically, this was not a typical product for a major label, and Hammond had to fight with Columbia's management to get the album released. Some of the higher-ups "were terribly upset that I was meddling in something that it was not fashionable to meddle in in 1940," Hammond recalled. Fears that the record would alienate southern record dealers were probably exacerbated by the fact that a chain-gang collection was a new concept and might not prove to be commercially viable even in the North. Hammond fought for it, however, and it proved a surprising success. Critics applauded the album, and it sold well all over the country.

Although the songs seem rather tame by later protest standards, *Chain Gang* was a major breakthrough for American topical music. The *New York Times* critic called it "vastly exciting" and described the songs as "surcharged with bitterness and a rising note of rebelliousness." He declared the album "a must for those who are not afraid to discover some of the dark places of life and those who care about music that rises spontaneously from the hearts and throats of humble and unfortunate men," and compared it to Woody Guthrie's *Dust Bowl Ballads,* recently released on Victor. Aside from that album and some of Robeson's work, it was the first release from the progressive folk music scene to come out on a major label, and even Robeson had never sung as direct a racial statement as the first verse of "Trouble":

> Well, I always been in trouble, 'cause I'm a black-skinned man.
> Said I hit a white man, [and they] locked me in the can
> They took me to the stockade, wouldn't give me no trial
> The judge said, "You black boy, forty years on the hard rock pile."
> Trouble, trouble, sure won't make me stay,
> Trouble, trouble, jail break due someday.

There is no reason to think that Josh had given much attention to politics before joining the *John Henry* cast, but he knew plenty about racism and was more than ready to speak out. Robeson's views and those of the people driving the folk scene were very much in keeping with his own experience, and the lyrics of "Trouble" were almost entirely his, barely overlapping with the song in Gellert's book. He later explained that he wrote them about an uncle who got in trouble with the law: "My Uncle Sonny was a very quick-tempered man, I believed then an evil man. He was driving a four-mule team and, you know, mules will balk at times, they'll sit down and won't do a darn thing. My Uncle Sonny, I guess he was in his grog or feeling kind of evil this morning, and when the mule would balk he would get down and hit the mule with his fist in the temple. Sometimes he'd knock them out — he's been known to kill a mule like that.

"[He was] in front of the station, and this man was driving two matched beautiful horses and he saw my uncle hit this mule and he jumped down on my Uncle Sonny's back and there was a big fight and Uncle Sonny sort of did him in. You know, he didn't know whether he was white, black, gray, or what; he was just angry that somebody jumped him from the back. So my uncle was sent to the chain gang, with no trial, and was given 99 years. And I wrote that song about Uncle Sonny."

Even before *Chain Gang* was released, in August 1940, Columbia had brought the Carolinians back into the studio to record a session of Negro spirituals. This was a natural choice, both because spirituals were a time-tested favorite with much of the white audience and because de Paur had such good training in the field. It was also a project that Carol White was enthusiastic about, and she helped put together some of the vocal arrangements, which were musically more complicated and swinging than most of the prison songs. After the novelty and power of *Chain Gang,* though, the traditionalism of the spirituals was anticlimactic. The two singles released on Columbia and a couple more on the smaller Harmony label attracted little attention.

*Chain Gang* not only impressed the white, liberal audience but also received favorable mention in the black press. The *Amsterdam News* described it as "one of the finest albums yet released . . . which no sensible person attuned to the conditions which go to make up America can be without." Later that fall the *News* ran a big picture of Josh singing into a CBS microphone and headlined "He's Newest Rage Downtown," with a caption describing how the Carolinians were "breaking things up nightly at Cafe Society." This popular club on Sheridan Square in Greenwich Village was the first fully integrated nightclub in New York. Its owner, Barney Josephson, had opened the room soon after the Spirituals to Swing concert and presented a similar range of music, much of it drawn from that program. He seems to have hired the Carolinians, on John Hammond's recommendation, as a spiritual group. He had just opened a second, larger club on East 58th Street, called Cafe Society Uptown, and the Golden Gate Quartet, his prime gospel group, had moved up there. To keep the "spirituals to swing" theme intact, the Carolinians were brought into the downtown location on November 26 on a bill with the blues singer Ida Cox, the boogie-woogie pianist Meade Lux Lewis, the jazz pianist Art Tatum, and Henry "Red" Allen's band. In later years, Cafe Society would become practically Josh's second home, but his first stay was short lived. A better-drawing religious singer, the Pentecostal guitarist and shouter Sister Rosetta Tharpe, showed up in early December and bumped the Carolinians off the program.

By then, however, Josh had got what he would later describe as his "really big break." It came through the efforts of Alan Lomax, the driving force behind much of the 1940s folk revival. Lomax, almost exactly a year younger than Josh, had started out in his teens as assistant to his father, John Lomax, dean of American folksong collectors. Where previous scholars had combed the Appalachians for survivals of old English ballads, John Lomax was equally interested in homegrown products. A native Texan, he compiled the first formal collection of cowboy songs in 1910. Then, in the burst of populist sentiment following Roosevelt's election, he received financing from the Library of Congress to make a wide sweep through the South, collecting folksongs of all kinds. From Appalachian homesteads to Texas prisons, he recorded hundreds of songs and eventually compiled a landmark book, *American Ballads and Folk Songs,* as well as "discovering" and publicizing Leadbelly.

Alan had gone along on many of these journeys and by the late 1930s was probably the most knowledgeable folksong aficionado in America. He was made director of the Library of Congress's Folk Song Archive, and while systematically cataloguing the raw materials that were being recorded through the New Deal's field programs, he organized concerts, wrote radio playlets, and did whatever he could to bring the music to the attention of a wider public. Unlike his father, who was politically conservative, Alan was wholeheartedly progressive, and he saw a direct link between his musical and political allegiances. He recalled an early collecting trip, when a black sharecropper, hearing that he was from the government in Washington, had sung a song about the economic plight of poor farmers and addressed it as a direct plea to the president. It was a defining experience in his life, and he saw his mission as providing a channel for the voices of people who would otherwise go unheard.

In 1940, Lomax and Nicholas Ray (who would later direct the film *Rebel without a Cause*) produced a groundbreaking radio show, *Back Where I Come From.* The show premiered in August, and by September it was airing three times a week on the CBS network. The regular cast included Josh, Woody Guthrie, Leadbelly, Burl Ives, and the Golden Gate Quartet. Each episode, fifteen minutes long, had scripted introductions framing traditional songs grouped around a particular theme. Josh both sang his own songs and acted as a sort of interpreter for Leadbelly; apparently, Ray considered the Louisianan's thick accent too difficult for listeners to understand, so he would sometimes have Josh read Leadbelly's song introductions. Josh remembered the opportunity to appear on *Back Where I Come From* as the key to all that followed. It gave him national exposure on a major network and broadened his appeal as an engaging and articulate interpreter of traditional songs. It also cemented his friendship with the Golden Gate Quartet, and he began to make occasional live appearances with them.

Lomax also used Josh on another CBS series, *The School of the Air.*

Although he often expressed mixed feelings about performers like Josh and Ives, whose polished approach was in stark contrast to the raw, earthy sound of a Guthrie or a Leadbelly, he understood their broader appeal and thoroughly admired their professionalism. Josh "was a jewel of a performer," he later said. "You could give him a song and it was just served up like strawberries with whipped cream! Josh became known to the whole country on these shows."

Lomax's sister, Bess Hawes, sometimes stopped by the *Back Where I Come From* broadcasts, and she recalls a wickedly humorous side of Josh's professionalism. "One of the things that he liked to do was to start to restring his guitar just minutes before air time. The directors would be sitting in the control room, and there would be Josh, ripping the strings off his guitar as the clock ticked around. Everybody would practically have a heart attack, and then he would whip the new ones on, tune them up by grabbing the strings and pulling them very hard, stretching them out as he tuned, and he was always in perfect tune just one second before air time. It was a great piece of show biz, and he enjoyed making everybody so nervous."

The story is indicative of more than Josh's uncanny musical ear and his sense of humor: it exemplifies his absolute confidence in his own abilities. Unlike most of the older, rurally raised singers — who never really understood the New York audience — or bright young novices like Pete Seeger and his friends, he was a practiced professional. He had, after all, been in show business of one kind or another since his childhood, was hanging around the offices of a national record company by his early teens, became a popular artist before he was twenty, and performed on the radio and at parties for wealthy white patrons before the folk scene existed. If some aspects of his new career surprised him, he did not let it show. Given the opportunity to appear on Broadway, at a fancy nightclub, or on a national radio show, he took it in stride, unfazed by the powerful figures around him.

For four years Josh's career had been on hold, but now opportunities were coming thick and fast. His daughter Bunny was then five years old, and her eyes still grow big when she talks about the changes in their life. "It was just awesome," she says. "I don't know why, but I remember we had red bulbs in our house, and all these strangers were coming in — I mean *strange* people; they were white, you know. And Leadbelly, with his raspy voice, and Paul Robeson."

Her father was making the most of his new popularity. His versatility meant that he could show up wherever he was wanted and perform at a moment's notice, and his new acquaintances took advantage of this to use him on their shows. Not all of these opportunities included the Carolinians, though, and Josh seems sometimes to have been less than straightforward with the group about his extracurricular excursions. De Paur would say that Josh "had been conditioned in the South so well that he just couldn't tell anybody the whole truth," and that his side projects "sort of undercut the esprit that held the group together." De Paur adds that in the long term there were no hard feelings, and the Carolinians continued to make occasional appearances together through the early months of 1941. Still, by the end of 1940, most of Josh's energies were being directed elsewhere.

Even the birth of his son did not slow him up. Joshua Donald White was born on November 30, 1940, and three weeks later Josh was in Washington, D.C., appearing with the Golden Gate Quartet in a concert for the Library of Congress to celebrate the seventy-fifth anniversary of the Emancipation Proclamation, then backing the quartet for an appearance at Franklin Roosevelt's third inaugural gala.

Josh had worked with "the Gates," as they were known in gospel circles, on *Back Where I Come From,* and they had used him as a guitarist for some of their concerts in the New York area. They were then at the height of their career, performing at Cafe Society's more prestigious uptown location, making regular radio appearances, and reigning as Columbia's most popular gospel recording artists. Like Josh, the Gates had first been stars for a black audience. In the mid-1930s they had taken the gospel world by storm with their impeccable rhythm and hot, jazzy arrangements. Their "jubilee" style was the foundation for generations of later quartets and influenced hot vocal groups in the pop world as well. Unlike most gospel groups, they had recorded occasional barbershop and pop numbers along with the religious material, thus increasing their appeal. The Spirituals to Swing concert had introduced them to a white audience, and their sophisticated approach made them natural stars of the nightclub circuit.

The teaming of Josh with the Gates was ideal; they were all young singers who mixed a knowledge of earlier traditions with modern, uptown arrangements. Orlandus Wilson, the Gates' leader and bass singer, who lived next door to the Whites, says that he and Josh were two of a kind, and their musical styles blended beautifully. The Library of Congress show was nonetheless a somewhat incongruous showcase for their talents. It was organized by Alan Lomax as a demonstration of African American folk styles, and he remembered it as "an enormous break with every tradition," the first time that the library had played host to anything resembling a folk concert. Remembering the singers' entrance on the stage of the Coolidge Auditorium, he said "it was an invitation only affair, the house was absolutely packed and . . . when the doors swung open . . . [where] usually some famous string quartet [would appear] . . . and the Golden Gate Quartet pranced through in their long tailed vest coats, the audience just gasped."

Lomax had designed a program that would showcase the performers and at the same time be thoroughly proper and educational. The musical pieces were fitted into scholarly lectures on the blues and spiritual traditions by two authorities on African American culture, Sterling Brown and Howard University's Alain Locke, and Lomax also played some of his own field recordings. The event succeeded beyond his wildest dreams: "People stood and applauded and cried and just wouldn't go away. . . . It was the first time the whole culture broke through the town. Everybody saw the magnificence of the thing, saw what an enormous contribution the blacks had made, and the blacks were delighted about the dignity and the authority of the event."

It is instructive to notice, considering the concert's importance and the emotional effect on its listeners, how stilted and patronizing it sounds today. Brown's long, wordy introduction commented on the "strong, peasant soul" of the Negro, and the singers never got to say a word, acting simply as animate lecture aids. As neither Josh nor the Gates were in any sense primitive folk artists, the attempt to fit their smooth, urbane approach into this scholarly context seems, in retrospect, rather forced. They did adapt their repertoire to the occasion, singing traditional spirituals and work songs (along with Josh's "Silicosis Blues"), and even reciting some rural rhymes and stories, but there is a clear disjunction between their polished professionalism and the audience's impression of them as untutored folk artists.

Nonetheless, the presentation was well suited to its time and venue, and it led to subsequent college dates with Lomax. It also provided the artists with the library's imprimatur of legitimacy as carriers of America's vital folk traditions. In later years Josh would laugh about being designated as "a repository of rare Southern music," but he played the role to the hilt, and his publicity handouts regularly, and inaccurately, described the library as having devoted several days to documenting his repertoire.

Significant and prestigious as this concert was from the performers' point of view, it was just an appetizer for the unprecedented invitation to perform at the inaugural gala. Eleanor Roosevelt had been much taken with the Gates on a visit to Cafe Society Uptown a few weeks earlier — the first time she had ever set foot in a nightclub — and they appeared on the program at her request. Held on January 19, 1941, at Constitution Hall, the gala was the most glittering event of Roosevelt's third inauguration and featured what the *Washington Post* called "a galaxy of distinguished artists," appearing for an audience of almost 4,000 people. The performers ranged from the National Symphony Orchestra to the popular tenor Nelson Eddy to Irving Berlin, who led the crowd in "God Bless America." Ethel Barrymore read Walt Whitman; Raymond Massey read Lincoln; Charlie Chaplin recited his final speech from *The Great Dictator*; and Mickey Rooney did impressions and played piano. The Gates appeared just before Chaplin, the evening's biggest star, and brought the house down with two songs, "Noah" and "Gospel Train," the latter featuring Josh's guitar.

As the Gates' Wilson points out, the most impressive thing about the evening was that they were on stage at Constitution Hall, the first black artists ever to break the room's strict racial barrier. Only the previous year, Marian Anderson had been refused permission to appear there by the hall's owners, the Daughters of the American Revolution, and Eleanor Roosevelt had resigned from the organization in protest. "They didn't want blacks on the stage there," Wilson remembers. "But Mrs. Roosevelt gave us the invitation to sing for the inauguration. It was a great thing for us." The historic importance of their appearance was not generally mentioned in the mainstream press, though the Washington *Daily News* ran a photo of Josh and the Gates over the headline "The D.A.R. didn't say Boo," and the breakthrough was duly heralded in black papers such as Baltimore's *Afro-American*.

A month later there was yet another Washington appearance. On February 17, Lomax brought Josh, the Gates, Burl Ives, and the North Carolina banjo player Wade Mainer to the White House for a "command performance" for President and Mrs. Roosevelt. This was Josh's first performance for the Roosevelts as anything more than the Gates' guitarist, and there is no reason to think that they singled him out for special attention, but in the next few years the First Family would come to play a major part in his life. As the Popular Front, comprising American liberals and radicals, gathered strength during the war years, Josh was perfectly suited to be a symbol of this unity. With folk music becoming a powerful voice in the war against fascism, Josh would undergo a transformation from ordinary entertainer to singing fighter for social justice. His reputation as a musical spokesman had been launched with *Chain Gang,* and 1941 would find him at the center of a newly vibrant American left.

# 6

# MARCHING DOWN FREEDOM'S ROAD (1941)

■ ■ ■ ■ ■ ■ ■ ■ ■ ■ ■ ■ ■ ■ ■ ■ ■ ■ ■ ■

The American left's involvement with folk music dates back at least to the 1910s and the organizing efforts of the Industrial Workers of the World, or IWW. Such IWW songwriters as Joe Hill and T-Bone Slim put new, socially conscious lyrics to familiar tunes, and the union's legendary *Little Red Songbook* set a pattern that remained long after the IWW itself had ceased to be a major factor in American labor politics. In the 1930s, folk music came to the fore again with the Popular Front. The Depression had united working-class Americans as never before, and the Communist Party had formed common cause with socialist groups and with the left wing of the Democratic Party in an attempt to create one solid American left.

In New York a group of leftist intellectuals sought to fuse politics and folk music, with an eye toward nurturing a homegrown working-class culture. Leadbelly became a great favorite of this circle and rewarded its attention by writing songs like "Bourgeois Blues" and an impassioned ballad defending the Scottsboro Boys, nine young black men whose multiple trials on charges of raping two white women had become a leftist cause célèbre. Classical composers such as Charles Seeger, inspired by artists like Leadbelly and Aunt Molly Jackson, turned from creating complex "proletarian" cantatas to collecting traditional American melodies. The dream was to find a true "people's music" that would be of and for the workers and could inspire and educate them to join the progressive fight.

In retrospect, many historians have specifically connected the folk-song movement to the Communist Party, and the Party certainly encouraged the creation of "people's art," both in Russia and abroad. This emphasis on the role of the Communists, though, is somewhat misleading. The CP was certainly the strongest wing of the far left, the only one that had actually won a revolution and hence had a strong international component and a government giving them support. Nonetheless, with the Popular Front strategy in effect, Party members formed or joined a wide range of groups that were not explicitly Communist: the American Youth Congress was a favorite of Mrs. Roosevelt; the League of American Writers included Archibald MacLeish, Ernest Hemingway, and John Steinbeck.

Communists were frequently the most zealous workers in these groups and would at times use their unity, as well as more coercive tactics, to force through Party-generated proposals and exercise a disproportionate degree of influence. Still, the groups can be dismissed as Communist fronts only when viewed through the distorted prism of the 1950s. There were non-Communists in all of them, and the Party's influence varied from organization to organization, issue to issue, and moment to moment. Furthermore, the Party's leaders were generally careful to keep their positions in line with the mainstream of progressive politics. The slogan of the day was "Communism is twentieth-century Americanism," and though historians have often dismissed this as pure cynicism, many of the people who were then joining in unprecedented numbers fervently believed in its truth.

In folk music, and folk culture in general, these progressives found an art that was irrefutably American and of the working people. The music of Mississippi sharecroppers and Appalachian miners was, to them, the true voice of America, and it was a voice calling for a new deal in every sense of the term. For New York's leftists, many of whom were first- or second-generation immigrants, immersion in this American workers' culture was not a cynical attempt at propaganda; it was an attempt to assimilate, to become part of an American tradition.

Alan Lomax, tracing the dawn of the folk revival, would say that Roosevelt wisely hitched his wagon to a new national self-awareness of which the folk scene was an integral part. Lomax felt that later historians who were "looking for reds under the bed" had mischaracterized the movement. "They have forgotten . . . the New Deal's connection with painting, photography, dance, art, theater, literature, history, sociology, research. The whole range of the humanities was a part and parcel of the whole New Deal activity. . . . It had nothing to do with politics or anything. It was because that was the period when America was discovering itself. The Roosevelts were clever and sensitive enough to know that that's where the country was going, and they went with it."

The command performance that Lomax organized for the Roosevelt White House was a perfect example of this interaction of folk music with larger ideals. He and Mrs. Roosevelt put it together with the aim of encouraging music in the armed forces. The idea was that the military, which was gearing up for what would become World War II, was bringing together Americans from all regions and all walks of life, and that these people would undoubtedly have a great variety of songs and musical skills. Encouraging them to sing would provide Lomax with a fertile ground for song collecting, of both older songs and new tunes about the war, and at the same time boost morale.

The concert, attended by the First Family and some seventy leading figures in Washington's military and cultural elite, began with brief addresses by Rear Admiral Chester Nimitz and his counterparts from the other services, followed by a first section featuring Sailor Dad, an old seaman who sang chanties. Then came Burl Ives, Wade Mainer and his Mountaineers, the Golden Gate Quartet, and Josh, who closed the professional part of the program with "There's a Man Goin' 'Round Takin' Names" and "John Henry." For the concert's second half, Lomax presented musical groups he had found on local military bases, from hillbilly bands to a Negro cavalry quartet.

This program perfectly illustrates Lomax's methods and explains why he worked so hard to forward the careers of artists like Josh and Burl Ives, helping them to find material and shaping their folk repertoires. Though he was personally drawn to rawer, more obviously rural singers like Leadbelly and Woody Guthrie, he was aware that the very roughness that attracted him to their work would make it hard for them to reach a wide audience, and that smoother, more professional interpreters would first have to pave the way. Leadbelly had achieved fame less for his musicianship than for his notoriety as a singing convict. Guthrie had become popular with progressives but largely as a sort of Will Rogers–style humorist and hayseed philosopher, as well known for his column in the *Daily Worker* as for his songs. In young singers such as Josh and Ives, Lomax saw the possibility of breaking through to mainstream America, and he made it his mission to teach them a well-chosen selection of songs and help them become America's first folk stars.

Josh and Ives were particularly suited to the job, as both had backgrounds in what were considered true folk cultures (Ives was from rural Illinois and had grown up singing traditional ballads before coming to New York in pursuit of a theater career). This set them apart from the previous urban popularizers of folk music, who had tended to be academics with formal training. In New York the early work of Charles Seeger had been carried on by classically trained composers and musicians: Elie Siegmeister formed a chorus called the American Ballad Singers, which sang formal settings of traditional songs; Earl Robinson not only sang old songs to his own guitar accompaniment but was beginning to work with progressive lyricists to compose new ones such as "Joe Hill" and "Ballad for Americans."

Lomax, with Nicholas Ray and other partners, pursued a less academic approach. He encouraged young people, whatever their backgrounds, to learn folk styles and to play music with one another. He occasionally performed the songs he had collected but preferred to act as a catalyst for others, and he became something of a mentor to a group of young, educated progressives who were interested in becoming folk musicians. (The very idea of "becoming" a folk musician, of course, was something new; traditionally, folk musicians were simply the untrained "folk" who made music.) This group included Charles Seeger's son Pete, who had worked with Lomax at the Library of Congress before taking off to travel with Guthrie; an Arkansas preacher's son named Lee Hays; and Millard Lampell, a Jewish leftist and intellectual from New Jersey. This trio rented a communal living space on 13th Street, which came to be known as Almanac House. It was a sort of free-form crash pad, providing temporary quarters to Guthrie, Ray, and an ever shifting group of young folk singers and fans. At the suggestion of John Hammond, who was familiar with the Harlem rent parties, they began holding loose, grab-bag concerts on Sunday afternoons.

"We rounded up Pete, Aunt Molly Jackson, and Josh to come and sing on Sunday at the loft," Lampell remembers. "That's when I first met him. He had all these slick tricks that we found fascinating. We were playing country, and he was playing what we now would call cool—your eyes would be absolutely fastened on that cigarette. And, of course, he had these marvelous blues runs. He would come down occasionally with Sam Gary, and we would have a few bucks for everybody, 'cause we charged admission.

"At that time, folk and even good blues singers were not in demand in New York City. It was jazz. That's where the money was. Everybody was struggling. Nobody had a following. Not Leadbelly and not Aunt Molly, and certainly not us. But it began to gather steam as people got to know about us. Earl Robinson would bring people. John Hammond would bring people from uptown, and before it was over we were even getting a smattering of Junior League debutantes who thought it was so colorful to go down to Greenwich Village and see these folk singers."

After a while, Lampell, Hays, and Seeger jelled into a core group known as the Almanac Singers. Although they made two albums of traditional folk songs, the Almanacs would become best known as political singers, building on the IWW tradition to become the first recording group devoted to composing agitprop anthems based on folk melodies and styles. It is unclear how many of the group ever became members of the Communist Party, and none was active in Party politics, but they were not simply New Dealers. Like Guthrie, a columnist for the *Daily Worker*, they were closely allied with the New York branch of the Party, and their musical statements tended to hew close to the accepted Party line.

Once again, this must be seen in the context of the times. By the 1950s, Communists would come to be seen by many Americans as superhuman incarnations of evil or Kremlin-controlled automatons. Whatever their faults, and they had many, they were never anything so simple. Nor were they a homogeneous group. There were many sorts of Communists, some more zealous than others; some were more devoted to the dream of the Soviet workers' state, and some more attracted by concrete work being done in the United States.

Unlike most of the later American far left, the Communists were not just sitting around debating theory. When the Scottsboro Boys' case came to trial, it was the CP that provided lawyers to defend them, and it was often the Communist component of New Deal groups that pushed those groups to include black members and support civil rights issues, reaching out in a way that no other white organization had done. Roi Ottley credited the Party with having a profound effect on blacks' self-perception, saying that many black activists "discovered themselves" through the prominent positions they were given in CP-dominated organizations. The Party's influence was equally important in the labor movement. This was the culminating period of the battle for industrial unionization, and Communist organizers played key roles at every level of the struggle. Although the Party always remained quite small numerically, its activist zeal earned it the respect — albeit mixed with fierce dislike — of most leftists.

Obviously, the Party was not operating in a spirit of pure altruism; it was attempting to build a world revolutionary movement that would overthrow the capitalist system and thus associated itself with causes that would attract new members. Those members, however, included a host of left-leaning activists, semi-activists, and would-be activists who, despite later propaganda, had no interest in creating a totalitarian state under the iron thumb of Joseph Stalin. If in retrospect their actions, and their unwillingness to hear hard truths about the Soviet Union, often seem bizarre and incomprehensible, it is important to remember that the shifting alliances and mythologies of the Western capitalist countries could be equally strange and self-serving. The American government would blockade Spain, cutting off Loyalist supplies even as Italy and Germany flew in massive aid to Franco's fascists; turn around and embrace the Soviet Union as a wartime ally in "the war against fascism"; then turn again to condemn those who had opposed Franco as "premature antifascists."

All this is by way of introducing the Almanac Singers' first record, *Songs for John Doe,* which would bring Josh still deeper into the orbit of the New York left. Josh had occasionally dropped by and performed at Almanac House and had frequently met the shifting cast of Almanacs at benefit concerts around New York. These were happening almost weekly, held to raise funds for everything from *New Masses* magazine to the New York Committee to Aid Agricultural Workers, and Josh was becoming a ubiquitous name on the circuit. Pete Seeger suggests that this was largely due to his friendship with Robeson, who was the most revered singer on the left. "Josh admired Robeson very much," Seeger says. "And perhaps sometimes when somebody called Robeson up, he said 'I can't make it, but why don't you ask Josh White.' Many of us found ourselves contributing our talents to raise money for Loyalist Spain or strikers here [in the United States]."

By March 1941 the Almanac Singers had scraped together enough financial support to record their first album, a collection of six "peace songs" opposing America's entry into the European war. The day before they were set to go into the studio, Seeger decided that they needed some stronger instrumental backing. "I realized it would sound so much better if we had a guitar with us, so I paid a nickel subway and went up to 126th Street [actually 151st] where Josh was living, knocked on his door and said, 'Josh I'm singing these peace songs with some others to make a record; will you come down and help us?'

"Without the slightest hesitation, he checked his book and said, 'Sure I can make it. Tomorrow? Sure, I'll be there at one o'clock.' And there he was, with his guitar, and without any rehearsal he just improvised great guitar accompaniments for this album of peace songs for us. I've forgotten if he got any pay at all. He probably got union minimum, $25. That's like $250 now, but it wasn't a lot."

The Communist Party, which had actively fought against fascism for most of the 1930s, made an about-face after Hitler and Stalin signed their pact of mutual noninterference in August 1939. For the next two years the *Daily Worker* was full of attacks on warmongering, especially by colonial empires such as England and France, and painted the European war as a replay of World War I, which most progressives had come to see as purely profit-driven and directed by capitalist leaders threatened by the spread of communism. Party publications did not support the fascist countries, but neither did they single them out for special condemnation. That stance that enraged many people on the left as well as the center and right, but others found it easy to excuse Russia's move on the grounds of self-preservation and to oppose a replay of what had only twenty years earlier been billed as "the war to end all war."

*Songs for John Doe* was ardently, indeed vitriolically, pacifist. One song, for example, had the chorus: "Franklin Roosevelt told the people how he felt, / We damn near believed what he said. / He said 'I hate war, and so does Eleanor / But we won't be safe till everybody's dead.'" Considering how popular Josh became with the Roosevelts, his involvement is a bit surprising, but at the time he probably gave the lyrics little thought. He was still a newcomer to the political scene and, as Seeger suggests, was at the session to help out his friends. He played guitar on most of the songs and sang on two, most prominently on "Billy Boy," a dialogue with Lampell. Josh would sing a question: "Don't you want to see the world, Billy boy, Billy boy? / Don't you want to see the world, charming Billy?" Then Lampell would reply, "No, it wouldn't be much thrill to die for Dupont in Brazil," and the Almanacs would all come in on "He's a young boy and cannot leave his mother!"

The album was recorded for Eric Bernay's Keynote Records, an outgrowth of the Keynote Theatre, a leftist revue produced by *New Masses*. Bernay owned a store called Eric Bernay's Music Room, on West 44th Street, and was a regular advertiser in the *Daily Worker*. It was he who, as treasurer for *New Masses*, had underwritten the Spirituals to Swing concert; and he joined with John Hammond and the composer Earl Robinson in financing *Songs for John Doe*. Once the album was recorded, however, he found it more controversial than he had expected and, rather than releasing it under the Keynote name, put it out on the one-shot Almanac label.

The album had a brief vogue in Communist circles and was reviled or dismissed by everyone else. Seeger heard a story that Roosevelt was incensed and inquired of Archibald MacLeish, then the Librarian of Congress, as to whether it could be suppressed. MacLeish is said to have responded, "Not unless you want to ignore the First Amendment," and Roosevelt consoled himself with the thought that "only a few left-wingers will ever hear it." Roosevelt was right. The album was released in May 1941 and sold almost exclusively in Communist bookstores. Then, on June 22, Hitler invaded the Soviet Union. Instantly, the Communist Party became an ardent supporter of American intervention, and Bernay pulled *Songs for John Doe* out of circulation.

Despite the album's brief life, it had got the Almanac Singers rolling. In May they went back into the Keynote studio and recorded their most popular album, *Talking Union*. Once again, Josh played guitar, showing off his best licks on the blues song "Get Thee Behind Me, Satan," and Carol White and the Carolinians' bass singer, Sam Gary, added their voices to the chorus of "Union Train," a reworking of an old southern spiritual.

Josh did not become a member of the Almanacs except on record, but those sessions were an important step for him and paved the way for his own Keynote album. *Southern Exposure*, in several ways a departure for him, marked his arrival as a mature solo artist. Like the Almanac albums it was explicitly political, but it had a polished and professional sound that was quite unlike the Almanacs' loose, sing-along style. It consisted entirely of original songs, cowritten by Josh and the Harlem Renaissance poet Waring Cuney, all attacking Jim Crow segregation and the hardships besetting rural, southern blacks. These were subjects with which Josh was intimately familiar, and apparently he provided the basic ideas for most of the songs. He talked the themes over with Cuney; then Cuney wrote poems that Josh set to music.

Musically, *Southern Exposure* was the first extended example of the musical approach Josh would use for the rest of his career. His voice had darkened and deepened, and he had developed a relaxed, easy phrasing. On guitar, he sounds strong and sure after a year of regular work. His accompaniments are spare and powerfully rhythmic, with none of the ragtime feel of his 1930s recordings. The guitar breaks show off his bright, singing tone and have gained a new warmth. There is less speed and more soul. Also, freed from the need to match current blues hits, Josh experiments more than on his old records and tailors his accompaniments to each song. For example, "Jim Crow Train" is set off with a show-stopping train imitation, a rumbling, highballing bass line that slowly picks up speed as high-note bends simulate a steam whistle.

Josh was a skillful musical editor, astutely selecting and discarding things from every stage of his musical career, and the songs on *Southern Exposure* frequently bring back echoes of his previous records. The title song is set to the tune of "Careless Love," using the arrangement Josh first recorded in 1933, but the playing is much stronger, the guitar functioning as an equal partner to the voice rather than simply as accompaniment. The singing is also both more powerful and subtler than the enthusiastic but somewhat callow sound of the earlier version.

The album's most musically impressive piece, and the one that remained most prominent in his repertoire, is "Hard Times Blues." Unlike the other songs, which are in traditional blues forms, "Hard Times" harks back to de Paur's rearrangements of chain-gang work songs. Josh opens with a driving bass figure that ends as he strums a single chord and starts singing a cappella in a polished variation on the southern field holler, then brings the guitar back in for a regular, rhythmic chorus. The lyrics, some of Cuney's best work, were later published in printed collections of his poetry:

> Went down home 'bout a year ago
> Things so bad, Lord, my heart was sore
> Folks had nothing, was a sin and a shame
> Everybody said hard times was to blame

*Chorus:*

    Great God A-Mighty, folks feeling bad;
        lost everything they ever had
    Great God A-Mighty, folks feeling bad;
        lost everything they ever had

    The sun was a-shining fourteen days and no rain
    Hoeing and planting was all in vain
    Hard, hard times, Lord, all around
    Meal barrels empty, crops burned to the ground

    Skinny-looking children, bellies poking out
    That old pellagra without a doubt
    Old folk hanging 'round the cabin door
    Ain't seen times this hard before

    I went to the boss at the commissary store
    Folks all starving, please don't close your door
    Want more food, a little more time to pay
    Boss man laughed and walked away

    Landlord coming 'round when the rent is due
    You ain't got the money, take your home from you;
    Take your mule and horse, even take your cow
    Says "Get off of my land, you're no good nohow."

The album was beautifully presented. The left side of the cover showed a pillared southern mansion, golden in the sunlight, but drawn so as to seem to be peeling off, allowing the true picture to emerge: a rundown wooden shack and a couple of leafless trees, wasting away under a cold night sky. The liner notes were by Richard Wright, then America's most famous black writer, solidifying the connection to the Harlem Renaissance as well as links to the African American left. Wright was an active Communist Party member and had been seeking a language that would reach out to a black working-class constituency. Clearly, *Southern Exposure* had a special appeal for him, as he explained in his notes.

Cultural leaders, both black and white, had often embraced spirituals as part of a rich Negro heritage while dismissing blues as lowlife pop music. Wright, in contrast, announced that blues were "the 'Spirituals' of the city . . . the songs of simple folk whose lives are caught and hurt in the brutal logic of modern industrial life." He added that "the blues, contrary to popular conception, are not always concerned with love, razors, dice, and death; they are concerned with every item of experience that disturbs and moves the imagination of the Negro folk. Hitherto, the best known blues songs have had love as their main theme, and, as a result, the public has gotten a rather one-sided impression of their real scope and function in Negro life. With the issuance of this album, SOUTHERN EXPOSURE, Keynote presents the 'other side' of the blues, the side that criticizes the environment, the side that has been long considered 'non-commercial' because of its social militancy. . . . SOUTHERN EXPOSURE contains the blues, the wailing blues, the moaning blues, the laughing-crying blues, the sad-happy blues. But it contains also the *fighting* blues."

Having established the blues as the true voice of African American resistance, Wright went on to argue for their universality. Asking rhetorically why the blues were so popular, he wrote: "Is it not that the Negro, in singing his spontaneous, blue songs, expresses in a large measure the deep hunger of millions of Americans for sensual expression, for the free play of impulse? Whatever the answer, this much is true: where the Negro cannot go, his blues songs have gone, affirming kinship in a nation teeming with differences, creating unity and solidarity where distance once reigned."

These sentiments, undoubtedly sincere, were also perfectly in keeping with the CP leadership's ever stronger emphasis on outreach. When Germany invaded the Soviet Union, the Popular Front ideals of the 1930s suddenly became mainstream reality. For the first time there was a common enemy whom almost everyone could agree on. With Russia now an official ally of the United States, Communism and patriotism could go hand in hand. Indeed, the Communists became such fervent supporters of the government that they came into conflict with some of their old allies, for the new Party line emphasized the primacy of the war effort, often to the neglect of industrial unionism and civil rights issues. Workers in the defense industry found their wages frozen while their bosses reaped enormous profits, and many blacks in the armed forces, relegated to segregated units and abused by racist officers, wondered what they were fighting for. But the Communists formed a united front with the government, opposing strikes and protests. While remaining theoretically supportive of fair wages and desegregation, for the duration of the war the Party would push these issues to the sidelines, and through this policy it lost much of the good will it had built up during the Depression years.

For many progressives, though, World War II was a blessedly unambiguous period, one in which the Soviet Union and the United States were fighting side by side, and leftists were faced with no difficult choices. A 1942 *Fortune* magazine poll found that 25 percent of Americans favored socialism, and another 35 percent had an open mind about it. In New York the numbers were likely even higher, and the CP's membership records are indicative of both the enthusiasm generated by the times and the frequent casualness of that enthusiasm: in April 1942 the Party had roughly 44,000 members, but even though 10,000 new recruits had joined in the previous year, there had been a net gain of only 1,500 members. Clearly, people were getting excited and joining, but few were remaining to become Party stalwarts.

This pattern was particularly true of the artistic community. Leftist organizations sponsored dances, cabarets, art expositions, and summer camps where not only children but urban adults could go for a while to socialize and escape the city's heat and humidity. There is an evocative photograph of Josh and Carol at an outdoor sing-along at Bear Mountain, with Huddie and Martha Ledbetter, Alan and Elizabeth Lomax, and Millard Lampell. Dizzy Gillespie, a musician not usually noted for his political radicalism, has written that he and his friends "used to play for all the communist dances. The communists used to hold a lot of them . . . [and] they were always trying to convert you. As a matter of fact, I signed one of those cards; I never went to a meeting, but I was a card-carrying communist because it was directly associated with my work, the dances, Camp Unity and all that kinda stuff."

For African Americans the general enthusiasm could be combined with other temptations. Sam Gary would later tell Josh Jr. that both he and Josh had briefly become Party members but that their joining had less to do with politics than with the free liquor and female companionship to be found at Party events. Since the early 1930s the CP had earned a reputation as the one white organization that welcomed African Americans not only politically but socially. Blacks, and black entertainers above all, were often treated with adulation in progressive circles. Richard Wright, who broke with the Party at the height of its wartime popularity, spoke with cynical bemusement of a black membership he perceived as growing by leaps and bounds: "I don't know whether they're going in for the Marxism and Communism or whether they're going in for the white women."

The New York left was certainly heady company for a black blues singer. In the 1930s Josh's fans had been rural, southern blacks, buying his records for twenty-five cents each from mail-order catalogues. In the 1940s they were white, urban, and often quite wealthy cafe-goers who, far from objecting to his strong stance on racial issues, applauded and lionized him as a spokesman for social justice and racial pride.

Josh was not a complex political theorist, but he was a passionate fighter for what he believed was right. He may have joined in the peace songs and union anthems of the Almanac Singers less because he had the same personal convictions than because the Almanacs seemed like good guys, but the songs against Jim Crow came from his heart, and he sang them wherever he went, regardless of any opposition he might face. There was nothing theoretical about the experiences that fueled such songs as "Bad Housing Blues" or "Jim Crow Train." The mobilization preceding U.S. entry into World War II, a "war to save democracy," drove home the ironies of American segregation, and he fought back with wry, angry songs such as "Defense Factory Blues" and "Uncle Sam Says."

In September 1940, Roosevelt had signed the Selective Service Act into law, and it included provisions that seemed to guarantee black recruits protection against some of the discriminatory practices they had faced in World War I. These guarantees were not backed up by any strong powers of enforcement, however, and Army Chief of Staff George C. Marshall expressed the War Department's prevailing opinion when he stated that integration was "fraught with danger to efficiency, discipline, and morale"; the department, said General Marshall, could not "ignore the social relationships between Negroes and whites which has [sic] been established by the American people through custom and habit." Roosevelt, apparently at his wife's urging, made some efforts to conciliate black leaders but on the whole showed no willingness to buck this tide, saying that it would be unwise to "confuse the issue of prompt preparedness with a new social experiment, however important and desirable it may be."

For northern blacks in particular, the issue was not that they wanted a "new social experiment" but simply that they did not want to return to the brutality and Jim Crow practices that had driven many of them out of the South in the first place. Draftees from Harlem were being sent to army camps in towns that responded to their arrival with front-page ads calling for new Ku Klux Klan volunteers, and assigned to segregated units commanded by officers whose sympathies were entirely with the locals. Up north, although the local townspeople might be less openly hostile, the conditions on base were insulting at best, as Josh was to see firsthand. When his brother Bill was drafted and sent to Fort Dix, New Jersey, for basic training, Josh visited him there and was taken aback by the different standards of living enjoyed by white and black GIs, the segregated mess halls and living accommodations. "We kept driving around, and I couldn't find my brother's barracks, but I began to notice . . . If you keep your eyes open, you'll notice things. First, there were all wooden barracks. Then there was half wood, and canvas-top. And finally it came down to just the pup tents, and that's where you found the Negroes."

When he finally located his brother, he asked whether any of the wooden barracks were for Negroes. Bill said no, they were not. "Well I shouldn't have been surprised," Josh recalled. "But I wasn't thinking. I felt that once we were preparing to fight an enemy we'd forget about these things and go ahead and get rid of the enemy, and then we'd start fighting this thing at home in a more orderly manner. So I went home, and I couldn't sleep. So I wrote a song. It wasn't a good song, a good tune, a good lyric, but it said what I had to say, what I wanted to say about Uncle Sam."

"Uncle Sam Says" is credited to Cuney and White, but there is no reason to doubt that it was inspired by Josh's experience:

Airplanes flying 'cross the land and sea
Everybody flying but a Negro like me
Uncle Sam says, "Your place is on the ground
When I fly my airplanes, don't want no Negro 'round."

The same thing for the Navy, when ships go to sea
All they got is a mess boy's job for me
Uncle Sam says, "Keep on your apron, son
You know I ain't gonna let you shoot my big Navy gun."

Got my long government letter, my time to go
When I got to the Army found the same old Jim Crow
Uncle Sam says, "Two camps for black and white"
But when trouble starts, we'll all be in that same big fight.

If you ask me, I think democracy is fine
I mean democracy without the color line.
Uncle Sam says, "We'll live the American way"
Let's get together and kill Jim Crow today.

While waiting for *Southern Exposure* to be released, Josh received an exciting invitation. The Mexican government was hosting a Pan American Conference of radio broadcasters and educators in Mexico City, and CBS sent Alan Lomax to present a demonstration of its *Wellsprings of Music* series (part of its larger *School of the Air*), featuring Josh and the Golden Gate Quartet.

On August 12 the group flew from Brownsville, Texas, to Mexico City. "It was the first time that any of us had been out of the United States," the Gates' Orlandus Wilson remembers. "And it was quite a festival for us, because we could clown around together, and we had time to ourselves to do sightseeing and that sort of thing. They gave us a couple of interpreters that traveled with us, and they took us on trips in small boats going around the canals, and we also went to some of the nightclubs; we just had fun laughing and talking together and seeing some of the shows."

Josh talked about that trip in an interview with the *Daily Worker* soon after his return. The paper had printed a photograph of the Carolinians in connection with *New Masses'* thirtieth anniversary celebration in February, but this was the first full-length article on Josh, prompted by the release of *Southern Exposure*. Under the headline "Blasting Jim-Crow with Song," it gave a brief synopsis of his life and a few verses from the album, then finished with several paragraphs on the Mexico trip. Apparently, the visit had been a huge success but marred by some of the same Jim Crow treatment that was all too familiar in the United States. The large hotels and resorts, which catered mostly to wealthy Americans, were doing what they could to keep these clients happy, and that included protecting them from contact with Josh and his companions: "One tourist ranch in Taxco phoned an invitation for the weekend and sent a car for the boys. When they arrived and the manager realized that they were Negroes, it all turned out to be a mistake. Not only were there no reservations, there was not so much as a sandwich to serve them before the long drive back to Mexico City." Still, the article added, there were plans afoot to send Josh on a further goodwill tour of all South America, and it ended on a note of ringing optimism: "Josh White and his guitar are a great symbol of America, singing and fighting her way toward real democracy."

*Southern Exposure* attracted even more attention than *Chain Gang.* Along with *Talking Union,* Robeson's *Ballad for Americans,* and the Spanish Civil War anthology *Six Songs for Democracy,* it became one of the handful of records found in virtually all progressive households. An album release party at a popular Harlem hangout, Ralph's Bar and Grill, attracted several hundred guests, including professors from Howard, Fisk, and Union Universities, the artist Romare Beardon, jazz pianist Teddy Wilson, Earl Robinson, Lee Hays, Burl Ives, and W. C. Handy, "the Father of the Blues." Handy, who had reportedly driven in from Chicago for the event, made a short speech, saying how glad he was that the blues tradition was being carried on by the younger generation, and "paid homage to Mr. White and Mr. Cuney after the former had sung the songs to the accompaniment of his famous guitar." Josh took full advantage of the occasion, though apparently it was no easy feat: one reporter noted that "he had just come back from Mexico, and he was tired and so sick he could hardly finger his guitar, but he stood for more than an hour responding to shouts for one song after another."

The album went on sale early in September and was praised everywhere from the *Daily Worker* to the *New York Times.* The *Amsterdam Star-News* devoted two articles to the release, one quoting liberally from Wright's notes and the second rating it as a major work that "no record library should be without." The reviewer emphasized the realness of the material, noting that "all of you know the guy who 'went to the defense factory trying to find some work to do.'" And "over there on 133d St. and Park Ave., and down in Mississippi and out in Minnesota, we all have a brother or a sister or a cousin who can wail: 'woke up this mornin' rain water in my bed. . . . There ain't no reason I should live this way. . . . I've lost my job, can't even get on the WPA.'"

Josh was becoming recognized as a musical spokesman for civil rights. His schedule of benefit concerts was growing ever busier and, when the New Theatre League decided to capitalize on the popularity of its weekly dances by hosting an antifascist nightclub, Chez Liberty, he was a featured performer on opening night and for the next three weeks. Indeed, for the next few months he and Sam Gary were ubiquitous on the left-wing circuit. Whether they actually made it to all the "all-star" benefit shows for which they were advertised is open to question, but they did more than their share.

Josh was also gaining stature with the African American cultural elite. Through *Southern Exposure* he had become associated with Cuney and Richard Wright, both leading lights of the Harlem Renaissance, and Fisk University reportedly invited him to Nashville to present him with an honorary degree in "Folk Anthology." W. C. Handy, whose "St. Louis Blues" had first put blues on the national map, also seems to have taken a special interest in his work. They likely met at the broadcast of a special "Music" segment of WEAF's *Freedom's People*, which featured them along with Robeson and the Leonard de Paur Chorus. Later, Josh was invited to perform with Robeson at a sixty-eighth birthday ceremony for the composer at the National Conference of Negro Youth in Washington, and then to play most of the music for Handy's radio biography.

To cement Josh's status as a "symbol of America," he also became a favorite of the Roosevelts. Someone had sent FDR a copy of *Southern Exposure*, and the president had been particularly taken with "Uncle Sam Says." To Josh's immense gratification, Roosevelt requested a private performance at the White House. "He said he wanted to see what I looked like singing the song to him," Josh said. "Because he knew I was talking about him when I was singing about Uncle Sam. . . . People said I should say I had laryngitis, because I shouldn't sing this to the president, but I figured if he wanted me to come down and sing the song, I was gonna go down and do it."

Josh recalled the visit years later. The reception room was full of "bigwigs," and the president was sitting in a chair, with Mrs. Roosevelt at his side. "I'd never thought of him as being a polio victim—it just didn't dawn on me, a lot of people didn't think about it. So I go over to shake his hand, before I go into my little bit, and I got my hand in his hand, but not the way it should have been, and he crunched down on it like a bear. I snatched it back, and 'God damn it,' I screamed out. He went 'kwa, kwa, kwa, kwa [*laughing*], well, let's do it again,' and this time I got it in his hand so he couldn't hurt me—I hate a fishy handshake anyhow, but I didn't get a chance to get *into* his hand when he came down on me. I said, 'I make my living with these things.' Probably I shouldn't have said that, but if it had been Jesus Christ God Almighty I would have said the same thing—it hurt, let's face it. He was a strong man, wow. And a good guy, too."

Josh gave a concert for the assembled guests, including all the songs from *Southern Exposure*, as well as a few spirituals. After it was all over, Roosevelt invited him back to his private chambers. "We were talking over coffee, with brandy—coffee royale. I brought up about this 'walking tax' bit in Greenville . . . and asked him why was this sort of thing so. And he says, 'Oh, there's no such thing. I'll look into it, but there's no such thing as a walking tax.' He explained to me, he said, 'Who are you talking about when you're singing "Uncle Sam Says"?' Well I told him, 'You're the president, you're Uncle Sam, I was singing about you.' He was a wonderful man, really, so he says, 'Well, you know, the president can be vetoed; he can't do everything.' I says, 'But we, as a whole, kind of think the president can damn near do everything.' And I talked to him like I talk to you—this is the kind of guy he was."

It was the first of many social visits with the Roosevelts, both at the White House and at their home in Hyde Park, where Josh's brother Bill would later get a job. Apparently, the First Family liked Josh not only as a musician but on a personal basis, and Eleanor Roosevelt became Josh Jr.'s godmother. The Roosevelt connection boosted Josh's prestige still further, and by the end of the war years he was being referred to as "the Presidential Minstrel."

# PARTNERSHIPS: LEADBELLY AND LIBBY HOLMAN 1941-1943

■ ■ ■ ■ ■ ■ ■ ■ ■ ■ ■ ■ ■ ■ ■ ■ ■ ■ ■ ■ ■ ■

Throughout the early 1940s most of the news articles on Josh focused on his political work, but politics by no means monopolized his life. Benefit concerts and appearances for the Roosevelts were getting his name out in front of the public but were not helping to feed what was now a family of five. Josh was not yet thirty, but he was in a very different position from the free-living bachelors and bohemian couples who surrounded him on the folk scene. The radio work paid him something, as did the recording sessions and the concerts with the Golden Gates, but he still did not have a regular source of income. So, along with the benefits and politically oriented material, he was also trying his hand at other kinds of songs and venues. Shortly before the first Almanac Singers session he recorded four sides for the Conqueror label, backed by bass, drums, and clarinetist Edmond Hall. The instrumentation and material indicate that these were aimed at the black pop market but they apparently failed to attract attention. (One, "Gotta Go," suggests the extent to which the *John Doe* antiwar songs were recorded simply to help the Almanacs and did not represent any strongly held personal convictions of Josh's: its first line is "I've gotta join the army.") He also appeared with Burl Ives and the actor Will Geer in a short folk music film, *Tall Tales,* which enjoyed a brief New York run.

He still had not found any regular work, but his next break was on the way. It came through his association with Leadbelly, which had started when the two appeared on Lomax's radio shows. Josh had since performed at an afternoon tribute to the older bluesman at Cafe Society Downtown and joined him to provide backing for a Spirituals to Swing–style dance program in November. Nicholas Ray was impressed by the way they worked as a team and suggested to Max Gordon, the owner of the Village Vanguard, that they would make a perfect act for his venue.

Ray's suggestion came at the right time for everyone concerned. Gordon's basement club, which the New Yorker described as "something like an air-raid shelter, except for the singers," had been a hangout for Greenwich Village bohemians since the mid-1930s. Over the previous year it had attracted a new degree of attention with the Revuers, a group of young musical comedians including Judy Holliday, Adolph Comden, and Betty Green. The Revuers had been lured away to the more profitable uptown clubs, and Gordon needed a new draw. Meanwhile, Leadbelly, despite his wide exposure on Lomax's radio programs and frequent college and folk concert appearances, had not managed to find the sort of regular work that could provide him with a decent living. Ray felt that "for a nightclub audience to take more than forty minutes of Leadbelly alone was risky" but that the addition of Josh would make for a perfect partnership: Josh's sophistication would balance Leadbelly's earthiness, while Leadbelly's deep traditional feel would lend weight to Josh's uptown sound.

Both singers were interested, and Gordon agreed that they could rehearse at the club in the daytime until they felt they were ready to open. "I turned on the work-lamp, wiped a table clean, and put a bottle of rye on the table," Gordon writes in his autobiography. "I hung around, watching and listening, saying nothing. Not until they finished the bottle did they say anything to me. So I put another bottle on the table. This went on for a week. And one day, twenty bottles later, Nick said he thought they were ready."

The duo's debut on November 25, 1941, attracted every folksinger in New York. Leadbelly and Josh were both great favorites, and the nightclub booking was a breakthrough for folk music as a whole. The two performers appeared on stage together but sang most of their songs as solos, each occasionally chiming in with the other on a vocal chorus, then finished up the night by trading verses and guitar solos on an improvised blues. Josh used the Vanguard's one microphone; Lead-belly's big voice and guitar easily filled the tiny club. "They were a great combination," remembers Pete Seeger, who was there for the opening night. "Leadbelly'd keep that great, thumping bass rhythm going, and Josh would get all the single strings going up in the top."

Woody Guthrie was also there that evening, and he wrote Gordon a long letter offering encouragement and suggesting a few improve-ments. He felt the show had "got all it takes to make night club history in New York . . . and open up a whole new field for entertainers of all colors, namely just plain, common, everyday American Music." Guth-rie clearly considered Leadbelly the deeper artist but was impressed by Josh's musicianship and easy stage presence: "Josh is an intelligent young guy, fast thinker, easy talker — friendly, and has made his living most of his life by being just that way. . . . Josh just happens to know the guitar and the blues 'from way back' — and this gives him the real feel-ing of what the blues is all about . . . the voice of the Negro people singing a worried song for all people. Josh remembers that Joe Louis is the best boxer the world ever had, and Josh wants to be the Joe Louis of the blues guitar. After lots of years of hard playing and singing Josh has got to be just that."

Getting down to specific criticisms, Guthrie suggested that Josh's portion of the show could do with a bit more variety, that his songs were all "too mush [*sic*] in the same movement and tempo . . . all too slow beat, and smooth and sweet." He also felt that Gordon should be care-ful to maintain the two singers' separate characters, suggesting he build them up "in exactly the same way that you'd say, Here's the boy from the Ukraine that destroyed a Hitler tank all by himself, and was honored with the order of Lenin. Or, here's the boy from Tennessee that sunk a German U-Boat singlehanded. . . .

"It is an entire way of life with both of them and their individual feelings about their individual work can't be anything but slowed down to work both of them together too much on a show. It cramps Josh's style, and cramps Leadbelly's. Both of them personally have told me that they had slightly different ways of doing their best, and that work-ing together as a team didn't allow their best to come through; and to present Josh and Huddie at any level but their best is wrong."

Josh and Leadbelly were indeed very different characters. Guthrie contrasted Leadbelly's "simplicity, roughness, honesty, strength, and volume" with Josh's "more refined, citified, educated, a little more complicated, but still mean and honest" approach, but the most dramatic difference between them was probably one of age. Leadbelly, born in 1888, was twice as old as Josh, and he had the habits and manner of another generation.

Leadbelly's admirers often spoke of him as a "primitive" genius, and reporters described his "country" dress as if this were a badge of genuineness. Some concert producers presented him in overalls or even prison garb. To those who were close to him, however, this was ridiculous and insulting. "Leadbelly was a dandy," says Josephine Premice, a Haitian dancer who would become a cabaret star and close friend of Josh. "He had this incredible cane that he carried, I think it had a gold head." Moses Asch, who recorded Leadbelly on his Asch and Disc labels, called him "the most formal human being that ever existed." The younger blues singer Brownie McGhee speaks of the lectures Leadbelly gave him on the importance of keeping up his personal appearance, wearing a tie, and always carrying his guitar in a case rather than just flinging it across his back. And Gordon writes that on opening night at the Vanguard, Leadbelly was "immaculately attired in a powder blue suit."

Leadbelly was certainly more countrified than Josh, but he was no backwoods hick. In black company he could sing rowdy songs that would get a party swinging even in an era when much of his style was considered dated. Unlike Josh, though, he had a lifetime of habits picked up as a black man in the deep South. Lee Hays's biographer writes of Hays's irritation that Leadbelly, though regarded as a master and teacher by young white singers, would always address them with the southern forms black people were supposed to use to white superiors, calling him "Mr. Lee" and Seeger "Mr. Pete." Onstage, Leadbelly drew on his decades of experience performing for white southern audiences, using a style that at times played on that audience's stereotypic expectations. His adeptness at entertaining white southerners had been what kept him alive in earlier years and allowed him to sing his way out of prison, but some of his techniques seemed to Josh archaic and demeaning. "He was a fine artist," Josh would say years later. "But Leadbelly was a clown. He . . . played up to the Uncle Tom image of the Negro."

Pete Seeger remembers: "A friend of mine was backstage at the Vanguard once and he heard Leadbelly and Josh arguing, very seriously. Josh was saying 'You do that once more and I'm gonna walk right off the stage and leave you there.' And Leadbelly says, 'Oh, come on, Josh — make a fool of yourself once in a while and take the while folks' money.' " Seeger rightly points out that Leadbelly's attitude was born of hard experience and had often been less a choice than a necessity, but he adds that "Josh was not going to make that kind of compromise."

Josh respected Leadbelly's work but had no interest in becoming a younger version of the primitive, southern archetype that Leadbelly represented in the folk world. In Bess Lomax's words, "Josh was much more of a Harlem man. He thought the other guys [Leadbelly and Sonny Terry] were kinda country, frankly. And they were." More important, he was not limited by the visions of the white folk promoters and musicians who had guided Leadbelly's career. When Josh and Leadbelly played the Village Vanguard, Leadbelly was still probably better known, but he had gone as far as he could go. Unlike the Golden Gate Quartet or the boogie-woogie pianists, he was never going to break the next barrier and attract a wealthy uptown audience. Josh was young, handsome, and supremely versatile, and for him the Vanguard was just another step up the ladder.

Whatever their differences, the pairing of Josh with Leadbelly had been a logical move. Josh's next teaming, though, startled almost all his musical acquaintances. The Vanguard engagement lasted through February 16, 1942, and within three days of closing Josh was in Boston, appearing at the Balinese Room of the Hotel Somerset as accompanist to a sultry white Broadway star and torch singer. Libby Holman was completely different from the other artists with whom Josh had been associated. Born Elizabeth Holzman in Cincinnati, she was ten years his senior and had come to New York in 1924 to seek her fortune in the theater. She quickly succeeded in a string of small, well-written revues, such as 1929's *The Little Show*, in which she starred with Clifton Webb and Fred Allen and introduced two standards, "Can't We Be Friends" and her trademark, "Moanin' Low." The same trio returned the next year in *Three's a Crowd*, and Holman debuted another soon-to-be-classic torch ballad, "Body and Soul."

Holman was famous for her smoky sex appeal, and her offstage life was pretty much in keeping with her professional image. She made her biggest headlines in 1932 when she married Zachary Smith Reynolds, the younger son of the tobacco magnate R. J. Reynolds, and he shortly died in mysterious circumstances after a drunken party at the Reynolds

family estate. Holman said that he had shot himself, but her explanation was widely doubted, and all the partygoers turned up at the inquest
telling vague, contradictory stories punctuated by strategic memory
gaps. Holman, pregnant with a child that many people believed was not
Reynolds's, was eventually put on trial for murder, but the charges were
dropped halfway through, leaving the case and her reputation in limbo.

Despite the scandalous circumstances and a protracted court battle,
Holman and her son inherited some $2 million from the Reynolds'
estate. By the time she met Josh, she controlled $7 million but, rather
than retiring to a life of luxury, had chosen to return to Broadway. After
a trial period in summer stock she took a starring role in a new operetta,
*Revenge with Music,* then spent some time doing a cabaret act before
returning to the stage in *You Never Know,* one of Cole Porter's least
successful musicals. Meanwhile, she lived the life of the rich and sophisticated, hobnobbing with the wilder Broadway and society crowd.

In the early 1940s Holman decided to lead a less frivolous life. She
took an interest in left-wing causes, hosting and appearing at several
benefits, and tried to improve her dramatic acting skills. She also concluded that her Broadway songs were facile and showy and resolved to
master a deeper repertoire. She had been a devotee of black music
since seeing Bessie Smith in Cincinnati, even hiring Billie Holiday and
the Benny Goodman Quartet to play for her son's sixth birthday party,
and had slavishly copied the mannerisms of such black singers as the
Duke Ellington band's Adelaide Hall. Now, with folk music coming to
the fore, she fell in love with the folk-blues sound. She went to the
Vanguard to see Josh and Leadbelly and was entranced with Josh's
singing. Already acquainted with Nicholas Ray, she insisted that he
introduce them, then asked Josh if he would teach her to sing the
blues.

Neither Josh nor Ray thought much of the idea. Ray considered
Holman an affected Broadway singer, and Josh expressed doubts as to
whether any white person could do justice to his music. Nonetheless,
Ray set up a date for the two to get together at Holman's Manhattan
apartment. She would later say that the meeting was "worse than any
audition I ever had on Broadway . . . his approval meant more to me
than a million dollars" (an odd figure of speech for a woman with seven
million). Whatever Josh may privately have thought of Holman's singing, he was complimentary and agreed to take her on as a student,

though he first said she would have to forget all her previous vocal training. In typically overblown style, she responded that she was "prepared to forget even more than that."

Josh had found a partner who could also serve as a patron. Although there is no record of the financial arrangements between them, Holman was clearly his main source of income for the duration of their time together. Free of money worries, he stopped searching out solo jobs and worked "six hours a day, every day," to teach Holman to sing the material. "It took me around twelve months to teach her eight songs. She wanted it to be just like it should be, every breath. Then I had to break her away from being me to being herself." In fact, though it would be another year before they settled into a regular engagement, the duo made their debut at the Somerset within a few months of their first meeting.

Since Holman had not made any appearances in two years, her return was news. Earl Wilson did an interview for the *New York Post,* and the Boston press turned out in force. She was the first established star to take up folk music, and although her comments on this new career trajectory often sounded patronizing and self-important, she was truly in love with the material. "I'm so happy I've found a place where my voice belongs," she told a *Boston Globe* interviewer. "I can't endure Tin Pan Alley melodies—I don't think I'm suited for opera or so-called classical numbers, and I wanted something that nobody else sang. So I looked for what America sang at her beginnings—what American people have felt through what they sang. Only songs of the past can illustrate the true American spirit. No amount of patriotic songs made up for the occasion can be a true barometer of American emotion. And I've picked from the high and the low, the good and the bad. That's how we can be sure of the real American touch."

Speaking of the war, she said, "It's time to sing, and I don't think that 'The Star Spangled Banner' and 'America, I Love You' mean quite as much to people as the songs that a whole nation has felt to be a part of their daily lives. This is real Americana which I have dug up. In the cases of some of the Negro songs, no white person has ever sung them in public. . . . Because you want to spill everything you have at a time like this, I can't stop singing—and with all these new songs I don't want to try to be a lady of leisure."

Josh was mentioned in only one paragraph of the article: "Her accompanist is a Negro — Joshua White — and Miss Holman says that at times he talks with his guitar. 'And sometimes I answer him in the same manner,' she insists. 'I'm not always certain whether it's the guitar or me.'"

Holman's enthusiasm about her new direction was not shared by all her fans, but the interviewer assured them that "Miss Holman doesn't rely entirely on her music — she is enough of a trouper to get a little dramatic setting into the picture. Mainbocher has designed her chocolate brown skirt and white blouse, which sounds simple but isn't." A brief review the day after the opening concert was positive, but it used most of its space to suggest that the audience wanted more of Holman's old hits, and to express a hope that "she'll sing a tin pan alley 'blues' song before she leaves the Somerset Hotel."

Later writers, and most of Josh's friends, stress the earthshaking novelty of Josh and Holman's interracial pairing, but the fact that Holman was appearing in a duo with a black man did not excite any particular comment from contemporary reporters. It did, however, cause immediate logistical problems. The Somerset made it clear that Holman would get lodging in the hotel, but Josh would have to stay elsewhere. Furthermore, he was not welcome in the Balinese Room except as a performer. "My brother [Bill] was at Fort Devens, near Boston," he recalled. "He came in, but we couldn't mingle — Libby wouldn't sit at a table with anyone since we couldn't."

To solve the problem, the three of them decided to meet in Holman's room after the show. "We had to go upstairs and see what we wanted to cut and what we should add," Josh said. "[But] they didn't appreciate my being upstairs and they called her to 'get those Negroes out of there . . .' She said, 'Mr. White happens to be my accompanist, whose brother is in the armed forces training to fight for America.' She wouldn't stand for it. So the next evening I came down and found Libby . . . picketing the Somerset Hotel, saying, 'Take down the American flag and put up a German swastika.'"

Despite the problems, Holman was thrilled with her new persona, and in March she and Josh went into the studio to record *Blues till Dawn,* a three-record album for Decca. Today, the album sounds pretty dreadful. Holman said that she was "not trying to copy the Negroes . . . just taking their feeling," but despite Josh's coaching, she had neither the sound nor the soul. Her singing has a forced affectation of passion;

her phrasing is marked by long, moaning slides that constantly waver off pitch. Josh's playing is fine, but his spare style, designed to set off his own vocals, does nothing to cover Holman's deficiencies.

For Josh's fans, however, the song selection is interesting. The album was made just before the War Production Board issued an order restricting domestic use of shellac, which was the main component of phonograph records. This restriction, combined with the American Federation of Musicians' recording ban, which went into effect in August, meant that virtually no records were made between 1942 and 1944. This was a key period in Josh's career, during which he made the transition from someone who was primarily a blues and gospel singer to a folk star whose taste in material stretched over three continents and several centuries. Virtually all the songs on *Blues till Dawn* would be staples of Josh's later repertoire, and one wonders to what extent they represent his own work of the period, which he was teaching to Holman, and to what extent the collaboration with Holman may have shaped his future direction. Certainly, Leroy Carr's "When the Sun Goes Down" came from his songbag, but it may well be through Holman that he was drawn to two women's laments, "House of the Rising Sun" and "Fare Thee Well" (a Lomax find originally known as "Dink's Song"), and to the Appalachian ballad "On Top of Old Smoky."

The album got good reviews, but Holman had to put her musical life temporarily on hold while she opened on Broadway in a new play, *Mexican Mural.* The play lasted only three weeks, but in those days before air conditioning, summer was the dead time for New York nightlife, so her big-city debut as a blues singer was put off till the fall. Meanwhile, she and Josh continued to rehearse, and he escaped the summer heat by spending much of his time at her Connecticut estate. Oscar Brand, a young folk singer recently arrived from Canada, remembers going to visit him out there and being amused to find all the rich women running after him. The rest of the White family members were also welcome, and Bunny still speaks with awe about her first sight of Holman reclining in a huge, sunken, black marble bathtub.

Josh kept on playing occasional benefit shows, and in August he and Sam Gary were treated to a testimonial dinner featuring Leadbelly, Albert Ammons, and Pete Johnson. But he was mostly working with Holman and marking time until their New York debut. They finally opened in late October at an uptown nightspot, La Vie Parisienne. This was an elegant room, known for its European talent and the murals of

Paris that adorned its walls. Though a long way from Josh's Greenwich Village turf, it was a logical venue for Holman's wealthy society crowd, which flocked to hear her sing her new repertoire. An out-of-town columnist who dropped by reported finding the club "so full I could barely squeeze in."

The New York press was generally effusive, although one finds the occasional gibe at the rural roots of Holman's material. The *Post*'s Earl Wilson declared Holman "on the way to becoming a national institution" and gushed over her voice, her dress, and the way she performed "the beautiful old folk songs she and Josh had gathered down in Noo Orleyuhns, Joejuh and elsewhere." Only the *New Yorker* failed to be bowled over by her transformation, declaring the whole show rather gloomy and disparaging the "sort of groan" to which Holman resorted in her low range. "There are moments when she gives up singing altogether and devotes herself to what might be an imitation of Marley's ghost, minus only the jingle jangle jingle of chains," the critic wrote, adding that this might be appropriate for the folk material but was absolute death to the more familiar torch songs.

Holman had added the torch songs only in response to the demands of old fans and was annoyed that she should now be criticized for singing them wrong. In her mind the problem was that the synthetic Broadway ballads simply did not stand up to the pure folk art. Responding to those who said she was not singing the old songs as well as she had in the past, she said, "I sing them better — I've got more voice now. [People] just don't want the old songs, though they don't know it."

The folk scene took an equally mixed view of what Holman and Josh were doing. The duo was a hit, and was exposing the music to an audience that had never heard it before, but many of Josh's early fans were purists who thought of him as a genuine folk artist and a partner of Leadbelly's, and they considered his new direction something of a betrayal. Brownie McGhee, who made a trip up from North Carolina to Washington in 1942 to act as accompanist for Sonny Terry, says that after the gig all the important folk people came over and told him that he had to move to New York because "they didn't have any blues singers up there; that Josh White was the only one, and he'd gone white." McGhee laughingly adds that when he got to New York and met Josh, "when I saw how much money he was making, I said, 'Hey, show me how to go white, too.' "

Whatever he might have been doing musically, Josh had by no means gone white, as the Vie Parisienne management quickly made clear. Just as in Boston, the club was happy to have Josh on its stage but did not want him or his family mingling with anyone out front. "They wanted Josh to come in the back door, play for Libby and leave," Carol White says. "And she said, 'You have really got to be kidding. I will not sing another note in this place. Josh White and his family come in the front door or I don't sing here.' And when I did go down there after that, I walked in the front door."

Such annoyances aside, Josh and Holman were well pleased with their success. They stayed at La Vie Parisienne for almost four months, then took a month's vacation and returned for a further two. By that time, Holman seems to have had her fill of nightclub life, and Josh was ready to strike out on his own, though the duo continued to make occasional special appearances at military bases along the East Coast. They also attempted to go abroad on a USO tour, but Holman was informed that a policy forbidding "mixed entertainment" made it impossible. She wrote to Eleanor Roosevelt, who in turn wrote to the USO director, but nothing came of the correspondence. For the next two years, Holman and Josh went their separate ways.

# 8

# CAFE SOCIETY
## 1943-1945
■ ■ ■ ■ ■ ■ ■ ■ ■ ■ ■ ■ ■ ■ ■ ■ ■ ■ ■ ■

JOSH WHITE

*. . . is a sly, winning smile and a burning cigarette cocked over one ear.*

*. . . is a charmer, a satyr and a fighter.*

*. . . is a soft insinuating voice that speaks directly to the heart.*

*. . . is a pair of lean hands that rustle over his guitar like brown hawk's wings.*

*. . . is a cafe singer and a poet and a proud American.*

*. . . is a voice for his people and for freedom-loving people everywhere.*

— Notes to *Folk Songs Sung by Josh White,* Asch album 358, 1944

The 1940s and 1950s were the golden age of New York cabaret. Television had not yet had its disastrous effect on the nightclub business, and New Yorkers took pride in the sophistication of the city's small entertainment rooms. The Village Vanguard had set the pattern in the 1930s, and it was followed by the more refined, European-flavored Ruban Bleu uptown, then a flood of new venues. Some lasted only a few months; others thrived for decades. Their sizes ranged from tiny to small, and entertainers were encouraged to provide an intimate, living-room feel.

It was a late-night scene; the clubs might start their first show at midnight, and few closed before three or four in the morning. They had fallen heir to the tradition of the prohibition-era speakeasies and after-hours joints, and customers cheerfully crowded together in an atmosphere thick with loud talk and cigarette smoke. Regulars took pride in knowing the performers personally, or at least in being greeted as old friends when they brought in dates they wanted to impress. Each club had its own special clientele, some noted for wealth and prestige, others for bohemian funkiness. All were very "New York," the pinnacle of metropolitan sophistication. Indeed, it was almost a point of pride that when popular local stars went on the road, they tended to bomb in such "backwaters" as Cleveland and Omaha.

The nightclub entertainers were a varied bunch. Typically, a club would have a comedian and a couple of musical acts, plus a pianist to play during breaks, but that was by no means a fixed rule. If the musical performers were strong enough and someone else was prepared to act as master of ceremonies, the comedian could sometimes be dispensed with, and other sorts of acts occasionally made their way into the mix. Dancers, if they were able to work on the tiny stages, could win devoted followings. The larger rooms might have a small dance floor, in which case there would also be a house band, a swing group of five or six pieces.

When Josh finished his stint with Holman at La Vie Parisienne, he had a reputation that no one else on the folk scene could match, and Max Gordon quickly booked him into the Blue Angel. The Angel was an uptown club, owned by Gordon and a Frenchman, Herbert Jacoby, who had made his name with the Ruban Bleu and specialized in continental performers. Ever since Josh and Leadbelly had opened up the Village Vanguard to folk music, Gordon had made it a staple of his downtown club, but the Angel had remained folk-free until Josh's debut there. His engagement lasted slightly over two weeks, and he blazed a trail for later folk performers—something he would do in a half-dozen rooms around New York. The uptown milieu never felt quite right for him, though, and he found his nightclub home back in Greenwich Village, at Cafe Society.

Cafe Society had been started in December 1938 by Barney Josephson, a native of New Jersey who had been working as a shoestore clerk in Atlantic City before he decided to go into the nightclub business. Josephson opened his club with the explicit intention of creating a space where black and white patrons could mix in an atmosphere of absolute equality. He had often been to the Cotton Club—the famous Harlem showcase for black entertainers, where the few black customers were seated in a special section at the back—and the Kit Kat Club, which had an all-black staff and entertainment policy but barred blacks from the audience. As a Jew, he was intimately familiar with the restrictive policies of such popular niteries as the Stork Club, which did its best to discourage Jewish, as well as black, custom. He thought New York was ready for a different kind of room and named his club in a satiric comment on the wealthy "cafe society" crowd. It is mildly ironic that to many people his own clientele would come to define the term.

Cafe Society was a small, L-shaped basement room that seated just over two hundred people. Its walls were decorated with murals by progressive New York artists, satirizing the society swells, and it aimed for an audience of artists, jazz fans, and college kids. It had inexpensive food and a small dance floor, and it presented three shows a night, at nine, twelve, and two in the morning. From the outset the club featured some of the best black musicians in the country, booked on the advice of John Hammond. In its first years it provided a home for the Spirituals to Swing stars plus such Hammond protégés as Billie Holiday and Teddy Wilson. In 1940, Josephson opened a second and larger branch on 58th Street, which he called Cafe Society Uptown. As a rule, he would break in acts at the downtown club, then move them uptown when they had attracted a large enough following, but if a performer such as the pianist Mary Lou Williams seemed better suited to the smaller, more relaxed room, she could play there on and off for years.

To the regular Cafe Society performers the club was much more than just another venue. "It was like a family," says Susan Reed, who would join Josh, Burl Ives, and Richard Dyer-Bennett as one of the big four of the 1940s folk world. "Barney was the most loving, caring person, an incredible man, and he created an environment that was so pleasant that when I later went to work in some other nightclubs I couldn't believe how awful they were. We were all treated nicely at Cafe Society, and of course you flourished."

Cafe Society was like nowhere else on earth. The customers could include Ernest Hemingway and Paulette Goddard one night, Ingrid Bergman or Eleanor Roosevelt the next. Joe Louis and Paul Robeson were regular visitors, and when Harlem's flamboyant Congressman Adam Clayton Powell married the pianist Hazel Scott, Josephson hosted their wedding party at his uptown venue. For the performers, the downtown club was the sort of room where you might hang out even if you were not working. Pearl Primus, a modern dancer who became a Cafe Society sensation and choreographed a dance to Josh's "Hard Time Blues," spoke glowingly of the parties the performers would have in the wee hours, after the customers had been sent home, when someone like Leadbelly might stop by and join an impromptu jam session with Josh and whoever else was there.

The Carolinians had appeared at Cafe Society Downtown toward the end of 1940 but had not made much of a splash (the *New Yorker*'s club listings for the period never even mentioned them). By the summer of 1943, though, Josh was something of a local name, and he opened on August 24 with second billing in the *New Yorker* listing, below Mary Lou Williams but ahead of Eddie Heywood's Orchestra and Pearl Primus. Within a few months he was the club's top act, and he would remain there, with a few brief breaks, for the next four years.

Josh and Cafe Society were a perfect match. A capsule review in the show business weekly *Variety* introduced him as "the guitar-strumming colored singer of blues who was former accompanist for Libby Holman" and noted that "in the Village let-your-hair-down spots he has already built up a considerable following, as evidenced by the reception he was accorded opening night." It goes on: "White's engaging personality is his strongest factor, though his fine voice and original compositions are no mean assets. . . . For the arty niteries, White is a natural. His appeal elsewhere would probably be limited." This final caveat would prove less than flawless as prophecy, but it reflected the degree to which Josh's show meshed with the room's intimate ambiance.

Despite the Carolinians' earlier visit, Josh's music was something new for the club. Cafe Society had always been the home of black music, whether gospel, blues, or jazz, but by 1943 Josh was no longer relying solely on black musical styles. His repertoire ranged over the breadth of what then constituted the folk genre, from old English ballads to the sort of contemporary "folk" art song that Earl Robinson was writing. Though newspaper articles continued to trace his romantic background as a lead boy for traveling bluesmen, when they talked of his material they were more likely to single out the "songs of social significance." It was his use of topical songs as much as his race that set him apart from the other well-known cabaret folksingers. Burl Ives, Richard Dyer-Bennet, and, later, Susan Reed were dedicated progressives and made regular appearances at benefits, but they tended to eschew explicitly political material. Josh thrived on it.

Throughout the 1940s, articles on Josh would always focus on this aspect of his repertoire. In one of his first extensive interviews, the *New York Post* said that although Josh was "famed as a singer of traditional spirituals and blues, he is not satisfied with singing in these forms alone. He cannot see why the Negro must be represented only by Tin-Pan Alley, or by Uncle Tom's cries to Heaven. He likes best to sing out directly and clearly against Jim Crow practices, as against everything else under the sun that stands in the way of Democracy, equality and justice for everybody. No night-club can dilute his fervor."

Josh's new emphasis was shown by the three songs noted in *Variety*'s review of his twelve-minute debut set: "Little Man Sitting on a Fence," "Blues in Berlin," and "The Cherry, the Chicken, and the Baby" (usually called "The Riddle Song" or "I Gave My Love a Cherry"). The first two were newly composed topical pieces; the third was a medieval English ballad. Blues, in the old sense, was not even represented. Of course, Josh had been singing protest songs since the 1930s, but the new numbers were still a departure for him. Though in interviews he would frequently disparage Tin Pan Alley pop, he was now himself a popular entertainer, and professional songwriters were pitching him material. It is hard to pin down authorship for the topical songs, many of which were pretty ephemeral, but often they came from the pens of the top Broadway and nightclub composers and lyricists and were musically no different from what standard pop performers were singing. "Blues In Berlin," for example, was a wartime rewrite of Harold Arlen's "Blues in the Night," with Nazis rather than women cast as the betrayers. "Little Man Sitting on a Fence" was about a character who had no political convictions, "tryin' to see the war from every point of view / 'cause after all a Nazi is a person too / While the Soviet Union goes ro-o-olling along."

Though he did virtually no songwriting once he moved beyond straightforward blues, journalists frequently credited Josh with authorship of the songs he introduced or popularized. For example, an interviewer for the left-leaning New York newspaper *PM* named him as the author of "Little Man," though it was actually by a writer named Eleanor Young. The extent to which Josh was complicit in this confusion of authorship is unclear, but he could certainly be cavalier about such matters and over the years he often took credit, or at least tacitly accepted it, for introducing songs that had previously been done by other artists.

In the folk world the issue of authorship has always been rather confusing. Although he wrote few songs, Josh tended to rework whatever he learned to fit his style. Telling an interviewer of how he came to compose one of his blues numbers, "Evil-Hearted Me," Josh would add, "When I say I wrote it, I mean I heard this before. But you take a song, and if the story just doesn't run true to form, then you sort of write into it; you add, and you subtract. And that's one thing about folk songs, you're at liberty to do this kind of thing. You don't have to sing them word for word. If the story doesn't make it, then you sort of make the story. You write into the story what you want."

Josh was adept at shaping his material, and he could always toss a blues together when the situation called for it. Few of these made it onto records, but an article in *Opportunity* magazine quotes from a ballad about Dorie Miller, a black naval messman who took over an antiaircraft gun during the Japanese attack on Pearl Harbor and was subsequently decorated for bravery. The rhyme scheme of the lyric suggests that it was a set of straight blues couplets of the sort Josh had often written in the 1930s, and there is no reason to think that the song was not his own composition. Unlike the clever wordplay of his night-club material, it was simple and straightforward: "They found Dorie Miller, behind that great big Navy gun / He made them wish they'd stayed in the land of the risin' sun."

"Dorie Miller" was Josh's contribution to an all-star "Folk Songs on the Firing Line" concert at Town Hall in June 1942, organized to aid the war effort. The lineup included Libby Holman, Leadbelly, the Almanacs, and pretty much everyone else on the New York folk scene, along with singers from the black 183d Regiment, the Coast Guard, the Royal Australian Air Force, and from China and the Soviet Union. (The Australians sang "Waltzing Matilda," and this may be where Josh picked up the song, which would become one of his favorite numbers.) The concert was only one of hundreds of benefits at which Josh performed during the war years and on through the 1940s. Susan Reed recalls that it was not unusual for Cafe Society performers to rush off to play a benefit between sets at the club: "Sometimes we would do six shows a night, three benefits and our regular sets, and we would sell war bonds." Josh was such a regular on the nonprofit circuit that by 1944 he was being referred to in print as "the Benefit Kid."

He was by no means alone in his dedication. The United States and the Soviet Union were fighting side by side, along with all the Western democracies, and the folk world had set itself to churning out patriotic songs. The thing that distinguished Josh from the other performers was that he continued to sing about the problems at home as well as the need for unity abroad. This was not the Party line but did represent a strong sentiment in the African American community. Black leaders were united in their opposition to Hitler's fascism, but they could not ignore the irony of sending their people abroad to fight for principles of freedom and racial equality which were denied them at home. As Roy Wilkins, then leader of the NAACP, wrote, "It sounded pretty foolish to be against park benches marked JUDE in Berlin, but to be *for* park benches marked COLORED in Tallahassee, Florida. It was grim, not foolish, to have a young black man in uniform get an orientation in the morning on wiping out Nazi bigotry and that same evening be told he could buy a soft drink only in the 'colored' post exchange."

Josh's performances were thoroughly patriotic, and he was soon recording morale-boosting programs for the Office of War Information (OWI) and the British Broadcasting Corporation (BBC) — sometimes as many as a dozen in one week — as well as playing shows at military bases and service canteens. Still, even at his most gung-ho, his songs maintained the note of protest he had struck in "Uncle Sam Says." "Dorie Miller," after recounting Miller's heroic acts, goes on to tell how he was sent "back to the messroom with the Navy Cross he'd won / They should have placed him right back behind that big Navy gun," and concludes: "Now if we want to win this war and sink these U-boats in the tide / We've got to have black and white sailors fightin' side by side."

Josh's wartime stance was best summed up in "Freedom Road," a song by Langston Hughes that he performed frequently throughout the war years and continued to sing off and on during the next two decades:

> Hand me my gun, let the bugle blow loud
> I'm on my way with my head up proud
> One objective I've got in view
> Is to keep ahold of freedom for me and you
>
> *Chorus:*
> That's why I'm marching, yes, I'm marching
> Marching down Freedom's Road
> Ain't nobody gonna stop me, nobody gonna keep me
> From marching down Freedom's Road

It ought to be plain as the nose on your face
There's room in this land for every race
Some folks think that freedom just ain't right
Those are the very people I want to fight

Now, Hitler may rant, Hirohito may rave
I'm going after freedom if it leads me to my grave
That's why I'm marching, yes, I'm marching
Marching down Freedom's Road

United we stand, divided we fall
Let's make this land safe for one and all
I've got a message and you know it's right
Black and white together, unite and fight!

Hughes was a friend of the Whites, and Josh narrated and sang most of the songs for his BBC radio play *The Man Who Went to War*. This was only one of Josh's many radio performances during the war years. He also starred in a radio biography of Dorie Miller, *Dorie Got His Medal*, by the writer and director Norman Corwin, and he was featured in several episodes of *New World A-Coming*, a program inspired by Roi Ottley's book of the same name. This history of Harlem, written with a strong racial sensibility, put forward the argument that if America wanted blacks to support the war effort, a lot of changes were going to have to be made at home. On one program the actor Canada Lee read a series of Hughes's stories of Jim Crow absurdities, titled "White Folks Do Some Funny Things," while Josh sang a mix of old and new songs that fit the theme.

On another broadcast, "Music at War," Josh told the story that had inspired "Uncle Sam Says," then acted in a skit based on his experience while singing on the "Lunchtime Follies" revue, a morale-boosting program at a munitions factory in New Jersey. He started by saying that though he and Cuney had written "Defense Factory Blues" some time earlier, he had not planned to sing that song in the revue, preferring to concentrate on patriotic material. Then, as the skit unfolded, Josh found a guard barring him from the factory's segregated restaurant when he went in to get a glass of milk before the show. First nonplussed, then furious, he ended by taking the stage and singing "Defense Factory," with its angry request that if blacks were to be enlisted in the defense of democracy, they be given "some democracy to defend."

"Yes, folks, that's a song I wish I never knew about," he said at the end. "If there was no discrimination against the colored man, I'd give up singing it in a minute. The songs I really enjoy singing are those that symbolize the kind of world we'd all like to live in — songs of hope — of the good people all over the world — they're songs that I like best — because that's what my brother Bill is out there in Italy fighting for."

This hopeful note was driven home by the final selection, "The House I Live In," which had become one of his most famous numbers. Written by Lewis Allan (the pen name of Abel Meeropol), with music by Earl Robinson, this was the progressive equivalent of "America the Beautiful," an evocation of the liberal dream. It begins with the question, "What is America to me?" The answer is a list including the mix of working people, races, and ethnicities, the many forms of democratic government, the words of Lincoln, Jefferson, and Thomas Paine, and the victories at Concord, Gettysburg, Midway, and Bataan. It ends, "A land that we call freedom, the home of liberty / With its promise for tomorrow, that's America to me."

At Cafe Society, Josh was seeing the possibility that this new world of universal brotherhood might be brought to life. The patrons were a blend of wealthy society people and starving artists, blacks and whites, Christians and Jews and atheists, and they were all applauding him and hanging on his every note. Nonetheless, the club was not sealed off from the problems of the larger society, and Josh never took its easygoing climate for granted. Robert Shelton wrote that "Josh had his little prejudice 'tests' for listeners at the Cafe. He would be invited to join them at their tables, then would take a drink from their glasses or a puff of their cigarettes when they were rested in ashtrays. If the patrons failed to return their glasses or cigarettes to their lips, Josh would know that some form of anti-Negro prejudice was stealthily at work, despite apparent friendship."

In some cases no subtle tests were necessary. As Josh became an ever more visible spokesman for racial equality, delivering his message more explicitly than any other nightclub performer of the time, he also became the focus of a lot of racist resentment. A story in the *Amsterdam News* tells how Josh's "long and amicable sojourn" at Cafe Society was being disturbed by "an influx of Southern servicemen who shout his numbers down. . . . [They] drape themselves around the Cafe Society bar and drool quietly until Josh's numbers begin. His songs require a noiseless and intimate environment. The boys at the bar usually know this. They immediately begin catcalls, yelling and hissing — 'they don't want to hear that n----- sing!'

"Being an artist and a rather sensitive one, Josh White was at first 'thrown' by this demonstration," the piece goes on. "But being progressive in his thinking and practical in his method of interpreting this form of sabotage, he has since found that . . . halting his singing while the typical Village patrons repudiate the resentful Southerners and embarrass them out of the place has worked to his advantage."

Sometimes the detractors were not so easily cowed, and there are many stories of fights that broke out at or near Cafe Society over racial issues. Mary Lou Williams remembered that "on several occasions when Josh agreed to escort me back to Harlem after the show, sometimes four or five white men, who had been viewing Josh's drinking with white women at their tables, would be waiting for him outside the club and he would have to fight them all off by himself before we could leave. Some nights, he would be cut and bruised pretty bad, but the other men would be really hurting, laying on the ground. He just accepted this . . . like it was just part of the job." Another friend remembered an evening when Alan Lomax and Josh were sitting at a table and Lomax floored a patron who made a remark about not wanting "to sit at the next table to a goddam nigger," while several female customers held Josh back to keep him from getting involved.

Josh often told of the night that seven servicemen attacked him outside the club during a break. As Josh Jr. tells the story, "He had a cold or something, and between sets he went out to the drugstore and he noticed these seven servicemen walking after him. He recognized them from being in the club, and right away you know [when you are going to have trouble]. So, he tried to give the high-sign to the druggist to maybe call or do something, and the man wasn't gonna get involved. Anyway, he finally had to go back to the club.

"He knew what was gonna happen, so he said that he got himself in a position where nobody was to his back, he was against the wall. And, as they came in, he said, 'I hit out first.' The best defense was his offense. A fight ensued, and when it was all over he was on the ground, but three other people were too." A friend recalls him showing up later at a party with his knuckles so swollen that he was unable to play guitar.

According to Josh Jr., the specific song that had enraged the southerners was "Strange Fruit," another Lewis Allan composition. The song paints a stark picture of southern lynching: "Black bodies swaying in the southern breeze / Strange fruit hanging from the poplar trees." It pulls no punches, ironically juxtaposing the "pastoral . . . gallant South," with the "bulging eyes and twisted mouth" of a hanged man, and the scent of magnolia blossoms with the "sudden smell of burning flesh."

"Strange Fruit" had been written in the late 1930s and performed at various left-wing cabarets before being introduced at Cafe Society by Billie Holiday shortly after the club opened. Five years later she still considered it her personal property, especially if it was going to be sung on that stage. After Josh added it to his repertoire, she came down to the club in a rage, accusing him of stealing her material. As he often told the story, she had a knife and was threatening to cut his throat, but "we talked and finally came downstairs peaceably together, and to everyone's surprise had a nice little dancing session." He explained to her that he admired her original version but believed "that song should be sung by everyone until it never had to be sung again."

Today, "Strange Fruit" sounds too graphic and brutal to have been popular nightclub fare, but in the early 1940s lynching was still one of the most immediate issues in the American racial struggle, and the song hit a nerve with Cafe Society's progressive clientele. As in World War I, there were a lot of white southerners who were irate at the thought of black men going abroad to shoot white men and, even worse, meeting white women. When black northern soldiers were sent to southern bases, the confrontations led to frequent fights and, in extreme cases, pitched gun battles. The black press was full of stories of soldiers being beaten or killed and white perpetrators who were not even brought to trial. Meanwhile, small-town southern newspapers printed calls for Klan action to keep the black soldiers in their place.

Josh's audiences included some people who were infuriated by songs like "Strange Fruit," but his performances also forced more than a few listeners to confront their prejudices. As he would say over and over again, "I'm no speech maker. All I can do is play a guitar and sing. [But] it's a pretty good way of making people listen to what I have to say. . . . You can so easily find your way into people's minds with music and make them start thinking."

Josh liked to stress the positive effect he was having, quoting a letter from southern fans or telling about someone who had been changed by his performance. "If I reach one person a month with what I have to say I think that's doing something," he said in a 1945 interview. "Take the time a southern Army major walked out on me while I was doing 'Strange Fruit'. . . . He came back a week later and said to me, 'I've returned because I wanted to know why I walked out before.' He sat all through it this time and earnestly tried to convince me that not all Southerners are jimcrowers. . . . About four months later he arrived at Cafe Society with his wife — a Southern woman filled with anti-Negro prejudices. The major had begged her to come to hear me sing without telling her I was a Negro. But she stayed, and later invited me to sit at her table. . . . Later in the evening she asked me to dance. . . . The major later told me that this was the first time in his wife's life that she had ever sat at the same table with a Negro.

"You see," Josh told the interviewer, "they had both learned something and that's a portent of the things to come."

The southern major's wife was not the only woman to be charmed by Josh's performances. Though the early newspaper reports tend to concentrate on the political power of his songs and his colorful background as an itinerant musician, virtually everyone who saw him perform speaks first of his sex appeal. Eartha Kitt wrote of the first time she heard him, at a dance rehearsal: "The sound of his guitar stirred me sensually. It was irresistible and enchanting and seductive. It tantalized my senses and wined my bitter blood. I watched his hands as they caressed the guitar, telling of love and hatred, of faithless women. His mouth moved as though he was making love to the words he spoke; his eyes had a come hither look that said, 'There's no woman I cannot have and any woman can have me.' "

Other listeners, though less eloquent, shared Kitt's feelings, and it was this more than anything else that set Josh apart from his folksinging compatriots. "Josh was a wonderfully sexy man," Lena Horne recalled, thinking back to her own Cafe Society days. "You used to have to beat your way through swarms of women just to say hello to him."

"He played sex to the hilt," Barney Josephson remembered. "He was bigger at this than anybody else I ever saw in show business. He knew exactly what he was doing — so that when he stroked his guitar strings, the women in his audience just sat there in heat and felt like he was stroking their vaginas." Josephson encouraged this aspect of Josh's performance, urging him to wear his shirts open to the chest. "When they saw that neck — all muscles and tendons — they wanted to bite it."

Josephine Premice laughs as she remembers the effect Josh had: "He would have his shirt buttoned, and then he'd unbutton and tease the ladies. He totally enjoyed watching the ladies look at him, and one felt sorry for the men they were with. Because the women would go crazy — 'Get out of my way! There he is!' He was a marvelous showman, and one clever thing he did was he would come on stage and take about five minutes tuning his guitar, but the tuning was all flexing his muscles. Every muscle rippled, and that's why he did it, because you know he had tuned his guitar before he left his dressing room. But he'd do this whole thing, and then everybody would applaud the tuning! He had all those white ladies chasing and putting gold watches on him, hanging on him far and wide — and they were not black ladies, they were white. He was a very impressive man, and from age eight to eighty, women were all in love with Josh White. They just swarmed around him like bees to honey."

"He was the first black person to use sex appeal on white audiences," Josh Jr. says today. "And he was lucky he didn't get killed for it. It was something that no other black entertainer had done. White women came to see them perform and might want to see what they could do with them afterwards, but he used it on stage. He was into women, and so he used it and he wasn't afraid, he didn't hold it back. I would be embarrassed for some women, especially if they were close in the front rows."

In addition to his sex appeal, suave and raw at the same time, friends, fans, and family recall the way he could instantly get an audience in the palm of his hand. Cabaret audiences were famous for talking throughout a performance, and there was something magic about the way Josh could quiet them down. He had at first doubted his ability to work the nightclub as a single act: "I told Barney, 'These people are here to eat and drink and socialize. They won't listen to me.' Barney didn't sympathize. He said, 'If you can't quiet them, you shouldn't be working here.' "

Josh would always recall his fear on that first night. "Barney, after introducing me, walked off the stage and I walked on. The noise in the place was terrible. I put my foot up on a chair. I smiled. They continued to talk. I started to tune the guitar, but they didn't listen. I started 'Evil-Hearted Man' without raising my voice one bit. I did about three verses and then it happened. They started to listen. They listened for years. It was the greatest goddam nightclub in the world."

"He demanded respect," his daughter Bunny says. "In a club, people have a tendency to chatter; the star comes out, the spotlight's on him, but they keep chattering. And my father would come out with a cigarette in his hand, stick it behind his ear, put his foot up on the chair and they'd be chattering. The spotlight's on him. And do you know what he'd do? He'd wait. He didn't say anything. He just demanded their attention in class: 'I'm a presence. You will respect me.' All of a sudden, the message would hit them, and they'd quiet right down."

It was a skill that left other performers astonished. Oscar Brand, then beginning his career as a nightclub folksinger, recalls what would happen when an unsuspecting customer began to talk during one of Josh's songs: "Josh would just stand there, and long sparks and lightening bolts would come out of his eyes, like out of a cartoon character. That person would feel it, maybe from the tension of the other people in the room, and he would turn around and see Josh's eyes and never talk again. I saw him just wither people."

When the look did not work, Josh had other methods. Sammy Benskin, who sometimes led the Cafe Society house band, recalled a time when the patrons at one table went on with their conversation, oblivious to Josh's glance. Josh stopped playing in midsong, walked over, and whispered something in the ear of one of the men. The whole room tensed, and the table instantly became quiet. When Benskin later asked what he had said, Josh explained, "I told him he was wearing a very pretty tie." As Benskin put it, "The psychology . . . was that he had taken a spotlight right to the table that was making noise and being rather kind to them so they realized that they were being offensive. And they were really a beautiful audience from then on."

Most nights, such special attention was not needed. Josh was drawing his own following, and fans came to his shows fully aware that, in *Cue* magazine's words, he was "as stern in his audience demands as a Toscanini." If his glance did not silence a noisy table, the other customers were ready to shush the malefactors into submission.

Josh was becoming a fixture of the New York entertainment world, famous for his unique repertoire and performance style. Time and again, people repeat the same memories: his stance, his right foot up on a box or a chair, the guitar resting on his knee, the lighted cigarette behind his ear surrounding his head with an atmospheric cloud of smoke. Josh explained that the cigarette placement was just a handy thing he had worked out, that the blind men had stuck their cigarettes between their guitar strings, and sometimes one would burn down and break a string, but that he could always feel the heat and remove it from his ear before it burned him. Handy or not, it was wonderful theater.

Even more theatrical, and remembered by every performer who worked with him, was the mileage Josh could get out of a broken string. When one popped, he would finish whatever number he was doing, then start singing George Gershwin's "Summertime." He would strum an occasional chord while removing the old string, replacing it, then tuning up the new string note by note in perfect, relaxed harmony with his vocal line. By the end of the song the guitar would be as good as new, and the audience would give him a wild ovation. It was so beautifully done that many performers insist that the whole routine was a setup, that Josh had somehow learned how to break guitar strings at will. Bill Lee, who was Josh's bass player off and on in the late 1950s, says that "Josh could tell when he might just be losing the audience a little bit, and then he would break a string, the G string, which he had already prepared for by giving me a spare to take on the stage in my pocket. When he'd break the string, he'd ask me for it and then start singing 'Summertime,' and the audience looked on in disbelief — singing, playing, and restringing the guitar at the same time. It would always work to get back their attention."

Josh Jr. is adamant that the broken strings were accidental and is amused by all the claims to the contrary. Despite the legend, he says, the strings did not always break at opportune moments; sometimes one would go when the whole audience was already enthralled and the interruption was an annoyance. When he began his own solo career, he adopted his father's trick (though he chose a different song), and he maintains that it is simply an elegant solution to a common problem. Once again, he says, it is a case of Josh's fans remembering him as larger than life. Everyone breaks a string sometimes, and the idea of singing while replacing it is simply a way of not losing the crowd. It was the flair of Josh's execution that made it seem like something more.

Among Josh's songs, the one most people recall as the centerpiece of his sets was "The Riddle Song," which *Variety* had mentioned as being one of the three numbers he did on his opening night. It would be hard to find a piece of material that was further from the upbeat blues of Josh's youth. One of the oldest songs in the English language, reaching back to at least the fifteenth century, it had been collected in the southern Appalachians by the folklorist Cecil Sharp and later recorded by Burl Ives.

Josh would introduce it very quietly, with careful pauses, as "a song about a cherry . . . a chicken . . . a story . . . and a baby." Then he would strum a gentle chord and sing about giving mysterious gifts to his love: a cherry that had no stone, a chicken that had no bone, a story that had no end, and a baby with no crying. The second verse posed the riddle, asking how these things could exist, and the third provided the answers.

On record it is a pretty piece, but there is little to suggest the haunting power that it apparently had on stage. It worked because it was so simple, and because Josh, rather than trying to make it fancier, emphasized that simplicity. He just presented the lyric, with minimal guitar accompaniment, and its gentleness and the ancient quality of the poetry provided an ideal balance to the toughness of his blues songs and the polemics of his topical material, creating a memorable moment of stillness in the middle of his generally upbeat sets.

By 1944, Josh was Cafe Society's top-billed act and rivaled Burl Ives as America's most popular folksinger. He had his own fifteen-minute radio show on WNEW every Sunday, as well as regular broadcasts for the OWI and frequent appearances as a guest on other programs. He had recorded a half-dozen songs on V-discs (special releases for the armed forces), and as the recording ban and shellac shortage eased up, he began making records for several commercial labels.

His first new recordings were part of an all-star leftist folk session organized by Alan Lomax, which included Pete Seeger, Brownie McGhee, Sonny Terry, Burl Ives, and Tom Glazer and was released under the nom de group the Union Boys. Josh sang "Little Man on a Fence" by himself, "Jim Crow" (a composition by Seeger and Lee Hays) with other singers humming in the background, and a duet with McGhee on "Move into Germany." He also led the group in "Hold On," a World War II rewrite of the old spiritual "Gospel Plow" (this song provides an example of the odd bedfellows made by the Allied war effort, with its chorus: "Hold on — Franklin D. / Hold on — Winston C. / Hold on — Chiang Kai-shek / Hold on — Joseph Stalin").

With the Union Boys' *Songs for Victory,* Josh began an association with Moe Asch, whose Asch label would release his next two albums. Asch, later to found Folkways Records, was an electrical engineer who had started out recording Jewish cantorial music before expanding into jazz and then folk, in which he would make his most valuable contribution. Over the years he amassed an unequaled catalogue of traditional and contemporary folk styles, including music from all over the world, and his label became the lifeblood of the folk and blues revivals of the 1960s.

Josh recorded some thirty-five sides for Asch, playing roughly the same songs he was featuring in his live shows, either as singles or in blues and folk anthologies. Asch also compiled two solo albums. These were beautifully packaged, with covers by David Stone Martin, who was then beginning to make his reputation as the peerless visual artist of the jazz world. The first, called simply *Songs by Josh White*, had liner notes by Langston Hughes that sum up the contemporary perception of Josh's work:

> You could call Josh White the Minstrel of the Blues, except that he is more than a Minstrel of the Blues. The Blues are Negro music, but, although he is a Negro, Josh is a fine folk-singer of anybody's songs — southern Negro or southern white, plantation work-songs or modern union songs, English or Irish ballads — any songs that come from the heart of the people. . . .
>
> Perhaps it was from Blind Lemmon [*sic*] that Josh absorbed the common loneliness of the folk song that binds one heart to all others — and all others to the one who sings the song. For Josh has a way of taking a song like Hard Time Blues and making folks who have never even had a hard time feel as though they had experienced poverty.
>
> The guitar that Josh White plays is as eloquent, as simple and direct as are his songs themselves. His guitar keeps a heart-beat rhythm that makes you feel his songs in your heart. His guitar has in it at one and the same time, sadness and gaiety, despair and faith. Sometimes his guitar laughs behind a sad song. Sometimes it cries behind a happy song. . . . Josh White and His Guitar used to be billed together. They are one and inseparable.
>
> Josh White sings with such ease that you never feel like he is trying. That is the secret of true folk-singing — for the folk-song never tries to get itself sung. If it just doesn't ease itself into your soul and then out of your mouth spontaneously, to stay singing around your head forever, then it isn't a folk-song. And if the singer tries too hard and gets nowhere with such a song, that singer isn't a folk-singer. . . . From Blind Lemmon [*sic*] to Burl Ives, from Bessie Smith to Aunt Molly Jackson there runs a wave of singing easy. Josh White also sings easy.

The Asch recordings show the range of sources on which Josh drew for his Cafe Society shows. There were songs from every previous stage of his career: "Mean Mistreatin' Woman" and "Motherless Children" from his early blues and gospel days; "I Got a Head like a Rock" from the *John Henry* score; "Jerry" and "Trouble" from *Chain Gang*; "Jim Crow Train" and "Hard Times" from *Southern Exposure*; and "Don't Lie Buddy," a duet with Leadbelly. Reflecting the Cafe Society milieu, there was also a contemporary patriotic song, "Minute Man," recorded with backing by the Mary Lou Williams Quartet. The other new additions were an interesting mix. Josh had begun venturing outside the American tradition: "Waltzing Matilda" had become a staple of his repertoire, as had "The Lass with the Delicate Air," a saucy English ballad reworked by the New York pop writers Hy Zaret (who would later write the lyric to "Unchained Melody") and Lou Singer. Meanwhile, he was keeping in touch with current blues trends, adopting "Outskirts of Town," a 1930s number that Louis Jordan had recently revived and made into a huge hit with his Tympany Five.

One particularly apt choice, showing the acuity with which Josh could spot material, was Cole Porter's "Miss Otis Regrets." Though this was exactly the sort of song that bothered his purist folk fans, it was ideally suited to Josh's delivery. A blues ballad of murder and hanging, told in the voice of a genteel sophisticate, it displayed both his sure musicianship and his wry, sexy humor. Other singers tend to sound overly arch or inappropriately bouncy when confronted with Porter's bizarre juxtaposition of events and tone, but for Josh it was a perfect fit; it was cafe blues, a style that he was inventing and of which he would be the sole successful practitioner.

After recording for Asch through the summer of 1944, in September Josh went back to Keynote, the label that had released *Southern Exposure,* for one album. Then, under Alan Lomax's auspices, he moved over to a major label, Decca, where he would stay for the next two years. In all, he recorded some sixty songs in 1944 alone, and particular favorites such as "The Riddle Song," "Strange Fruit," and the comically tough "Evil-Hearted Man" showed up on all three labels.

Surprisingly, Josh's most popular number, and the one that would catapult him to national fame, was commercially recorded only for Asch. That song was "One Meat Ball," a seriocomic ballad about a "little man" with only fifteen cents to his name who went to a restaurant and found he could afford only one meatball. When he asked humbly if he might have some bread with it, the waiter "hollered down the hall" the refusal that would forever haunt his dreams: "You gets no bread with one meat ball!"

The song was copyrighted by Zaret and Singer, who had already given Josh "The Lass with the Delicate Air," and Josh recorded it on V-disc, then twice for Asch, making it the leadoff song for his first postwar album. It was a startling success. *Billboard,* the music industry's bible, reported that although "most of his tune singing is for the followers of the folk trail, . . . this 'Meat Ball' routine is good for any juke," adding that "Asch's limited pressings, no doubt, will keep this out of the top 10 in the juke pop chart—but wherever it's going to be played it's going to do a top nickel gathering job."

Of course, as with any pop song of the day, Josh did not have "One Meat Ball" to himself. Jimmy Savo, a singing pantomimist at Cafe Society Uptown, made it into an intricate mime routine that was a highlight of his act. Soon the orchestra leader Tony Pastor covered the song, and the Andrews Sisters picked it up as well, putting it on the flip side of "Rum and Coca-Cola" and taking it to number fifteen on the pop charts. The competition seems to have been fierce but friendly: a publicity photograph shows the sisters recoiling in mock horror from Savo's pantomime while Josh strums along on guitar.

The sheet music for "One Meat Ball," copyrighted in 1944, features cover photos of Josh and Savo on either side of a checked tablecloth emblazoned with the words "Presented by BARNEY JOSEPHSON at his famous twin edition night club." Dates for both the music and Josh's recording suggest that he must have been doing the song by the summer of 1944, but if so, it attracted relatively little attention at that time. Though Josh was then getting his first taste of large-scale press coverage (including an impressive profile in *Current Biography,* which had generally ignored black performers), none of the stories include the song in their lists of favorite material. The first mention is in a black newspaper, the *Missouri Call,* in a review of a December concert in Chicago with Libby Holman. The critic refers to it as "an old Irish sea song said to be about 400 years old," which "painted a picture of the poverty-stricken Irish by bringing out the point that the character's last 15 cents could buy only one meatball, without bread or spaghetti."

This colorful genealogy presents perplexing questions, such as what the sixteenth-century Irish would have been doing with spaghetti, cents, or, for that matter, waiters. Clearly, it was the invention of a press agent rather than a folklorist, and as the song climbed the charts and became ubiquitous on jukeboxes, all sorts of arguments surfaced as to its origin. *PM* finally devoted a full page to exploring the question, interviewing everyone concerned and tracing a more recent but equally bizarre history. The song, it said, had begun its life as a burlesque epic poem, "The Lay of the Lone Fish Ball," apparently written by a Latin professor at Harvard University around 1850. Two other Harvard men, the poet James Russell Lowell and the folklorist Francis J. Child, then transformed it into a burlesque Italian opera, *Il Pescebello*. Zaret and Singer heard someone sing a partial version of "One Fish Ball" at a party and were inspired to write a modern song on the same theme, using many of the original lines but putting them to a new tune and removing the mock-heroic language. Zaret explained that they had given the song to Josh in the summer and had not even bothered to publish it until several months later, when they arranged for him to make the V-disc recording and it was also picked up by Savo. The *PM* story concluded by noting that the Andrews Sisters' record had recently sold its millionth copy and that "a judge in the Bronx Police Court fined the proprietor of a music shop $2 for playing 'One Meat Ball' over and over on meatless Tuesday."

Though the Andrews version was the one that made the charts, and Savo was featured in a *PM* picture spread on the song, most people regarded it as Josh's property. *Down Beat* sniffed that "the three girls do no better with Meat Ball than Pastor, for Josh's version will always remain the best." A *New Yorker* critic, in the magazine's "Tables for Two" nightclub column, wrote, "Listening . . . to Josh White apply his expert talent to 'One Meat Ball' (which is getting to be something of a nuisance around town), I was moved to wish that the city would make it a crime for anyone else to attempt it. Come to think of it, it already is."

"One Meat Ball" was Josh's one national hit, and it came at just the right time. In the summer of 1944 he had gotten back together with Libby Holman; the duo had signed with Columbia Concert Management, one of the most prominent New York booking agencies, and set to work planning a national tour. In August they made their first formal concert appearance, at the Hedgerow Theater in Philadelphia, then went on to New York and Chicago. Holman had commissioned a theatrical stage designer, who put together a setting that simulated the back porch of a southern country shack. She would sit on a low stool, silhouetted by atmospherically dim lighting, while Josh sat on the step below her.

This time around, Josh was a popular artist in his own right. He received equal billing with Holman and sang his own songs as well as accompanying hers and joining in a handful of duets. A *Chicago Daily News* columnist declared that he "achieved something little short of tragic greatness" in his portion of a duet on "Strange Fruit." The *Chicago Tribune*'s critic gushed that during the program "a kind of molten mesmerism hung tingling in the throbbing air"; astonished to discover that Holman's accompanist was the Josh White of her "cherished 'Chain Gang' album," she dubbed him the "man with a Svengali guitar." The *Chicago Defender* put the crowd in the Civic Theatre at 5,000 people and wondered why the show had been booked for only one night.

Josh and Libby played a concert at Cornell University in February 1945, then headed across country at the beginning of March. After a gig in Detroit they drove straight to Los Angeles, where they packed the Wilshire Ebell Theater and garnered more rave reviews. Two nights later they were equally successful at San Francisco's Geary Theater, then made their way back down the coast, playing benefits at military canteens and hospitals. The tour finished up with a nightclub run at the popular Ciro's in Hollywood.

While in Hollywood, Josh also made his first film appearance. "One Meat Ball" was a national rage, and Universal Pictures signed him to sing it in a B-level crime film, *The Crimson Canary*. He appeared in a nightclub sequence, following a jazz band led by Coleman Hawkins and Oscar Pettiford. After a hot bop jam the band leaves for a break, and Josh strides onto the stage in dark slacks and a white shirt, carrying his guitar in his left hand and a chair in his right. Placing the chair at center stage, he puts his right foot up on it, takes the cigarette from his mouth, parks it behind his ear, and goes into "Joshua Fit the Battle of Jericho." The listeners, all white and well dressed, tap their fingers on tabletops and applaud enthusiastically as he puts a capo on his third fret and swings into "One Meat Ball." He seems completely relaxed, smiling and teasing the notes, moving his whole arm as he strikes ringing chords. Then, quickly picking up the chair, he exits, and the movie goes back to its convoluted plot: a drunken Noah Beery Jr., out of work and framed on a murder charge, sums up his feelings by growling to his partner that they are "strictly one meat ball kind of guys."

All in all, the trip out west opened up a world of new opportunities, and Josh felt that he and Holman had made an important breakthrough. "The idea of a Negro and white artist joining for a tour is really something," he told an interviewer for the *Daily Worker.* "And the responses we received all over the country were heartwarming. You mustn't forget that most of the people we sang to had never before heard folk songs and songs of protest. They were mixed audiences and it was a new experience and a splendid one for them."

Josh was particularly proud of his and Holman's duet version of "Strange Fruit." He described it as "the strongest thing that we did. . . . Can you imagine a Negro and a white person singing that as a duet, and especially a white woman and a Negro man? She sang the hell out of this thing, and with the two of these races mixing into this song — well, I wish we had recorded it."

Happy as Josh was with the artistic aspects of the tour, Holman's biographer reports that the relationship between them was becoming strained. There were the usual problems of petty racism surrounding them at every turn, and these were augmented by persistent rumors that the pair were lovers as well as musical partners. Both singers would always deny this, though Holman freely admitted that she had been tempted, and several of Josh's friends will testify that they were indeed romantically linked. (One tells a complex story in which Holman gave Josh a Buick Roadmaster and two wolfhounds, bought Carol a mink coat, and paid for Josh's mother to come up from South Carolina for a visit, only to break off the relationship after finding him in bed with a younger woman.) Either way, the rumors marked the end of their partnership. Holman continued to harbor hopes for the future, telling an interviewer that she was making plans for another national tour with Josh in the fall, but aside from some scattered appearances at benefits the duo performed together only once more, in 1948, to record a song for the soundtrack of the surrealist film *Dreams That Money Can Buy.*

Back in New York, Hollywood's call was followed by Broadway's. Josh was added to the cast of *Blue Holiday,* a new revue created as a showcase for Ethel Waters which opened at the Belasco Theatre on May 21, 1945. He had second billing in a cast that included Willie Bryant, the Katherine Dunham Dancers, the Hall Johnson Choir, Mary Lou Williams, and Josephine Premice. Unfortunately, the whole was markedly inferior to the sum of its parts. A typical review, in the *New York World-Telegram,* was headlined "Vaudeville at Its Dullest," and the show, despite having been postponed three days for last-minute doctoring, was dismissed as a hopeless hodgepodge.

Josh, however, was unanimously hailed as *Blue Holiday*'s saving grace. He sang a quartet of Cafe Society favorites: "Hard Time Blues," "Evil-Hearted Man," "The House I Live In," and, of course, "One Meat Ball." Then he closed the show in a duet with Timmie Rodgers, a popular comedian, of "The Free and Equal Blues," a bitingly funny dialogue of universal brotherhood by Earl Robinson and E. Y. Harburg, sung with the backing of the entire company. The *Herald Tribune* called him "easily the most successful of the performers," and the *Post* reviewer, apparently seeing Josh for the first time, described him as a "favorite of the evening . . . a serious-minded, intensely socially-conscious young man with a guitar and a trick of tossing his voice around until it sometimes approaches a refined, somewhat muted, yodel, if there is such a thing."

Like *John Henry, Blue Holiday* lasted barely a week, but it further increased Josh's stature as a New York star. During its run he had continued his late shows at Cafe Society, rushing down from Broadway as soon as the curtain fell. When the show closed, Josephson acknowledged Josh's growing popularity by moving him into the larger uptown room. He was first paired with Jimmy Savo, then with the cabaret singers Paula Laurence and Georgia Gibbs on a bill the *New Yorker* declared "the best thing in town." During this run he also gave his first formal concert, appearing at Town Hall in a program of "Songs of the Land and Blues" together with a singer named Elwood Smith, and in October he returned to the hall on his own as part of a new folk series.

In November, Decca brought Josh back into the studio and tried to broaden his appeal as a recording artist by cutting two sides with an eight-piece jazz band led by Edmond Hall, the same clarinetist who had backed him on his 1941 Conqueror sides. Josh left the guitar at home for a change and proved to be an effective singer in the then current blues-jazz style; his vocals show a power and range he never rose to in quieter settings, and the record makes one wish he had done more work with bands. Still, it is easy to understand why he did not: there were plenty of strong band singers on the pop scene but no one else who could do his solo act.

For Josh, the Broadway and concert appearances provided a taste of something he wanted to do a lot more of. Master though he was of nightclub entertaining, he relished the opportunity to work in places where "a singer doesn't have to worry about cash registers ringing, glasses clinking." He also liked the fact that concert audiences were there specifically to hear him, and he did not risk offending people who had just dropped in for a drink. In a concert, he said, "you sing what you want. People can walk out if they don't like it." The nightclub scene had been good to him, but with a Hollywood production and a Broadway show under his belt, he was looking for new worlds to conquer. By the spring of 1946 he had signed with a manager, Mary Chase, and a booking agency, Metropolitan Musical Bureau (a division of Columbia Concerts), and plans were being made for his own national tour, with a European visit to follow.

# 9

# THE HOUSE
# I LIVE IN

■ ■ ■ ■ ■ ■ ■ ■ ■ ■ ■ ■ ■ ■ ■ ■ ■ ■ ■ ■ ■

While Josh's career was monopolizing much of his attention, there was also plenty happening at home. The White family remembers the Cafe Society years as something of a golden age. When he started there in 1943, he was reportedly earning $75 a week, but by 1946 he was getting $500 weekly, plus whatever he made from concerts, radio, and recordings. There were no financial worries, and during this period, unlike the later years when he would be touring heavily, he was at home. A third daughter, Fern, was born on March 3, 1944, and the following year the family moved into a bigger apartment at 539 West 150th Street.

With Josh doing so well the two older girls, Bunny and Beverly, were pulled out of the neighborhood public school and transferred to Downtown Community School. As Bunny explains it, the move was in part necessitated by Josh's celebrity: as he became a popular star, the local bullies began to pick on his kids, trying to cut them down to size.

"I didn't know my father was famous," she says. "He was special to me because he was my father. But when they found out that my father was Josh White and he was in show business and he was appearing downtown, it was like, 'Now I know why she thinks she's so cute.' See, my mother used to have me in pinafores, with a big, beautiful bow—I mean cutesy-poo. I didn't try to be, I wasn't a teacher's pet. It's just that was the way my mama said, 'You represent me.' So I was just too perfect, and then I had a famous father. You know what I'm saying? Well, they chased me from the school, all these classmates that were gonna kick my ass because I was who I was. And there were trolley cars then, and they were chasing me, and a trolley car missed me by a hair. I didn't go home and tell my mom, but a friend of hers told her. And my mother had always told me never to fight. She said 'Never stoop to their level.' But guess what? My mother said, 'The next time you run away, if you don't kick her ass, I'm kickin' yours.' "

Bunny stood up to the bullies and proved her mettle, but Carol did not want her children growing up in that kind of environment. "She said 'To hell with that,' " Bunny says. "And that's when we went to Downtown Community School." When Josh Jr. started school the following year, he went downtown as well.

To Josh, it was important that his children receive the best possible education and that they always carry themselves with dignity and propriety. Though he often presented himself to the world, both onstage and off, as a partygoer, a heavy drinker, and a womanizer, he was a surprisingly strict and traditional father. He and Carol insisted that their children be thoroughly presentable young people. Bunny remembers being instructed from her earliest years that she was a representative of her parents and must always comport herself well. In fact, when she heard her father's early blues recordings for the first time, in 1996, her immediate reaction was amazement at his country speech patterns and the slang he used.

"I never heard my father with a southern accent," she says firmly. "And he didn't allow improper English. I could not say, 'can I,' when I was asking for something; it had to be, 'may I,' or I would not get what I was asking for. 'Ain't' is something I am not comfortable with today, because 'ain't' was not a part of our language. I remember as a child, a little tiny one, when you're allowed to have baby language, I loved bread and butter. If my grandmother or my mother was there, I'd say, 'Sa bed pease,' and they would give it to me. I couldn't get it if Daddy was around. If Daddy was there, he'd say, 'A piece of bread, please,' and I could not get it unless I said it exactly like that."

Josh Jr. also stresses his parents' insistence on proper speech and behavior, and although he can understand and appreciate their motives, he clearly feels that it distanced him from other black children. Downtown Community School was not only a good school; it was also a white school. Beverly likes to describe it as multicultural and multiracial but thinks that she and her siblings were the first blacks to enroll. For Josh Jr., in particular, that bore a heavy burden of responsibility. "We would get ribbed by some people out in the black society," he says. "You know, like 'Who do you think you are, talking white?' But the old man wanted to show 'them' that we all don't speak that way — that we can be just as educated, we can speak just as well as you can. He was always trying to show 'them.'"

It was a reasonable stance, but could be hard for a child. "You're a black person to begin with, and you're dealing in a white society," Josh Jr. says. "And then you're also Josh White's son or daughter. So we had a lot of weight on our shoulders. You could never really be yourself, because you would not be judged by the individual you were but by who you belonged to and who you represented. I don't know if we felt it at the time, but it was like it was kind of being on guard, making sure you are always proper, not really letting your hair down. In school as teenagers, kids would go walking off and do slightly naughty things, but we felt we should not attempt to disgrace the black race or Josh White's kids."

Josh was going to make sure that his children had a very different youth from his own, with a solid home life and all the opportunities he had lacked. He was fighting to build a better world for them outside the family and was doing his best to prepare them for it. He was also trying to create a solid place for himself, one where he could truly feel as if he belonged. "Basically, what he was looking for was a home," Carol says. "Because that was something that he had never had."

Josh's background had not prepared him well for the role of a good husband and father, but he had long since proved his ability to shape and adapt himself to new situations. Carol came from a warm, firmly grounded family, and he seems to have learned a great deal from her. His own childhood had also taught him something about firm parenting, though as much by showing him what not to do as by providing him with models. Although at first glance the kids' stories about Josh's strict rules seem to echo his own upbringing, Carol and his children instantly reject the parallel. Indeed, the New York Whites are unanimously agreed that the Greenville Whites were, in modern parlance, a severely dysfunctional family.

Josh and Carol's house was full of rules but also of love; their children do not tell tales of harsh punishments, only of scoldings. By contrast, Elizabeth White never mellowed. Bunny's memory of Josh's mother is defined by a single incident: the elder Mrs. White, on a visit to New York, was sitting across the table from Josh when he lit a cigarette, and she reached over and smacked him as if he were still an errant schoolboy. "She was a piece of work," Bunny says, her voice rising with indignation. "Here's my father, with three kids, and he smoked a cigarette and she slapped him, in front of my mother."

Josh continued to visit his mother occasionally, and she came up to New York a couple of times, but she would not go to see him perform and made no bones about her disappointment that he was singing "reels" rather than sacred songs. "To this day, Mama has never heard me sing the blues," he would say in the early 1960s. "I can't send her my blues albums. She won't have them in the house. She's seventy-nine years old now, and she's never seen me work on stage other than in church when I was a kid." Friends in Greenville remember that when he sent an LP to his sister Deborah, he included a note telling her to avoid playing one track, "Sam Hall," around the house, because it included the words "God damn."

As for his father, Josh hardly mentioned him except as a strong preacher and the victim of a racist power structure. There were no stories that suggested a close, personal relationship between father and son. Furthermore, Josh seems to have felt a degree of shame at the fact that Dennis White had ended up in an insane asylum. Though he was quite open about the history when talking with Robert Shelton in the 1960s, telling of his father's escapes and final death in the institution, Carol says she had the impression that Josh never saw his father again after the arrest and beating. Bunny says that she first heard of her grandfather's commitment secondhand, that Josh never spoke of it in her presence until she was fully grown.

To Carol and the children, Josh's background was a frightening, foreign thing. His memories of violent racism, lynching, and the hardships of traveling as a lead boy were more like ghost tales or nightmares than reality. Carol emphasizes how sheltered her life had been compared to his. "Whatever was not pleasing about my family leaving the South, it might have been discussed once or twice, but they never dwelled on it," she says. "When I would hear Josh speaking with my parents, I thought. 'Oh, I don't even believe this guy. I don't believe things like this happen.' When he'd sit down and begin to tell how hard it was when he was playing with the blind men, and how he'd have to wrap his hands and his feet in any kind of rags that he could just to keep warm, it was really devastating to me."

Josh's own feelings about his hometown were hardly more pleasant than his family's imaginings. Carol says that when she first went south with him, in 1946, she had to beg him to take her along. "He was afraid for me," she says. "He didn't want me to go in the wrong place. And the first time I saw the signs, it was like being mesmerized; I had to sit and look and say, 'That really does say *white,* and that does say *colored.*' It was unreal for me; I could not believe it. And then I could see what he was talking about, that all the things he had been telling me were really true."

On another trip a year or two later, the party included the three eldest kids, plus Josh's brother Bill and his wife. Carol had made them a basket of food so they would not have to search out a restaurant that would serve them, but they pulled over for a brief stop in the ominously named Lynchburg, Virginia. A large car full of black people, with New York plates, instantly attracted the attention of the local police, who shone a light in their eyes, then escorted them to the edge of town. "This is my first time south," Bunny remembers. "I've heard all of the horrible things that happen to black people, so I am a little bit nervous. And now we have a police car following us. I'm terrified. The adults in the front are aware. Donny [Josh Jr.] and those dummies, they're sleeping. When they flashed that light, I thought it was all over, I thought they were going to lynch us. So that was scary.

"Then we were at my father's mother's house. Now, Uncle Billy was in the service after Pearl Harbor. He went with a beautiful head full of hair, came back bald, OK? And they went into town and a cracker said for my Uncle Billy to take his hat off — 'cause he wore a hat to cover the bald spot. And Uncle Billy wouldn't do it. So something went down whereby we had to leave Greenville on two wheels! 'Cause Uncle Billy would not kowtow, he wouldn't kiss ass. He wasn't gonna go along with whatever was said to him by this cracker. And so, when they came back to the house, the word got back to Grandma and she packed food. 'Leave!' We had to get out of town in a hurry."

For Carol and the children, these were isolated moments, adventurous or horrifying but not part of real life. For Josh, they were things that he lived with every day and that were always in his mind, no matter how famous he became. Many of his friends stress the anger that he carried around with him. They always add, though, that it was legitimate anger, not bitterness or hatred. Somehow, despite his early experiences with white prejudice and the frequent slights that reinforced those lessons year after year, Josh was firm in his belief that the problem was a racist system, not an evil inherent in white people. "He had every right to have [his children be] five screaming bigots," Josh Jr. says. "But he didn't do it. He taught us to take an individual as an individual, and if that particular white person did something against you, it is that particular person, not the race. My hat always goes off to him for that, 'cause we could have been very angry black people."

Music provided Josh with some release, allowing him to go on stage and present his side of the story, flaunting his defiance of the racial caste system and his strength as a proud black artist. Still, he kept a lot of anger bottled up inside, and by the early 1940s he was suffering severely from ulcers. Of course, ulcers are a typical drinker's problem, and Josh was famous for his capacity for alcohol, but no one who knew him hesitates to ascribe his illness largely to frustration with the society around him.

About 1943, Oscar Brand was a section chief at the induction station at Grand Central Station and remembers Josh coming in for his draft board physical. "He sent a message to me, and he said, 'Get me through this fast. I'm dying.' His ulcers were killing him." Brand rushed him through the usual lines and red tape, and once the doctors had seen his condition, it was clear that he was in no shape to join the army. As soon as they had run the medical gauntlet, Brand took Josh to the apartment he had nearby. "I gave him milk and anything that I could find that might be soothing," he says. "He swallowed everything down. He was really in excruciating pain. And it made me see him a little differently, because I had always seen him as being adamantine — hard, tough. I saw that he was really covering a lot of pain and a lot of problems."

It was a side of Josh that would become more visible as his health got worse in later years but that few saw in the 1940s. Whatever problems he had physically, he carefully concealed them from his fans, both on and offstage. The partying and the drinking went on, ulcers or no ulcers. Even when his doctor advised him to change his habits, he made a relatively open secret of his backsliding. "At Cafe Society, both uptown and downtown, he would go to the bar between sets and the bartender would hand him a glass of milk," Susan Reed recalls. "And everybody thought, 'Isn't that nice.' Of course, they didn't know there was whiskey in the milk."

Josh liked to project a larger-than-life image. Josh Jr. will say that his father always reminded him of John Wayne. He was a solidly built man and in addition to playing football in high school, he would tell reporters that during his Chicago days he had been a Golden Gloves boxer. Some of his friends are dubious about this story, but others find it easy to believe. Either way, in his early thirties he remained in generally good physical condition. The ulcers flared up from time to time, but he got out for regular exercise, balancing the long nights of smoking and drinking with a fondness for tennis, which was becoming a popular recreation for Harlem's middle class. There was a court across the street from the apartment, and Carol remembers that he was a good player and would cheerfully play all day against neighborhood acquaintances.

His preferred recreation at home, though, was cards. He would play whist or bridge, but pinochle was his favorite, and the children remember going to bed to the sound of cards being shuffled and dealt, then waking up and going to school with the game still in progress. Carol says that he also read a lot and could spend days at a time sitting in a corner with a paperback. In general, he read westerns and crime novels, but Bunny says that he gave her both MacKinlay Kantor's *Andersonville* and Ayn Rand's *Atlas Shrugged,* which she found tough going but he had apparently enjoyed.

At home with his family, Josh could relax and drop the performer's mask. "He was not a talker," Carol often says. "The only time you really heard Josh do a lot of talking, he had to have his guitar and maybe a drink. But otherwise he was a very quiet man." The broad, brash stage persona could come out instantly, though, if an audience appeared. "My old man was a pretty laid-back dude at home," Josh Jr. says. "But he was one of those performers who, not unlike a lot of us, kind of liked the attention. If it were just us or my mom's good friends or Sam [Gary] or whatever, Dad was just Dad, but have someone other than that come in, and that other kind of persona would come out."

Carol remembers all too many visitors in Josh's glory days and believes that they often had a detrimental effect on his health and the family's sanity. The children clearly agree but also remember the excitement of seeing Paul Robeson and Joe Louis, Langston Hughes or the gospel singer James Cleveland. They also remember the White family shows, given for the neighborhood on Christmas, Thanksgiving, or any time they felt like throwing a party. All the kids sang, and Josh would accompany each one for his or her special numbers. Carol led gospel songs; Bunny liked to sing blues; Beverly favored the gentler folk styles.

As for Josh Jr., his specialties were soon on display not only in the living room but out in public. As Josh would later tell the story, "One night [at Cafe Society] I suddenly heard this little baby voice pipe up with a song. It was Josh Jr., sitting in the audience. When the lights went up, they put a spotlight on him and everybody forgot about me. It was unexpected and very disturbing."

The story may be as apocryphal as it is cute, but however he started, Josh Jr. was soon a regular part of the act. "No one has ever explained to me what I was doing in Cafe Society at four years old," he says today. "But that's when I started singing with him. He was very proud that he had a son, having two girls first—which he loved, but he wanted a son—and I guess I had an instinct for singing, as we all did, and maybe was not as shy at singing publicly as the others, or I could be coerced very easily.

"When the old man was at Cafe Society for those five years, a special stool was made for him, and I remember standing on that, sharing that with his right foot and singing 'One Meat Ball,' and 'Mr. Frog Went A-Courtin'.' It didn't take long to enjoy doing that. I'm not saying I was that good; I didn't have the talent that Michael Jackson did at that age. But I could hold a tune, and I was cute, and whenever I sang I was with the old man. How could we go wrong? Josh plays, and then his little son comes out and plays. My goodness! Josh gets the accolades, I get some. It was easy. And it was fun; as a kid you get all of this attention and instant gratification. And, for me, my old man could do no wrong."

A surviving tape of a Mildred Bailey radio program from Christmas 1944 shows the father and son duo at the outset of their partnership. The song they perform is, naturally, "One Meat Ball," and Josh proudly introduces his son as "the real singing star of the White family." The performance, as Josh Jr. indicates, is more cute than musically impressive: he sings his part in a childish quaver, his father regularly chiming in with a gently supportive obbligato and singing for the four-year-old to pipe up "a little louder." The result is sweet and disorganized, and the studio audience eats it up, punctuating the performance with frequent laughter and applauding loudly at the end, as Bailey presents the boy with a pair of diminutive boxing gloves as a Christmas present.

It was as Josh's tiny alter ego that Donny, as he is still known to friends and family, began to be called Josh Jr. To the cabaret crowd he was adorable, and a *PM* photo shows him standing on the arm of his father's chair, his hands clasped together and a serious expression on his face, singing out to Big Josh's accompaniment. The accompanying text says that he had already been signed by Warner Brothers for a film career, with "the express stipulation that he will not be thrust into any Farina-type parts" (a reference to the raggedy black child in the "Our Gang" comedies).

Nothing came of the film offer, but Josh Jr. went on to some success as a child actor on Broadway and would become a quite successful folk singer. The other White children also took occasional turns on stage. Beverly was her father's traveling companion on several tours, and Bunny, though she never much liked performing, sometimes joined him for a song or two at Cafe Society. "There were certain times Daddy would just bring the family down," she says. "And we'd all do our little shtick. There would be other people there too, and they were good, but I wouldn't clap. And they'd say, 'Why?' And I said, ''Cause I only clap for my daddy.' "

Of the children, Bunny has the strongest memories of the Cafe Society days. Four years older than Beverly and five years older than Josh Jr., she turned ten in 1945. Whereas the others' memories are largely of the 1950s, when Josh was spending months on the road, she had him at home for most of her childhood. Whether because of this or simply because of her different temperament, she seems to share a unique bond with her father. Though she was the only White child who never pursued a show business career, she has a broader, more animated style than her younger siblings, who have more of Carol's reserve, and her stories about Josh have a special intimacy.

"I could always talk to my father about anything," she says. "And I mean *anything*. I was a little bit more careful with Mom, 'cause Mom was kind of like sheltered, and I understood that already when I was little. I'll never forget, Daddy would stop at Sherman's Ribs [down the street from the apartment] and wake me up and maybe it'd be three or four clock in the morning and he and I would sit and eat pig's feet, potato salad, cole slaw, or ribs and we would just talk. That was just his and our time and I knew that anything that I asked him he would answer. Like about sex — no, it was 'in-ter-course' — well, I had heard this stuff on the street, but I felt this was something that a parent's supposed to tell me. I remember coming home and saying 'intercourse' to my mother, and she said don't even talk to her again, 'cause she didn't know how to relate. So I put my father through it. I asked him 'Daddy, how are babies born?' I made him go through the whole thing, and he did it well. It was a little uncomfortable for him, but he did it well. Never backed down on any question that I asked him. Then I said to him, 'Daddy, I knew, but I wanted you guys to tell me.' "

This was in marked contrast with Josh's own upbringing. "My parents never told me about anything," he said. "Of course, I wasn't there long enough, but if I had been — the only thing my mother said to me is this: 'Never have anything to do with a girl until you are twenty-one, because if you do your children will be born imbeciles.' This kind of thing."

As his oldest daughter reached puberty, he did his best to be honest and helpful to her. "I think I was about ten or eleven," Bunny says. "That's about the time. And who bought me my first bra? My first pair of high heels? Who, when I got my period, stayed with me all night long, rubbed my stomach? Mommy, who wasn't prepared, cried, 'cause now I was a woman, and I had gone too fast. You know, like I wasn't the baby anymore. And I was in a lot of pain. So Daddy was the one that sat with me all night and rubbed my stomach and brought me hot water bottles.

"I'll tell you something else about Daddy. Daddy had the most excellent taste. I remember later, he was in England and he had a dress made for my mother that fit her to a T. And it was baaad! Daddy could go and buy pantyhose or stockings and have the right shade. He asked me one year, 'What do you want to wear for Easter?' He picked out the perfect outfit. He was fantastic. I mean he knew the sizes, he knew the color, everything."

Bunny's eyes light up, and her voice and gestures become animated as she talks about her father. "Daddy was a piece of work," she almost shouts. "I don't have a driver's license, I don't drive. But when I was grown, out of the house, I'd be in the Bronx hanging out and I'd know he was at Cafe Society, the Vanguard, or one of those clubs, and I'd decide to surprise him and go. And I'd come in and then we'd leave together when the club closed. Now, under the West Side Highway, Daddy decided to teach me how to damn drive. Middle of the night. And we had had a couple of cocktails, naturally. And that's how I learned how to drive."

There are plenty of other memories of good times. Beverly recalls with pleasure her own late-night barbecue feasts with her father, her mother scolding him for keeping the kids up, but her loving every minute. Josh Jr. tells how Josh would get up and fix breakfast for the family, making a great show of preparing the perfect bowl of Cream of Wheat. "He was the only one who could do it. It was the mixing of the butter and the sugar — that had to be just right, without milk. That was the deal, to make a batch for a number of people and do it slowly enough that it has no lumps. All of this was very important." Josh enjoyed cooking other meals as well on occasion, grilling up big pans of liver and onions and showing off his special technique of using a bit of sugar to caramelize the onions. All the kids remember the special way he would whistle when he came home from a trip, and the big Afghan hound named Tosh, who would hear the whistle a block away and alert them to his homecoming.

Every member of the White family has a story of Josh's flamboyant generosity. Carol tells of going Easter shopping, back when they had very little money, and taking a boy off the street into a shoestore and buying him a pair of new shoes. The kids remember that whatever Josh bought them he was likely to buy for everyone around. "If the truck came by with the watermelons, he didn't just buy watermelon for us but for all the children on the block," Bunny says. "There was a place in the Bronx where we knew the owner and we would go for heroes — I have not had a hero [sandwich] like that since — and he would take not just us but whoever was out there. If he bought one, he bought one for everybody."

It was the sort of gesture Josh loved and that would be remembered by many of his friends. He liked to pick up the tab for a night's drinking, or to give small gifts. Manny Greenhill — later a well-known concert promoter and agent, who took some guitar lessons from Josh in the early 1940s — says that when he and some other young fans were mobilized into the army and sent overseas, Josh went into a little "make your own record" booth and recorded a going-away song for each of them. Performers who were close to him were amazed at the freedom with which he would teach his trademark songs to other people, regardless of the fact that they might be regarded as his competitors. "He taught everybody and God his material," says his sometime touring partner Josephine Premice. "If you said, 'Josh, I love that song, I'd like to learn it,' he'd pull out his guitar and he would show it to you. [His manager] used to fight with him all the time because of his generosity with people. She'd say, 'You can't do that! Why are you teaching people your songs?' "

Josh was equally free with stage tips and advice, and numerous younger folksingers speak of lessons he taught them. His most common advice was the same that he gave his children. He often said that he was a storyteller, not a singer, and he would tell young performers to concentrate on getting the lyrics across rather than on vocal technique. "There were two things he told all of us who sang," Josh Jr. says. "One was, 'If you go to sing a song, make sure you believe it. Because if you don't believe the song you're singing, the people you're singing to won't believe it.' The other was, 'If you go to sing a song, make sure you articulate, make sure they can understand you. It's not going to work if they can't understand what the hell you're saying.' He never told me that I should sing blues, or that I shouldn't sing this or that song. Those were the only rules."

Like any performer, Josh had to be many things to many people. Unlike many, though, he managed, with Carol's help, to keep his different lives in some kind of balance. People who saw him out in the world could never imagine him as a solid family man, but even when he became a national and international touring artist, on the road for months at a time, he always kept a part of himself at home.

"He called home just about every day," Carol says, "just to make sure everything was OK. He would talk to each of the children, ask them about their homework, how they were doing in school. If we had a big decision to make, I never made it alone. We always called him. I always let them know that I was not *the* parent; I was part of a team that they had to answer to, and whatever we had to share, we had to share with him."

# 10

## APPLES, PEACHES, AND CHERRIES
### 1946-1947
■ ■ ■ ■ ■ ■ ■ ■ ■ ■ ■ ■ ■ ■ ■ ■ ■ ■ ■ ■ ■ ■

By 1945 Josh had become a national name. "One Meat Ball" was on the jukeboxes, the radio, and in a Hollywood film. He was on a major record label, and to many Americans he was, in Pete Seeger's words, "Mr. Folk Music." Though Libby Holman had hoped for another tour together, he was now big enough to make his own way. The moment was right for him to start touring as a solo headliner, and he had a new manager whose ambition more than matched his own.

Mary D. Chase, a New York writer with several books to her credit, met Josh through her daughter Beverly, who had seen him at Cafe Society. Although Beverly Chase does not remember how the first meeting took place or what made her mother go into personal management, it must have been during or shortly after the run of *Blue Holiday,* for Chase picked up not only Josh but two lesser known cast members: Josephine Premice, a Haitian dancer who had received good notices for her "Voodoo in Haiti" number, and a young member of the Katherine Dunham troupe named Eartha Kitt, Premice's understudy, who had already become something of a protégé of Josh's.

Of the three, Josh was far and away the biggest name, and Chase was not only his manager but also his number one fan. As Carol puts it, "We talk about the pied piper, but this woman, once she met Josh . . . Mary would always worry about him; she never wanted him to hurt his hands or anything, and she would run out into the street and stop the traffic so he could pass. It was unreal—you know, we really felt 'The lady's not together. You cannot stop traffic for people.' But she loved him dearly and we loved her."

Carol's affection for Chase appears to be very much a minority opinion. Premice speaks highly of her, both as a manager and as a person, but the reactions of Josh's other friends and acquaintances range from mild dislike to active hatred. Oscar Brand, for example, says, "She was a horror. She was a terrible person to deal with—though she might have been good in many ways for Josh, I don't know. Certainly, he respected her and her dedication to him, but he knew that she turned off a lot of people."

Even her worst detractors agree that Chase worked unbelievably hard for Josh. Beverly Chase, who would follow her mother into personal management, feels that her mother's devotion to Josh went so far that it became unprofessional. For example, she says that Mary Chase took over all of the White family's finances. "Josh had no concept of money. It was 'I want, give me, buy me, and get me.' So she would dole out his allowance and get all his bills." He also became a regular guest at her apartment, sitting around the living room in the evening, playing pinochle with Mary and her husband.

Now that Josh had a manager, the first order of business was to capitalize on his national exposure. Metropolitan Musical Bureau, a national booking agency, began making plans for his first coast-to-coast tour as a headliner, with Premice as a supporting artist. Meanwhile, he continued at Cafe Society Downtown, having come back there from the uptown branch when Susan Reed, a lovely, long-haired, teenage folksinger, got such a flood of press that Josephson had to move her into the larger room. In March 1946 he went into the studio for a pair of Decca sessions, recording a superb version of a new song called "Sometime" (or "Watcha Gonna Do When the Meat Gives Out"), with Brownie McGhee adding lead guitar lines and Sonny Terry blowing harmonica and whooping his encouragement. Josh later explained that he had wanted to use Terry before but had been discouraged by the record company. This time, Terry happened to drop by to see Alan Lomax, who was producing the session, and Josh persuaded him to sit in on the song.

April brought the first testing of Josh's out-of-town strength: a concert, supported by Premice, at the Detroit Art Institute. The show was well attended, and the press was excellent, giving him a strong advance buildup and a review that praised his varied repertoire, his informally engaging manner, and his skill at getting the audience to sing along with him. He had proved that he could appeal to audiences outside the intimate nightclub setting, and when Cafe Society closed for the summer in July, he moved up to one of New York City's few remaining vaudeville houses, Loew's State, for a week as a headliner. In September he played a week at a Philadelphia vaudeville house, the Earle Theater, earning $1,500 at the top of a bill that also included Ella Fitzgerald and Benny Carter. While there, he also acted the title role in *The Story of a Great Musician,* a radio biography of the black conductor Dean Dixon.

By October, Josh was ready to begin his tour, and press releases went out to all the New York papers. The trip started with a tiring zigzag: Josh and Premice drove to Montreal for a show on October 15, played Toronto two days later, and two days after that were back in Philadelphia. From there, things improved considerably. The pair moved around the Northeast for a week, playing at Dartmouth College in New Hampshire and doing two concerts at Boston's Jordan Hall with an Albany date in between, then ducked down to Norfolk, Virginia, before heading west through Pittsburgh to Zanesville, Ohio, and on to Detroit and three different dates around Chicago.

Josh soon found that the topical repertoire applauded by the Greenwich Village audiences was distinctly controversial outside New York. In Newcastle, Pennsylvania, a man interrupted his introduction to "Strange Fruit" by jumping up and shouting, "Yeah, that song was written by a nigger lover."

"I got hot under the collar," Josh told a reporter. "But I started to sing. While I was singing, this guy started down the aisle and other people joined him. They went through a door at the side leading backstage. I was sure there was going to be trouble. 'One Meat Ball' was supposed to be my next number, but my manager signaled from the wings to sing 'The House I Live In.' There was no applause for 'Strange Fruit' and little for 'House.' Then I went off stage and outside. Those fellows were standing together under a tree looking for me. But I just walked on by and nothing happened."

For middle America, Josh's show was a departure from anything previously presented, and it must have caught quite a few people by surprise. Metropolitan Musical Bureau handled Paul Robeson but also such apolitical acts as the Paul Whiteman Orchestra and Moran and

Mack, one of the most notorious blackface comedy teams. The brochure that Metropolitan sent to prospective promoters described Josh as "that great rarity — a *medium-priced drawing card*" and stressed the success of "One Meat Ball" and his popularity with the college crowd. In a paragraph that one assumes Josh never saw, it added, "Few personalities of the concert platform today possess the eloquence of this simple Negro, whose songs run the full gamut of the emotions of his race — from the poignant misery of impoverishment to the gay humor of ingenuous pleasures." With that sort of advance work, it is hardly surprising that Josh's topical material raised some eyebrows.

The tour included everything from performances in lodge halls and high school auditoriums to a USO show at the Norfolk Auditorium Arena and formal concerts in such venues as Carnegie Music Hall in Pittsburgh. Unlike folk concerts today, they followed a printed program, with brief notes on each selection. An entire concert lasted two to two and a half hours. It would start with Josh singing "Got a Head like a Rock," "Waltzing Matilda," "Joshua Fit the Battle of Jericho," and a blues. Then Premice came out with her drummer, Indio Macurije, to sing a song and perform dances from Cuba and Brazil. Josh returned for five songs, including "The Riddle Song" and "Strange Fruit," before ending the first half with "One Meat Ball."

The second half was similarly distributed, with Josh starting things off and Premice taking up the middle portion with a set of Creole and calypso songs. Josh would end his second set with "The House I Live In," and then he and Premice would do a final two numbers together: he backed her on a Haitian song, "Chacoune," and she joined him on the upbeat spiritual "Dip Your Fingers in the Water."

In Chicago, Josh not only played at Orchestra Hall, plus doing separate concerts in Evanston and Rockford, but also showed up at a fundraising party for a new organization, People's Songs. Started in New York, People's Songs was the brainchild of Lee Hays and Pete Seeger, and Josh had been one of the twenty or so singers present at its founding meeting. Intended as a sort of general clearinghouse for progressive music, it published a regular newsletter and acted as a central booking agency for union and political benefit shows. The party, featured in a picture spread in *Down Beat* magazine, was given in Josh's honor and included appearances by Woody Guthrie and Leadbelly, the former dressed in a rumpled work shirt, the latter dapper as ever in a pin-striped suit and polka-dot bowtie.

The
Sensation
of the
South

## JOSHUA WHITE
### *The Singing Christian*

NOW SINGS CHRISTIAN SONGS FOR
THE COLORED PEOPLE

0264 { LAY SOME FLOWERS ON MY GRAVE
THERE'S A MAN GOING AROUND
TAKING NAMES

0263 { PURE RELIGION HALLILU
I DON'T INTEND TO DIE IN EGYPTLAND

0258 { JESUS GONNA MAKE UP MY DYING BED
MOTHERLESS CHILDREN

## 25c PERFECT RECORDS 25c

PRODUCT OF AMERICAN RECORD CORPORATION

Advertisement for Josh's first gospel releases, c. 1933.
Courtesy of Lawrence Cohn.

FORM 64 6-31 1M

## RECORD ( ) CARD

| MATRIX NO. | RECORD NO. | BACKING MATRIX NO. |
|---|---|---|
| Cameo 11690 | 6-05-63 | (Good Gal) |
| Perfect | | 11691 |
| Regal | | |
| Banner | | |

Date Recorded 4/4/32
Title Greenville Sheik
Writers —
Artist Joshua White Pinewood Tom
Publisher W. R. Calaway   Style Vocal –
1 hold   5 Guitar acc
2 O/K   6
3   7
4   8

Month Released   Remarks
Cameo
Perfect

Original ARC file card for Josh's recording of "Greenville Sheik." The recording was made in 1932, when his blues releases were still under the name Joshua White, but released in 1936, by which time he was known as Pinewood Tom. Courtesy of Sony Music International.

Josh White and his Carolinians harmonizing, c. 1940.
*From left:* Bill White, Josh, Carrington Lewis, Bayard Rustin (standing), Sam Gary.
All photos not otherwise credited are courtesy of the White family.

Contact prints for publicity photos, c. 1940.
(*left*) Josh and Sam Gary. (*right*) Josh solo with the trademark cigarette behind his ear.

# They Appeared On Inaugural Program

Josh playing with the Golden Gate Quartet at Franklin D. Roosevelt's inaugural ball, January 1941. *From left:* Josh, Orlandus Wilson, Clyde Riddick, Henry Owens, and Willie Johnson. From *Atlanta Daily World*, used by permission.

Josh and Leadbelly at a party of folk fans, c. 1941. *Clockwise from bottom center:* Burl Ives, Leadbelly, Sonny Terry, Brownie McGhee, unidentified, unidentified, Bess Lomax, unidentified, Alan Lomax, unidentified, Josh, unidentified. Courtesy of John Reynolds and Lawrence Cohn.

Josh and Libby Holman, probably at a World War II benefit show, early 1940s.

Josh, Josh Jr., and Carol.

(*left*) In early 1945,
"One Meat Ball" became
a national hit, with versions
by Josh, Tony Pastor's
Orchestra, the Andrews
Sisters, and Jimmy Savo.
Author's collection.

(*below*) As this publicity
shot with the Sisters and
Savo makes clear, the rivalry
was friendly. The song was
Josh's first, though, and most
people continue to associate
it with him. Photograph
by Albert A. Freeman.

(*opposite*) Three generations of Whites: Josh with his mother and children. Bunny is
standing behind Mrs. White with Beverly next to her and Fern on her grandmother's
lap. On the floor is Tosh, the family's Afghan hound.

Josh, Beverly, and Josh Jr. at Cafe Society. Note that father and son are wearing matching slacks and velvet shirts, though Josh Sr.'s shirt is unbuttoned a good deal farther.

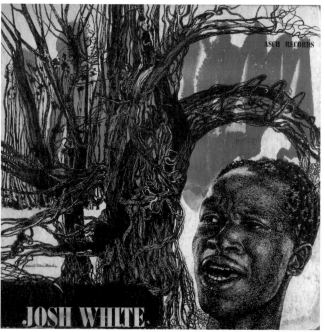

David Stone Martin, soon to become one of the most popular album cover artists in the jazz world, did several early covers for Asch Records, including this one for Josh's first Asch album. "One Meat Ball" was the leadoff song; the liner notes were by Langston Hughes. Author's collection.

The singing White family at home: Judy, Beverly, Josh, Josh Jr., and Fern.

(*above*) The final scene of *The Walking Hills*, with Randolph Scott (on horseback), Ella Raines, and the other gold miners, including Josh (second from right).

(*left*) *Our World* was a competitor of *Ebony* and featured Josh on the cover when *The Walking Hills* was released. Courtesy of Rene Dannen.

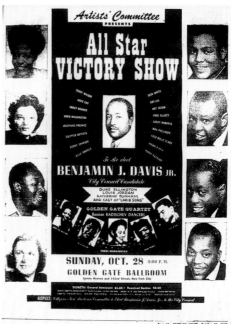

Two advertisements for benefit shows of the sort that led to Josh's downfall. Paul Draper was blacklisted, destroying his career. Benjamin J. Davis Jr. was the Communist Party's City Councilor for New York, and the array of stars booked for his reelection benefit included Billie Holiday, Duke Ellington, Louis Jordan, Katherine Dunham, Art Tatum, Mary Lou Williams, Teddy Wilson, Josephine Premice, the Golden Gate Quartet, and the Russian Radischev Dancers. Josh is pictured at left.

In happier times, Josh with Paul Robeson and friends. Photograph by Albert A. Freeman.

Good times in England.

(*left*) Josh and Beverly in one of the many newspaper clippings from their first tour together.

(*below*) The London gang: Don and Sandra Luck, Josh, and Rene Gordon out nightclubbing, with dedications from Josh and Gordon.
Courtesy of Don and Sandra Luck.

Relaxing in Hawaii with Sam Gary.

LEONARD
RIPLEY
and
JAC
HOLZMAN
present

JOSH WHITE

with the talents of

SAM GARY vocal

AL HALL bass

**TOWN HALL**
**Friday Evening, May 4, 1956 at 8:40**
TICKETS: $1.75, $2.50, $3.00

The two sides of the Josh White image: sexy and serious album covers for Elektra Records. Author's collection.

1 - JOSHUA
2 - Lass with the delicate air
3 - St James Infirmary
4 - Nobody knows the trouble I've seen
6 5 -> Out there of town
6 - Molly Malone
7 - Whats everybody made of
8 - Rising Sun
9 - John Henry

1 - Back Water Blues
2 - Foggy Dew
3 - I don't know what in the hell
to sing frankly I am stumped
please some one help this bastard out
of this fix. yes?

A handwritten set list. After number 3 of the second set, Josh has written: "I don't know what in the hell to sing frankly I am stumped please some-one help this bastard out of this fix, yes?" Courtesy of Rene Dannen.

(*opposite*) The poster for the 1956 Town Hall concert, featuring the cover art for *Josh At Midnight,* Josh's best-selling LP. This marked the beginning of Josh's climb back to the top of the folk scene

Still traveling in the 1960s.
(*left*) On tour with Judy in London. Photograph by and courtesy of Bengt Ohlson.
(*right*) With Josh Jr. and Beverly in Sweden.

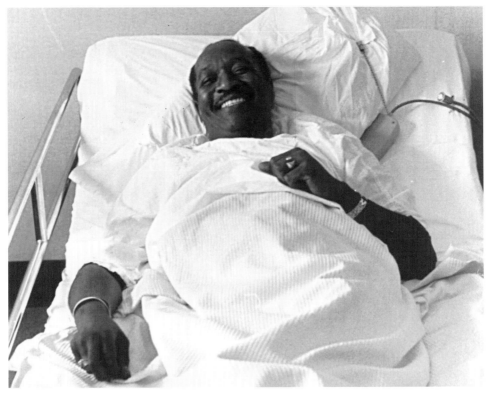

Looking good till the end: Josh in the hospital in California during his final illness.
Photo by and courtesy of Gerry Waitz.

Josh was in an odd situation relative to his politically oriented peers. He continued to sing topical numbers and to take a strong stance on civil rights issues, but he now had a mass audience that knew him for "One Meat Ball," and many of the new fans were unaware that he was anything more than an entertaining pop-folk stylist. Mary Chase was sometimes unsure how to deal with this situation. At a show for high school students in Winnetka, Illinois, she advised him not to sing "Free and Equal Blues," "Strange Fruit," or "Foggy, Foggy Dew," which was considered a bit racy. As it happened, the older students sent him notes before the show requesting these very songs, and then the principal asked him to sing the two political numbers in a separate show for junior high students, as they would be educational. Josh wholeheartedly agreed. "Kids are no dummies," he said, when he told the story to reporters. "They know what it's all about."

From Chicago, Josh and Premice headed out through the northern plains and up into the Rocky Mountains, moving into territory that was far off the normal folk and cabaret artists' itineraries. In those days before television and discos, it was not unusual for big dance bands such as Duke Ellington's or Count Basie's to tour through even the most out-of-the-way regions, but Josh seems to have been the first black solo artist to attempt anything of this kind. Though Premice says she remembers nothing about the journey, she and Josh must have been a truly exotic offering as they moved through Madison and Minneapolis and on into North Dakota, Montana, and the Idaho panhandle. The concerts were mostly in college towns such as Fargo and Moscow, but in the late 1940s, folk music had made only the most minor inroads into the college scene away from the coasts, and a strong, black guitarist and singer was something completely new. As for a Haitian dancer, it is hard to imagine anything further from the normal Dakota or Idaho fare.

Whether because of the success of "One Meat Ball" or simply the novelty of the offering, the tour drew large crowds wherever it touched down. The *Forum,* bulletin of North Dakota Agricultural College, reported that the Fargo concert, though on a Monday night, drew 1,200 people — all of them students "except for a few lucky townspeople who knew what was up."

A lot of people were learning "what was up." As Josh hit Fargo, the new issue of *Collier's* magazine came out with a three-page feature hailing him as "the nearest approach that we have to the strolling minstrel of the Middle Ages." This was not the *Daily Worker* or the *Amsterdam*

*News* but the voice of mainstream America. To be featured in a full-size article in *Collier's* signaled that Josh had arrived at the top of his profession. It was quickly followed by a feature in *Mademoiselle*, in which perky young co-eds were sent out as reporters, and Margo Stratton, UCLA '47, reported on Cafe Society and its "main attraction, Josh White, who can create a sensation with the lift of an eyebrow."

The *Collier's* piece, titled "Preacher in Song," was everything Josh and Mary Chase could have wished for, a respectful profile with none of the condescension often used in reference to black celebrities: "Medium tall, with a slow, mischievous smile, and dressed in sports slacks and corduroy shirt, Josh White held forth for three years in New York at Cafe Society Uptown and its twin Downtown, where Josh and his guitar were one and inseparable and were always billed together. His fame spread swiftly, and now he has just begun his first formal concert tour, which will take him to 31 American and Canadian cities from coast to coast."

The story gave a somewhat romanticized version of Josh's life story, with strong emphasis on his days with the blind men and especially on his tutelage by the legendary Blind "Lemmon" Jefferson. It went on to trace his early career in New York, switching a few events but giving a generally accurate picture. Toward the end, though, it veered into fiction as it detailed Josh's folk scholarship, painting him as a practiced field researcher who was also one of the folk, a sort of mythic blend of Alan Lomax and Leadbelly. It spoke of the effort with which he had painstakingly transcribed the *Chain Gang* songs from the singing of southern convicts and declared that "specialists in musical Americana were recognizing, in Josh White's repertoire, songs that they had heard about . . . which for years have been believed irretrievably lost."

Josh himself led the way to this romanticized interpretation. He told how "for years [he'd] been haunted by certain songs that Georgia chain-gang prisoners sang in low, frightened voices when their guards walked down the road a ways, out of hearing." Speaking of the excitement his repertoire created among folklorists, he said, "I soon heard myself called 'a repository' of rare Southern music. That's quite something, don't you think, to call a man who just loves to sing old songs?" One can only imagine how Lomax, who had taught Josh many more songs than he had learned from him, took this. Still, it was no further from the truth than the way Burl Ives, another "wandering minstrel," was being described, and it was perfect *Collier's* copy.

Indeed, Josh was proving to be singularly astute in the way he handled the press. Talking to a *Daily Worker* or *PM* reporter, he would say that he disliked Negro spirituals, considering them an archaic relic of slavery days, and would toss in a word of support for Ben Davis, Harlem's black Communist city councilor. For *Collier's,* he spoke admiringly of Lemon Jefferson's repertoire of "pre–Civil War songs, and very rare spirituals," which Jefferson had never recorded but had passed on to him. If a newspaper wanted a proud social activist, he was comfortable in that role. If it wanted a genuine folk minstrel, he could handle that part as well.

All in all, Josh was an ideal ambassador for folk music, and *Collier's* reported that the business was treating him very well. The magazine said that "Josh's annual income from his best-seller records alone zooms into five figures. Add the fees from his concert tour, his private-party and radio engagements and the lessons he gives in folk-song singing, and it becomes a high-bracket income." (How much Josh actually made from record sales is open to question, but this was the year that "One Meat Ball" was on the charts and would in any case have been exceptional.)

The *Collier's* interview attracted plenty of attention and was already being quoted by other reporters by the time Josh and Premice reached the West Coast. These were still the days when every town of any size had at least two or three papers, and Josh was important enough to justify coverage in every one of them. As interview followed interview, he began to have something of a set statement, combining the folkloric and activist sides of his persona: "People who have heard of me as a 'blues singer' generally expect something like Ol Black Joe, or the customary melancholy wail of a defeated people," he told a reporter for the *Tacoma* (Washington) *Times.* "That's not for me. Contrary to popular conception, the blues are not always concerned with love, razors, dice and death. I strive to present the other side of the blues, the blues that criticize man's inhumanity to man, the side that has long been regarded as non-commercial because of its social militancy." Ten days later, in an interview for the *Denver Post,* Josh repeated the "love, razors, dice, and death" line, which came from Richard Wright's *Southern Exposure* liner notes, and added Wright's contention that blues are "the spirituals of the city."

Josh and Premice traveled north from Seattle and Tacoma to Vancouver, then doubled back through Portland and Corvallis, Oregon, before heading east via Colorado Springs and Denver to Waterloo, Iowa, and Cleveland, Ohio. They ended the year with a homecoming concert at Columbia University's MacMillan Theater. The tour had been another milestone for Josh, and he was clearly aware of the fact. Though the combination of constant travel and multiple performances had left him with a bad case of laryngitis, when he was interviewed for the new American Negro Press (ANP) wire service he proudly gave a precise odometer reading for the trip: 16,923 miles.

Along with the ANP story, Josh was welcomed home with a cover article in the January issue of the year-old *People's Songs* bulletin. "The career of Josh White is of great significance for People's Songs members," it began. "Just as Paul Robeson has shown that a concert singer can increase his stature by singing songs of freedom . . . Josh has also become a great people's singer precisely because he has sung songs of protest, and has never conceded an inch to Jim Crow or Uncle Tom. . . . In spite of the sage advice from some oldsters that it would be wiser to lay off these songs, he insisted upon singing them (and was backed up by his manager, Mary Chase). And it turned out that of all songs, these were the ones that got *best* notices from the critics, and cheers from the audience."

The article went on to advertise an upcoming concert at Town Hall, which was also previewed in a *Daily Worker* piece. That story, except for its opening paragraph, consisted of direct quotation from Josh and demonstrates how well he knew the *Worker* audience (though some of the rather stilted phrases, in that era before tape recorders, are not necessarily to be taken as verbatim):

> "Music is my weapon," said Josh, "and I use it every opportunity I get. Come on down to Town Hall, Saturday night, Jan. 18, and you'll see what I mean. People's Songs is sponsoring my concert and they write and publish the songs I use as a weapon.
>
> "When I sing 'White, Brown and Black Blues' or 'Free and Equal Blues' I'm wielding a mighty sword, and when I sing 'Strange Fruit' or 'Talking Atomic Blues' I feel as powerful as an M-4 tank.
>
> "Why, in Louisville, Ky., I sang 'Strange Fruit' which is the most potent anti-lynch propaganda ever written. Mind you, this was in a Southern town — a representative Southern town — and the people caught the message and reacted accordingly. Their reception was loud and long.

"A song sung with the weight of a man's beliefs behind it carries a tougher punch than a speech with the most powerful words in Mr. Webster's big book in it.

"The attention of an audience to a song is held by the accompaniment of the guitar, the sound of the voice, the lilt and swing of the tempo of the song, and the forcefulness of the words lifts them out of their seats onto a magic carpet to where the words tell about.

"And in their minds and hearts they, too, are singing with me, believing with me what the words say. Believe me, a song is a helluva potent weapon."

The *Daily Worker* still regarded Josh as one of its fighting heroes, but the relationship would soon begin to show some cracks. Times had changed considerably since the Popular Front years, and American politics was already drifting toward the polarization of the McCarthy era and the Cold War. The shift can be ascribed to numerous factors, from postwar prosperity to international rivalries, and there had also been major upheavals within the Communist Party itself. In the interest of furthering the integration of progressive politics into the Roosevelt mainstream, General Secretary Earl Browder had dissolved the Party in May 1944 and reformed it as the Communist Political Association, with the aim of influencing rather than competing with the Democratic Party. This move was bitterly opposed by Party hard-liners, and in 1946 they seized control: Browder was cast onto the proverbial dustheap of history, and the Party took a hard left turn.

At the same time, the American right was beginning to level its full weight and power on the destruction of Communism, both at home and abroad. This was not surprising or unexpected, but to the dismay of progressives, many liberals joined the attack. The American Communists had been hard workers, but their authoritarian and high-handed manner had earned them plenty of enemies among their erstwhile allies. Meanwhile, the Soviet Union was behaving more and more like a police state intent on complete domination of its neighbors. In March 1946, Winston Churchill gave a speech in Fulton, Missouri, announcing that "an iron curtain has descended across the [European] Continent." That same year, voters elected the first Republican-majority Congress since 1932.

The Democratic Party, meanwhile, was making it very clear that its honeymoon with the left was over. In March 1947, President Harry Truman pronounced the Truman Doctrine, defining the United States as protector of Europe against Soviet dominance and saying that the world "must choose between alternative ways of life." Two weeks later he issued an executive order to investigate "infiltration of disloyal persons" in the U.S. government. That summer the Taft-Hartley Act (passed over Truman's veto) crippled the labor movement by severely limiting rights to strike, boycott, or organize union shops. It was the beginning of the Cold War, and with the toughening international line came a crackdown on domestic dissent. The CP's new hard-line leadership reacted by turning inward, sending its top cadre underground and expelling what some historians have estimated as several thousand members. (Others dispute this figure, saying that most of the losses came from people quitting the Party for a variety of reasons. Either way, it shrank to a fraction of its previous size.) Any thought of Communism as twentieth-century Americanism was over for good.

Of course, in many areas these changes were relatively gradual. New Dealers were still prominent in the Democratic Party, and the full-scale anti-Communist assault of the "red scare" would arrive only with the Korean War. In the middle to late 1940s the most visible signs of what was to come were a few high-profile investigations and trials of New Deal political figures — most famously, Alger Hiss — and of the group of screenwriters known as the Hollywood Ten. It was not until 1950 that these investigations spilled over significantly into the rest of the entertainment world, bringing widespread blacklisting.

By chance, though, Cafe Society was caught in the first wave of the anti-Communist assault. Early in 1947 a German exile named Gerhardt Eisler, who had been active in the Communist Party since the 1920s, was called before the House Committee on Un-American Activities (commonly abbreviated HUAC) and accused of having been the main liaison between the Soviet Comintern and the American Communist Party. He refused to testify and was cited for contempt in a resolution presented by Richard Nixon, then a freshman congressman making his maiden speech. A few days later, on March 5, HUAC called Leon Josephson, Barney Josephson's brother, and accused him of having helped Eisler obtain a fake U.S. passport.

Leon, who had been a leading lawyer for the International Labor Defense, a progressive legal organization, refused to testify. He argued that HUAC had no authority to question him and that committee member John Rankin's presence made the proceedings invalid, as

Rankin had gained his House seat in a Mississippi election that illegally barred blacks from voting (Rankin had been elected by only 5 percent of his district's population). Josephson was found guilty of contempt of Congress and given the maximum sentence of a $1,000 fine and a year in jail.

Leon had also been working for his brother, and in a later interview Barney Josephson recalled the effects of his testimony: "My life turned inside out," he said. Leon's case "was front-page stuff, and since no one knew who Leon Josephson was, he was always mentioned in the papers as the brother of Barney Josephson, the owner of Cafe Society Uptown and Cafe Society Downtown. The Hearst press . . . took off, and the innuendo, the guilt-by-association, began. [Westbrook] Pegler devoted a column to Leon implying that he was a drug addict, and the last line was 'And there is much to be said about his brother Barney. . . .' So I was the brother of a Communist drug addict, I allowed Negroes in my clubs, I had introduced inflammatory songs like 'Strange Fruit' and 'The House I Live In,' and on and on. It ruined my clubs. Three weeks after the first uproar, business at the Uptown dropped 45 percent."

Cafe Society Uptown closed in December 1947, but the downtown club, with its smaller size and less conventional clientele, was able to continue for almost another two years before Josephson was forced to sell out to new owners. Even here, though, the publicity was scaring a lot of customers away. There were constant jibes in the nightclub columns of Walter Winchell, Lee Mortimer, and Dorothy Kilgallen. "Kilgallen would write things like 'the Moscow-line nightclub Cafe Society' or 'that proletarian hangout,' " Josephson recalled. "And after I finally had to go out of business, [she wrote that] 'Cafe Society, "the place where the races mixed," is no longer there — no longer do you have to go in and hear Teddy Wilson's orchestra playing the Red marching song. . . .'

"The only paper that didn't attack me was the *New York Times*. A reporter from the *New York Tribune* wrote a favorable review of one of my acts and the editor told him, 'Don't you know better than to give Cafe Society a favorable review?' The reporter told me he wouldn't be coming in any more and he literally started crying in his glass of scotch. . . .

"I was not able to get press reviews for new talent, and reviews were crucial. I decided to bring in established names who would not be dependent on reviews, but they wouldn't talk to me, as they were fearful they would be blacklisted if they appeared in my clubs."

The fears were, at least to some extent, justified. Guilt by association was the order of the day, and anyone who worked at the club could be fitted into the tenuous chain of suspicion. A textbook example of the way this chain was forged can be found in a sentence from HUAC's 1947 report on the Southern Conference for Human Welfare: "Entertainer at the Washington meeting [of the Conference] was Susan Reed, employed by Cafe Society, a night club, owned by Barney Josephson, brother of Leon Josephson, leading Communist, Soviet Secret Service operative, charged with passport frauds."

Josh was among the first "established names" to cut his ties with Cafe Society, as well as with any other group whose red taint might adversely affect his reputation. He had his name removed from the People's Songs advisory board, and to protect against possible future problems he and Mary Chase contacted Howard Rushmore, a onetime writer for the *Daily Worker* who had become a columnist on the right-wing *Journal-American*. They explained to Rushmore that they had only recently learned, with the publication of the attorney general's list of "subversive" organizations, that many of the groups for which Josh had played were "Communist fronts." They asked his support in backing up Josh's Americanism and also in advising them as to which benefit concerts were and were not "safe." "[Mary] would talk with Howard Rushmore about all the requests for me to perform," Josh later said. "And he would say yes or no."

This wariness was in marked contrast to the strong and unambiguous stance Josh had always taken on political issues, and to his characterization of a folksinger as someone who expresses the hopes and battles of the common people against the forces of racism and oppression. The speed of his capitulation to right-wing pressure and his willingness to turn his back on Josephson and Cafe Society, which had supported him throughout his early years as a folk performer, was intensely disturbing to his old leftist friends and admirers, and the ill feeling would increase over the next few years. Some people close to Josh prefer to blame Chase, who had big plans for Josh's future and had always felt that he was playing too many benefits and not concentrating enough on building his career. But even if Chase was behind his new stance, it is not clear that Josh would have needed much urging. After all, there was plenty to be wary of: his employer's brother had just been hauled off to jail, and his workplace was being described as a den of iniquity and international intrigue.

Josh's political views were strongly held but not particularly complex. They were centered on the American civil rights struggle, and he had been aligned with the far left, as he was aligned with the New Dealers, to the extent that they supported this struggle. Although he gave lip service to internationalism and had tended to echo the slogans of the people around him, he was never the sort to go to meetings, and no one ever took him for a subtle political theorist. His friends were puzzled and angry when he gave in to political pressures, and he must have at times had some misgivings, but on the whole he saw no contradiction in maintaining his strong position as a singer of "fighting songs" even as he distanced himself from many of his old associates. Except for a few "win the war" numbers, all his topical material had been directed toward combatting racial discrimination, a position in which he believed as strongly as ever. He may have been playing a smaller proportion of topical songs in his concerts, but he continued to end the first segment with "Strange Fruit" and the second with "Freedom Road." To the liberals, he remained a symbol and a hero, and if the Communists felt betrayed, many people considered them to have made their own problems with their hard-line stance.

Even before the Josephson investigation, Josh had been drifting away from the far left as it diverged more and more drastically from the Roosevelt center. He would show up at the occasional "hootenanny" and still appeared with some frequency at events featuring his more radical peers, but by 1947 people like Pete Seeger and Woody Guthrie were no longer coming by the house or spending much time hanging out with him after hours. Josh did continue to play a lot of benefits even after leaving Cafe Society. Despite the overtures made to Howard Rushmore, he would sing for pretty much any cause that requested his help. Indeed, to Chase and Carol White it sometimes seemed as if Josh simply lacked the ability to say no. "If you were giving your favorite rat a party and you asked Josh to play, he'd play," Carol says, with bitter humor. He genuinely loved to entertain people and be the center of attention, whether at a party, a nightclub, or a political rally, and if the free concerts were an annoyance to some of his more business-minded associates, it is by no means clear that they hurt him professionally. Although they brought in no direct payment, his openness and accessibility won him a lot of ardent admirers.

Foremost among those admirers were the liberal leaders of the New Deal, for although the red-baiters tended to highlight the most "subversive" organizations that Josh played for, his strongest links were to the Roosevelt camp. His reputation as minstrel to the president had continued to grow after FDR's death, through his firm ties to Eleanor Roosevelt. This cut no ice with the red-hunters, whose attacks on Communism were, to a great extent, simply covers for their primary aim of discrediting the remaining New Dealers. Indeed, there is a letter to Josh from Mrs. Roosevelt in which she declines to vouch for him on a passport application, writing that "it might do you more harm than good to have a letter from me as I am not looked upon with favor in some quarters." Nonetheless, Josh always took pride in Mrs. Roosevelt's patronage, and the relationship continued to develop into the 1950s.

In 1945, Mrs. Roosevelt had invited Josh, along with Carol and Josh Jr., to her Hyde Park residence for the first of what became a series of annual Christmas performances for the boys at Wiltwyck, a nearby boarding school for juvenile delinquents in which she had taken an interest. The Whites would stay at Hyde Park, and according to Carol, "At dinner Mrs. Roosevelt would be right there heaping your plate at the buffet; at night, she made sure we had hot water bottles in our beds." Mrs. Roosevelt also invited Josh to come and sing on other occasions, and early in 1947 she asked him to premiere a special song, written in FDR's memory by MacKinlay Kantor, at the President's Birthday Ball in New York. The song was called "The Man Who Couldn't Walk Around," and all royalties were dedicated to the Infantile Paralysis Foundation. Josh said that this occasion was the only time he ever saw Mrs. Roosevelt cry, and he made the song a regular part of his concert programs. According to a *Variety* blurb, "its message is to polio victims to take heart from the example of the late President Roosevelt and it makes a perfect addition to the White repertoire of folk and pseudo-folk tunes."

*PM* took a rather different view, calling it "one of the most mawkish and maudlin songs ever written about a great man." The *PM* piece, a review of Josh's concert that September at Town Hall, was representative of a newly critical attitude toward his work, especially in the progressive press. "It was a little disturbing to find that Mr. White is beginning to lose some of his former simplicity and directness in projecting some of the numbers in his repertoire," the reviewer wrote. "And he is too good an artist to need the complicated variety of floodlights and colored spotlights, which he used at Town Hall, to build up the mood of his offerings."

Having become an established artist, Josh could no longer expect the sweetheart press he had received as a newcomer. Writers who had found his work fresh and unusual five years earlier were beginning to wish for something new. By 1946 the *New Yorker* listings had begun to describe him as "singing in his now slightly stylized fashion," and three months after the *PM* piece a *New York Times* reviewer remarked that he had "become very mannered over the years." Clearly, the honeymoon was over.

Both *PM* and the *Times* singled out Josh's handling of non-blues material for special criticism. This opinion, which would become more pervasive through the years, has some obvious justice. There were plenty of other people on the folk scene who specialized in traditional ballads, from classical purists such as Richard Dyer-Bennett to popularizers such as Burl Ives and the young and effervescent Susan Reed. Although none of these singers gave a raw, traditional rendition of the material, neither had any of them adapted and reshaped it to the extent that Josh did. Josh's treatment of English ballads stopped short of transforming them into blues, but he was influenced by his blues and gospel training, and some critics found both his vocal and instrumental style inappropriate.

That said, these criticisms tend to beg the question. No one on the New York cabaret scene was presenting the pure folk tradition, and Josh's approach was as valid as any other. In Afro-American as in Euro-American styles, he had always been a master illusionist rather than a musicologist. His chain-gang songs sounded nothing like the singing of southern convicts, and it would be hard to come up with an acoustic blues player who was farther from the rough and idiosyncratic brilliance of someone like Blind Lemon Jefferson, however often Josh might cite Jefferson as his teacher.

Josh was a consummate professional, and had been since his teens. Critics who accused him of becoming slick were off the mark; he had always been slick, in the sense of polished and studied, and never more so than in 1934, when he had been turning out adept covers of the latest pop-blues hits. Josh's blues performances had actually become tougher with the years. His voice was darker and his guitar work far more varied and distinctive than during his days on the race labels. Meanwhile, his overall style had become more, not less, original. Adapting techniques from his blues background to material that had never before been played that way, he had melded disparate traditions into something that, though by no means folklorically "genuine," proved its validity in front of enthusiastic audiences every time he stepped on stage.

It is hard not to see an element of racism in some of the critiques. To some people Josh's job was to be not just a folk stylist but a black folk stylist, so the idea of his singing "Molly Malone," "Waltzing Matilda," or "On Top of Old Smoky" was unacceptable. This is not to say that in the late 1940s Josh's material left no grounds for criticism. Many of the newer songs in his repertoire were pretty lightweight and forgettable. "The Man Who Couldn't Walk Around" deserved everything *PM* said about it, and its flip side, "Apples, Peaches, and Cherries," a sappy imitation ballad from the pen of Lewis Allan, was no better. Josh was a nightclub singer, not a folk artist, and the "pseudo-folk" songs being written for him often came from the same writers who were churning out material for other cafe chanteurs and chanteuses. Applied to such songs, "folk" was a marketing term rather than a musical description. Like the Elizabethan pastorals, they were romantic songs that spoke of a working-class or peasant folk but were written by and performed for the educated, urban elite. Some were quite good, but on average, like most compositions of the "folk revivals" of the 1950s, 1960s, and later (or most mainstream pop fare), they would not survive their time.

Josh's performance style had also changed as he adapted to the cabaret audience. If no "slicker" than in his youth, he was certainly silkier; the way he caressed a lyric like "Molly Malone" or "The Riddle Song" was closer to Julie London's midnight whisper than to the raw sound of Leadbelly or Woody Guthrie. He had a habit of swooping up to notes which many of his critics found mannered and annoying, especially when applied to the simple melodies of the old ballads. And he was nothing if not stylized. His songs were theatrical set pieces; he would vary them to suit his mood and his audience, but he knew where every note, breath, and facial expression should be placed. Though surrounded by some of the most adept improvisers in jazz, he chose to polish rather than explore his material. If he sang "The Lass with the Delicate Air" a hundred times, the same sexy "ow!" would precede the word "delicate" every time.

Which is to say, he knew exactly what he was doing — and had to accept that what he was doing was not to everyone's taste. The negative comments he was beginning to receive in the mainstream press simply echoed what the hard-core folk crowd had been saying for years, but were largely irrelevant to the audience that loved upbeat, entertaining tunes like "The Lass with the Delicate Air" and "One Meat Ball." He had found a formula that worked, and he could apply it to a range of material that none of his peers would have attempted. And he made it all seem utterly natural and relaxed. The veteran jazz and pop producer Milt Gabler, who supervised Josh's Decca recordings, sums him up when asked what Josh was like to work with in the studio: "He was a professional," Gabler growls, annoyed to be asked such a stupid question. "He was one of the great ones, and the great ones are always easy."

# 11

## TRAVELS, WHISKEY, AND WOMEN

■ ■ ■ ■ ■ ■ ■ ■ ■ ■ ■ ■ ■ ■ ■ ■ ■ ■ ■ ■ ■ ■

Though political pressures certainly played a part in Josh's decision to quit Cafe Society, they were not his only reason. By 1947 he was regularly telling interviewers that he had had his fill of nightclub work. He was getting more concert bookings, and their advantages were obvious: "No waiters, no dishes, no sweat—more bread." He was also ready to capitalize on his success by branching out beyond the music world. He had become a celebrity, with the press covering him not only in reviews and feature interviews but also in puff pieces such as the *Our World* cover story in which a popular model listed "the ten most handsome American Negro men."

Even if his immediate reasons for leaving Cafe Society were related to political pressures, then, it was a move he had been considering for some time. When his final, two-month stint at the downtown room ended in April 1947, he did not search for another nightclub home. Instead, for the next two years he devoted himself to concerts, touring, and acting and remained completely absent from the New York cabaret scene.

At almost the same time, with no apparent explanation, he stopped recording. His last Decca session was in May, after which he recorded two singles for the Apollo label, and that was it for the rest of the decade. No one can remember the reason for this change. It may have been related to his political break with old contacts, or may simply reflect a lack of new material or a preoccupation with other projects. Whatever the reason, it did not reflect any general slowing down in his career. In October he played a two-day stint at the 92nd Street YMHA, including an afternoon show with Josh Jr., then headed off on another national tour. With his brother Bill as a traveling partner he drove out to the West Coast for a concert at the Philharmonic Auditorium in Los Angeles and then a two-week residency at the California Theater Club in San Francisco. Bill had become a frequent companion, recording several duets with Josh at the last Decca session, including a "Josh and Bill Blues" that had them trading off standard blues verses. His singing was less distinctive than Josh's, but he sounded very similar, and the two had a close personal relationship. "They were very definitely brothers," remembers Katie Lee, a young singer and friend, "though Billy was not as nervous as Josh; the vitality and the energy did not flow through him like it did Josh."

Josh enjoyed traveling, but he always liked to have some company. Even though he did not need anyone else onstage, he would often bring a second singer along for the ride: Bill White or Sam Gary or, in later years, Josh Jr. or Beverly. When there was no musical companion available, Mary Chase's son Jay might go along. Jay Chase was barely out of high school when he first went out as Josh's road companion, and he looks back on the trips as exciting adventures. "Josh was a very fast driver," he says admiringly. "Josh liked a big automobile, and he liked to do ninety miles an hour."

The nice cars and high speeds were remembered by everyone who ever had the opportunity to be Josh's passenger. Josh Jr., who shares this passion, tells of traveling with him in the 1950s and early 1960s and of switching places at the wheel while roaring down the highway. He still laughs about a trip with Albert Grossman, then owner of Chicago's Gate of Horn, who was so terrified by their high-speed shenanigans that he flew home rather than ride with them again.

Jay Chase points out that the impressive cars were not simply a projection of Josh's high spirits. "You have to remember the times," he says. "We couldn't go to the average motel and stay. We couldn't go into the average eating place and get a meal. So it was a matter of getting to the next stop quickly, where those arrangements were made." He adds that as with any other black artist, it could happen that Josh would be stranded in a town that had no "colored" hotel and have to sleep in that big car.

In one late 1940s interview Josh talked about the difficulties of traveling, even in the supposedly liberal North. Describing one cross-country trip with his brother, he told how "just out of Zanesville, Ohio, we had to stop for gas. The gas attendants didn't get up to serve us. So I called them, and one of them said, 'There's a gas shortage.' I said I didn't believe it. Besides, I carried a credit card. Finally, one attendant said, 'We don't sell to blacks.' I jumped out of the car. I was so mad! But what's the use.

"Later we picked up two hitchhikers. Then, when we'd stop for gas, I'd pretend I was the chauffeur and the white hitchhikers the owners. That's how we got gas."

Josh went on to recount how five St. Louis restaurants refused to sell him a cup of coffee. "Finally, one waitress begged her boss to let me have some in the kitchen and he said, 'What'll we serve it in?' " Such insults were constant, and although most might have been petty enough by themselves, the totality could be crippling. In Portland, Oregon, a hotel accepted his reservation with the proviso that he not use the dining room or have visitors. "I told them to go to hell," he said.

By the time they got to the West Coast, Josh was so tired and upset that he had to go to a nerve specialist. His old hand injury had started acting up, and one of his fingers was paralyzed.

Josh's wife and children were well aware of the pressures he was under on the road and often cite them to explain the more troubling sides of his personality: the constant drinking and womanizing. It was not that Josh turned to drink and women in some sort of secret, depressed escape from his normal life; these habits were not private, but integral to the persona he projected in public. The folksinger Jackie Washington, who would become friends with both Josh and Josh Jr. in the late 1950s, was even drawn to wonder whether they were more for show than for pleasure. They seemed so much part of the "Josh White" image that he found them slightly unreal.

Certainly, there was an air of theatricality to Josh's excesses. He would drink whiskey or vodka by the tumbler, and there is story after story about his capacity. An English friend remembers him being served whiskey in a water glass, tapping the glass to indicate that he needed a larger shot, then tapping again, and again, till the glass was almost full and the bartender was staring, before finally picking it up and tossing the liquor back in one gulp. As if the amounts themselves were not striking enough, he developed the habit of gargling his drinks before he swallowed. In the 1950s he even recorded the gargle, using it as an introduction to his Elektra recording of "Jelly Jelly." Enrico Banducci, who frequently employed Josh at his San Francisco club, the Hungry i, recalls expressing his astonishment that Josh would gargle whiskey right before going on stage, and Josh replying, "Clears my throat. Clears my throat."

Constant as the drinking was, though, no one in the White family seems to feel that Josh had a "problem" in the popular sense of the term. When he was home, Carol would try to keep the partying to a minimum, simply to give him a rest, but she says he was never more than a social drinker: "It kind of went along with the guitar. It helped him to relax, so he didn't turn it down. And after a while there were people that might say, 'Oh, if you didn't have a bottle Josh wasn't there,' but that's not true. The thing about Josh was, even as much as Josh drank, it was his sham, it was his curtain. And once Josh left that stage and came home, he did not have to pretend. When he was home, he would sometimes have something, but he didn't *need* a drink."

Josh Jr., a longtime A.A. member who is quite open about his own difficulties with alcohol, also believes that his father managed to keep that part of his life under control. He says that he could always tell how much Josh had drunk before he went onstage and that it might somewhat affect Josh's timing, but he adds that despite all the drinking he saw him do over the years, he never saw his father drunk.

Beverly concurs and emphasizes that from the family's point of view the drinking was not a big deal. "We always had alcohol in our home, and it was never a problem for us as children," she says. "Some people have memories where the parents had to be put to bed, or became violent or something, and we had nothing like that. It was just there, and when he drank, my mother drank, years ago. And to me, it did nothing significant that changed his personality. You knew that he had imbibed, but someone seeing him would not say, 'There goes so and so, he's drunk again.' If anything, he might be a little more benevolent than usual, and more long-winded, but that's about all."

People who knew Josh less intimately, his fellow performers and the club owners he met over the years, tended to be impressed rather than concerned by his liquor intake and still enjoy telling stories of his capacity and how little it affected him. Many of them get more nervous, though, when it comes to talking about the women who constantly surrounded him. Person after person, asked for reminiscences, would ask if Carol was still alive, then politely explain that out of respect for her feelings they had no anecdotes that they were prepared to repeat for publication. The White family is, rather surprisingly, more open about the subject. They were, of course, aware of his philandering, whether or not they had specific details, and they were not happy about it, but over the years they learned to come to terms with it in their own ways.

Bunny, as usual, is the most outspoken. "Daddy was a sexy man, a handsome man," she says. "They threw their bodies at him, and he was much too polite to turn it down. But he always gave my mom respect. And, to a great extent, she went along with the program because he gave her the respect."

The sex appeal was so integral to Josh's public image that the actual extent of his womanizing may sometimes have been exaggerated. Jo Mapes, who met him in the 1950s when she was just starting out as a cabaret folksinger, recalls that he was "very arrogant about being a ladykiller, a real womanizer." She says that she liked him nonetheless but, knowing him only as an occasional acquaintance, was horrified when, onstage at a Greenwich Village coffeehouse, he openly implied that they were lovers. "He started caressing the guitar and making allusions to a woman's body and to having slept with me. I was so angry . . . everybody looking would have sworn we had just gotten out of bed. And I was furious with him. I told him, 'If you ever do that again, you silly son of a bitch, I'll break your own guitar over your head.' "

Josh had more than his share of conquests, but the sex appeal was also part of his public image. Jackie Washington remembers that when Josh sat down at a table where there was a woman he had never met, he would always take a sip from her glass with a courtly "Do you mind?" or take a puff from her cigarette and then place it back between her lips. Robert Shelton described such gestures as a form of racial testing, but by the time Washington was seeing them they had become purely theatrical exercises in seduction. "It was a come-on. And all of that was a great thrill to him. It was so much fun. I don't believe the fucking was the real fun — *looking* like you're fucking, being seen emerging from the hotel room with the woman in the background, was even more important."

Josh's other friends are quite certain that he took pleasure in the acts themselves, but all agree that he was a showman from the tips of his alligator shoes to the cigarette burning behind his ear, and that it was generally impossible to sort out the reality from the pose. There is not one woman with whom he was associated over the years, whether through professional or personal attachments, whom someone will not cite as having been his lover. From Libby Holman to Lena Horne, Josephine Premice, and Eartha Kitt, to later friends such as Katie Lee, Cynthia Gooding, and the silver-haired cabaret singer Joyce Bryant, and even his manager Mary Chase, the rumors always circulated, sometimes at reasonably reliable first hand but often at three or four removes. Talking about him today, almost every female friend finds it necessary to mention that there was nothing romantic between them. As Lee puts it, "I was a good-looking woman, but never once in all our relationship was there even the slightest hint that Josh wanted to spend any time with me in a prone position." Other friends laugh at these denials, and even those who are most adamant about the platonic nature of their own relationships with Josh agree that his reputation was well deserved. Indeed, several said that they believed themselves to be the only close female friends with whom Josh did *not* have a sexual relationship.

As for Carol, she is surprisingly forthright on this subject. "All the fellows that played wherever Josh was, they made fun of him," she says. "Because they said 'All the white women run after him.' Well, there were no black women there *to* run after him. But there was no question that girls would flock all over him. There was just no question about it. And he was like any other normal man. Come *on*. He was human. He *was human*. He was really a very virile-looking man. He was terrible! Women would just die."

Looking back, Carol cannot help laughing, but she is serious about her feelings. She was not happy with the situation, but she managed to make her peace with it. "I was always the kind of person that felt that if a woman has a husband and she loves him, she does all that she can," she says. "You have to be a strong person to be married to a guy like him. You have to make up your mind that this person whom you fell in love with and married, if he ever walked away it would be because *he* wanted to, not because of anything you might have done along the way. That was always my motto. And of course it was difficult sometimes.

"It takes a special kind of person, and I say this modestly, but see, I went through it from the age of sixteen, seventeen. And I have learned through the years. I told my first daughter-in-law, and I told this one [Josh Jr.'s current wife]: 'You're gonna have to love him more than you think he loves you. He'll love you that much, but you're gonna have to show it more. And if you're not ready for it, you have to leave it alone, because it's not easy.' "

It is obvious that Josh's philandering was a lot harder to deal with at the time, but at this remove Carol can discuss it with understanding and at times even laugh and joke about it. She took a degree of pride in Josh's attractiveness and could find a lot of humor in the angry jealousy of the powerful white men who suddenly found their women friends ignoring them.

Carol also understood that Josh's sex appeal was integral to his professional success. "I know perfectly well that if these women didn't run after him, I wouldn't have this house," she says, looking around at her comfortable duplex in a pleasant area of Queens. And like Bunny, she insists that whatever his extracurricular activities, he always gave her the respect she needed. If she went to Cafe Society, she was never confronted with the sight of him exchanging intimacies with another woman, and he never let his affairs interfere with his duties as a father. "I knew he loved his children," she says. "And I knew he loved me."

If Carol was resigned to Josh's affairs during the Cafe Society days, she is genuinely sympathetic about his behavior once he went out on the road. "A lot of people in show business are the most lonely people in the world," she says. "Thousands could come to hear you sing, and then it's 'Thanks, Josh, for a good evening,' and they all go home to their house and you're there in a hotel by yourself. And sure, then you want to have company. They go home to their families, and you're just there. It's not easy. So, when you closed the door, you at least had someone."

As for Josh himself, he derived plenty of enjoyment from the drinking, the parties, and the attention, intimate or otherwise. Many friends speculate that the affairs with white women were, in part, a way of asserting his manliness in a racist society and of getting back for the insults and abuse he had suffered. Yet he seems to have conducted all of them in a respectful and loving way and to have genuinely liked the women involved. Carol will always point out how little love and affection he had received in his childhood, and the insatiable appetite he showed for it later seems completely natural to her, even if it was not always pleasant.

It must be added that Josh was able to have close friendships with women whether or not they were or had been his lovers. Jo Mapes, for example, finishes her story by saying that Josh never again made any suggestion of an intimate relationship between them and that he was always a complete pleasure to be around. "He was a dear man," she says. "And he was a good man." Indeed, virtually all his female friends and acquaintances speak well of him and tell of the help and moral support he gave them. Eartha Kitt, in one of her several autobiographies, says he was the only New York friend to accompany her down south to the funeral of her closest relative. Josephine Premice speaks of the openness and generosity with which he encouraged her and other young performers. Katie Lee remembers him comforting her after a cabaret patron had made a nasty remark and bolstering her sagging confidence. He liked camaraderie, regardless of sex, and any particular intimacy was a pleasant addition to that.

On the road, the people he met at various venues were already familiar with his reputation, and it only burnished the legend if he happened to arrive with a pretty young woman who had "needed a ride from Chicago." As for his male traveling companions, they could either share in the partying or discreetly absent themselves. On a tape made at a Los Angeles party one hears Sam Gary snoring quietly in the background as Josh plays guitar for Katie Lee and another young woman. Josh was virtually indefatigable as long as there was an audience. Carol did her best to see to it that he got some rest when he was home, but on the road he was always ready to have a good time.

# 12

## BROADWAY, HOLLYWOOD, AND BEYOND
## 1947-1950

■ ■ ■ ■ ■ ■ ■ ■ ■ ■ ■ ■ ■ ■ ■ ■ ■ ■ ■ ■ ■

The details of Josh's schedule for the late 1940s are not easily pieced together, especially fifty years after the fact. When he and Bill finished their tour in Los Angeles at the end of 1947, he sold the car and flew back to New York, arriving four days after the birth of his youngest child, a fourth daughter, named Judith. His first job back home was as a special guest of the vaudeville stars Paul Draper and Larry Adler in their annual children's Christmas show at the New York City Center. After that, his comings and goings are hard to trace with any degree of accuracy. There were frequent shows in New York or in New Jersey or Philadelphia, regular trips to Chicago and Detroit, and annual cross-country tours, but the surviving records are only the tip of the iceberg. Whereas Josh's first trip to any town was news, the fact that he was back six months later might not be, so the newspaper files cannot be counted on, and neither the Whites nor the people involved in his booking and management have kept records of his appearances.

If Josh's concert career was no longer news, his branching out into other activities attracted greater attention. He had always aspired to be more than just a singer and guitar player, and in the late 1940s he began to expand into acting. His first nonsinging appearance came in February 1948 with an off-Broadway group appropriately named the Experimental Theatre. The play, titled *A Long Way from Home*, was an all-black adaptation of Maxim Gorki's *Lower Depths*. The playwrights, Randolph Goodman and Walter Carroll, had shifted the scene of the action from turn-of-the-century Russia to present-day Durham, North Carolina, where a mingled assemblage of riffraff lived in basement quarters under a pool hall. The story involved a visit from an itinerant preacher, which transformed the characters in various ways, uplifting some but leading others into tragic missteps.

Josh played Joebuck, a crook who is having an affair with the landlord's wife but, after the preacher's arrival, decides to go straight and marry the landlord's daughter instead. As the *Daily Worker* reviewer described the ensuing mayhem, "The landlord's wife, in a fit of jealousy, practically scalds the feet off the daughter. The crook, who previously had rejected the wife's appeal to kill her husband, now does so in an attempt to come to the aid of the daughter. The wife betrays him to the cop, and the cop, knowing of her desire to have her husband murdered, takes her to jail along with the crook."

The *New York Times* made clear where its interest lay by illustrating its review with an old picture of Josh and his guitar. The reviewer was kind, describing the play as "fascinating" and the individual performances, including the debut of a young Ruby Dee, as "excellent." That said, though, he added that "the performance as a whole strikes the strident note too insistently . . . the transitions of mood are too swift . . . and the overall impression is too clamorous."

One possible problem can be deduced from the fact that Josh was in Chicago, giving a solo concert at Orchestra Hall, eight days before the play opened. Even if he just drove out for the weekend, he would have missed at least a couple of key rehearsals and was probably exhausted on his return. His personal reviews were all right, though, and his absence can hardly be blamed for the fact that like his previous theatrical ventures, *A Long Way from Home* closed in a week.

For Josh, the play was a valuable experience, but the main event of 1948 was his debut as a film actor. For years he had had his sights set on Hollywood, and he was encouraged by the inclusion of his cabaret act in *The Crimson Canary*, but he had never found an acting part that he considered acceptable. As early as 1944 he was saying that he had refused the exorbitant sum of $87,000 in one year because of the stereotyped roles being offered him.

This was a frequent complaint of the era when Bill "Bojangles"

Robinson and Stepin Fetchit defined Hollywood's perception of black male performers. Like Paul Robeson, Josh was not willing to take a job that would cast him as a singing butler or a comically lazy rapscallion. "I'd like to do things like Dooley Wilson did with Humphrey Bogart in *Casablanca,*" he told one interviewer. "But those are one in a million and I won't do bit parts. If our 'Tom actors' would only stay away from the roles they do, Negroes could get somewhere in Hollywood."

The right sort of role finally came Josh's way in the summer of 1948, when he was signed by Columbia Pictures to play a part in a modern-day western, *The Walking Hills.* The story involved a group of border-town characters who set off into the desert in search of a lost and buried gold caravan. It starred Randolph Scott and Ella Raines and was the directorial debut of John Sturges, who would go on to make *Bad Day at Black Rock* and *The Magnificent Seven.*

Josh's part was not much of a stretch for him. He played a character named Josh, a saloon guitarist who happens to be hanging around a backroom poker game when the secret of the lost caravan is revealed. One of the players, suspicious of betrayal, suggests that everyone in the room had better go along on the treasure hunt, whether they like it or not. Josh wryly responds, "If you're looking at me, I've turned down a few things in my life, but I'd never turn down a million bucks."

It is one of his two lines, both of which come in the first ten minutes of the picture. He also has four songs, one of them a work song that he performs a cappella while digging in the sands of Death Valley, and the other three integrated into the convoluted love story that forms a sub-plot of the film's first half. His last number is "The Riddle Song," sung beside the campfire as the gold hunters sit around after dinner on the second day. Then the plot gets even more complex, and there is no time for music. Instead there are fistfights, shootings, and two battles with shovels. Three suspected murderers and a money-crazed detective face off, while Scott acts as midwife to a horse. Then Scott kills the worst of the murderers in a final shootout during a sandstorm, Raines rides off with her young, righteously innocent paramour to face his accusers, and the titles scroll as the orchestra plays a sweeping reprise of "The Riddle Song."

Josh's part was relatively small and seems to have been further re-duced in the editing, for a story in *Ebony* lists him as having sung three more numbers, one of them an original composition by eight-year-old Josh Jr. In an interview with the New York *Post,* Josh explained that he would have done more, but was unable to work for nine days because of a fall from a horse, and after that he had to leave for a concert tour. By modern standards it is hard to see what was so unusual or politically advanced about his role, since, even compared with Wilson's rather minor part in Casablanca, it involves little interaction with the other actors. In 1947, though, it was still rare for a black man to appear in a western as anything but a cowardly, pop-eyed clown. Josh's character, extraneous as he was to the story, was an equal member of the gold-hunting party, not a servant or sidekick, and the part involved no ste-reotyped mannerisms, kowtowing, or self-abasement of any kind. As he told the *Post,* "I don't talk in dialect, my complexion never turns white with fright or foolishness, my hair doesn't, even when I'm dead scared of anything, stand up on end. When I read the script of 'Walking Hills' I realized that the role had been written in especially for me ... it doesn't matter that I'm a Negro and the others are white; we're all together with a common destiny. I felt that it was an expression of what one world should be. And I was happy to accept the part—for its stand, rather than its merit as a movie."

The *Ebony* piece echoed this opinion but was mostly a picture spread, running three pages.

For Josh, the *Ebony* story must have been doubly welcome. Not only was it a feature spread in a major magazine, heralding his new career as a movie actor, but it was a rare sign of appreciation from the African American community. The black press had covered him well for the first couple of years after *John Henry,* but its interest had soon waned, and the black media had virtually ignored his later successes. Even though his songs were the strongest racial "issue" material being per-formed at the time, almost all his fans were white. Apparently, his work was too sedate and not danceable enough for the thousands of young black record buyers who supported blues singers such as Louis Jordan, and too sexy and pop-oriented for the growing black middle class that hailed Paul Robeson and Marian Anderson as models of respectable African American artistry. When he was occasionally mentioned in the *Amsterdam News,* it was as a celebrity of the white world, and his records were hardly ever advertised in black newspapers. The few advertise-ments that did appear were not for his hard-hitting protest songs but for risqué blues such as "Jelly Jelly."

The music Josh played was simply not of much interest to the Har-lem audience. His uptown neighbors might appreciate his professional success, but they regarded his material as "country," a reminder of hard times down south. What is more, his polished approach and clear diction made it sound to a lot of people's ears like *white* country music. Carol never got over her irritation at the "ignorant" reaction he would get from the guys on the block. "They referred to folk songs as 'hillbilly' music," she says. "You know, some of the fellas in the neighborhood, they'd be 'Hey, is Josh still playing that hillbilly music?' I'd just look at them and say, 'Yes, and living good.' "

This was not a subject Josh often talked about to the press, but his family remembers that it weighed on his mind, and he touched on it at some length in the *Ebony* piece. Speaking of his 1947 tour, he said that his two-week engagement at the California Theater Club in San Francisco was the first time in his career that he had been booked into a black nightclub. "When I started [there], the customers were 85 per cent Negro," he said. "A week later it was a fifty-fifty percentage. When I finished, the trade was 85 per cent white.

"I don't draw Negroes much," he continued. "I feel bad about it. When I sing songs like 'Strange Fruit' or 'Free and Equal Blues' or 'The House I Live In,' my own people don't even quiet down. But white people lean back and concentrate and really go with me. I don't know why this is. Negro bobby-soxers just want to hear 'Jelly Jelly,' 'Outskirts of Town,' 'Did You Ever love a Woman.' I wish they'd like to hear songs that really mean something to us. Maybe they don't want to face facts but I feel they should. There's nothing to be afraid of and it makes you feel better to stand up instead of escaping all the time."

Two months before the *Ebony* article hit the stands, Josh had received his first booking at Harlem's most popular musical showcase, the Apollo Theatre. He had played a week there, alternating with a rather bizarre film, *Miracle in Harlem,* which starred Stepin Fetchit and bore the advertising line "They accused her of MURDER . . . but her crime was LOVE!" The stage show featured Josh in the middle slot, between the jazz trumpeter Roy Eldridge and the pianist Sonny "Long Gone" Thompson.

The Apollo poster described Josh as "the famous record, concert, stage and screen star" and emphasized the fact that he was making his first Harlem appearance. As he had been living in Harlem for seventeen years, this must have rankled, and Josh must also have been hurt by the fact that his appearance was completely ignored by New York's two black newspapers. *Variety* did have a short review, mentioning his fine performance of "Outskirts of Town" backed by the Eldridge band, but if he hoped the booking would give him a new presence in his home community, it can only have been a disappointment. The family remembers that the Apollo audience had never been as white as it was during Josh's stay.

For Josh the performer, Harlem would always remain foreign turf. His normal venues, when out of the nightclubs, were classical concert houses such as Town Hall, Boston's Jordan Hall, and Chicago's Orchestra Hall. He appeared at all three in the last months of 1948, sometimes with Josh Jr. in tow, and the concerts were written up in mainstream dailies: the *New York Times*, the *Chicago Tribune*, the *Christian Science Monitor*. Indeed, to much of the white world, he was likely to be named alongside Robeson, both as a proud black man and as a respectable concert artist.

As the artistic differences between the two men were considerable, their pairing could sometimes lead to confusion. When the *Monitor* covered Josh's Boston appearance, the critic obviously had expected something more in the semiclassical "art song" vein of Robeson or Richard Dyer-Bennett. "In only a few spots did the evening rise above the atmospheric level of the nightclub," the writer sniffed. "Many songs seem crude and often bordering on the vulgar, without any relation to the rich charm of the folk song." Nonetheless, it had to be granted that "the singer showed marked ability in the handling of his guitar [and] he was never at a loss for harmonic and rhythmic nuance in the style of jazz that reflects the atmosphere of the deep South."

Though it was rarely put so bluntly, the perception that Josh's show was better suited to the nightclubs than the concert halls seems to have been shared by many of his fans as well. The halls had advantages from a performer's point of view: they provided a quiet, attentive audience and much higher pay for an evening's work. Nonetheless, there was an intimacy to Josh's small-club appearances that people missed when they saw him in larger rooms. Other benefits were that a club booking could last for months, and he could live at home rather than driving from hotel to hotel. Thus, in 1949 he returned to the Village Vanguard — which he had not played since his days with Leadbelly — and stayed there from April to July, then went back briefly to his old stomping grounds at Cafe Society.

The intervening years had seen a drastic change in the club. The political pressures had finally forced Barney Josephson to sell out. He had held on for almost two years, even taking out a defiant ad in *Bill-board:* a full page with only the small, centered sentence "My head is bloodied but not bowed — Barney Josephson." In February 1949, though, the New York State Liquor Authority canceled his liquor license after determining that he had made a "false material statement in a renewal application . . . as to whether any officers, stockholders or directors [of the business] had ever been arrested, indicted or served a summons for a crime or offense other than traffic violations." He sold the business to Louis Lewis and Max Mansch and shortly thereafter opened a reasonably successful string of restaurants, but he would not book any live entertainment again until the late 1970s.

With Josephson gone, Cafe Society was once again "safe" to play, but Josh's return was only for a two-week stint, on a bill with the young blues belter Ruth Brown. Then he took three months off the cabaret scene before returning as the debut act at a new club, the Shelburne Lounge.

The return to clubs did not greatly interfere with Josh's concert career, as he continued to do the occasional Town Hall show and to duck off for weekends in Chicago and other relatively nearby cities. He made an appearance on a sadder occasion, as well, singing "Precious Lord" at Leadbelly's funeral in December. The clubs were a convenience, providing regular income while he continued to pursue his greater aspirations. At the end of 1949 he was planning a tour that would take him to forty-two cities in the United States and then on to Europe, but he canceled it at the last moment when he got an offer to appear in his first starring role on Broadway.

The play was called *How Long till Summer,* and Josh came to it in a rather roundabout manner. Josh Jr. had been attracting attention as a child performer, and the play's producers had approached the Whites about casting him in a leading role. He was to play Josh Jeffers, the son of a prominent black lawyer who is running for congressional office with the backing of some white gangsters; Jeffers Sr. hopes, by becoming wealthy and influential, to better the position of his race and protect his son from the horrors of racism. Unfortunately, protection is not to be had. Young Jeffers, playing in the alley with his best friend, a white boy, is suddenly accosted by the friend's drunken, loutish father, who calls him a "black bastard" and threatens to lynch him. From then on he is terrified by nightmares of being spat upon, lynched, and caged in a zoo. The nightmares are played out on one side of the stage, while on the other the lawyer's wife and a wise family doctor attempt to extricate the lawyer from the mobsters' coils.

The play's message was full of resonance for Josh, and the part offered to Josh Jr. was exceptionally good, the longest and meatiest child role on Broadway that year. Josh and Carol were thrilled but also a bit apprehensive. Like the parents in the play, they felt that they had so far been successful in protecting Josh Jr. from any sort of racial abuse, and they were not sure what effect it might have on him to live out the racist persecution and nightmares of Josh Jeffers.

Eventually, they consulted Josh Jr.'s godmother, Eleanor Roosevelt. She was impressed with the play but echoed their concern for the effect it might have on him. As a way of cushioning him, she suggested, it might be helpful if Josh could play the part of the boy's father and guide him through it. Josh was tempted by the opportunity, and his paternal pride turned the trick. "I got to thinking . . . that I would be in Europe on the boy's opening," he told a reporter, "and that decided me to stay." Postponing his tour, Josh signed a run-of-the-play contract and settled into rehearsals. "This is a gamble for me," he said. "But I know it will do wonders for the boy. We study our lines together and I have managed to make the whole thing a game for him. That's how we've got over the bad spots. It's just a game."

It was a game at which Josh Jr. proved singularly adept. When *How Long till Summer* opened at the Playhouse on December 27, he received universal raves. The *New York Post* called him "charming" and "talented"; the *New Yorker* found his performance "remarkably touching"; and the *Daily News* said he was the play's "best feature . . . a grand little boy with a lot of drive and talent." The *Times* critic said both he and Charles Taylor, who played his white friend, were "frank, artless and attractive," and promised that if anyone would devote a whole play to them, "this column will guarantee every consideration that is ethically possible."

As for the play itself, the less said the better. The *Post* review was headlined "A Well-Intentioned Catastrophe," and that about summed up the critical opinion. It was badly written, badly directed, and, with the exception of the child roles, not very well acted. Josh Sr.'s performance was variously described as "vigorous," "competent," and "confusing," and the rest of the cast fared little better. Like Josh's previous theatrical ventures, *How Long till Summer* was gone before most theatergoers were even aware of its existence. If it did nothing else, though, it clearly established who the actor was in the White family. Josh Jr. won an award as the year's best child actor, and by the end of January 1951 he was on Broadway again, in a play starring the silent film star Dorothy Gish. Meanwhile, Josh headed back to Cafe Society and rekindled his European tour plans.

Although *How Long till Summer* had done less for Josh's career than he must have hoped, it had at least been a starring role on Broadway, which set him apart from other black nightclub performers and, together with his role in *The Walking Hills*, established him as a figure to be reckoned with in the broader entertainment world. He was also beginning to make frequent appearances on the new national medium, television, which at that time was centered entirely in New York and heavily weighted toward local talent. When *Ebony* published a piece on the relative absence of racial barriers in the video world, the four artists mentioned as appearing with "great frequency" were Ethel Waters, Pearl Bailey, Billy Eckstine, and Josh White.

Black listeners might continue to ignore Josh's music, but no one could ignore the fact that he was making impressive inroads into previously white preserves and blazing the way for other black artists. His celebrity was a source of pride for a lot of black Americans, even if they rarely bought his records. Josh was very conscious of this, and it was extremely important to him. He made special efforts to help black causes, going so far as to take several weeks of art lessons just so he could contribute a picture to an exhibit and benefit auction of celebrity paintings for the Urban League. "Guitar," a painting of a guitar resting on its case, was one of the half-dozen works reproduced in the *Ebony* spread on the show. The caption said that it had sold for $20 and that Josh had shown up for the auction and purchased a painting by the movie star Cornel Wilde.

By the summer of 1950 the European tour was ready to get under way. Its first leg was part of a goodwill mission to Scandinavia headed by Eleanor Roosevelt, followed by a series of bookings in France and Great Britain. The White family had become even closer to Mrs. Roosevelt in the previous year. Along with Josh and Josh Jr.'s annual Christmas visit to play for the boys at the Wiltwyck school, Josh had responded to her request for a man who could stay and work at her Hyde Park residence by recommending his brother Bill.

As Roosevelt wrote later in a piece for *Ebony* (titled, in a phrase that would come to be synonymous with a patronizing, white liberal attitude, "Some of My Best Friends Are Negro"), "At first I did not think William would like it too well. He had been in the entertainment world a long time with Josh I knew. . . . I said to him: 'It will be very difficult for you to do housework, to drive a car.' William said, 'No, Mrs. Roosevelt, since the war, I don't feel like singing any more." She added that some of her Negro friends feared she was "creating what they call a social problem by having one brother as a rather frequent guest and another brother as a servant, more or less." To her, though, it was all very simple and straightforward: "I never saw that as a problem. Each has a dignified, necessary contribution to make."

The European tour group included Mrs. Roosevelt, her son Elliott, and his children. Josh would say that Mrs. Roosevelt invited him as a musical symbol of America's virtues: "She thought that I was the one American who could show the true America in Europe through song." She also seems to have taken an interest in his career, and hoped that he would establish connections that might be useful in the future. In a letter written shortly after arriving in Stockholm, she mentioned that Josh would be singing after the American Embassy dinner that night and added, "That should help him, as he will meet the Crown Prince and Princess."

Josh's trip started badly. He left home with a severe cold and high fever, and burst an eardrum on the transatlantic flight. Hospitalized on his arrival in Oslo, he was delivered to his first concert in an ambulance. From there on, though, the tour was a triumph. As well as accompanying Eleanor Roosevelt to embassy events in each capital, Josh gave concerts and met a glittering array of dignitaries. He particularly remembered one evening in Stockholm. After the concert there was a special dinner for Mrs. Roosevelt, and a local architect who was also an amateur folksinger sang some Swedish songs. Then Josh took over. "There was King Gustav and his two sisters — or one sister — and they had really big plush rugs, and it finally wound up with people sitting on the floor, and I was teaching them songs. They were singing in broken English, like 'When the Saints Go Marching In' and 'On Top of Old Smoky.' We were having a really crazy time, you know, and the old man, King Gustav was I think singing — anyhow, he was enjoying himself." That evening would be written up by Mrs. Roosevelt in her "My Day" newspaper column — with unexpected and troublesome results.

For the time being, however, the trip was turning out wonderfully.

According to some reports, Josh's early concerts were not well attended because American recordings had been unavailable during the war, but his reputation spread quickly, and the crowds were soon all he could have hoped for and more. In Goteborg, Sweden, he caused such a sensation that a reported 15,000 people gathered outside the hall where he was singing. Speakers were rigged to transmit his music to them, and afterward he came out and sang two songs on the steps. In Copenhagen he gave an outdoor concert in the Tivoli Gardens and was amazed to see a huge audience stand in the rain through his whole performance. He was bowled over by all the attention and enjoyed it to the fullest, though the form of his enjoyment seems to have been a bit of an annoyance to his staid sponsor. "Josh White is drinking, but gave a good concert last night, I'm told," Mrs. Roosevelt wrote to a friend. "I think I will have to be severe in Denmark when we meet again."

This remark gives a somewhat different picture of her relationship with Josh than either indicated in public pronouncements. They always spoke of each other as friends, but if so, it was hardly an equal friendship. It was a relationship of artist and patron, black performer and white sponsor, and in her private communications Mrs. Roosevelt could write of Josh as if he were an erring child. Whether or not, in the end, she chose to scold him about his drinking, Josh continued to accompany her through the Scandinavian countries and on to Holland. With that, her part of the tour was finished, and one suspects that, much as he appreciated her patronage, Josh must have felt a degree of relief at being on his own. He went first to France, where an article in the French journal *Jazz Hot* says that his arrival was not much noticed, as he only gave two shows and neither was open to the public. The music community was excited, though, and Vogue records brought him into the studio for his first recordings in three years. Backed by a French rhythm section, he recut four of his old favorites and two new songs: "I Want You," which he had introduced in *The Walking Hills,* and "The Blind Man Stood on the Road and Cried," a spiritual with obvious resonance from his early days, which he would continue to feature in his live shows.

If Josh's French visit attracted little notice, his English stay more than made up for it. He was already well known to English blues and jazz fans from his many wartime radio broadcasts. *The Walking Hills* had also recently appeared in Great Britain, and there had been a number of articles over the years in the music press. For the English jazz community, his arrival was a major event, the first time a folk-blues singer had made it across the Atlantic. The country had a large coterie of record collectors, some of whom had ordered entire catalogues of race recordings, but Josh was a taste of the real thing, and they turned out in droves.

*Melody Maker,* Britain's reigning pop music journal, published a dozen articles on his visit. There were three anticipatory stories before he flew from Paris to Manchester on July 9 for his debut at the Hippodrome, and his concert there the following evening received an undiluted rave: "On Monday night I saw the impossible happen!" wrote the jazz critic Dennis Preston. "An artist on his first appearance in this country, and not even a name to the average British music-hall patron, held just such an audience spellbound with a twenty-minute selection of unfamiliar folk songs and ballads sung in a most unfamiliar manner."

Preston interviewed Josh backstage, and his piece is interesting for its marked divergence from the way Josh had always been handled by the U.S. press. American critics had either hailed Josh's music as a wonderful manifestation of the folk tradition or attacked it for failing to be just that. Preston, by contrast, heard that Josh was putting a unique spin on the older material and, rather than passing judgment, was fascinated. "Josh White, by the very breadth of his repertoire and highly mannered style of singing, presents a challenge to every would-be critic, amateur or professional, long-hair or crew-cut," he wrote. Then, instead of launching into his own theories, he proceeded to interview Josh with a degree of knowledgeable respect that was a complete change from previous published pieces. Whereas American writers had treated Josh as a colorful character, a political symbol, a pop celebrity, or all three, Preston approached him as a serious, intelligent musician.

When Josh described himself as simply a folksinger, Preston pressed him to explain just what he meant. Josh started with his standard boilerplate: "I sing songs of the people, popular songs in the best sense of the word. Not manufactured hits." Preston, though, was not just looking for a pretty quote; he really wanted to know what Josh meant. What, he asked, would be the dividing line between a folksinger and a blues or jazz singer?

"When the folk singers leave the countryside and move into town, like so many of the Chicago blues men, they right away start imitating the kind of jazz they hear all around and that way soon lose the folk touch," Josh responded. "You see that to a certain extent in Leadbelly's later work, and in such men as Big Bill Broonzy and Tampa Red. Blind Blake is about the best example of a borderline blues and folk man. Blind Lemon Jefferson, another blind man I used to lead around when I was a kid, is a straight folk singer."

It is not clear where exactly Josh placed his own work on this spectrum, but it was a new thing for anyone to want to hear him expound on the subject and to press him for further opinions. "How much of jazz, if any, is folk music?" Preston asked.

"Not that bebop — [unprintable epithet]," Josh replied. "That's not folk. But something like [Sidney] Bechet's music — that's folk. Like my own music it isn't confined to just one kind of thing. There's a lot that sounds like Hungarian gypsy in Sidney's playing."

Preston noted that an academic folk music authority had made a very similar comment on Bechet's work, then asked Josh if he thought Negro jazz was the only true jazz. "No," Josh said. "And there's some pretty terrible Negro musicians, just as there's some pretty wonderful white musicians.

"But it does seem to me that the Negro musicians manage to get those in-between tones, that sort of strained intonation, better than any white musician can. Maybe because he's usually self-taught, like me, while the white boys often have the advantage of some academic schooling on their instruments."

Clearly, Josh was enjoying the chance to expound his musical views and to find someone who was interested in publishing opinions he had previously stated only to friends and acquaintances. The English fans, far more knowledgeable than the American nightclub crowd, viewed him not simply as an artist but as a musical authority. As he moved on to London and a week-long stay at a variety house, the Chiswick Empire, he became the center of a crowd of admiring musicians, some of whom had traveled the length of the country to hear him.

American jazz musicians had been visiting Britain for years, but Josh was the first blues guitarist to make the trip, and the hard-core cognoscenti who knew him only from his records were pleasantly surprised by his live shows. *Jazz Journal* reported that "before the excellent Josh arrived," blues lovers had dismissed him as overly sophisticated, but "that hectic week at Chiswick did quite a lot to dispel that fable." Max Jones, editor of the *Jazz Music* and *Folk* magazines, who had written the definitive British article on Josh during the 1940s, reported that half the audience would head back to Josh's dressing room after each performance, including the cream of the British jazz community, people like the jazz vocalist George Melly (who gave Josh a photo inscribed "To a great singer from a small one"). Unlike Preston, Jones felt that Josh's music went over the heads of the "variety public" but added that "happily, there was nearly always a sufficient muster of jazz lovers to ensure him a cordial reception."

The live shows were not Josh's most important performances in Britain, however. If the coterie of jazz fans was not large enough to pack the concert halls, it was influential enough to keep him busy in the radio and recording studios. The BBC broke precedent by recording shows for all three of its networks, the "Home" (highbrow), "Light" (pop), and "Third" (special or experimental) programs. The producers mixed the music with interviews and historical background, bringing Preston on board to write the narration.

Meanwhile, English Decca rushed a half-dozen of Josh's American recordings into print, the Melodisc label reissued an Asch 78, and London Records brought Josh into the studio for a session backed by an English combo of piano, rhythm guitar, bass, and drums. The English musicians played with care and sensitivity, adding bowed bass or tinkling celeste behind the ballads, then rolling out some fair blues chops on "Outskirts of Town." In a funny aside, pianist Steve Race recalled that for the work song "Like a Natural Man," Josh wanted the grunts of a work crew to punctuate his verses. Rather than doing them himself, he placed Race beside him at the microphone and punched the pianist in the stomach at the appropriate moments.

Josh made a short trip back to Paris before the session, then returned for a whirlwind weekend that included two radio shows, a private performance with Humphrey Lyttelton's jazz band, and the London recording date. He had meant to fly home immediately after that but postponed his departure another four days so that he could record a forty-five-minute biographical program for the BBC.

All in all, the visit was a huge success. Josh had reached a wider range of listeners than ever before, and the British promoters were already making plans for a full-scale tour in 1951. Josh scrawled a brief note of thanks to the English public, which was reproduced in the magazine *Jazz Review:* "I have met so many wonderful people since my arrival and I'd like to thank each one, and here it is. I hope I'm able to see you every year, your pal, Josh."

Max Jones added the final note in an August record review, printing the impressions of a Liverpool fan who had been treated to one of Josh's post-concert dressing-room sessions: "The atmosphere was informal, the recital spontaneous. Someone would mention a song, Josh would strum a few introductory chords, and we were away . . . we sat at his elbow watching the subtle changes in expression as he sang, listening at close quarters to his beautifully controlled voice and eloquent guitar comments. He has a charm of manner and an incredible ease of delivery which cannot be described at second hand. His is a personality not easily to be forgotten."

It was a touching testimonial, but by August, Josh was in no position to enjoy it. Just before leaving London, he had received a panicked call from Mary Chase. *Red Channels* had listed him as a dangerous subversive, and everything he had built up over the last decade was threatened with collapse.

# 13

## UN-AMERICAN ACTIVITIES
### 1950
■ ■ ■ ■ ■ ■ ■ ■ ■ ■ ■ ■ ■ ■ ■ ■ ■ ■ ■ ■

*Red Channels* was subtitled *The Report of Communist Influence in Radio and Television.* Often called "the bible of the blacklist," it was a compilation of information drawn from the pages of *Counterattack,* a weekly newsletter of "Facts to Combat Communism," and the files of Vincent Hartnett, who operated a red-hunting outfit called Aware, Inc. An inexpensive paperback (a dollar per copy, with reductions for bulk orders), decorated with lightning bolts and a red hand reaching to seize a broadcast microphone, it was published by the innocent-sounding American Business Consultants on Thursday, June 22, 1950. It is easy to give the exact date, because the book instantly attracted a lot of attention.

Appearing just as the Korean War hit the headlines, *Red Channels* sent the broadcasting world into a panic. It listed 151 people in radio and television who should be considered Communists or Communist sympathizers, together with each person's supposed Communist-front affiliations. The roster was prefaced with the disclaimer that the listed activities and organizations might be innocent of subversive intent, that *Red Channels* was simply detailing the artists' affiliations with them without passing judgment. This was *Counterattack*'s version of printing "the truth." It would not, for legal reasons, accuse anyone of being a Communist; it only reported that someone had been reported elsewhere as associating with a group that had been described as a Communist front. If readers understood this to be an implication of guilt, or artists lost their jobs because of a *Red Channels* entry, that was not the newsletter's fault. The authors were merely repeating information in the public record.

If this position seems bizarre, the degree to which it was accepted in official circles was even more so. When Hazel Scott, a popular Cafe Society pianist and the wife of Congressman Adam Clayton Powell, testified before HUAC in an attempt to discredit *Counterattack,* the interchanges were often surreal. Scott would point out that she had never even heard of an organization with which she was linked in *Red Channels.* The committee member would feign misunderstanding, asking her if she was saying that she had never been mentioned by the organization as a sponsor or member. She would reply that she did not know, but that if she had been, then the statement was false, and *Red Channels* should not have repeated it without first attempting to find out if it was true.

In a typical interchange, Congressman Burr Harrison, of Virginia, responded, "They do nothing that I see in here but simply quote from official records."

"But, don't you see," Scott pleaded, "if those records are false, how can you prove it?"

"If they are false, they were false in the original sources," the congressman said.

"Exactly," Scott said, thinking she had made her point.

"Then," the congressman said, "the publication is not false."

There was no legal recourse in this situation. *Red Channels* was only printing the facts, the facts looked pretty damning, and the onus was on the named artists to explain how and why they had come to have their names, accurately or inaccurately, associated with groups that might, or might not, be subversive.

Josh's *Red Channels* entry was typical. It described him as a "Singer of Folk Songs" and reported that he had been listed on the Advisory Committee of People's Songs and as an entertainer or performer for ten suspect organizations, ranging from the Communist Party to the New Theatre League, American Relief for Greek Democracy, and the Veterans against Discrimination of Civil Rights Congress. All the listings were at least three years old, and most had simply been copied from *Daily Worker* advertisements and concert reviews.

Josh was in excellent company. His entry followed an impressively long one for Orson Welles, and among other names included were Leonard Bernstein, Aaron Copland, Dashiell Hammett, Lillian Hellman, Judy Holliday, Lena Horne, Langston Hughes, Gypsy Rose Lee, Zero Mostel, Dorothy Parker, Edward G. Robinson, Artie Shaw, and every folksinger popular enough to attract notice. At first, there was some doubt as to just what effect the book would have. Many of the people it named had already been having some trouble, especially if they worked in Hollywood. For the others, how much difference could it make that a ten-year-old appearance for Spanish War Relief was now public knowledge? In Josh's case the answer was quickly forthcoming. *Red Channels* had been only the opening salvo in what was about to become a full-fledged bombardment. The July 28 issue of *Counterattack* included an article headlined "U S CONSULAR OFFICIAL FEATURES ENTERTAINER FOR COMMUNIST PARTY." In its trademark style, designed to catch the eye of a busy executive, the newsletter plumbed the depths of consular treachery:

> In one of her "My Day" columns, written during her trip to Sweden last month, Mrs ELEANOR ROOSEVELT revealed that she had attended a very pleasant dinner party given by the Counselor of the U S Stockholm Embassy and his wife.
>
> After dinner the guests relaxed while they were entertained by a Swedish architect, who played the guitar and sang native folk songs, and by "an American artist, JOSH WHITE," as Mrs Roosevelt wrote.
>
> WHITE evidently made a hit. Americans attending the party joined in with him when he sang Negro spirituals . . . just as many U S Communist leaders did in 1945, when JOSH WHITE entertained at a Communist celebration in honor of convicted CP leader BEN DAVIS.
>
> Other organizations, all officially cited as Communist fronts, for which JOSH WHITE has entertained, are listed in RED CHANNELS.
>
> Why doesn't State Dept keep its foreign service officers informed of the Communist front backgrounds of Americans who travel abroad?
>
> What's the sense of fighting Communism and Communist fronts here, and in Korea, if State Dept officials feature front supporters as entertainers in foreign countries?

Josh's name had appeared in *Counterattack* before, in a report on Oscar Brand's radio show, but this was the first story to single him out as a dangerous subversive. Reading it, Mary Chase saw the writing on the wall. As Josh told the story, "I got a telephone call from [Mary] in New York, and she says, 'Josh, I want to read something to you.'

"This is my money she's spending, so I said, 'Don't read it, baby, send it to me and I can read it, you know. Like, mail it.'

" 'No, it's important, I want you to listen to this.'

" 'OK, I'll listen.' "

Chase read about half the piece, and Josh got the idea. "I said, 'That's enough, I'll be home.' I hadn't finished my tour because I had left Mrs. Roosevelt in Paris, and I was on my own in England. Well, I left London the next afternoon."

In fact, he seems to have stayed another week to finish up his radio commitments (though he gave up any plans of putting together a longer British tour), then headed home to try to sort things out. His welcome was anything but congenial. He had bought a cowboy-style gun as a present for Josh Jr., which the customs agents used as an excuse to take him aside and send him off to a small room, where he was kept for over three hours while they telephoned Washington to see what should be done with him.

"There was no place to sit down," he said, "and I don't know why they're keeping me in this friggin' place. . . . I came back mainly to see this *Red Channels,* this lie that was being passed around about me. So finally I sent a note by a redcap to my manager and my wife: 'What the hell am I . . .? Why can't I get out? 'Cause I want a drink, you know, or let me sit down, let me talk with the kids. I had nothing to declare, so why am I being held here?' So finally somebody says I could leave Customs and go home."

The next day, Josh went to the offices of American Business Consultants to talk with the editor, an ex-FBI agent named Theodore Kirkpatrick. As with all his stories of this period, Josh's description of this interview paints his attitude as proudly confrontational, but the fact that he was talking with the red-hunters at all, and would continue to do so, suggests that at the time he was treading a good deal more carefully than he would later recall. "I was hot and bothered," he said. "Because this thing didn't make sense. . . . Mary Chase says, 'Josh, I think you should write down what you're going to say.' I didn't want to write anything down. What I was going to say was straight goods, and I didn't have to write it down. But I said, 'I promise I won't get angry.' "

Josh met with Kirkpatrick and another man, whose name he did not recall. "Kirkpatrick says to me 'You got here kind of fast.'

"I say, 'I got here fast as I could.' I say, 'First of all, I don't know where you got this lie, which *is* a lie, that I was in Europe fronting for the Communist Party. . . . Like, I care less about the Communist Party. I am an American, I was born here. But, first of all, let me tell you about myself.' And I started from when I was a child . . . about the fear that the average Negro has for the uniform, the brass buttons, the brutality. The South — I can't even tell you. It's hard to imagine what it's been like. I told him about the lynchings, about the walking tax, I told him about my daddy, I told him the whole bloody thing.

"And then he says to me, 'You worked at Cafe Society quite a few years. You know that was run by the Communist Party.' And I says, 'No, I don't. I know I went there, I think my first paycheck was seventy-five dollars a week, $125 a week, and I was taking care of my family. I didn't go to Barney Josephson and ask him what his relations, or what his feelings were. You don't go ask your boss. No, you don't. This was my job.'"

Josh recalled that two FBI agents were present at this meeting, but as the FBI has no records of any interview with him for another month, it is almost certain that, in retrospect, he was collapsing two interviews into one. His biographer reported still another, two days after the first, at which Josh met Alvin W. Stokes, HUAC's specialist on Communist influence in the black community. Whatever the exact number of meetings, Josh talked to several different interviewers, and it is not surprising that he should have got them mixed up, as he was always asked the same questions. What everyone wanted to hear was why, if Josh was not a Communist or at least a sympathizer, he kept showing up at all the Communist-sponsored benefits.

His response was twofold: in the first place he often had not been at the benefits where he was listed, and in the second place they seemed innocent, even laudable. "There were many times when I was working at Cafe Society where my name was put down, it was in the paper I was supposed to be here, be there," he remembered saying. "It was impossible. I was doing three shows a night. I never even said I was going to be there. If I *could* make some of them, I would go if I thought it was for a good thing. I says, 'Do you have down the things I did for — Christ Almighty, you name them — B'nai, Catholic organizations, I did them all. . . . Bundles for Britain. And at that time, Russia was our ally.'"

The interviewers questioned Josh about a benefit he had played for Isaac Woodward, a black soldier who had been blinded in a beating by police in South Carolina after he tried to use a "white" restroom. At a concert held in Harlem for funds to set Woodward up with a restaurant, many leading artists, black and white, liberal and progressive, had performed. "It was supposed to be run by the *Amsterdam News,*" Josh said. "They wanted money, so, some people that had money, they gave; I didn't have money, I gave [my services]. Now they said that this thing was run by the Communist Party. I said, 'The *Amsterdam News* was a Negro paper, this was all I knew.' "

Going on the offensive, Josh asked his interviewers why the FBI had not been doing more to combat things like the blinding of Woodward. "I said, 'Let me ask you one thing: Why is it that you don't fight against this kind of thing . . .? Why do you say that it's always the Communist party?'

"He said, 'Because they [the Communists] take the play away from us.'

"I said, 'Ain't that a hell of an answer to tell me?' I said, 'I'll tell you one thing—if [the Woodward case] happened again, I would do [the benefit] again. I didn't like what happened, and I think it's a very poor answer to give, saying "Because they take the play away from us." It is a screwy answer!' "

The interviewers pressed Josh to name some names, asking who had invited him to come and sing at the various benefits. He replied that he couldn't possibly remember what had happened that long ago. As he reported the conversation, they then asked him if he wanted to take the Fifth Amendment (an unlikely question, since he was not under oath, but they may have been asking how he would react if subpoenaed). "I said, 'I just cannot answer because *I don't know,*' and I *don't* know. If they were gonna hang me, I wouldn't know."

The conversation then moved to Paul Robeson, who had become for many people the symbol of an African American in the international left.

"He says, 'You know Robeson very well.'

"I said, 'Yes, I do.'

"He said, 'Did he ever tell you to join the Communist Party?'

" 'He did not. He never mentioned the Communist Party.' Which he never has. I said, 'Look, let me say this to you. If this man is what you say he is—my son was sitting on his knee at uptown Cafe Society. He was rehearsing for *Othello*. He said this to me, he said, "Josh, don't be connected with any kind of organization and party. You're doing a great job for your country as you are." Now, if he was so bad, why did he say these words to me?' "

Josh said that his interviewers told him they would clear him if he would attack Robeson. "I told them I didn't come to attack Robeson. I was there to squash a lie. I'm going to attack him? Crap! I'm not built that way."

Josh's memory of the interviews shows a fighting, confrontational stance that was in perfect keeping with his professional reputation but seems somewhat unlikely, or at least overstated, in the context of his previous abandonment of Cafe Society and his later actions. Indeed, there was only one reason why an entertainer would go for a private talk with the publisher of *Counterattack,* or to the Aware office, and that was to begin the mysterious process known as "clearance."

Like so much of what has come to be known as the McCarthy era, "clearance" was a term out of Lewis Carroll's looking-glass world or a Kafka novel. The blacklist was never a single, organized list, nor was it administered by a single person or group. Often an obscure, self-appointed consumer watchdog might start the whole process, writing to a breakfast cereal company, for example, and threatening a boycott if a certain "red" continued to appear on a program the company was sponsoring (American Business Consultants, as the name suggests, was designed with sponsors rather than networks in mind). Thus, getting on or off the lists could be an incredibly convoluted and ambiguous process, with an unexplained system of ever changing rules. This was particularly true in the summer of 1950, when *Red Channels* had just appeared and no one yet knew what effect it would have. Two or three years later the blacklist had so evolved that television networks and advertising firms employed experts to vet cast lists, pass judgments, and arrange "clearance" procedures, but in 1950 there were no such guides; the landscape of accusation, penalties, and redemption was still largely terra incognita.

Still, if Josh was something of a pioneer, he was on a path that would soon be extremely well trod. As the blacklist became institutionalized, the same people who were smearing artists with accusations of Communist sympathies became active in the process of "clearing" them. In both cases the process involved not fact but perception. If the American Legion, Aware, or *Counterattack* named someone as a "pink" or "fellow traveler," that person was, by definition, "controversial" and would be avoided by television and radio networks. If the same organizations declared that the person had heroically stood up against his or her Communist associates, that individual was on the road to clearance, but it was still an open question whether he or she would, in fact, get work. Sometimes it was enough just to repudiate one's previous appearances at "Communist-front" events. Sometimes it was necessary to repudiate liberal or New Deal positions that could be construed as supportive of a pink sensibility. Often it was necessary to "name names" — of people one had known to be Communists or simply knew to have been present at left-wing events — as proof that one was truly converted to the side of anti-Communism.

Where one did these things could also be an issue. Some artists, particularly those who were prized and sponsored by a major television network or film studio, were able to clear themselves simply by having a private meeting with someone like Theodore Kirkpatrick or Aware's Vincent Hartnett, who had written the introduction to *Red Channels*. Others had to make their break with the left in public, writing a magazine article condemning Communism or testifying before HUAC about their leftist associates.

Josh made his break in all three ways. Shortly after his private interviews he took the unusual step of appearing voluntarily before HUAC, then published his testimony in *Negro Digest* (the black equivalent of *Reader's Digest*) under the title "I Was a Sucker for the Communists." Why, at this early stage, Josh went to the extremes he did to "clear" his name is something of a mystery. His own later explanations suggest that he was simply overcome by righteous indignation at being falsely accused, but this does not ring altogether true. If, as he says, he was reacting with the fury of an innocent man, it is odd that, rather than denouncing his accusers, he met with them for private conversations in their offices and then made public apologies for having been led astray by his former acquaintances.

Of course, many other people capitulated to the red-hunters, but most of them waited another year or two until the blacklist was in force and they were being barred from work. Even then, few went so far as to testify publicly before the committee unless obligated by a subpoena. Even when the blacklist was at its height, neither the New York nightclubs nor the Broadway stage made anything like a universal practice of barring "named" performers, and many artists managed to weather the storm. Josh's livelihood was certainly threatened; Barney Josephson had been forced to transfer ownership of Cafe Society in 1949, and there was no telling what the future held there. Meanwhile, Columbia Artists Management, whose Metropolitan Music Bureau had booked Josh's American tours since his days with Libby Holman, had been forced to cancel Paul Robeson's last tour because of pressure on the concert promoters. The blacklist had already flooded Hollywood and was overflowing into radio and television, threatening Josh's gains of the previous few years. Still, in August 1950 there was no way to know what effect his *Red Channels* listing was going to have on his income or professional prospects, and plenty of reason to be hesitant about alienating his supporters and further opening his political views to public scrutiny by testifying in front of HUAC.

Josh's family, friends, and acquaintances have given a wide range of explanations for his choice. One is that it was Mary Chase who panicked and pushed him to testify. There is undoubtedly some truth to this, as she had been actively involved in his attempt to distance himself from his old leftist companions at the time of Leon Josephson's conviction and the smearing of Cafe Society. Chase certainly supported Josh's decision to testify, and she may well have pushed him in that direction, but his friends' impressions must be balanced by the fact that since Chase was widely disliked, they would understandably be eager to shift the blame from Josh to her.

Another explanation, repeated by several of his more radical friends, is that Josh was blackmailed by the FBI. Pete Seeger thinks something of this kind happened and relates a conversation he understands to have taken place between Josh and Paul Robeson. "Paul told me that Josh called him up the night before he testified and said, 'Paul, I have to tell you. Tomorrow I have to go down to Washington and make a heel of myself before the Un-American Activities Committee.' And Paul says, 'Why do you have to?' He says, 'I don't have any alternative, Paul. I just have to.' My guess is that the FBI or something presented him with some pictures and said, 'Mr. White, you won't just be out of a job, you'll be in jail.'"

Michael Loring, an activist and sometime folksinger who had known Josh since the *John Henry* days, would later tell Dave Samuelson, a folksong researcher, that Josh had privately told him that the FBI was ready to bring him up on a Mann Act charge (transporting a woman over state lines for immoral purposes). Loring's son says that his father was generally contemptuous of those who had testified but believed that Josh had been in a particularly difficult position.

While not impossible, the story that Josh was being directly blackmailed is probably nothing more than a particularly strong rationalization, an explanation that made something unthinkable a bit less so. To those who had always admired Josh's fighting spirit, his behavior in this situation seemed inexplicable, and some are still looking for excuses. In fact, it was all too easy to explain.

Everyone agrees that Josh was not a particularly political person. He had strong views on segregation and civil rights issues and a general admiration for the struggle of the underdog, but he made no deep analyses of national or world events and had no dedication to any theory or system. He had frequently found himself allied with the Communists, but that was almost automatic on the early New York folk scene. Throughout the war years he had moved with the liberal center represented by the Roosevelts, and when the CP took its hard-line turn in the late 1940s, he stayed firmly with the New Dealers.

Although the Communist Party frequently had been the most influential agent for progressive change in the United States and the strongest supporter of black and union issues, it could also be doctrinaire, dictatorial, and manipulative. According to Pete Seeger, who views the CP with the ambivalence of a man who has seen it at both its best and its worst, "Josh had seen the seamy side of the Communist Party, which like any organization bent on power had power-hungry people in it. While it was better than many organizations in many ways, it was probably as bad as many organizations in some ways."

Whereas Josh tended to be reticent in later years about his motivations, at the time he testified he also made himself available to conservative columnists and struck a strongly anti-Communist note. Obviously, these interviews were part of his efforts to get on the good side of the blacklisters, and it is unclear how well they reflected his deeper views, but they suggest a pretty active dislike of the CP. "I began to see what harm they were doing to the United States when I traveled through Europe," he told one interviewer. "I talked with some folks who believed that every day on streets in America there were Negro lynchings. . . . I was surprised and dismayed to find so much enmity for Americans in Europe." He added that if indeed he had become involved with organizations that were un-American, that was because he did not know any better. "It isn't surprising that a lot of entertainers like myself fell into the traps set by those who wanted to use us for their own subversive plans," he said. "How could we find out things like that? We're simple people who are mostly dominated by our emotions."

The protestation of childlike innocence is a bit extreme, but if Josh's progressive friends felt betrayed by him, he certainly felt equally let down by them. There was no way that anyone singing for the American Rescue Ship Mission or a Spanish refugee appeal in the early 1940s could have imagined that having done so would one day threaten his livelihood. The situation was unexpected, and vicious. It is easy to say that the viciousness was coming from the right and that Josh should have confronted his true enemies, the red-hunters, rather than distancing himself from those he had once considered his friends and allies. On the other hand, Josh felt that many of those friends had been less than honest with him. The Communists had always claimed an almost prophetic ability to foresee where events were heading; if the things they were asking him to do were far more dangerous than they seemed, he must have wondered, why did they give him no warning?

This position, that they had been betrayed first by the Communists, was frequently taken by liberal "fellow travelers." They felt that the left was asking them to sacrifice their careers to protect people they had barely known and often heartily disliked. For Josh, the decision to testify was made still easier by an unwritten rule of the red-scare years. For most of those who went before HUAC, to "name names" publicly was an integral part of the procedure, a ritual of self-degradation that provided the one sure proof that a witness had truly cast off all ties to his or her old associates. African American witnesses, however, were rarely forced to go through this ritual. Apparently, the red-hunters were worried about being seen as racist (not without reason: John Stephens Wood, the Georgia representative who was HUAC's chairman at the time Josh appeared, had won office in a Jim Crow election with the support of less than 6 percent of his district's potential voters, and when asked why HUAC was not investigating the Ku Klux Klan, he replied, "The threats and intimidations of the Klan are an old American custom like illegal whiskey-making"). They did not want to humiliate black leaders publicly or to force black sports or entertainment figures to behave in an unmanly fashion by betraying their friends. Therefore, as Victor Navasky reports in his classic study *Naming Names*, the key act generally demanded of them was that they distance themselves from Paul Robeson.

Jackie Robinson, who had broken baseball's color line when he joined the Brooklyn Dodgers, had set the pattern a year before Josh's appearance. Called before HUAC, he reaffirmed his strong feelings about racial discrimination but went on to say, "I've been asked to express my views on Paul Robeson's statement in Paris to the effect that American Negroes would refuse to fight in any war against Russia because we love Russia so much. I haven't any comment to make on that statement except that if Mr. Robeson actually made it, it sounds very silly to me." Following Robinson's testimony he was thanked by the committee members, and Congressman Morgan Moulder of Missouri pointed out that "it is not the purpose of this Committee in conducting these hearings to question the loyalty of the Negro race. There is no question about that. It is to give an opportunity to you and others to combat the idea Paul Robeson had given by his statements. I think you have rendered a great service to your country and to your people."

The statement in question, made by Robeson in April 1949 at a peace conference in Paris, had been widely and inaccurately repeated in the American press. What he said was that the wealth of America was built "on the backs of the white workers from Europe . . . and on the backs of millions of blacks . . . And we shall not put up with any hysterical raving that urges us to make war on anyone. Our will to fight for peace is strong. We shall not make war on anyone. We shall not make war on the Soviet Union." The Associated Press reworked this to read, "It is unthinkable that American Negroes would go to war on behalf of those who have oppressed us for generations against a country [the Soviet Union] which in one generation has raised our people to the full dignity of mankind."

The American right instantly leaped on Robeson's reported remark, blazoned it far and wide, and for the first time was joined by all the liberals. Virtually the full spectrum of prominent black leaders rallied to condemn, and distance themselves from, Robeson's statement. The effect on his standing as the most respected and admired black man in America was profound. Everyone continued to speak of him as a great artist but balanced this praise with the insistence that he was not a spokesman for anyone but himself and, apparently, the Communist Party.

To repudiate Robeson's remark as it was reported in the mainstream press was extremely easy. Robinson was careful to hedge his repudiation with the caveat "if he actually said it," but it was obvious that if

Robeson really believed that no African Americans would fight for the United States in a U.S.-Soviet war, he was living in a dream world. Like Robinson, Josh was always careful to state his admiration for Robeson, but he had no reason to back up an absurd position. Josh and Robinson were not just disagreeing with Robeson in private conversations, however, or even on public stages. They were testifying against him in front of HUAC, an official body investigating anti-American subversion.

Josh went before the committee on September 1, 1950. He had written a full statement, and his daughter Bunny remembers driving to Hyde Park with him to get Mrs. Roosevelt's reaction, and her making a few suggestions but giving her overall approval. Unlike Robinson and most of the other artists who testified over the years, Josh had not been asked to appear. The idea had certainly been suggested by Kirkpatrick and Stokes, and Josh recalled Stokes even threatening him with a subpoena, but he went voluntarily. To the members of his family, this is a sign of his strength: he did not get dragged there under duress but went proudly and of his own volition. They are also proud of the statement he made.

Emphasizing the fact that he had nothing to hide, Josh did not even bring a lawyer. He had only Carol by his side. He started by thanking the committee for giving him "this opportunity to clear up some misunderstandings about myself in some quarters."

Josh's testimony showed a man doing his best to walk a narrow line between pride and capitulation. He explained that "artists are not often smart about politics . . . [and] know mighty little about the ins and outs of 'movements' and parties. But we're apt to have strong feelings and therefore are easy prey for anyone who appeals to our sense of justice and decency."

While he had "never knowingly belonged to or supported any organization designed to overthrow the Government of the United States," he had frequently appeared at events for what he had believed to be "worthwhile causes," never suspecting that they might be Communist-inspired. "I did on some occasions sign petitions against lynching or poll tax or other evils," he said, but "dozens of other artists of all races and colors, I have no doubt, have also given their names and talent and time under the innocent impression that they were on the side of charity and equality."

"Let me make it clear, if I can, that I am still on that side," he added, echoing Robinson's testimony. "The fact that Communists are exploiting grievances for their own purposes does not make those grievances any less real. As I've said, I am no politician. On the other hand, I do know what injustice and discrimination and Jim-Crowism mean. I know these things not as theories but as cruel facts that I've seen and suffered in my own life. Against those things I have protested and will go on protesting, because I love my country and want to see it a better, more tolerant, place to live in. I'm proud of the fact that under our system of freedom everyone is able to speak out — or in my case, to sing out — against what we consider wrong and for what we consider right."

Josh explained that to him a folksinger must be "the voice and the conscience of his time and his audience." He would continue to sing the feelings of those around him "as long as there is suffering and discrimination around me and freedom and equality to be won," he said. "That's not Communism, even if Communists try to use us for their own foul ends. As I see it, it's simply Christianity. And I say this as the son of a minister brought up in a religious family. I say this as the father of four daughters and a son whom my wife and I are trying to bring up as patriotic and religious Americans — which is to say, as decent human beings."

He went on to trace his life from the time he left home with the blind men up to his appearance in *John Henry* and his first meeting with Paul Robeson. "I have a great admiration for Mr. Robeson as an actor and a great singer," he said. "And if what I read in the papers is true, I feel sad over the help he's been giving to people who despise America. He has a right to his own opinions, but when he, or anybody, pretends to talk for a whole race, he's kidding himself. His statement that the Negroes would not fight for their country, against Soviet Russia or any other enemy, is both wrong and an insult; because I stand ready to fight Russia or any enemy of America.

"There are some Communists among Negroes, as I am told, just as there are among other Americans. But they don't speak for the rest of us, any more than white Communists speak for white Americans. I am told that the proportion of Negro members in the Communist fold is even smaller than the proportions of other races; and that says a lot for their common sense."

Josh continued his autobiography, speaking of his early successes in the music business. He explained that once his name became somewhat valuable, he was frequently asked to sing at benefits and was happy to do so. Unfortunately, through ignorance, he had sung for many organizations that were "phony, false-face political rackets." He had only discovered this in 1947, when the attorney general published a list of "subversive" organizations and he found, to his horror, that many were familiar sponsors of events at which he had appeared. "It was an awful blow," he said. "I realized that I had been played for a sucker. There I was, a devoted American who had let himself be used." His one consolation was that he had never sung anything he did not believe. He had often sung "Strange Fruit," but "why shouldn't a Negro artist — and for that matter any decent person — raise his voice against lynching?" Furthermore, he always followed it with "The House I Live In," which "expressed the other side of the story — my profound love for our America."

Josh then recited the lyrics to both songs, saying that "I believe that no one who sings such songs honestly, from the heart, can be Communist." He added that he had always refused requests to sing "Strange Fruit" abroad, because "it's our family affair, to be solved by Americans in the peaceful, democratic American way." When the European press had asked him about Robeson's remark, "I spoke of my pride in our country, and denied the libel that my people would not fight and die to defend America." He had therefore been horrified to find that he was being attacked in the American press as "fronting for the Communists." He had cut his tour short and hurried home to bury the lie. He had seen too many smears directed against him and had even read assertions that his son was a Communist after Josh Jr. sang "Freedom Road" (and "The Lord's Prayer") at a Chicago concert. He was not only personally insulted but also felt he had "a duty to other folk singers and artists in general, especially young people just getting started.

"I hope they will give themselves to good causes as generously as I have tried to do," he said. "But I hope also they will be more careful who uses them and why. My advice to them is plain and clear: Be sure to look under the label."

Josh ended his testimony on a ringing note: "Personally I have little to retract or regret, other than the auspices under which I have sometimes appeared. As long as my voice and spirit hold out, I shall keep on singing of the hope, joys, and grievances of ordinary folk. I shall stand shoulder to shoulder with those who are pushed around and humiliated and discriminated against, no matter what their race or their creed may be. That, as I see it, is the least I can do for the country we all cherish.

"But those who would tear down our America, those who hold a double allegiance, those who turn words upside down and inside out in support of foreign tyranny — they're my enemies. Better than most people in this room I know the blemishes on our American civilization. I think we should all devote ourselves to removing them, not merely because they give aid and comfort to the Communists, but because they're wrong in themselves."

Josh believed that in the context of the times his testimony was firmly in the middle of the road. It was reasonably honest and could even be interpreted as tough and moderately confrontational. He was disingenuous about his earlier political affiliations but stood strongly behind his "fighting songs" and continued to attack the evils he had always attacked on stage. He had named no names, and had spoken of his admiration for Paul Robeson. If the papers had reported Robeson's words correctly, he disagreed, but Robeson had "a right to his own opinions." If he had been misled into singing his songs for organizations that were inimical to America, he was upset about that, but he had done so in the belief that they were supporting the "ordinary folk," and he was still proudly on that side.

If that was the impression Josh was trying to convey, however, his testimony was a miserable failure. The *New York Daily Mirror* headline was "Josh White Hits Robeson for Aiding Foes of U.S." The *Washington Times Herald* had "Red Quiz Told Robeson 'Slur' Riles Negroes." The report in the *Amsterdam News* — with a photo of him and Carol before HUAC and captioned "SINGER REPUDIATES PAUL ROBESON" — said that "White volunteered to come before the House group and tell how he was 'exploited' by the Communists. He charged that Paul Robeson is giving help to 'people who despise America' by endorsing Communist causes." The *News* article did at least go on to quote Josh's affirmation of his old fighting stance, but most stories simply repeated his explanation that he had been duped and his condemnation of Robeson.

The unfortunate fact was that Josh was trying to take the middle ground in a battle that had none. Appearances before HUAC were purely pro forma proceedings. Despite its purported aim, the committee was not in fact digging up information about Communist infiltration of the entertainment industry; there was little Josh or his fellow witnesses could tell them that was not long since old news. What the committee wanted was "cooperation" — an antiseptic word that could mean anything from minor assistance to complete personal abasement, groveling, and the betrayal of one's friends and relations — and, by extension, an acknowledgment from progressive figures that all their good works, and by implication all the optimism and victories of the New Deal, were inextricably intertwined and tainted with the treasonous machinations of the red devils who were killing American boys in Korea.

In general, both the left and right regarded the naming of names as the litmus test for "cooperation." Whatever else one might say before the committee, all that finally mattered was one's willingness to place other people at the scene of one's supposed peccadilloes. Strong as one's denunciations of Communism might be, eager as one might be to espouse the strongest right-wing positions, the moment of truth would come when a congressman asked, "Can you tell us who else was present at this event?"

Josh had long since dissociated himself from the CP, and his career was at stake, but his self-image made the idea of outright betrayal utterly repugnant, and he was proud that he had not ratted on anyone else. In distancing himself from Robeson he had carefully avoided admitting any direct knowledge of Robeson's allegedly "disloyal" views, merely giving his personal reaction to reports in the newspapers. In this, he echoed the public pronouncements of virtually every black leader in America and, arguably, the advice of Robeson himself: Robeson's biographer quotes the black Communist organizer Revels Cayton's report of a final conversation in which Josh told Robeson, "They've got me in a vise; I'm going to have to talk." Robeson is supposed to have replied, "Do what you have to but don't name names."

Since the rules for black witnesses were, in practice, different from those for whites, the Josh Whites and Jackie Robinsons who appeared before HUAC were never asked the fatal question. Instead, they were simply required to distance themselves from the Communists and, especially, from Robeson. This subtlety, not explicitly remarked until Navasky's book was published in 1980, made it possible for someone like Josh to feel that he was to some extent keeping his honor intact. Over a decade later he was still making the point, complaining to Shelton that "people said I went to Washington and called names, even though I didn't." This was certainly true. Few leftists bothered to read Josh's full testimony, and the fact that his appearance was accepted by the committee as cooperative led many to conclude that he *had* named names. Several still think of him as having betrayed Barney Josephson, and Eartha Kitt even repeated this charge in one of her autobiographies.

As it happened, he had not, but that mattered to no one but him. Both the right and the left treated the committee's thanks for his friendly testimony as a sign that he had chosen up sides. *Counterattack* cited him again on September 13, this time as proof that the system worked. The newsletter had been coming under attack in the mainstream press, accused of smearing people through false accusations. Jean Muir, an actress who had just been signed for a major role in an NBC television series, had been named in *Red Channels* and, after the station and sponsor received a handful of threatening letters, summarily dropped from the show. This was the first major television blacklist case, and it made national headlines. Kirkpatrick was widely vilified as an irresponsible scandalmonger, and a lot of important people vowed that his listings would not be allowed to destroy people's lives.

*Counterattack* snapped back with a special six-page issue. It repeated the argument that it was merely reprinting information available elsewhere, in the interest of a better-informed American public. Far from wishing to "police the airwaves," the newsletter's publisher firmly believed "that NO individual should have the right to 'absolve' or convict anyone . . . of pro-Communist leanings." However, *Counterattack*'s editors would of course be happy to help anyone who had "innocently or otherwise aided the Communist cause" to set the record straight, and would give "assistance in getting straightened out, securing a job, etc."

Josh was exhibit A in this argument:

> JOSH WHITE, the folk singer, is a recent example of this. He approached COUNTERATTACK voluntarily and explained his problem. COUNTERATTACK brought his case to the attention of the House Committee on Un-American Activities. As a result, in the middle of the JEAN MUIR controversy, he gave public testimony before the Committee, told how he had been duped into supporting Communist fronts, and dealt an effective propaganda counterblow against the CP and its deception agencies. The public was given the opportunity to judge the facts for themselves.

The point is that whatever Josh intended, and however real his dislike of the Communist Party, he made his HUAC appearance at a key time and with severe consequences. His testimony was widely disseminated — *Billboard* printed it in full — and by going as early as he did, years before anyone in the folk music scene was subpoenaed, he became an exemplary pioneer in granting the premise that people named in *Red Channels* had the responsibility to explain their pasts. The obvious corollary, regularly stated by the red-hunters, was that those who did not testify must have something to hide. In this view, anyone who was blacklisted and not a Communist should stand up for America and do whatever was necessary to confound her enemies; all others deserved to remain on the blacklist, and did. Once this premise was accepted, there were effectively only two sides: with the Woods and Kirkpatricks, or with the Communists.

# 14

## STRANGE FRUIT
■ ■ ■ ■ ■ ■ ■ ■ ■ ■ ■ ■ ■ ■ ■ ■ ■ ■ ■

*Confidential Informant [name blacked out] of unknown reliability, on September 14, 1950, stated that he had heard that* JOSH WHITE *since his appearance before the House Committee on Un-American Activities has been snubbed by the Communists and anti-Communists in the entertainment field; that apparently the Communists snubbed him because of his having been critical of his former Communist Party connections, and that the anti-Communists snubbed him because of these connections.*
—FBI report on Josh White, January 23, 1951

Josh's old friends on the left had no doubt about which side he had chosen. Pete Seeger was "shocked" that Josh would give friendly testimony in front of the "Dixiecrat" racists he had always hated and condemned. "I sat down the moment I got that news and I said 'The Josh White I know would have died before he went to testify for a guy named Rankin,'" Seeger says, confusing Chairman Wood with his even more notorious Mississippi predecessor. "And I wrote him a letter, with a little sketch of a guitar broken in half, in two pieces."

Seeger goes on to say that other people took a more nuanced view of Josh's actions. Lee Hays happened to be in the room when Seeger was drawing his message to Josh.

"Lee said, 'Pete what are you writing?'"

"I said, 'I'm writing a letter to Josh.'"

"He read it and said 'Pete, don't mail it.' He says, 'Do you know yourself what pressure Josh is under?'"

"I said, 'I still think I should send it.'

"He said, 'You can't dream in your own life of the pressures that Josh has faced in his life.' And Lee and Ronnie [Gilbert], and Toshi [Seeger] also, said 'Don't mail that letter.'

"So I didn't mail it. But I kept it; I came across it years later. I may have destroyed it now. Because they were right." Hays remembered Josh always helping him out, encouraging him and giving him money when he was destitute, and he understood that Josh's situation was very different from that of Seeger, a younger, white folksinger, who did not have five children to support. Hays was sad rather than angry about Josh's behavior. Nonetheless, in his case as well the friendship was over, and the two no longer met.

Those who had never known Josh personally saw no reason to be charitable. The *Daily Worker*'s report on his testimony was headlined "Time of the Toad," a phrase borrowed from the blacklisted screenwriter Dalton Trumbo. It bitterly declared that Josh had "earned the contempt of all who honor human dignity when he cringed before the riding bosses in Congress," and described his "abject performance" as "a slap in the face" to his old fans. "Whatever White told the witchhunters about his being 'duped' and 'used' by the Communists, the fact remains that the Left first discovered his talent, provided his audience, and created an atmosphere in white supremacist America receptive to his songs of Negro protest. . . . He may call this being 'duped' and 'used' if he pleases, but American culture would be infinitely richer if the plutocrats who monopolize the radio, stage, concert hall, television, and motion picture industries would 'dupe' and 'use' talented Negroes in such a way."

There was a note of condescension in this attack but also a good deal of truth. Although Josh might have come to feel that he had been used by the Communists to further their own interests, his relationship with the left had unquestionably been symbiotic. The *Worker* had provided some of his earliest press coverage, and progressives — Party members or not — had been his most ardent and influential supporters. Josh had gained as much from his political associations as any political group had gained from him, and if he had some justification for feeling used, they had at least an equal right to resent his willingness to play along with the blacklisters.

Resent it they did. Josh had taken sides with the people who had driven Cafe Society out of business and were hounding hundreds of his coworkers out of their jobs. There are stories of old friends turning their backs on him, nasty remarks, waiters refusing to take his orders. Friends who were politically liberal, as opposed to "progressive," remember that he seemed almost pitifully grateful when they were still friendly. Ed McCurdy, a ballad singer who replaced Richard Dyer-Bennett at the Village Vanguard late in 1950, remembers Josh coming over to see him between sets at Cafe Society: "I'm sure it was just so he'd have someone to shake hands with," McCurdy says. "Because he was in the doghouse; everybody thought he went down and ratted on his friends."

What made things even worse was that Josh himself was unhappy with his behavior. He believed he had had no choice, but the interviews with Kirkpatrick and the testimony before HUAC had been thoroughly unpleasant experiences. He had always been able to make proud, unambiguous declarations in support of racial and economic justice, and this was central to his identity, both private and public. Now, he had denied much of his past and severely compromised his present and future. He might say that he still stood for all the things he had always stood for, but his old allies condemned him as a traitor, and he would never again be able to sing at a benefit or make a statement of support for a cause without thinking twice.

Oscar Brand, who had also been named in *Counterattack* and *Red Channels* but managed to avoid ever having to testify, offers some insight into Josh's feelings. Though frequently associated with the progressives, Brand was always something of a political maverick and remained firmly distant from the Communist Party. Indeed, the leaders of People's Songs sometimes cited his name as an example of the group's non-Communist membership. Brand feels that Josh made a bad mistake, but he can easily understand the reasons: "He was forced into it, in part by his agent, in part by his family. Family pressure can be tremendous." Brand speaks from experience. During the blacklist period his sister told him that their father was dying because of the attacks being made on him as a left-winger.

Brand believes that, all things considered, Josh behaved quite well in front of HUAC and that much of his guilt and unhappiness was undeserved. Nonetheless, he concludes that those feelings were inescapable. "A man as proud as he was, as powerful as he was personally, who gives any part of himself to the other side, to the people he despises, is not going to be happy for the rest of his life," Brand says. "Burl Ives [who did name names before HUAC] was the worst. He's never been happy since that happened. Very few people are. There's a piece of you that you never forget, a piece that you handed out to them. I don't think Josh deserved to excoriate himself the way he did . . . But the kind of person he was made it impossible for him to ignore the fact that he acted against his own personal feelings. It was something in his stomach — it wasn't the ulcer at this time, but it was an ulcer America had handed him — part of him that said, 'You gave in to the bastards. You let them suck you in.' "

If Josh had expected his troubles to end with his HUAC appearance, he was mistaken. As the first cooperative witness from the folk music scene or Cafe Society, he was viewed by the red-hunters as a source of testimony with which they could pressure other potential witnesses. The FBI, which had begun keeping loose tabs on him in the early 1940s and made him the subject of a pending investigation in 1947, had prepared a full-scale file on him in July while he was in Europe with Mrs. Roosevelt. It was 191 pages long, though many pages contained only a single, brief paragraph (often a single sentence) of information gleaned from one or another newspaper or, occasionally, from a confidential informant. Almost all the entries simply mentioned his appearance at benefit concerts or public events sponsored by suspect organizations; some were completely devoid of political interest, just listing a concert date at, for example, the Detroit Art Institute.

The FBI was quick to follow up Josh's HUAC appearance. On September 12, 1950, a letter went to the New York bureau director, instructing him to have Josh interviewed by two experienced agents. "The initial interview should be confined to White's own activities with regard to Communist Party matters," it said, "and in the event he proves cooperative, subsequent interviews should be arranged for the purpose of obtaining from him information concerning the identities, background and activities of the numerous Communist Party officials and members with whom he came in contact during the years he was associating with such individuals."

As it happened, Josh had gone back to England right after his HUAC appearance, to wrap up some unfinished business, and on his return he left immediately for a West Coast tour. By November, though, he was back at the new Cafe Society, and the FBI set up an interview with two agents. While the bureau's interest was mostly informational, the agents had been instructed to review Josh's HUAC testimony thoroughly and to watch out for any discrepancies that would leave him open to a perjury charge (for example, an admission that he had at any time been a CP member).

The FBI's summary of the interview ran only four pages. As expected, Josh said that he had never been a Communist, nor had he ever been asked or had any desire to join the Party. He said he had played many benefits, for all sorts of groups, but could not recall anyone in particular who had invited him to do so, and he could not recall ever having joined any of the sponsoring organizations. He vehemently denied any connection with People's Songs, saying that he had only gone to "one song fest," had been disgusted by the songs because they were all about Russia, and had left at intermission; "his current policy," the agents reported, "is that he will not appear with any artist whom he knows to be sponsored by this organization."

Josh told the agents that HUAC's Alvin Stokes had questioned him about his earlier associations but that he simply could not remember "the organizations or the dates or any of the other artists who might have appeared with him." The only person he had ever known to be a Communist was Benjamin Davis, who had run for the New York City Council as an official CP candidate, and he knew that only from public statements.

For the present, Josh said, he was doing everything in his power to avoid appearing in any suspect forum, but it was often very difficult to tell when a performance might be chancy. He cited as an example an invitation to a folk festival which he only later learned was being sponsored by People's Songs. As a precaution, he was now checking all invitations with *Counterattack*'s Kirkpatrick or the conservative columnists Howard Rushmore and Eugene Lyons, "to obtain their advice as to the worthiness of the organization."

At the end of the interview, Josh said he was willing to come back as needed. The agents felt that he had been cooperative but could be of no further use. They concluded their report by saying that unless advised to the contrary they would conduct no more interviews with him, and suggesting "that the Security Index Card on the subject be canceled."

Josh would have liked nothing better, but FBI headquarters took a far less rosy view of his performance. It fired off a letter to the New York office saying that with his long history of appearances for organizations that were widely publicized as Communist fronts, Josh could hardly have been as innocent of their nature as he claimed: "In view of this it would seem that White has not been entirely truthful or cooperative." The letter added that although no further interviews needed to be scheduled, the New York office should keep in close touch with its informants to make sure that Josh had truly severed his Communist connections.

The early 1950s were the heyday of "red" investigations, and information kept flowing in to the FBI, but little of it was contemporary. For almost four years after he was first interviewed the bureau regularly updated its Josh White file, but all the "new" information related to his behavior in the early 1940s. In 1951 a confidential informant "of known reliability," describing himself as a former CP functionary who had resigned in 1945, said Josh had regularly been referred to as an "adherent of the Communist Party." A sample of the informant's reliability is that he described Josh as a "folk singer and cartoonist."

In 1954 Josh's file was closed, then almost instantly reopened. Apparently, even though there was no evidence that he had retained any connection with subversive elements, his status as a "prominent individual" was such that he warranted continued attention. In July of that year the New York office was directed to interview him a second time, "in order that [his] present and past Communist Party affiliation and sympathies may be more definitely determined."

The interview was conducted on September 20, and this time the agents were not satisfied with generalities. For almost four hours they grilled him, asking him who had arranged each separate event mentioned in his file and who had been present at it. Faced with such direct queries, Josh demonstrated what can only be considered a praiseworthy amnesia: he said that he vaguely remembered some of the events but had no memory of anyone else who might have been involved with them.

A half-dozen times the FBI agents asked Josh about specific people, from Paul Robeson to the left-wing cartoonist Bill Gropper, and in all but one case Josh responded that he did not know them to be Communists. The exception, as in his previous interview, was Ben Davis, whom he had supported in a campaign for a New York City Council seat. Josh said he had known that Davis was the Communist Party candidate but added that he had supported Davis because "they were both Negroes rather than [from] any desire to support the Communist platform."

The only names that led to extended questioning were those of Barney and Leon Josephson. Josh said that he did not know the Josephsons to be Communist Party members, although he did recall Leon's prison sentence for contempt of Congress. Asked whether Barney had urged him to appear at benefits, Josh first said he did not recall his doing so; then "he stated after some reflection that he is quite sure Barney Josephson had not asked him or directed him to play before any groups since he can recall Barney Josephson having been critical of him for appearing at benefits . . . [because] such performances hurt the business at the Cafes."

According to other Cafe Society performers, Josephson always encouraged benefit performances, so this can only be taken as Josh's attempt to shield his old employer. Since the accepted gossip among Cafe Society entertainers is that Josh betrayed Josephson, this is significant. In the next paragraph the FBI agents reported Josh as saying that during World War II "Josephson had told him he was not to sing his ballads 'Strange Fruit' or 'The Free and Equal Blues' because such songs might cause dissension among Negroes in the Armed Forces," but that he had insisted on playing whatever songs he chose. This declaration is a bit more ambiguous, as the CP often joined the American government in trying to stifle racial struggles during the war, but it is hardly a betrayal.

At the end of the four-hour interview, Josh said that if the agents had any further questions he would always be available. Once again, the interviewers described him as cooperative, and in April 1955 Josh was finally dropped from the FBI's Security Index.

Three years later, Josh was to have a third and final interview with the FBI — this time at his request. His testimony before HUAC had succeeded in getting him favorable mention in *Counterattack* and in alienating most of his old friends in the music world, but it had not gotten him off the film and television blacklists. Unlike Burl Ives, who named names and went on to a profitable film career (though his betrayal made him anathema on the folk scene), Josh had always made his politics an integral part of his public persona, and rejecting his past Communist affiliations was not enough to separate him from that image. Communist or not, he was still something of a racial activist and, as such, controversial. A television show that broadcast nationally might worry about complaints from southern viewers if Josh appeared, and a film company could not be certain that someone, somewhere, would not picket a film that had his name in the credits.

Since the blacklist was a matter of perception and fear rather than a single concrete list, there was no way a performer could ever know exactly why he or she was on it, or what would have to be done to get off. Becoming "safe" was an intricate and amorphous process of trying to persuade one network or film company to take a chance, then hoping that there would be no adverse reactions and that others might follow suit. For Josh, the attempt to figure out exactly how and why he was being barred from the airwaves was made more difficult by the fact that, being black, his opportunities would have been limited even if the only organization he had ever sung for was the American Legion.

Grasping at straws, in June 1958 Josh called Ausa Parsons, director of the FBI's Chicago office, asking how he could "clear his name" and "implying listings were hurting him in his profession." An interview took place on June 20 but was unsatisfactory to all concerned. Josh said there was nothing he could add to what he had told the bureau in 1954, and he was informed that "the FBI could make no recommendation publicly or otherwise to clear his name of any Communist connections."

Thus, Josh remained in limbo. He was not absolutely barred as a leftist — indeed, he would on occasion be hailed as an outspoken liberal who had bravely stood up to the Communists — but neither was he considered completely "safe." The result was a situation that could be tantalizing, with possibilities constantly visible but just out of reach. For example, a five-page memorandum written by Jac Holzman of Elektra records details two months of correspondence about a job offer that could have transformed Josh's career. In late January 1956, Holzman received a call from a Mr. Paul Marshal of the New York chapter of the National Republican Club, asking if Josh could appear on March 20 as one of four performers at a banquet being given at the Waldorf-Astoria for President Dwight Eisenhower and his cabinet. Holzman cabled Josh, who was in London; Josh instantly called back to accept; and Holzman conveyed his acceptance to Marshal, who said he was delighted — though he did add that because of Josh's appearance before HUAC, final clearance would have to come from Washington.

Holzman arranged for Josh and Marshal to meet at his house for dinner as soon as Josh got home. Josh "told his story to Marshal, giving him a complete blow-by-blow description of his statement" to HUAC, and Marshal seemed completely satisfied. Indeed, he called back a few days later to say that the chief counsel for the Senate investigating committee had sent him a transcript of Josh's testimony, and everything was fine.

Then all communication ceased. Holzman tried to reach Marshal on the phone but consistently failed. He finally got through in late February, only be told by Marshal that "everybody was anxious in the Club for Josh to appear but that they thought he was a controversial figure." They talked some more and seemed to have reached an agreement, but once again Holzman found himself unable to get further news. Finally, on March 6, he got a call from the head of the entertainment committee for the banquet, saying that the entire program had been canceled.

Reaching Marshal later that day, Holzman was told that the members of the club had "overwhelmingly voted in favor of having Josh on the program," but this decision had been vetoed by a Republican congressman, Frederic René Coudert Jr. Marshal said that he and "many other people" resigned from the club as a result, and that because Josh was not appearing he had also pulled out the other performers — an opera singer, a flamenco dancer, and the pop star Pat Boone.

Holzman's memo concludes: "I felt that this thing stunk and needed a public airing but I was loath to instigate same because I felt that the publicity would be harmful to Josh and would only reinforce the opinions of some people that he was a 'controversial' character. Paul Marshal agreed but said that as far as the Club was concerned, he was making this a political issue inside the Club. I told him he could do whatever he wanted but to keep it out of the papers."

So it went. Publicly, Josh's best strategy, and that of the other performers in his position, was to pretend that everything was fine, since any complaint would only exacerbate the problem. Meanwhile, jobs were quietly denied him, in most cases without ever reaching the stage where he could be sure of what was happening. He continued to work, and even appeared on television from time to time, but the taint of "controversy" would never disappear. Even late in the 1960s his name turned up on lists circulated by American Legion–style groups as someone to be avoided by patriotic Americans. Liberals decried these lists but all too often also shied away from situations that could lead to confrontations with the red-baiters.

A chillingly polite correspondence from 1955 between Len Rosenfeld, soon to be Josh's manager, and Ed Sullivan demonstrates just how difficult the situation could be. The Sullivan show was television's top variety program, and the combination of its importance and Sullivan's reputation as a staunchly anti-Communist liberal led many to consider an appearance on it as a sort of de facto clearance from the blacklist. For an artist in Josh's position it thus had a value far beyond its normal function as a national showcase. That Rosenfeld clearly saw it this way is demonstrated by the fact that he filed this correspondence not with his regular business papers but with the Holzman memorandum on the Republican Club affair. The first letter, from January 6, finds Rosenfeld thanking Sullivan for the courtesy extended in a recent telephone conversation "when we discussed very briefly the general problems of artists and Red Channels, and, more specifically, the problem of Josh White."

Rosenfeld then gives a synopsis of Josh's political past: the performances at benefits, the appearances before the FBI and HUAC, and so forth, pointing out that since the *Red Channels* listing, Josh and those like him had found it "virtually impossible" to get television work, despite their willingness to cooperate with investigators and the general understanding that they were "innocent dupes" of the Communists. Then Rosenfeld comes to the crux of the matter:

"Because Mr. White's case is the most effective example of an artist being deprived of work as a result of his being used as a 'dupe,' and knowing of your interest in this overall problem, I ask you pointblank if you will have Mr. White on your show and thereby take the lead in breaking the back of this problem—a problem which, until now, has not been resolved."

Sullivan's reply came a month later:

> Dear Leonard,
> When spring or summer arrives, I'll certainly use Josh White and the youngsters on our show.
> At the moment, because of the tremendous competition, I am using only big names, but this should ease off.
> Sincerely, Ed Sullivan

By July, Josh still had not been offered an appearance, and Rosenfeld was writing letters reminding Sullivan of the earlier correspondence and complaining that he had failed "on numerous occasions" to reach Sullivan's office by telephone. By September he was quoting Sullivan's letter back to him, then pitifully writing, "Needless to say, Josh was overjoyed when I communicated this information to him, and needless to say, as so many of us have had to do, he, too, has learned to accept disappointment." Still trying to salvage the situation, he ended by saying that Josh would be in the country until late October, if Sullivan wanted him, and pointing out the good reception Josh Jr. and Beverly had recently received on a muscular dystrophy telethon.

Josh would eventually appear on several network shows, but it would take many years; Oscar Brand recalls being forbidden to use him as late as 1963. At that time, Brand was the music director of *Exploring,* an NBC children's program. Though he had also been blacklisted, Brand was working only behind the scenes and therefore not attracting much attention. Getting a questionable performer's appearance on screen was trickier.

"I couldn't get Josh on for love or money," Brand says. "And the fellow who was running the show was an honest, straightforward, marvelous guy. I was able to get other people who were considered troublesome, controversial. I put Theo Bikel on it; Dyer-Bennet I tried to get on it, but he refused for the money I was able to offer. But Josh I couldn't get on. He was considered a troublemaker. I caused some difficulty with what they called the 'Continuity Acceptance People' — that's a lawyer who has a copy of *Red Channels.*"

Brand has no doubt that race played a major role in Josh's remaining persona non grata. "He was too proud," Brand says. "An uppity Negro. That was the description of Josh White. And they knew who Josh was. He wasn't small enough; like I got Phil Ochs on. Now, Phil was much more radical than Josh, but they didn't know Phil Ochs."

The left was almost as unforgiving as the right. A year after his HUAC appearance the *Daily Worker* headed a column "The New 'Safe' Josh White," excoriating him yet again for his betrayal and pointing out that his art had crumbled along with his convictions. Quoting a recent *New York Times* review, which was generally favorable but bemoaned the loss of Josh's old fighting spirit and the replacement of his "earthy lyrics" with new ones that "sound a little smutty, as if . . . created to please a fashionable public," the *Worker* was bitterly sarcastic: "This is our new, non-political Josh White. He is not a dupe now; he's not being 'used.' He's artistically dead, otherwise he's just the same."

The animosity of the left was less harmful in a strictly professional sense than that of the right, as progressives did not wield anything like commensurate power in the American media. Nonetheless, Josh's reputation as someone who had knuckled under to the red-baiters cost him more than goodwill. The folk music movement, though slowed by the blacklist, remained vital and growing throughout the 1950s, but Josh was often left on the outside. The reasons were not entirely political; the young "traditionalist" singers often attacked him on purely musical grounds. Still, politics was a big part of it. The *People's Songs* bulletin, though its supporting organization was wiped out by the red hunt, was reborn as the slim magazine *Sing Out!* and became the voice of the burgeoning folk revival. Edited by Irwin Silber, who fearlessly championed progressive causes through the worst of the McCarthy era, *Sing Out!* was by no means purely political; it included positive reviews and friendly interviews of plenty of apolitical and even conservative performers. Yet within its pages Josh was a nonperson. Except in paid advertisements the magazine avoided mentioning his name in any context until after his death. Even when it printed his old specialty "Jerry the Mule (Timber)," it gave no suggestion as to the song's source.

Though there is no way to come up with any numbers, there were also concert promoters who remembered Josh as a traitor to his friends and passed him over because of it. Especially in the later part of the 1950s, as the red scare waned, the blacklisted were openly applauded on college campuses as heroes. Pete Seeger, who had appeared before HUAC and, rather than taking the Fifth Amendment, had taken the First, arguing that freedom of speech implied freedom of silence, was now the dean of the folk movement. He would not have denied Josh a job for political reasons, being all too conscious of the evils of blacklisting, but other people were not always aware of his tolerance. Manny Greenhill, who had taken guitar lessons from Josh in the early 1940s and became a concert promoter in the 1950s, remembers consulting Seeger before hiring Josh to appear in a concert series—for fear that Josh's participation might preclude Seeger's—and finding that Seeger had no problem at all with including Josh. Younger promoters, however, would have been less willing to trouble the great man with such questions, and may simply have avoided the issue by leaving Josh off their programs.

The loss of a concert here or there was bearable, but the general loss of respect was crippling. Josh had been a hero not only to audiences but to many young performers. Along with the host of young women he mentored, and in whom he at times took a more than strictly artistic interest, there had been such budding stars as Sidney Poitier and Harry Belafonte. "I spent many, many hours with him in the years of my early development," Belafonte would say. "He had a profound influence on my style. At the time I came along he was the only popular black folk singer and . . . exposed America to a wealth of material about the life and the conditions of black people that had not been sung by any other artist." Carol remembered Belafonte as a frequent visitor to their home, and when the young singer turned from jazz to folk music, his act was clearly modeled on Josh's. The shirt was unbuttoned another couple of buttons, but the basic appeal was nearly identical, and critics commented on the similarity so frequently that one suspects Belafonte must have at times found it mildly annoying.

Belafonte was too young to have been in the thick of the Popular Front, and although his sympathies were with the left, he managed to avoid the worst of the blacklist without actually having to testify. Having taken Josh as something of an artistic father figure, though, he seems to have been particularly hurt by his mentor's behavior. Over the years, while doing a generally fine job of pointing up his predecessors and keeping their memories fresh, he rarely mentioned Josh's name. Even today, his polite note of refusal to an interview request gives as a reason that "Mr. White's betrayal of his friends and colleagues at the height of the tragic period of McCarthyism still sadly resonates in the memories of many."

Josh, as he himself often pointed out, was not a talker. He did not tend to unburden himself, even to close friends and family, so any attempt to figure out his feelings about the limbo in which he found himself after his HUAC testimony must be largely speculative. There is no question that he felt isolated and hurt, and that he never really understood how he had simultaneously alienated both ends of the political spectrum. Caught in the middle of a battle between extremes, he felt that both had betrayed him. As far as anyone remembers, he never expressed any regrets either for testifying that he had been duped by the Communists or for refusing to cooperate more fully with the FBI. It seems clear that in his own mind he had had no choice in either case. He had tried to bend without breaking, to cooperate with his enemies without betraying his old friends, and the result had satisfied no one.

More accurately, it had satisfied no one in the political world or the blacklist-conscious entertainment industry. To Josh's family, and his friends in the neighborhood, he remained the same heroic figure he had always been. As Jackie Washington puts it, "Many, many black people would consider that the way he kissed off Josephson and all those people was just taking care of business. The way you deal with white people and the white world is something that white people just don't understand. Now, Eartha Kitt and Harry Belafonte are not regular black folks. To most black folks, the important thing is being clever enough to get by, and Josh White found a way to maneuver through."

Josh certainly felt that he had done what he had to do and gotten by as best he could. He would live the rest of his life with the sense that he had been falsely attacked by both sides, that despite his testimony he was one of the most complete victims of the red scare. Some of the people who held out against the committee and the blacklisters will object strenuously to this idea. Certainly, there were other artists who suffered more severely, and Josh did make an effort to go along and to save himself at a time when other people who were equally devoid of strong Party ties were holding fast. Nonetheless, it is hard to argue that he did not suffer, or that he brought all his suffering on himself. Like the vast majority of the blacklisted, he had never done anything faintly "subversive," but his partial cooperation with the red-hunters was not enough to put his career back on track. He was not destroyed, but his life would never be the same. Some nightclub and concert dates kept coming in, at least for a while, but the good months would be interspersed with long dry periods. Josh remained a folk star for the rest of his life, and the folk revival of the 1960s even brought him back a measure of commercial success, but he would never again break out of that insular world. There would be no more national hits or major magazine spreads, no Broadway shows or Hollywood film roles.

# 15

## ACROSS THE ATLANTIC
### 1951

■ ■ ■ ■ ■ ■ ■ ■ ■ ■ ■ ■ ■ ■ ■ ■ ■ ■ ■ ■ ■

There was one front on which Josh still had some victories coming. His first visit to Britain had stirred up a lot of interest, and the English entertainment world was unconcerned with the byzantine vagaries of America's Cold War politics. Josh closed out 1950 with a two-month stint at Cafe Society, then headed across the Atlantic, with Mary Chase's son Jay riding shotgun.

This time, the British booking agents had done a superb job. Josh arrived in England on January 30, 1951, welcomed with a front-page picture in *Melody Maker,* and went into a schedule that had him racing up and down the island, playing twenty-eight shows in thirty days and returning to London for a concert each Sunday. The tour was a wild success. The Weavers were taking folk music to the top of the hit parade back home, but there was no one abroad who could do anything comparable. The British public loved his blues and spirituals and were equally enthusiastic about his versions of old English numbers like "The Riddle Song" and "Molly Malone."

"To us, he was just a singer," says Charles Chilton, a BBC producer who would record dozens of shows with Josh. "We couldn't really categorize him. He could do blues and American folk, but he did English folk songs as well, and anything else that came along. And he did them in a way that was so refreshing. I mean, we sang these songs at school, with the usual stiff piano accompaniment, and then to hear them sung in this style was absolutely fascinating. It had great attraction to English people. His programs were among the best-liked programs that we broadcast over the BBC. I couldn't do enough of them."

This level of professional respect was a nice change for Josh, and he was welcomed with equal warmth offstage. The English musical community found him uniquely approachable, happy to talk with anyone who came back to his dressing room and always ready to pull out his guitar and sing a few songs. *Melody Maker* not only covered his tour but gave a brief squib on his birthday party, a gala affair at the home of Don and Sandra Luck.

Josh had met the Lucks during his first visit to England and had made their house his London base. As Don Luck tells the story, Josh had originally been staying in a flat near the Haymarket, and then had been adopted by a wealthy couple with a house in Wimbledon. "He wasn't very happy there, because [the lady of the house] had big eyes for him and she wasn't a very attractive lady," Luck says. "He wanted to get out. So one night, when we went to Chiswick to hear him, he invited us back to their flat for a party. Josh did his normal cabaret act and everything, and when we said we were going he suddenly stood up and said, 'I'm coming with you.' "

The Lucks were a vibrant, bohemian couple and reveled in Josh's company. Sandra Luck remembers that he would not even call before he came. He would just show up and yell through their letter box, and they were always glad to see him. They threw parties and went around with him to take in the London night life.

After the trials of the preceding year, England was just what Josh needed, and he responded to the wave of affection by becoming something of an Anglophile, at least in sartorial matters. He had his foot size registered with a company whose letterhead proclaimed it shoemakers to the Royal Family and later had pairs of shoes custom made and sent to him in America. He also took to wearing briefs — not yet common in the States — and for years afterward would receive his underwear by transatlantic mail.

The only problems Josh experienced on the British tour were physical. He had a swollen right hand which, he explained, had been injured when he fought off a couple of muggers in Philadelphia just before leaving the United States, and a minor car accident during the first week in Britain left him unhurt but somewhat shaken. Worst, though, was an ingrown toenail, which got so bad that in Birmingham he had to be rushed to the hospital for a midnight operation. Jay Chase recalls with admiration Josh's insistence that the show must go on, despite the fact that his foot was "bandaged up till it looked like a large forearm" and he had to be wheeled onstage.

Between concerts, Josh was hurried in and out of various radio and recording studios. He did two record sessions, one of them fairly typical but the other verging on the bizarre. In America the Weavers had conquered the pop charts by backing their banjo, guitar, and four-part harmonies with an orchestra and chorus. Their latest hit was "On Top of Old Smoky," which Pete Seeger says had been adapted directly from Josh's stage version, right down to his habit of "lining out" the lyric with spoken cues to help the audience sing along. London Records could see no reason why the same formula would not work in Britain, so Josh was paired with Bill Hill's Orchestra and a popular vocal group, the Stargazers, for "Black Girl," "On Top of Old Smoky," and a new version of "Free and Equal Blues." Folk fans today wince at the over-orchestrated Weavers records, but what Hill and the Stargazers did to "Old Smoky" was in a class by itself. The strings waltz along in a perkily Viennese manner, while youthful voices swell up and overwhelm Josh on every other phrase, and a female singer does a sort of winsome Swiss descant behind his solos.

He was more fortunate in the accompaniment for his radio performances. Charles Chilton was not only a producer but a fan. He had a special love for American folklore and had broadcast a half-hour of Josh and Leadbelly on his *Radio Rhythm* series in the 1940s, though the program had been recorded in New York and he had not actually met the musicians. The chance to produce Josh live was something of a dream come true. "The head of my department rang me up and said 'Josh White's in town, how about doing some programs with him.'" Chilton remembers. "I said 'What kind?' and he said 'Well, go and see him and see what kind of things you can think up.'

"I went to meet Josh, and asked him what kind of thing he'd like to do. It was around about Easter time, and we decided to do an hour's program with the George Mitchell Choir on Easter, of American Negro folk music, the spirituals. We did it on Good Friday, and this turned out to be quite a sensational program. I think the *Church Times* and the

*Catholic Times* wrote it up and said how wonderful it was. Josh was like God to these people.

"That convinced the BBC that there was more to Josh than they'd realized, and they said, 'We'll do a series.' So I did various series. The first one I did was *The Glory Road,* which was American Negro folk music with the choir and Josh; then we did a history of the Negro in America through folk music. We went out of our way, and I think we were among the first people, to actively combat racial prejudice with these programs. And for that reason we got an awful lot of support from British people and a lot of insults, mainly from American soldiers stationed in Europe. These programs were very, very popular — among the best-liked programs that we broadcast over the BBC — and Josh became quite a hero to a lot of people."

Chilton wrote a script for each program, combining music, narration, and excerpts from the works of African American poets such as Langston Hughes and James Weldon Johnson. He remembers that Josh, though a smooth and fluent speaker, was not very good at reading from a script, so he gave most of the narration to an American actor, Guy Kingsley Pointer. The Mitchell Choir was English and had little experience with the sort of music Josh was doing, but Chilton wisely put the singers in Josh's hands. Josh would go over each song with them, singing the parts he wanted, and then they would go off and practice until they had a sound that suited him.

Josh stayed in England until early in April, busily recording programs to be broadcast in his absence. Mary Chase had joined him and was making plans for another European tour in the fall, including more than a month of Scandinavian appearances. As in America, she seems to have rubbed most of Josh's associates the wrong way. Chilton found her irritating and takes a certain relish in remembering her constant references to the *Negro Anthology* series he and Josh were compiling as "Negro Anthropology" (a mistake she would continue to make in publicity releases), and in recalling her terror on Good Friday because she had heard that Europeans celebrated the day by hunting and killing Jews.

Josh gave a farewell concert for some 1,500 listeners at Kingsway Hall on April 7, then a last cabaret show, which drew a celebrity audience that included Hoagy Carmichael and Judy Garland. As a finishing touch he penned a goodbye letter to *Melody Maker,* thanking his fans, producers, and backing musicians. "I want to come back to Britain before the year ends," he wrote, "and again every year after."

Back in the United States, Josh played a month at Cafe Society and then various gigs around the Northeast, ending with a stint at the Surf Club in Provincetown, Massachusetts. In June he gave a midnight concert at Town Hall, which led the *New York Times* to suggest that although the audiences were still turning out and Josh was "still a knowing interpreter," much of the verve and passion seemed to have gone out of the folk scene. It was with relief that Josh once more headed across the Atlantic in August.

This time, Europe held more for him than simply the promise of work. On his previous visit he had made the acquaintance of a young Englishwoman named Rene Dannen. She had actually been introduced to Josh during a visit to New York in 1948 but says that their first meeting was unpromising. A groups of friends who were amateur folksingers had taken her to see his show, and when he came over to their table, "I was extremely rude to him," Dannen remembers. "Only being stroppy, because he obviously expected every girl in the place to fall down flat in front of him. That really annoyed me, so I was very unpleasant to him. I think, on reflection, he probably thought I was being extremely silly and funny."

Dannen was friends with the black actor Canada Lee, who was also having blacklisting problems and spending time abroad. Lee and Josh had been friends since the 1940s, and as Lee was leaving London shortly before Josh was due to arrive in January, he had asked Dannen to go see Josh and say hello for him. "Josh was staying at a hotel in Piccadilly called the Atheneum," Dannen says. "And there was a huge fuss in the paper because he'd been dancing with some white woman, and some Americans objected and made a stink about it. I was outraged at this and went to the hotel where he was staying. I went and knocked on the door, and Jay opened the door. It was about lunch time, and Josh had obviously just got out of bed and he had his dressing gown on, and he came out and he said, 'Come on in,' and then we started talking. He was very upset about this hoo-hah in the paper, he was really angry. And we just stayed and we talked. We must have talked from about lunch time till somewhere late, late in the evening. And that was it. It started from then."

Dannen remains a striking and vibrant woman, slim and pretty, with long dark hair and a sharp, incisive wit. She recalls Josh with great affection and says that she took to him immediately but at first did not consider their relationship a very big deal. When he was due back in London, the Lucks invited her to come along and meet his plane, and she says she went with some misgivings. "I thought, 'He's not going to remember me. He must have millions of girls everytime he goes anywhere; he can't remember them all.' And then, when he came off the plane, the first thing he did was he just pushed everybody aside and looked for me, and when he found me he just came straight over and picked me up and flung his arms around me and whizzed me round and round and all the rest of it. It just took off again from that, and from that time everytime he went away he would phone and he would write reams of letters."

Dannen and Josh would be lovers off and on for the next seven years, and his letters to her provide unique insights into his feelings over that period. In general, he was not a letter writer. He might dash off a page to Carol or his mother from time to time, but he preferred simply to call or send a telegram. For some reason, though, Dannen sparked a writing urge, and his letters would often be three, four, or even eight pages long. He was as surprised as anyone by this; at one point, when he had sent Dannen four letters in a little over a week, he wrote, "If anyone had told me I'd be writing one letter a week I would have said you, my friend, must be out of your head in other words you're a Goddam liar." Another letter, running five pages, ends with the sentence, "I have never written this much to my mother. Hell I must be crazy, yes crazy about my crazy baby."

Though he regularly bemoaned his lack of a proper education and complained about the difficulties of writing, Josh's letters are clear and conversational. He made some spelling errors, and his punctuation was idiosyncratic, but his handwriting was smooth and easy and his language articulate. The letters reveal a sensitivity and a loneliness that never surfaced in his public pronouncements or even in most of his social interactions. Dannen says that she was attracted to him by his gentleness and vulnerability rather than by his public persona, the superman character, which turned her off. She felt that he needed her support and that much of the showy sexiness was a cover for insecurities. "It was very important for him, in front of other people, to be seen having a girl very attached to him. He sometimes behaved outrageously when I was with him — it was quite adolescent, the hugging and the kissing and the innuendos and all of that sort of big sexy number. A lot of singers, when they're working, they don't want their woman with them. They want to get on with the work. With Josh, it was exactly the other way around. Every time he did a recording, even at the BBC with the studio musicians, he insisted that I be there with him, sit on his lap and have a cuddle, and every concert I had to be standing in the wings. It was very important for him to have that one person there for him."

Josh clearly enjoyed being pampered, but out of the limelight he also liked to have someone with whom he could relax and stop being the superman. In his letters he sometimes seems to be wallowing in misery, pointing up his loneliness, his health problems, or his financial worries. He even took to signing himself, only half jokingly, "your Trouble Baby." Of course, much of what he wrote referred to the relationship itself, which was not without its difficulties as well as its pleasures. Dannen was barely twenty; Josh was thirty-seven — still described in the papers as youthful and handsome, but in many ways old beyond his years. While the relationship provided him with a pressure valve, a supportive figure, an ego boost, and an antidote to all his troubles back home, he often worried about what it was doing to Dannen. Her father was anything but pleased to find her involved with an older, married, black musician, and even though she insisted that this did not matter to her, Josh was concerned. As he wrote in one early letter:

> Baby I am so sorry that you had to be hurt on my account you will never know how much it is worrying me. I try but I cant forget I watched your face yesterday especially your eyes and your forehead. First your eyes sunk deep and got very dark and soft then your forehead wrinkled up. Only for a second but I caught it you were hurt so bad that was when mummie said your dad turned your picture around. Honey whats gonna happen when I leave? Do you think it is worth loosing him I know what you are gonna say but I want you to think very hard about it. I still think we can pretend you have come to your self and say to him you have had enough of J.W. I cant see you all alone after I've gone.

Such moments of doubt and concern would surface regularly in his correspondence, though always balanced with professions of love and pleas that Dannen not leave him. These perhaps reflected an ambivalence about what he was doing, but both the concern and the protestations showed his tender feelings for her and helped further the intimacy between them. As in all his relationships, Josh's behavior with her was a strange mix. Over the years he would go to great lengths to insist that, aside from Carol, she was the only woman in his life, and she even had moments when she hoped he might one day marry her, though today she says that was never a real possibility. "He couldn't ever have left Carol," she says. "And quite right, too." As to other women, his letters often included, along with protestations of love, involved denials of the latest affair of which news had come to her ears. Looking back, Dannen gives these denials little credence, nor does she seem upset at his behavior. "For all I know, there was another girl coming in the door as soon as I left," she says, but for her, as for other women in Josh's life, the great thing about him was that when he was with her, he was with her 100 percent.

Josh wrote his first letter to Dannen shortly after their reunion, on the first leg of a month-long tour of Scandinavia. He had apparently needed a second foot operation in London, and things had not gone well; the infection had spread up his leg, and he had been forced to undergo still another operation when he arrived in Stockholm. "Altho I dident miss a show as yet my life has been miserable," he wrote at one-thirty in the morning, his style affected by the late hour and the medication he had been given. "The papers are raving about your baby, but I think they are feeling sorry because of my condition."

The Swedish papers revealed no hint that his health was affecting his performances, but a long interview in the music publication *Orkester Journalen* described him sitting in his hotel room with his foot bandaged and protected by pillows. Like the English reporters, the Swedes let Josh go on at some length about his musical tastes, praising Louis Armstrong and Ella Fitzgerald, Mahalia Jackson and Bessie Smith, then moving on to favorite blues singers. Not surprisingly, his list included the most uptown and popular of the early stars: Lonnie Johnson, Tampa Red, Leroy Carr, and the hokum comedian Frankie "Half Pint" Jaxon. He also praised Oscar Moore, the guitarist with the King Cole Trio: "He uses amplifiers, but he has done unbelievable blues with his brother Buddy Moore's quartet. And when he sings—I wish I could sing the way he does. . . . You've got to hear it—and if you don't like it you can go to hell."

Sweden would become one of Josh's favorite countries. He told English interviewers that he considered the Scandinavian audiences, and especially the Swedes, the best in the world. On this first solo tour he reported playing "about" seventy-two concerts. He stayed until the end of September, then flew back to London.

This time, the contingent that met him at the airport included not just his English friends but several visitors from home. Sam Gary and Mary Chase had come over, but the most excited new arrival was his daughter Beverly, who had flown in just hours before. The BBC had suggested that Josh bring Josh Jr. over, but at eleven he was still too young to appear professionally in Britain. Beverly was twelve, which fulfilled most of the British legal requirements, so she was elected instead. She was the first entertainer ever to be flown across the Atlantic at the BBC's expense, and the British press greeted her with wild enthusiasm. Newspapers ran pictures of her waving as she stepped off the airplane holding her carry-on luggage, a shoebox tied with string. They dubbed her "Miss Melody," describing her as an American TV and radio star and saying that, with Josh Jr., she had been earning a quite unbelievable £800 a week in New York theaters. Though hyperbolic, this report had more than a germ of truth. Since 1949 the White kids had been making quite a splash, both with and without their father. Beverly had distinguished herself on the Arthur Godfrey show, singing "Molly Malone" so beautifully that Godfrey had cried, and along with Bunny and Josh Jr. she had been featured in an *Ebony* article on the new crop of popular child entertainers.

Immediately after arriving in England, Josh and Beverly set off on a two-week tour, accompanied by Mary Chase and her assistant, Lenore Leonard, and by Dannen, who was introduced to the press as Beverly's tutor. Dannen says that Josh was extremely circumspect about keeping up appearances in front of his daughter, but Beverly had no illusions about what was going on. Nonetheless, her memories of the trip are mostly of the excitement of being a young star in a foreign country. She arrived almost deaf from the flight, but the tour was due to start immediately, and she did the best she could. The first time she stepped onstage, the overwhelming crowd reaction caught her completely off guard. "I walked out on the middle of the stage, never knowing that I was going to receive flowers," she says. "That was their tradition, of course, but I thought only for older people, not for me. So there I was, wearing my little mary jane shoes and nylon ruffle socks and crinoline under my skirts, and I walked out and sang my little song and I curtseyed and thought, 'The kids should see me now.' Then I turned to walk off and I tripped and fell. It was terrible; I mean it was like a season getting to the wings, crawling. They applauded and stood and I cried."

The English treated her as she had never dreamed of being treated, but Josh made sure it did not go to her head. "I was spoiled. It was always 'Miss Beverly,' and my Dad would say, 'You are Miss Beverly to them, but you are going to be here for three weeks or so, and when we get up in the morning you will make up your bed. Even if they're going to do it for you, you'll do this.'" She also had to keep up with her schoolwork, and a Manchester reporter found her doing three hours of lessons in the private lounge of a local hotel before going into "a bedroom strewn with wires and microphones [where] she spent two hours rehearsing and recording for a thirty-minute broadcast of Negro blues and folk songs." (The paper reported that she was doing the lessons with her tutor, but if Dannen was supervising, she has forgotten the fact, and Beverly just rolls her eyes at the idea of Dannen doing any such job.)

Josh was trying to do his duty as a strict parent, but Beverly soon proved that two could play at that game. One of her favorite memories of the trip is of waking Josh and Sam Gary after a night of drinking. "I had my own room, and I would go to wake them up in the mornings. I'd have the maid open the door, and I'd go sneaking around and put all the bottles of vodka or gin or whatever on the sink. Then I'd call them, and as they opened their eyes I'm pouring it all down the sink."

Back in London, Beverly and Josh would record a session of duets in a light folk-pop vein, accompanied by an English orchestra, but their main work was live concerts and performances for the BBC, including a second series of *Glory Road* programs. These featured many of the same performers who had joined Josh on the first series, along with Beverly and Sam Gary. The scripts were tailored to highlight Beverly's precocious self-assuredness, often leaving Josh to make brief comments that she would expand into impressively intellectual song introductions. These were a favorite device on the show, though whether originally of Chilton's or Josh's devising is unclear. Josh himself employed the technique on one program, introducing Leadbelly's old "Ballad of the Boll Weevil" with a flourish of Latin:

If anybody ever told you they'd just seen an *Anthonomus grandis*, I guess you'd think he was crazy or he'd been down to the museum to see one of those enormous skeletons of a prehistoric animal. Well, you'd be wrong, because the *Anthonomous grandis* is just a little fellow, a black bug no more than a quarter of an inch long, and more than half that length is taken up by his nose. But, believe me, that little black bug can do more damage in a year than General Sherman did to Georgia in his march to the sea.

Clearly, Josh was warming to his work, and Chilton took advantage of this by adapting Langston Hughes's "Simple" stories into short radio playlets, featuring Josh in the Hughes role and Sam Gary as his hip Harlem friend, "Simple."

Once again, the main problems of the trip were related to Josh's health. This time, he was suffering from bad migraines. A Bristol paper reported that he collapsed in his dressing room after his concert there and had to be carried to his car, and Beverly recalls that the attacks dogged him throughout the tour. In Scotland she was barred from appearing on stage because of her age and sang her songs from the audience. "I would sit in the front row, and toward the end of the concert I could just see the strain, and I would always go to the exit, so that when he came off we'd be together. I became used to the tones of his voice, and if the twang at the top was a little off, I knew that maybe a migraine was coming, and many times as the curtain closed I just caught him." Finally, she remembers, a doctor had to come to his hotel room and perform an operation to clear out his sinuses.

Other than that, the tour was a great success. Josh was by now an established star in Britain, and the audiences were large and enthusiastic, charmed both by his music and by the casual ease with which he led them through concerts that regularly lasted two and a half or even three hours. In Birmingham, he and Beverly were not allowed to leave the stage until they had taken eight encores. The only cooling was among the hard-core jazz crowd, which was devoting more attention to the first European appearance of Big Bill Broonzy. One of the biggest pop-blues recording stars of the 1930s, Broonzy had seen his fortunes decline with the end of the blues boom. Though he had been featured on the 1939 Spirituals to Swing concert, he had never managed to capture a substantial white audience in the United States. In Europe, however, he was lionized as "the last of the Mississippi blues singers," and English and French critics were quick to compare his and Josh's approaches, counterposing Broonzy's pure, earthy sound with Josh's more sophisticated style. The jazz buffs preferred Broonzy, and the fact that the wider public disagreed only strengthened their view. "We felt Josh was a bit sweet for our taste," says the English writer Karl Dallas. "Big Bill Broonzy played the country boy, whereas Josh played the cabaret star."

Humphrey Lyttelton writes of going to see Broonzy on a night when Josh was in the audience, and of Broonzy ribbing Josh all through the show: "He cain't sing the blues! He's from the North — ain't never heard no one from the North sing the blues." Lyttelton says that he, along with the other jazz fans in the room, was more than ready to agree with Broonzy's comments and was rather shocked to hear from Broonzy a few weeks later that in fact much of his traditional blues and folk repertoire consisted of songs he had learned or relearned at the request of his European promoter.

Indeed, as Dallas's wording suggests, the differences between Josh and Broonzy were often less a matter of musical approach than of presentation. Broonzy was some twenty years older than Josh, and although he had been a very slick performer in his heyday, he could not equal Josh's easy, sexy rapport with white audiences. Having been a much bigger star than Josh in the 1930s, he seems to have been a bit perplexed and resentful at Josh's success, and his solution (or that of his promoters) was to present himself as more "genuine," a Delta farmer singing the music of his home. Broonzy's music did sound deeper and more "country" than Josh's, but it is hard to say whether that would have continued to be true if he had found a more profitable approach to pursue. Be that as it may, the two men always got along well offstage. Don Luck recalls their hanging out together in London, drinking, swapping songs, and exchanging compliments. "There was no temperament or jealousy at all," he says. "They just seemed pleased to see each other."

Broonzy would spend much of the 1950s in Europe, especially Paris, where he was treated with a respect he had never enjoyed in the United States. In the postwar years, Paris had become something of a mecca for African American artists and developed a thriving jazz scene featuring many of Josh's old Cafe Society friends. The Golden Gate Quartet made the city their permanent home (they are still based there today), and top American bands were coming through on regular tours. In late

November 1951, Charles Chilton decided to take advantage of this talent pool by recording a Christmas special with an all–African American cast, and he and Josh flew across the Channel.

Chilton remembers the trip with some amusement. First of all, a wealthy American woman who had fallen in love with Josh had made up her mind that she would go with them. Since Josh had no interest in her company, both he and Chilton carefully avoided telling her what flight they would take, but she booked a seat on every single plane leaving for Paris and waited at the airport until they arrived. Then, in Paris, the situation was complicated further by Josh's reunion with Eartha Kitt.

Kitt had become something of a protégé of Josh's during their appearance in *Blue Holiday*, five years earlier, and writes that he had "taken a fancy" to her, buying her dresses and shoes to wear as he and his friends escorted her around New York. Jay Chase remembers that Josh also worked with her on her singing: "He helped her tremendously in terms of phrasing and feeling and understanding — not style, because Kitty was a great artist, but he worked very diligently on perfecting her career." Since that time she had become a Parisian star but remained in touch with him. When she was forced to return to the United States in 1950, to arrange the funeral of the aunt who had raised her, Josh was the only one of her friends to accompany her back to South Carolina for the burial service, and she writes that he shocked the ultratraditional congregation by bringing his guitar into the church to sing "Precious Lord."

Kitt has written three autobiographies, and they give rather different pictures of Josh and her interactions with him. In the first two, all is friendly. In the third, he and Mary Chase play a rather disturbing role. According to Chase's family and other clients, she had become Kitt's manager during *Blue Holiday*, but the relationship broke up because of their mutually forceful personalities. According to Kitt's third book, the trouble came to a head after Josh's testimony before HUAC; she says Josh was economically destroyed by it and that Chase came to her for money to support him. "Remembering how good Josh had been to [her]," Kitt not only gave Chase a check for the amount requested but said she had more money on the West Coast. Chase "rubbed her hands and said, 'You must get on a plane right away and go get it.' " Josh took her to the airport; she flew to Los Angeles, drew out her money, was met by Josh on her return, and handed over all her savings to him and Chase.

As if this were not enough, Kitt writes that the little cash she had left after buying a boat ticket back to Paris went to paying off "one of Josh's girlfriends at Cafe Society who claimed she was pregnant with his child." Then, on reaching her stateroom, she found that Mary Chase was traveling to Paris as her roommate. Finally, on arrival, Chase had the taxi take them to one of the most expensive hotels in town, presumably on Kitt's tab.

Kitt at this point got a major break, being selected by Orson Welles to star opposite him in his experimental production of *Dr. Faust*. She tells a funny story about Josh showing up in town, coming to the theater, and almost getting in a fight with Welles after Welles bit her lip during a love scene. (In her second book, Welles drives off before Josh can find him, and Josh then orders her to "stay away from Orson off stage," which she does, "knowing Josh's temper." In her third, "Josh calmed down quite easily when he realized that Orson was twice his size.") Kitt suggests that Welles bit her out of jealousy, believing Josh was her lover, though she says she was not romantically involved with either of them.

Josh's friends, whatever they may think of the rest of this story, are quite positive that Kitt and Josh were lovers. Chilton says he had to spirit off the wealthy admirer so that Josh and Kitt could be alone and that these maneuvers got in the way of putting the radio show together. Kitt also spent some time in England during Josh's visit, suggesting a romantic situation that must have been complicated, to say the least, since Dannen and Josh were seeing each other. To add to the confusion, Dannen says that Mary Chase was trying to fix Josh up with her friend Lenore Leonard. "Lenore had a lot of money, and she was very snobbish, swarming around in mink coats and all that jazz. They [Leonard and Kitt] were two very sophisticated women, very streetwise, stagewise, and everything-elsewise. I felt like a hick from the sticks in comparison to them. I can remember one time they reduced me to floods of tears. I went to the BBC, and I knew Josh was due to come, and I just sat in the lobby there, sort of snuffling and sniffing. He came and asked what had happened, and he was furious. He phoned them straightaway and he tore into them, because he was really angry, which made me feel much much better."

Kitt's current response to an interview request is to say that she "hardly knew" Josh, which everyone else involved finds utterly baffling. Whatever the truth of the story, their friendship would not last beyond the mid-1950s.

Josh spent some time in Paris in November and again in December. Chilton says that his Christmas program was recorded on the first trip and, along with Josh, featured Hazel Scott, Josephine Premice, and the Peters Sisters, a trio of singers who were starring at the Folies Bergères. Chilton recalls the Peterses with special affection: "We went to see them in their dressing room," he says. "The show was on, and at one particular point one of them said to me, 'Open the door, Charles, let's see the steps.' So I did, and at that point all the girls in the Folies Bergères chorus came down, every one stark naked, and as each one went by she bowed and said 'Bon soir, bon soir,' and went on down to the stage. And that of course is why she had the door open, because she knew at this point the girls always came down to the stage. It was quite startling, and Josh was sitting there with his eyes wide."

Back in England for a few dates at the end of November, Josh was the star of a "History of Jazz" program at the Gaumont State Theatre, a London variety house. While there, he showed that he was still as ready as ever to fight over racial issues. Though Europe was, in general, a haven from American-style racism, problems could still surface. There was the dancing incident that Dannen remembers, and a newspaper story quotes Josh as opening a cabaret show at one club by saying, "I am allowed to do only a strictly limited selection of songs, and, although many of my friends want me to drink at their tables, I won't be able to. Perhaps my skin is the wrong colour." The reporter criticizes this remark, saying that other "coloured" performers had eaten at the club, and asks why Josh must "bring his prejudices to a country where precious little colour bar exists." It is impossible, however, that Josh would have made such a remark without provocation.

At the Gaumont, Josh faced a different problem: he arrived to find that one of the other performers on the bill intended to do a blackface tribute to Al Jolson — apparently considered an integral part of jazz history. Josh was offended and threatened to withdraw unless the program was changed. "I explained that I would never have consented to do the concert had I known that an act of that kind was on the bill," he told a reporter. "Please understand that I don't want to interfere with anybody's livelihood, but I know that this black-faced minstrel routine — often practised quite innocently — has been, and is, detrimental to the interests of coloured Americans . . . I know I can't stop this kind of performance going on, but I do not have to support it by playing in the same bill. People who think I've got 'a chip on my shoulder' about this should look into the subject and learn something of its effects before they criticize."

The English managers seem to have been supportive of Josh's stance, though rather than confronting the issue directly, the Gaumont side-stepped it by unearthing an old regulation that forbade the wearing of makeup on Sunday. This allowed everyone to keep his dignity intact, and the program went on without the blackface sketch.

On December 5, Josh recorded the last of his *Glory Road* programs, and then he and Sam Gary went back to France. It is not clear exactly what he hoped to do there, but the visit was a disappointing contrast to his English success. No work was forthcoming, and the bleak reception led to an unprecedented flood of letter writing. He seems to have written Dannen every day or two, though it is hard to know exactly, since none of the letters is dated. Once again, he advises her to be considerate of her parents' feelings, pointing out that asking her mother to mail one of her letters to him was "rubbing it a little to hard," and he describes himself as feeling "guilty as hell" for getting her into the whole affair. Then, as usual, he balances the guilt with effusions of sentiment: "God must love you because he only made one of you and I am just selfish enough to think he made you for me. Am I a poor fool. Its a funny thing I never realized before that a letter could be so satisfying yet leaving one so hungry and at the same time miserabley happy." He goes on to insist that he has not been involved with anyone else, despite what she has apparently been told.

Josh's letters were not limited to discussions of the relationship. Much of the space is given over to describing what was happening in his life, the comings and goings of Sam Gary, Charles Chilton, and their other mutual friends (including Eleanor Roosevelt, who was apparently passing through Paris), and the bad situation in which he found himself: "I might as well tell you a few of things that's bugging me. 1 – No money here. Mary writes to Bev [Beverly Chase, Mary's daughter, in Paris with Josephine Premice] and tells her not to spend any money on me but Mary told me the day she left that I should come to Paris because she had money here and I wouldent have to take any from London. Love I can only say one thing if trouble was money I'd be a rich mother------"

In his next letter he wrote that Sam Gary had left but that he could not see Sam off at the airport because he did not have enough money. "Charles is having no luck," he continued. "Every body is doing all they can for me but up to now nothing is happening. I can only wait till tomorrow." There was an Italian tour coming up, but meanwhile he was struggling to get by. There was one bright note, however: "I haven't had a drink since the night I arrived and what's more dont intend to. Your baby is going to take care of his self for you. ok?"

After a couple of bad weeks, Josh finally got off to Italy. He played in Milan and in Lecco, on Lake Como, and was a great hit. But as the money troubles abated, his health started bothering him again, and he also had to contend with the problems of being in a foreign country by himself. On other tours he had always had one of the Chases or Charles Chilton near at hand, but, probably to cut costs, he went to Italy on his own and was not happy about it. His first Italian letter is headlined "Mood Evil — Nasty and in a great deal of pain."

> Right now I am some goddam place in Italy waiting for a train. I had to call Milan, the office so they could talk to the man here, he cant understand me I cant understand him so I dident know when the train would arrive since my train was late we missed connections now I wait about 2 hours and I hope the bastard remembers to put me on the right train. Never again will I go through this shit and I do mean *shit*. About the concert. I dont know how it went I just wont talk about it altho they say it was wonderful. I cant read the paper so honey I dont know. I do know that Josh dident like himself and I'm not joking there were reasons why. a) the chair was dancing all over the dam stage and b) they were sitting on the floor *on stage* while I'm trying to sing takeing pictures. c) I forgot my cappo and had to sing the first half without it. Even if I had asked for it no one would have known what I was saying but the second half I was once again J.W. . . .
>
> All I have to do is stand up there and grin huh? How in the hell can I grin? What have I got to grin about? I could tell you a lie and make you feel better, but you wouldent like that would you honey? so I'll shoot straight with you. You remember how my head was on the tour. Thats right it has started acting up again I pray to God it wont be that bad but right now it hurts like hell this time it started on the right side and my eye is aching like oh well cross your fingers. I wish I could lie in your arms put my head on your brest throw my leg over you kiss your brest and go to sleep. I wouldent have no worry then.

By December 16 he had reached Rome, only to find that there were no letters waiting for him. He wrote that his plans had changed again, and he would not be leaving for London until the December 22, which meant that he would not be able to get back to Carol and the kids in time for Christmas. And what was Dannen up to? He understood that Canada Lee was back in London and insinuated that this might be keeping her too busy to write. (Since Lee normally traveled with his wife, who was also a friend of Dannen's, it is a bit hard to sort out what, exactly, Josh was implying.) On the other hand, he understood that she might simply have failed to get his letters, and so might not have his Rome address. Whatever the reason for her silence, he was feeling annoyed and lonely.

Amid all the pain and worries, Josh managed to record an album in Italy, essentially a "greatest hits" package of all his apolitical nightclub standards, plus a couple of new gospel numbers. Then he flew back to London, where he found Dannen waiting as always. He spent only a couple of days there, though, before boarding another plane and heading for the United States. He had been away five months.

# 16

## YOU KNOW BABY
## 1952-1953
▪ ▪ ▪ ▪ ▪ ▪ ▪ ▪ ▪ ▪ ▪ ▪ ▪ ▪ ▪ ▪ ▪ ▪ ▪ ▪

The European trip, or at least the English leg of it, had been something of a vacation for Josh, not from work but from the problem of looking for it and of facing the fact that the professional structure he had built up at home over the last decade was in serious disrepair. He returned to the United States with new energy, and his situation must have seemed less bleak than it had a year before. Indeed, for a while it was almost like old times. He celebrated his return with a month-long stay at Cafe Society, then a stint at Boston's top jazz club, Storyville. In May 1952, Cafe Society closed again, but Josh's situation was not materially affected. He moved into the Blue Angel, Max Gordon's uptown club, on a bill with Eartha Kitt and the comedian Orson Bean. This was considered a more prestigious room, on a par with the old Cafe Society Uptown. In earlier years Josh had never been able to equal his Greenwich Village success in the bigger uptown venues, but this time everything clicked. Initially signed for a two-week run, he was held over for three months, and Mary Chase took out a full-page ad in *Variety* announcing that he was "<u>again</u> making <u>new</u> box office history . . . keeping the Blue Angel open all summer for the first time in its history!"

Offstage, life was still difficult. Josh's first letter to Dannen, written shortly after his homecoming, starts out by saying, "I arrived safe and found everything as bad as I expected if not a little worse . . . I just cant pretend to C[arol]. I try but honey I cant and you know she is such a wonderful woman. She has suffered so much. Why cant I? If I could get <u>you</u> out of <u>my mind</u> for a little while <u>maby.</u>"

Of course, such letters must be understood in the context of a married man writing to a lover. Whether things were really as bad at home as he indicates is open to doubt. Josh and Carol's relationship was complicated but always included a great deal of mutual respect and a commitment to be there for each other and for the children. While in Europe he had remained in close touch with his family, and the fact that his letters to Dannen survive while other correspondence does not should not overly skew the picture of his emotional commitments. In fact, even as he was writing to her, he was embarking on yet another relationship, an on-again, off-again affair with a young woman named Devon McGovern.

A seventeen-year-old New Yorker from a show business family, McGovern first saw Josh at Cafe Society when she was dating a saxophone player in the house band. As she recalls their meeting, one of the other girls in her roominghouse wanted Josh's autograph, so McGovern went backstage between sets and asked if he would sign a picture for her. "He said OK, and he pulled one out and he said 'To who?' I forget the girl's name, but he autographed it and I said thank you. And then he grabbed me and he kissed me. That was the end. That was all she wrote."

Soon McGovern became friends with Sam Gary and his wife, Sue, and a regular visitor at their home. The Garys lived on 151st Street, just around the corner from the Whites' apartment, and would regularly drop by the Whites', where Sam would sit for hours playing pinochle and drinking. Sue Gary and Carol White never hit it off, however. Sue was a sportier type who seems to have regarded Carol as snooty, and she did nothing to discourage Josh's extramarital romances. Indeed, the first time that McGovern visited the Garys, Sue insisted that they go over to Josh's house. "Of course, he almost died when he saw me," McGovern remembers. "Suzanne was a shit stirrer. So, we went back around to her place, and she said, 'Wait, he'll be here,' and of course he came. And he said, 'What are you doing here?' And I said, 'I just came up to visit Suzanne.' So we sat and talked for about an hour, I guess, and I went home and he went back to his own home, and I didn't see him again until that fall."

McGovern would be involved with Josh off and on through the 1950s, but she did not have any written correspondence with him, and he seems not to have made the sort of commitments to her that he made to Dannen. Living in the same city with him, and coming from a sophisticated theatrical family, she never had any illusions about his faithfulness to her; she just liked being with him. "He was the most exciting man I've ever known," she says today. "The way he laughed — my God, it was wonderful. You have to have heard it to know. He had such joy in living." As with all his girlfriends, Josh made McGovern feel that she was special, whatever he might do when they were apart. "I knew that I mattered to him," she says. "I know that he cared a great deal about me, and it didn't matter who else there was. He was worth it. He was a very loving person and a very giving person. He gave so much that it was worth it."

Carol would say much the same thing at times, though for her the situation was much more difficult. She stayed with Josh through thick and thin, but then she had very little choice. She was at home with the children and could neither control Josh's behavior nor support the family on her own. For her, the bottom line was that whatever else happened, he continued to do his duty as a father. Meanwhile, she represented the solid rock in his life, the person and place he could always come home to, a refuge from the stresses and wildness of the nightlife and touring.

As for the other people in Josh's life, they all seem to have accepted his dual commitment to his family and his extracurricular activities. Once he walked out of his apartment, everyone took it for granted that he would be accompanied by pretty companions, some of them for one-night stands but others for periods of years. Many of Josh's friends rather enjoyed the spectacle, and virtually all his business associates doubled as social secretaries, receiving his romantic correspondence and relaying messages. Dannen at first sent her letters in care of Mary Chase, which led to yet another contretemps. As Josh explained in a letter to her that June, Chase's landlords had been interfering with his mail as part of a general objection to his visits: "They have been trying to get her out because they would rather Negros to ride the service elevator. They dont want them comming in the building at all so the Law[y]ers told us that they said I even had my mail coming there so you see I hadent been receiveing my mail. Any way Mary is selling her place and getting another."

This sort of problem was becoming routine for Josh. Even though the northern version of segregation was less institutionalized than its southern counterpart, there were plenty of places that did not want black people coming in and out, especially if they were black men visiting white women. During a club residency in Chicago the singer Katie Lee was asked to leave her hotel after she refused to stop having Josh come by to give her guitar lessons. That time, the story had its humorous side, though the humor was pretty bitter. Josh and his brother Bill were driving Lee around town to look for a new place, Lee recalls, "and I said, 'God, Josh, this is really white of you.'

"He slammed on the brakes, pulled over to the side, and said, 'Do you know what you just said?'

"I said, 'What's the matter?'

"He said, 'What if I said, "That's black of you?"'

"I said, 'I'm sorry.'

"He said, 'You don't know what you're saying, do you?'

"I said, 'No.'

"Billy's sitting in the back, and he starts laughing, and Josh said, 'Billy, that ain't funny.'

"And I said, 'No, I guess it's really not funny.' But as I look back on it, it was pretty funny.

"Josh just shook his head: 'Oh God, you white folks.' "

The quick return to Europe Josh had planned kept being postponed, so in September Dannen flew over to the States. He had promised to meet her plane but was once again in the hospital, this time in Boston, so instead he sent Bill to pick her up and bring her to him. Looking back, Dannen thinks this hospitalization was for ulcers, but she is not sure. The fact is, Josh seemed to be going into hospitals a lot in the 1950s, and most of his friends came to view the visits as another sort of act, the flip side of the invulnerability he projected onstage. Dannen thinks he was a bit of a hypochondriac, and she is far from alone. She adds that shortly after her arrival in America she decided to study nursing, and Josh was instantly and amusingly enthusiastic about the idea: "He thought it would be splendid, because then as he got older and more ill I would be well qualified to look after him."

It was not that Josh had no genuine health problems. The ulcers that had troubled him for a decade must have been exacerbated by the stresses of political, financial, and romantic complications, as well as by his constant drinking. "He was always chewing endless packets of antiacids," Dannen remembers. "And he thought that if he drank his scotch with milk it would be better for him, so he would do that. And something else he used to do, he wouldn't put salt on his food; he put lemon juice. That wouldn't be so great for the ulcer, but he thought it was better for him."

Josh was also beginning to suffer from psoriasis of his fingernails, which made his fingers crack and bleed when he played guitar, and at times this condition spread to other extremities as well. Since at least the mid-1940s he had been troubled by recurring bouts of laryngitis, and by the end of the 1950s he had developed still another problem, severe bursitis in his shoulder, which at times made it almost impossible for him to hold his instrument. Then there were the migraines and the foot problems. And yet, night after night, the show had to go on.

"I ain't never seen that man refuse to get up there; I don't care how bad he felt or how tired he was," says Bill Lee, who regularly played bass for Josh in the late 1950s. "I've seen him with laryngitis so he couldn't talk, and he had that disease of the fingernails and he'd be showing me the blood and he couldn't touch the guitar, and all of this would be happening backstage and the managers would just be sick. He'd be saying, 'I don't think I'll be able . . . I don't think I'll be able to . . . call the doctor,' and as soon as the announcer calls, 'Ladies and gentlemen, the Bitter End—or the Round Table or wherever it was—is proud to present Josh White!' he'd hit the stage singing about Jerry, that old mule and all of the rest of the songs. I mean, his fingers were bleeding, but when he got on the stage it was like nothing."

After weeks of concerts, with every concert followed by another night of partying, Josh could look on a hospital as something of a haven. Virtually everyone agrees that the frequency of his visits in the 1950s was out of proportion to the seriousness of his illnesses, but that was not the point. "A lot of times, when Josh would come home, the doctor would put him in the hospital just to make him be quiet," Carol says. "To keep him quiet, and also to kind of eliminate some company. When he was on the road he would neglect himself, and by the time he got home he was just so out, so tired, so run down. He never knew how to say, 'No, I can't go tonight, I have to go back to my hotel and go to sleep.' So the doctor would put him in just to cleanse him. He had to be disciplined, because he never had time to rest."

After the Boston gig, Dannen settled in New York as a guest of Sam and Sue Gary, remaining with them for some eight or nine months.

Josh would get away from home when he could to spend time with her, and sometimes he took her along to visit his brother Bill at Eleanor Roosevelt's house in Hyde Park, or when he went out on the road. He also insisted, to her surprise and discomfiture, that she come by the family apartment to meet Carol and the children. "Carol was very nice," Dannen says. "She must have seen through the act—she wasn't stupid, she was very clever—but she was perfectly polite."

Dannen tried her best to make friends with the family, even allowing Josh Jr. to put his pet white mice up her pants leg (she still shudders at the memory), but she naturally felt uncomfortable about the visits and is a bit puzzled as to why they happened. For Josh, though, this seems to have been standard procedure. He did not like to sneak around, and over the years he never made any great effort to conceal his multiple female companions, especially those who were of any importance in his life. He simply introduced them as friends, and as long as the women behaved properly, everyone else went along with that explanation. Many, if not all, of his serious girlfriends would be invited to the White home, and some returned the favor, inviting the family to visit for a weekend out of town, or taking one or two of the kids to dinner. As long as appearances were maintained, this seemed to make the situation easier for everyone. In later years, Carol continued to speak with affection of several women whom other people identify as Josh's longtime lovers, and the open "friendships" made it possible for him to keep his home and social lives at least somewhat cohesive.

Of course, things were easier when he was on the road. That fall brought a Canadian tour, followed by a several-month residency in Chicago, where he was the first act booked at a new club, the Black Orchid, and played to packed houses night after night for ten weeks. Though the dates are not completely clear, Dannen and McGovern each seem to have joined him for part of this visit. A magazine piece shows him at the Orchid, sitting on stage with his foot in a cast, and tells how he broke his left ankle falling down the stairs in his Chicago apartment. It notes that he was spending his spare time studying Italian in preparation for going to Italy to star in a version of *Porgy and Bess* to be produced by the film director Roberto Rossellini, but this plan soon fell by the wayside—if indeed it was ever seriously considered and not simply a vague idea mentioned to a reporter.

In April 1953, Josh returned to New York for a month at the Blue Angel, then was booked as the opening artist in what would be Cafe

Society's last comeback attempt. Judging by the *New Yorker* listings, which come and go without explanation, the return was shaky from the outset. The club seems to have staggered along with frequent openings and closings, then finally breathed its last in mid-December. Josh appeared intermittently through these months, sharing the bill with jazz artists such as Roy Eldridge and Wingy Manone, but they must, all in all, have been depressing gigs.

The worst blow of 1953, though, was the loss of Mary Chase, who died suddenly on April 5 while she was in Chicago with Josephine Premice. Chase had alienated many people, but she had been absolutely devoted to Josh. She had also been someone with big ideas, whose view of the entertainment world and his place in it was in no way limited to the folk scene. To her, he was a brilliant entertainer whose work transcended genre, and she imagined him as an all-around cabaret and concert star, and an actor on Broadway and in Hollywood. As long as she was out there fighting for him, there was still hope that he could climb back to where he had been before *Red Channels*. With her gone, he would continue to work, but there was no one to make grand gestures like taking out full-page advertisements in *Variety,* or pursuing a career for him outside the folk and cabaret worlds.

Chase's death came at a critical time. Aside from Josh's personal run-in with the red scare, the country's new conservatism was having a deadening effect on the folk scene in general. What had been hailed as wholesome, all-American fare was now associated in many people's minds with subversion, and nightclub audiences that had cheered the Popular Front idealism of the Roosevelt years were sticking to the safer, assembly-line product of Tin Pan Alley. Some critics would argue that folk music had simply run its course as a popular nightclub style, but the Weavers' hits argue against that conclusion and suggest that its sudden decline after 1951 was due specifically to political pressures. It never entirely disappeared, but by the end of 1953 it had ceased to be a staple of New York nightlife. Josh and Burl Ives were pretty much the only folksingers left on the cabaret scene, and their bookings grew fewer and further between. Ives's burgeoning success as an actor made up for his reduced club dates, but that route would have been difficult for Josh even had Chase been alive and fighting for him. With her gone, the situation was crippling.

Politics aside, Josh's career was also hitting the midlife doldrums. In February 1954 he celebrated his fortieth birthday, and though still a commanding presence, he was no longer the hot show-business property he had been a decade earlier. Audiences kept coming, but he had ceased to be particularly newsworthy. The ink was going to newer, younger names, in particular his sometime protégé and friend Harry Belafonte, who was singing "Timber" in an open-necked shirt and knocking the ladies dead. A year earlier, *Variety* could still say that "Belafonte has a lot of s.a. [sex appeal] for the dames, but he has a long way to go to assume the authority that Josh White projects with more or less the same kind of numbers." Soon, however, Belafonte would be America's most popular black performer, with hit records and a booming film career. His act was built largely on a foundation Josh had constructed, but Belafonte was a fresh, new face, and the fact that he did not play guitar freed him to bring an even greater physicality to his performances.

Josh was also suffering from his own artistic conservatism or, as his critics would have it, his laziness. He continued to learn the occasional new song, but the body of his repertoire had not changed in a decade. Old fans were satisfied to hear "One Meat Ball," "Jelly Jelly," "Joshua Fit the Battle of Jericho," or "The Riddle Song" yet again, and they might even bring along a few new customers, but there was nothing to excite the press or to kick his career back into high gear. He was still a celebrity, but the fact that he was giving one more concert was no longer newsworthy. As if to drive this home, of the four *Ebony* articles that mentioned him in 1953 and 1954, none was about his music. One was about the black friends of Eleanor Roosevelt; another was about how various performers dealt with hecklers, and two were actually about his kids: Beverly, Josh Jr., and Judith were celebrity models for a summer picture spread on ice cream sundaes, and Josh Jr. and Beverly were prominently featured in a piece on the Professional Children's School.

Both Josh Jr. and Beverly were frequent guests on Josh's shows and would sometimes accompany him on tours out of town when school and other commitments permitted. Josh Jr. was also doing well as a child actor, appearing in several more plays as the decade progressed. It was an exciting time for him but also the beginning of a difficult relationship with his father, who took the "Josh Jr." business seriously and often seemed to be trying to make his son into a younger model of himself. "I have always wondered what would have happened if I couldn't sing," Josh Jr. says. "I also wonder how life would have gone had they waited for me to show an interest in show business. I think I enjoy music too much not to have eventually done it, but it was never up to me. Like getting a guitar at eleven was not my choosing. That was the old man and Mary Chase. You know, I was singing with him at four — now, 'Wouldn't it be cuter at eleven if he had a guitar?' I was big enough to wear that same black velour shirt, open, and the same pants. 'Isn't that cuter?' She looked at it in that way, and I understand it. But I will always credit them for me not playing as much guitar as I could, because they put it on me instead of waiting for me to ask. From eleven till twenty-one, when I went out on my own, I learned songs for the stage, but I never just took the guitar and said, 'Let me try and see what I can do.' "

If Josh had pushed his son to imitate him only onstage, that might have been manageable, but he extended the process into more serious areas. "I was eleven years old when he arranged for me to start my sexual experiences with an older woman in her twenties," Josh Jr. remembers. "I have a feeling maybe it was something that had happened to him when he was that age, and I think also the old man was a bit homophobic, that having two sisters older than me and then two on the other end, he wanted to make sure that his little boy remained a little boy. Then, as I got to be a teenager, a lot of women came my way through the old man. There's the album *Empty Bed Blues* of his, with a white woman on the cover. I was at that session, and I got set up by her because she said she had a girlfriend who would just love me."

Josh Jr. says he considered the sexual episodes a perk that helped ease the burden of always having to be a younger version of his father. Still, he does not doubt that they were, in their own way, damaging. He was reaching adolescence just as his father was beginning to show signs of age in both body and career, and he hypothesizes that this might have created a degree of subconscious sexual competitiveness. Certainly, Josh's behavior toward him on this front was anything but consistent. At the same time that Josh was setting his son up with women, and even in a couple of cases sharing his own girlfriends, he could turn around and act like a protective father. Vivienne Stenson, a folk promoter in Toronto, remembers that when Josh Jr. went out on a date with the younger sister of one of her friends, Josh not only insisted on knowing exactly where they were going but drove by the restaurant, "making quite sure that they were sitting demurely and behaving themselves."

The mixed messages can only have increased the normal confusion, frustration, and excitement of adolescence. As the years went on and Josh Jr. developed his own career, he would always be under the pressure of being compared with his father. Josh tried to be supportive, encouraging Josh Jr. to find his own style and never pushing him to do blues or other typical Josh White numbers, but he could also subtly undermine his son's independence. Jackie Washington remembers seeing Josh Jr. onstage performing and Josh reaching up from a front table in the middle of a song to retune one of his son's guitar strings.

Whatever damage all this may have done, it would not surface until later. Thinking back to the early 1950s, both Josh Jr. and Beverly remember the biggest headache of traveling with their father to have been the endless parties to which he dragged them. Sometimes, to their embarrassment, he would single out a woman and sing one of his more romantic songs — often "You Know Baby (All I Want from You Is a Kiss)" — directly at her, as the whole party looked on and she turned bright red. Even if he was not attempting a musical seduction, he would always be "on," continuing the night's performance rather than just relaxing and being sociable.

"Once he started playing, he wanted quiet," Josh Jr. says. "All of a sudden, the party had to cease being a fun-loving thing, people talking, and everyone had to be quiet and hear Josh sing."

"He was a show-off," Beverly chimes in. "Anybody who didn't make it to the concert wouldn't have to worry about it, 'cause afterwards there would be some place where they would congregate, and he would just keep going."

"He'd bring out the guitar for another damn two hours," Josh Jr. agrees. "We'd sing and he'd drink and be more debonair, and we'd be like, 'Come on, Dad, let's go home, jeez.' "

On the whole, though, their memories of life at that time are good — surprisingly so, considering the state of their father's professional life. After Chase's death, Josh went through a very difficult time. Chase's husband, Harry "Jay" Gruber — known in the White family as "Big Jay," as distinguished from her son, "Little Jay" — took over partial management of Josh's affairs, but no one remembers him doing much more than keeping up with the phone calls that came in, and some suggest that he did not even do a particularly good job at that. The New York cabaret bookings dried up, and although there were still occasional residencies in L.A. or Chicago, hotel shows in the Catskills, and some college dates, things were slow. Still, Josh seems to have managed to keep his family reasonably ignorant of these difficulties, and none of the children remember any economic hardship. They do not doubt that times were hard, but they never went hungry, and as long as major disasters were averted, there was no reason for them to know that the bills were overdue.

# 17

## JOSH AT MIDNIGHT
### 1954-1958

∎ ∎ ∎ ∎ ∎ ∎ ∎ ∎ ∎ ∎ ∎ ∎ ∎ ∎ ∎ ∎ ∎ ∎ ∎ ∎ ∎ ∎ ∎

Bad as things were, there were a few rays of light on the horizon. The Weavers had reached a national audience with their bright, engaging style and had inspired a lot of young people to pick up guitars and banjos. Throughout the 1950s there would be a growing groundswell of interest in folk music. College campuses nurtured folksong societies and provided work that, although not as lucrative or regular as the long-term nightclub engagements of the past, carried the better-known performers through the bad times. People's Songs was gone, but *Sing Out!* was getting off the ground. The magazine might assiduously avoid mentioning Josh's name, but many young folk fans still regarded him as a giant.

Indeed, Josh's status throughout the 1950s would often be that of a big fish in a small pond. The major labels, films, and network television shows were barred to him, but the newer, smaller folk promoters considered him an established star, and some, at least, assumed that his price would be out of their reach. When they discovered otherwise, many were thrilled to be able to present an artist with his experience and name recognition, and he continued to comport himself with the same assurance and command as in his glory years. Any discouragement was kept private; his admirers saw only the confident, masterful performer he had always been.

One such admirer was Jac Holzman, who had started a small New York record company called Elektra. Holzman was dedicated to releasing well-recorded, well-packaged records of music that he personally liked. Like Musicraft's Samuel Pruner back in the 1930s, he had first toyed with the idea of recording classical chamber music, but he quickly settled on doing folk.

"There was a very practical sense to folk music," Holzman explains. "Although I was a big baroque music fan, no matter what I did, somebody else could come out with a competitive version. I didn't want to deal with that, so I figured that I could afford to record folk music, which is essentially one or two people and their instruments, and there is only one Josh White, so you have exclusivity."

By 1954, Holzman had recorded several folk and international artists, including Sonny Terry, Oscar Brand, Ed McCurdy, and Susan Reed. He had known Josh's work since his student days and, when he heard rumors that Josh was interested in recording, was excited at the prospect of having a major "name artist" on his fledgling label. He got in touch through mutual acquaintances and arranged a meeting with Josh and Jay Gruber. "We certainly had no budget for recording an artist of Josh's stature and I explained this to his manager," Holzman later wrote. "The best I could do was a hundred dollar advance, but we did promise Josh that he could record his music his way."

The money was hardly better than Josh had received for his first solo sessions more than two decades earlier, but, not having made an American record in seven years, he was hardly in a position to bargain. Whatever the immediate payment, a new record would be helpful in generating some publicity and might lead to better things. Also, Josh had an idea that might make the release something of an event. Since it was roughly twenty-five years since he had begun his recording career with Joe Taggart, he suggested doing an anniversary album.

Josh's Elektra debut was both a departure and a return to palmier days. The long-playing record had come on the scene and, especially for the upscale jazz and classical markets, had begun to replace 78 rpm albums as the format of choice. These first LPs were ten-inch discs, the same size as most 78s, but they ran at 33 rpm and held some twelve to fifteen minutes of music on each side. Introduced in 1949, these records allowed classical compositions or jazz jam sessions to be played without interruptions every three minutes (though most pop and folk recordings would continue to be tailored to the three-minute, single format favored for juke box and radio play). Josh's first Elektra effort was one of the few folk or pop albums to take full advantage of this new development. It consisted of a double set of ten-inch LPs, one a mix of old and new songs, and the other a twenty-three-minute retelling of the John Henry story.

The symbolism was obvious. Once before, Josh had been crushed by circumstance, and his appearance in the Broadway *John Henry* had revived his career and taken him to new heights. Now, he must have hoped that lightning would strike twice. Called "The Story of John Henry . . . a musical narrative," the piece was an extended monologue interspersed with songs. The record label credits it to Jacques Wolfe and Roark Bradford, authors of the Broadway show, but Holzman insists that it was Josh's own work. "He totally put that together," he says. "He told me the sequence; we recorded all the parts; and then I strung everything together in the editing afterwards." Unlike the play, which had made John Henry a river roustabout, the record follows the old folk legend, portraying him as a steel-driving man on the railroad. The musical interludes include a couple of Bradford and Wolfe's songs but also bits and pieces Josh had picked up throughout his life: Leroy Carr's "In the Evening," work songs learned from Leadbelly, and "Baby, Baby" from the Libby Holman album. The piece ends with the traditional "John Henry" ballad, a highlight of Josh's Cafe Society shows.

"The Story of John Henry" was an unusual project, quite different from what other folk performers were attempting. It was perfectly suited to Josh's relaxed manner and became something of a classic on the scene. The companion record was also exceptionally well done. It included old favorites such as "Black Girl" and "Free and Equal Blues," but half the songs were new, and Josh was playing and singing with renewed energy. Compared with his recent European albums, it sounded fresher and tougher. His playing was particularly strong, and Elektra's high sound quality brought it out beautifully.

Holzman was very happy with the result and quickly cut two more albums. The exact dates are a bit sketchy, but *The Story of John Henry* seems to have come out early in 1955, followed by *Josh at Midnight* toward the end of the year and *Josh Sings Ballads and Blues* in 1956. The latter two were released in the new twelve-inch LP format (*Josh at*

*Midnight* was Elektra's first twelve-inch disc), and their success was at least in part due to the situation created by the technological changeover. With 78s out of fashion, Josh's earlier recordings were now obsolete, so Elektra had a ready-made audience for new versions of the old standbys. *Josh at Midnight,* the biggest seller of his Elektra albums, was a "greatest hits" package, with new versions of "One Meat Ball," "Timber (Jerry the Mule)," and "St. James Infirmary," among other favorites. In one important way, though, it departed from his previous albums: it was overwhelmingly devoted to blues and blues-related material.

This was a fundamental change and would mark Josh's musical approach for the rest of his career. He recorded over a dozen more LPs, representing roughly a third of his lifetime output, but none of them included "The Riddle Song," though it continued to be featured in his live shows and is often remembered as his most popular number. There would still be occasional English ballads, but they were rarities, and especially on Elektra, Josh was no longer marketed as a multifaceted folk singer; instead, he would be known for blues, spirituals, and other African American styles.

Artistically, it was not a bad choice; Josh's guitar work, especially, had always been strongest on blues and gospel material, where it could act as an equal partner rather than simply framing his vocals. For marketing, it also made a good deal of sense. When Josh joined Elektra, it was well on its way to becoming the premier label for cabaret-style folksong. Holzman was an astute salesman, finding strategies that highlighted the unique qualities of his artists. Jean Ritchie was the traditional ballad singer. Oscar Brand was the funny-song man, recording albums of light ditties by and about sailors, doctors, members of the various branches of the armed services, and even skiers (unlikely as this last concept may seem, Elektra also released a ski album by Bob Gibson). Ed McCurdy became the expert on historical erotica, recording a multivolume series titled *When Dalliance Was in Flower and Maidens Lost Their Heads,* which became ubiquitous on college campuses. Theodore Bikel was a one-man United Nations, singing songs from all over the globe, and Cynthia Gooding was his female counterpart.

With this niche-oriented strategy it was natural that the label would promote Josh as its bluesman, and the approach worked better than even Holzman had expected: "He did very well, relative to (a) what the marketplace was at the time, (b) what our expectation was, and

(c) what the costs were. The records sold nicely, and continued to sell over the years. I have no idea what the numbers were, but they were enormously satisfactory. He was right up there at the top; the only artist who did better was Theo Bikel."

With the new emphasis on blues, Elektra also to some extent reshaped Josh's public image. Both *John Henry* and *Josh at Midnight* had back-cover photos that showed him stripped to the waist, emphasizing a more primal sex appeal than the silk-shirt, Cafe Society look. Still, Elektra did not go overboard in the direction of rootsiness. Josh's sophistication, if not his devotion to medieval balladry, remained a selling point, and his third album for the label teamed him with a jazz rhythm section and leavened the blues material with moody readings of the late-night cafe standard "One for My Baby" and the Billie Holiday specialty "Gloomy Sunday." Although neither is a masterpiece, they provide an interesting glimpse of Josh's approach to a sort of music that was never a major part of his stage act but must have often been sung at the after-hours sessions of Cafe Society musicians.

Holzman says that both the sidemen and the songs were Josh's idea: "He wanted to see if he could expand his repertoire base a bit, and I was inclined to let him do it." Indeed, Holzman remembers that Josh pretty much called the shots on all his records. "I just followed the music," he says. "He always came in prepared, and he was a joy to work with. In the studio, we kidded around a lot; we knew it would take us a couple of nights to record each album, and we just tried to keep the mood elevated. I would turn off the lights and light candles — he loved that. The only problem we ever had was if there was a pretty girl around the studio. He would either chase her all around, or he would sing the songs to her, which could be a real plus."

The Elektra records sold well by Holzman's standards, but in the mid-1950s that was nothing earthshaking, and by no means enough to remove Josh's financial worries. His letters reveal a constant preoccupation with money. In November 1955 he was back in England, but even there he was running into trouble. In his one surviving letter home he first reassures Carol that his headaches are not bad and his health is fine but then goes on to say,

Baby I wish I could tell you that every thing is wonderful, but I cant so I must tell you the facts. The people that are paying me or should I say that are supposed to diden't live up the contract. I am supposed to recieve weekly $1,000 and my 11th + 12th week salary in cash given to the Foster agency [which handled his British bookings], even before I start working. Well this is what happened they gave Fosters a post dated check which we know now will bounce so if they dont get the cash by monday I am taking them to court meaning this I wont be working for them after today. Thats why no more has been sent to New York and baby I am not the one to send it. Thats Fosters job. . . . I am now going to fix a Army tour. I'll know by Wed. They wanted me last month for 13 weeks but Jack Fallon and Charles Chilton had to say no because of the contract Jay [Gruber] had sign witch means hands off. Maby it isent to late now so they are phoneing the people for Germany & France. No matter what I'll let you know at once [and] if its no then I'll be home in 2 weeks. So be sure to take care of you for me please.

As it turned out, Josh did find work, both in concerts and on radio. His visit also yielded two interesting record albums and a book that would influence a generation of British guitarists. The first record was *Sam Gary Sings,* the only solo recording of Josh's longtime friend and musical partner. Issued on London's Esquire Records and in the States on the short-lived Transition label, it purports to feature one Dean Laurence on guitar, and to have been recorded in Cambridge, Massachusetts, but Laurence plays on only two cuts, and the dates would seem to place Josh and Gary in England. Wherever the record was made, most of it features Josh, tastefully framing Gary's vocals and adding vocal responses on "Scandalize My Name," a rewrite of "Scandalous and a Shame," the song with which Josh had made his recording debut at age fourteen. Josh often backed Gary at parties and gave him solo spots on stage, but this was the only time Gary stepped out of his sideman role on disc.

The other album was recorded for the English Marble Arch label and shortly reissued in the States on Mercury Records' jazz subsidiary, Emarcy. It includes several of Josh's standard numbers but also four tracks with a full horn section, including trumpeter Kenny Baker and three saxophones. Two of the band cuts are blues standards, but there is also a wry number by the New Orleans singer and guitarist Danny Barker, "I Had to Stoop to Conquer You Baby," and a nice jumping version of the 1951 Clovers rhythm-and-blues hit "One Mint Julep." As always when singing in a jazz setting, Josh sounds thoroughly at home.

He was not a great jazz or R & B singer, but his relaxed, informal style could easily be adapted to other genres, and his forays out of the folk-blues mainstream were clearly a pleasure for him, even if they never made much impression on the public.

More important than either record, at least in Britain, was *The Josh White Guitar Method,* not only the first book of Josh's music but the first blues guitar instruction book ever published. It was the brainchild of Ivor Mairants, a jazz and classical guitarist, teacher, and musical entrepreneur who was working with a London music store and publisher, Boosey and Hawkes. Mairants, who had been bowled over by Josh's guitar tone ever since hearing him on a wartime radio broadcast, met him at a recording session for London Decca. As he listened to him more, Mairants was impressed by the harmonic complexity of Josh's work: "He was a master of the art of linking chords by means of suspensions or passing chords . . . quite unlike the other folk or blues singers of his day who used no such sophistications." Caught up with the idea of learning Josh's style, Mairants proposed that they get together and that he make transcriptions of some of Josh's pieces.

Josh at first demurred, saying that it would be too time-consuming, but was finally persuaded, and Mairants came around to his apartment in Airway House near the Haymarket. A "beautiful chick" answered the door and explained that Josh was sick in bed. Mairants called a doctor friend who happened to be a Josh White fan and got him taken care of, then came by for a few hours every day for the next week and made transcriptions from Josh's playing. "There were no short cuts," Mairants would later write. "We selected a suitable tune which he sang and played while I wrote down both the vocal melody and accompaniment which I then played back to him from my manuscript. His ear was infallible. I never heard him play a wrong note nor would he pass one."

The *Guitar Method* was published by Boosey and Hawkes in 1956, with Josh and Mairants listed as coauthors. Charles Chilton, an enthusiastic amateur guitarist, acted as guinea pig for the transcriptions and wrote a foreword, and Josh penned a brief note of appreciation: "I want to commend and thank Ivor Mairants for accomplishing what has heretofore been known as 'the task impossible.' In other words, to set into musical copy the notions of a completely unorthodox 'musician' — one who, technically, can neither read nor write a single note of music as it is known to the world today. The remarkable part of all this is the fact that during the one week that we had to work on this book, I had to do four shows for the BBC with the George Mitchell Choir, rehearsing with them, writing with Charles Chilton and his Girl Friday, Sheila, not forgetting the dozens of telephone interruptions plus being overtaken by the 'flu, all at the same time."

The book, which comprised a basic guide to Josh's style and complete accompaniments to seven songs, offered a window into the world of blues guitar for young players on both sides of the Atlantic. Stefan Grossman, who would become the dean of blues guitar instruction authors, and John Renbourn, among the most important guitarists to come out of the British folk revival, both started out with it. Renbourn says that he had first become caught up in blues after being taken to Josh's concerts by his mother and that Josh's was the only good instruction book available, providing the basis for most of the players of his generation. This was particularly significant because the book had not only blues but such British ballads as "Molly Malone" and "The Riddle Song." In the 1960s the young English musicians would take Josh's idea of using blues techniques to play English traditional songs, and expand and develop it to create a European fingerpicking style that overflowed into rock, pop, and jazz and continues to dominate the European folk scene.

Mairants was very pleased with the book's success and further capitalized on Josh's reputation by commissioning a German guitarmaker, Oscar Teller, to make copies of the Martin 0021 guitar Josh favored. Mairants brought one of the new guitars to Josh and, with his approval, was soon marketing it under the Zenith brand name as the Josh White model.

Josh flew back to New York in mid-February 1956, and his reception was once again in harsh contrast to his English success. His first letter to Dannen apologized for not writing sooner, but "I found things so bad I hadent the heart to write . . . I have no phone and no loot so couldent cable." He added that he had been in bed for eight days with the flu and that Jac Holzman had delivered her letters, now being addressed care of Elektra, and would mail this one.

The next few letters were largely taken up with denying rumored romantic affairs, but they also mentioned business problems that had not been cleared up in England; Josh asked Dannen to contact Charles Chilton and make sure that any monies due from the BBC shows be paid directly to Josh rather than to the Fosters agency, which would only forward it to another English agent, Gale, to whom he owed

$1,000, presumably in unrealized advance payments. As for the American scene, at the end of March he was still writing "I havent work as of yet, no phone, no gas or electric and no loot to pay rent. I am in a fucking fix no matter what happens." In June he wrote that he had a four-day engagement in Boston, his first since returning to the States, but nothing else until a Detroit booking at the end of July. "You know what its like when one doesn't work especially me," he wrote. "You can imagine how tough things are."

If all his complaints were true, it is something of a mystery just how the Whites survived this period. Even Carol could not answer the question. "I did not really know, as far as hard times were concerned," she said. "Because whatever happened, Josh always saw that we had everything. And, of course, if he didn't work, I was very happy to have him home. So it might have been slow, but we lived good."

Friends pitched in with some financial help; Elektra continued to come through with occasional advances on royalties; and there are also stories of guitars being pawned and loans taken out (one reportedly cosigned by Eleanor Roosevelt). Then there were the women, some of whom were a good deal richer than Dannen or McGovern. McGovern says that with her, at least, Josh was quite open about the economic component of his relationships. "A great many of the women that he was with had money, and that was his purpose," she says. "I'm being blunt about this, but he would be the first to tell you. He'd say to me, 'I have to spend some time with this so-and-so,' and suddenly he would have money again to take care of everything. It sounds brutal, but it's true. He did what he had to do to survive. Because he knew that he had responsibilities. He had his children, he had his car, there were things that had to be done and this was the only way he could do it."

The good news was that in 1956 Josh had reached the low point of his career and begun his climb back to popularity. Indeed, his reports to Dannen are at least in part misleading: nightclub bookings were still few and far between, but concert gigs were picking up some of the slack. In April, Holzman and Leonard Ripley produced a solo show at Town Hall, Josh's first appearance there in five years, and it was well received. The records were selling, and he was beginning to draw a new audience along with the older fans. Elektra was a small label, but it was respected and popular with the college crowd. For a lot of undergraduates, *Josh at Midnight* was the deep, sensuous counterpart to Ed Mc-Curdy's whitebread ribaldry, and its packaging made the most of Josh's sex appeal, the cover shiny black with a beautiful drawing of Josh by the artist W. S. Harvey, and its liner notes speaking of "stars throb[bing] in a black sky overcast with spirals of smoke."

The worst of the red scare was over, and folk music was bouncing back with surprising force. Belafonte would have his first hit in October with "Jamaica Farewell," and at roughly the same time the Tarriers put both "Cindy, Oh Cindy" and "The Banana Boat Song" in the top ten. Despite Holzman's desire for "exclusivity," he had not signed a long-term contract with Josh, and as the folk movement picked up, other labels came knocking. The first was a small outfit, Period, which had recorded a ten-inch LP in February 1956.

Period's liner notes indicate that it was one of the new "hi-fi" outfits that were springing up with the advances in recording technology. "The recording techniques used, despite their novelty, were quickly understood and accepted by Josh who made an easy and effortless adjustment to an exacting set of recording standards which, at the outset, were new to him," Period's producer wrote. "We invited him to listen to some of our other recordings and see the unorthodox methods we employed. On the first playback of one of our records his face was the guarantee that here, indeed, was the beginning of another terrific date. He grinned at the right places, liked what we liked, didn't say a word until it was all over. Then he virtually yelled, 'That's it!' He wanted to know how it was done, how long it had been going on, what else we had to play back. . . . Josh was our kind of musician from the word go. He knew how to listen."

It is interesting to contrast the notes on Josh's release with those on Period's Big Bill Broonzy album, with which it would be combined when the label went from the ten- to the twelve-inch LP format. Though he was a longtime blues star, had been king of the early Chicago scene, and now made his home in Paris, Broonzy was described as a "shy, tall farmer" from Arkansas whose "virile, profoundly simple style . . . was merely the natural expression of a normal function . . . a relaxing outlet for him after a full day's work in the field." Broonzy was a great artist, but not the sort of person one would demonstrate one's recording technology to. Josh, by contrast, was "a celebrity who 'needs no intro-duction,'" a show-business giant whom they were lucky enough to sign to their label. After the hi-fi listening session, they had pursued him for weeks, as Josh "kept delaying his decision on various aspects of the date.

We didn't mind because by that time we knew he was taking this just as seriously as we." In the end, Josh brought in Beverly, Bill, Sam Gary, and a rhythm section and recorded the album in one evening, before leaving for Hollywood.

Within a month of the Period date, Josh was picked up by a larger label. ABC-Paramount, a new company with little reputation but strong corporate backing, would soon become a major player, with Lloyd Price and Ray Charles bringing a string of hits, but when Josh recorded for the label, it was still searching for an identity. His appearance seems to have been due to the personal whim of Creed Taylor, a celebrated jazz producer who had enjoyed Josh's London Records album. "I became interested by virtue of that recording, and I just gave him a call," he says. Inspired by the small combo sound of the English recording, Taylor assembled a similar lineup: Cafe Society pianist Sammy Benskin, bassist Leonard Gaskin, and the veteran jazz drummer Panama Francis.

The first ABC release was *The Josh White Stories,* yet another collection of Josh's familiar standards. There was little to distinguish the album from his previous recordings, and the appearance of more Josh White material right on the heels of the Elektra albums is a bit surprising. Decca and Folkways had released roughly simultaneous albums of his work back in the 1940s, but he had at that time been at the peak of his career. Now, he was just making ends meet, and the only thing that made it feasible for Elektra, ABC, or Period to record him was that, relative to his name recognition, he was so easy — and inexpensive — to work with. His fee was reasonably low — his ABC-Paramount contract called for him to be paid union scale, plus three advance installments totaling $1,000 — and he provided his own material, knew it backward and forward, and played the main part of the instrumental accompaniment. Other singers needed musical arrangers, but Josh, even if he used sidemen, just sat down with them and whipped up "head" arrangements on the spot. Holzman remembers that most of Josh's albums were recorded in a couple of sessions, and even the more ambitious projects cost no more than $2,000, including recording expenses, musicians, and Josh's advance. As for Taylor, he says that the sessions required virtually no rehearsal and rarely more than one take per song. "Josh came by my house, and so did the other players, for parties a couple of times, and we recorded some of the same stuff that they would sing at the parties," he says. "It was very quick, just like Stan Getz.

He just sang the songs, and I would get the best sound possible. What more was there to do? Josh White was a work of art; I put a frame around it."

Taylor bridles at the idea that his recordings of Josh should be classified as folk, insisting that to him Josh was just a great performer, and genre was irrelevant. "Obviously it would end up in that bin in the record store," he says. "But he used to sing at Cafe Society. Billie Holiday sang there a lot, too, and I would put the two of them in the same pocket. That's the regard I have for him." Taylor enjoyed Josh as a person, as well, and recalls going with his wife to the Whites' for dinner a few times.

ABC was happy enough with Josh's work to bring him back into the studio for four more sessions in November 1956 and February 1957, released as *The Josh White Stories, Volume Two*. This album is chiefly notable for including Beverly's American recording debut: she sings "Sometimes I Feel like a Motherless Child" and a duet with Josh on "I Know Moonlight," her voice sounding strong, if rather stiff and careful on the gospel number. "Moonlight" and another pop-flavored composition, "Don't Smoke in Bed," were new additions to Josh's recorded repertoire, though he had been singing the latter for years and had even performed it as a special request for Princess Margaret on his first English visit. Both had quite ordinary lyrics set to melodies that were not really Josh's meat, and they fit rather badly with the rest of the album, which is mostly blues. Indeed, it must be said that on the whole the ABC albums are no match for Josh's Elektra work, either in musical terms or in the way they were packaged and marketed. For instance, where Elektra brought in prominent critics to write liner notes, ABC just printed the song lyrics on the back cover. This would become something of a folk cliché, pioneered by Mitch Miller on his "sing-along" albums, but it is hard to imagine many people sitting in their living rooms and singing along with Josh's rendition of "Trouble in Mind" or "Strange Fruit."

Josh had now recorded seven albums in a bit over two years, and even if the club dates were not coming as they used to, the situation was clearly improving. The Gate of Horn in Chicago and the Hungry i in San Francisco had started featuring folk music, and Josh was doing annual, month-long residencies at both. Les Brown, co-owner of the Gate, recalls that they first took Josh because his price was surprisingly low but that he did not do as well as more traditional performers like

Big Bill Broonzy: "He was a bit slick for our clientele, a little more a nightclub performer than a folk singer." Nonetheless, he would keep coming back to the room well into the 1960s. A particularly poignant residency came in the winter of 1957–58: Broonzy was dying of lung cancer and wrote to an English friend that Josh had come to Chicago to see him. Reportedly, "he was singing in a club just round the corner and coming in regularly to help look after Bill. He was also giving Bill money to tide him over his hospital expenses."

If Brown remembers Josh's Chicago reception as mixed, Josh's San Francisco employer reports a very different situation. Enrico Banducci, owner of the Hungry i, says that Josh was always one of his best draws. "He'd call me and say, 'Listen, I want to spend a little time in Frisco; can I stay a month?' And I'd say, 'When do you want to come?' So he'd give me his date and we'd make it up. He would stay for as long as he wanted to stay—a month, two months. All the liberals in San Francisco would be there, and there were quite a few of them. There's 450 seats in that room, and they used to fill it. The Gateway Singers would probably open the show, and then Mort Sahl would be in the middle, and then Josh would close it. They'd do sometimes four shows a night, and sometimes five on Saturday. He was wonderful, I gotta tell you, and he developed a big following there. Christ, I used to just take a little ad—one column and one inch—say, 'Josh White: Hungry i.' That's all I'd have to say and, boom, they'd come in."

San Francisco would become, much like Chicago, something of a home away from home for Josh. In both cities he developed not only a professional base but a circle of friends among whom he could relax. As in New York, these people tended to be black and from outside the entertainment world. In Chicago he still had his cousin Marie Miles, who would cook up big meals of "soul food," greens and chitlins, and reminisce about the days when she had found him freezing on the streets with Blind Joe Taggart. He also spent days at a time with a friend named Wardell Murphy, whom he referred to as his "brother." Murphy was an auto mechanic and would work on Josh's cars, but mostly they would sit around and play cards with Sam Gary or Josh's brother Bill, or make the rounds of the night spots. In San Francisco he became friends with a younger black folksinger, Stan Wilson, who adopted many of his stage techniques and would become something of a West Coast Josh White. Wilson recalls that Josh was unfailingly helpful and encouraging to him, but that as far as socializing went, Josh was as likely to spend the evenings quietly playing pinochle with Wilson's father as to do anything related to the entertainment world.

As folk music began to resurface, Josh also got some jobs a bit farther afield. In the summer of 1957, for example, he played a two-month residency at the Waikiki Tavern and Inn in Hawaii. Wilson was in Hawaii at the time, as was a young guitarist named Bob Shane, who knew both of them from his college days in the Bay area. Shane, who would soon form the Kingston Trio and usher in the next folk revival, recalls that the three of them would meet after their shows at an all-night restaurant, the Captain's Diner. He remembers showing up there with his first six-string guitar (having decided to switch over from a four-string, tenor model) and Josh taking two hours to show him the new fingerings.

Of course, Josh's social life was by no means confined to male friends. McGovern went with him for the Waikiki residency, and in his off time he wrote to Dannen as well. As usual, his letters reveal more worries than optimism. His psoriasis was acting up, and he wrote that "right now my fingers are like boils." Then, in an eight-page letter — his longest ever and the last that Dannen has — he begged her not to stop loving him and wrote that he and Carol were growing further apart. From there, he segued directly into talk of the next European tour and asked her to look into why his English record, now apparently available in the States, had not paid him anything despite an agreement that he would get 50 percent of the American sales.

On page five he turned to a new problem. Apparently, a reporter from *Confidential*, the popular scandal magazine, had appeared on Dannen's doorstep, looking for dirt, and Josh was concerned: "Baby what made this guy come to you about confidential? Tell me all about it next time please? And you know I know you wouden't give him or any one the time of day if it was going to hurt me because if it hurt me then it would have to affect you the same way. Why? Because you are me and I am you." He filled the next page denying a story Dannen had evidently heard about him and "a dame in Churchill's," and revealing yet another side of his musical taste as he recalled making love with Dannen while listening to Erroll Garner records. Then he returned to the first theme: "Doll if that story got out then I don't know how bad it would be for me. As far as home is concerned she knows but I wouldent want the kids to know yet so I hope I have answered your question as far as the public, it wouldent do me much good ok?"

The *Confidential* story never happened, but Dannen was beginning to realize that the future she had contemplated with Josh was largely, if not completely, illusory. "He always said when Judith was older, was thirteen — that was always the point he made — then he felt he could leave Carol and we could be together and all the rest of it," she says. "And half of me believed it and the other half — the sensible half — didn't. And a tiny bit of him probably meant it, in fantasyland." In real life, things were rather different. In 1956 she had met someone else and wrote Josh about it. His letter shows that the news had upset him, but she knew he was not going to leave Carol, so Dannen faced the facts and ended the affair. Despite his initial protestations, she says that Josh behaved beautifully. "He was great. It was sort of, 'Oh, well, it's probably the best thing for you, and make sure you're happy,' and all the rest of it. He was very sweet. His main concern was always, was it OK, was I happy."

This was typical for Josh. Within the limits of what was possible for someone who was married and carrying on multiple affairs, he tried to behave decently, and both Carol and his ladyfriends tend to point up how much better he acted than a lot of the other men around him. A striking example would come in 1959 when, near the end of their affair, McGovern had a son by him. Like Dannen, McGovern had finally had enough of dealing with the confusion of her relationship with Josh. "I had gotten married to somebody in my workplace, simply because I could no longer stand the pressure anymore," she says. "I got married and we moved in a new apartment uptown and all of that, and it was fine. And then for some reason or other Josh was at the Gate of Horn [in Chicago]. I'd been married maybe three months, but I called him. He said, 'I thought I'd never hear from you again.' And I said, 'You're hearing from me.' He said, 'When are you coming?' and I said, 'I'll be there at the weekend.' I made an elaborate lie up to my then husband, and I went out to Chicago, and that's when I got pregnant.

"I guess I got pregnant in June, and he drove me home in November. He drove me to my parents' house, and he walked in and said, 'She's pregnant.' He didn't make any bones about it and say, 'It's not mine." He said, 'She's pregnant and it's my child.' My mother wasn't horrified, she was like, 'I see . . .' But he was totally good about it. He didn't hesitate to commit to relationships."

McGovern went back to Chicago, working as a waitress and selling advertising for a newspaper, until the baby was born. "Danny wasn't due until the 17th of March, but he was born on the 20th of February. Josh came into town, it was about the 10th or 6th of March, and he was running late, so he called me from the road and said, 'Call [the club], tell them I'm running late and I'll be there.' I said, 'All right.' He walked in with all his clothes, and I forget who was with him, I think a bass player. And he said, 'Where can I put these, I'm in a terrible hurry, and did you call them?' And I said, 'Yes,' and I said, 'Put [the clothes] in the bedroom on the bed and I'll take care of it.' He walked through the bedroom, and the crib was over there, and he walked in and put the clothes on the bed, and he turned around and walked out the door, and he stopped dead and said, 'Whose baby is that?' And I said, 'Whose do you think, you asshole?'

"He picked him up and he said, 'Oh, my God.' And I said, 'There he is.' He said, 'I thought . . .' And I said, 'No, he was born six days ago.' He was very pleased."

Josh's sense of responsibility did not extend to recognizing the child in front of his own family or the world at large, but McGovern insists that he did all he could. "You know, it was '59, darling," she says, with absolute conviction. "He could hardly acknowledge him. In those days it would have been just ridiculous. But he saw him a number of times. He would come and see him at my father's house. He was a very loving parent."

While his personal life continued to be supremely complicated, Josh's professional career was finally getting straightened out. Back from Hawaii, he got another booking that pointed to better times ahead. In Boston, Manny Greenhill had formed the Folklore Society, and he opened his first concert series by presenting Josh at Jordan Hall, the auditorium of the New England Conservatory, where he had not played since the 1940s. A rave review in the *Christian Science Monitor* praised Josh's sure showmanship, his efforts as "an unrelenting voice of conscience for the plight of the Negro," and his "great contribution to American folklore."

By this time, Josh had also acquired a new manager. Len Rosenfeld had been booking and running a club at the Coonamesset Playhouse, near Falmouth, Massachusetts, and when Josh appeared there, the two hit it off immediately. "He asked me to help him out," Rosenfeld recalled. "We talked about it, and I decided to give it a try." The first sign of Rosenfeld's involvement was the aforementioned correspondence with Ed Sullivan, initiated in 1955 while Josh was still being managed by Gruber. It is not clear exactly how the transfer worked, but shortly thereafter, Gruber was out of the picture and Rosenfeld was in. Though he had no experience as an artist's manager, he liked Josh personally and was prepared to learn as he went along.

Rosenfeld handled the managerial chores for the rest of Josh's life, and he expanded his stable over the years to include many other folk artists, both big names — Odetta, Bob Gibson, Buffy Ste. Marie — and smaller acts such as Lisa Kindred and the guitar ace Dick Rosmini. Unlike Mary Chase, he was completely devoted to the folk music scene, which was both a benefit and a limitation for his clients. If he had been more inclined toward mainstream show business, he would never have taken most of them on, but he was not the sort of person who would turn a career around or make someone into a star. Though by all accounts a brilliant man, he was not particularly ambitious, and he never pushed either himself or his clients very hard. Nonetheless, he was a much better manager than Gruber, and he began to find Josh dates at colleges and clubs around the country.

Shortly after signing with Rosenfeld, Josh added an energetic partner to the management team. Marty Erlichman met Josh when he booked him, along with Oscar Brand, Theo Bikel, and others, for a hootenanny at Carnegie Hall on Thanksgiving Eve, 1957. "I woke up in Josh's house the next day," Erlichman recalls. "And he introduced me to his family as his manager. After Thanksgiving dinner we walked up Harlem, and I asked him what he had meant by that. He said that we had had a couple of drinks last night, and I had told him that I had bought him for less money than I thought he was worth [for the Carnegie date], and that if I was his manager I would have gotten more money for him, and while I had never managed before, I was in the business, producing concerts, and I was bright and from Brooklyn.

" 'I remember saying all that,' I said, 'But I don't remember saying I was going to be your manager.'

"He said, 'Hey, we both had an extra drink, it was the whiskey talking. That's OK.'

"I thought about it, and that was a Thursday, and I called him on Monday and said 'Let's start it.' "

Erlichman's memory is that within the first couple of years he and Rosenfeld between them had tripled Josh's income. Meanwhile, yet another manager was to appear on the scene, albeit rather briefly. A contract from March 1958 finds Josh signing on with Albert Grossman, whose shift from running the Gate of Horn to handling artists would culminate with his signing of Peter, Paul and Mary and Bob Dylan. The Grossman contract seems to have been designed to deal mostly with concert performances in the Midwest, however, and it was dissolved by Josh the following year after Grossman failed to book the thirty annual concert dates specified as his minimum responsibility.

With two or three managers and a bunch of new records, Josh was doing as well as or better than all but a handful of folksingers and even beginning to pick up some television exposure, at least in New York. Still, for the folk scene the mid-1950s were the calm before the storm, economically if not artistically; there was plenty of music but not yet a lot of money being earned. In Greenwich Village another revival was brewing, but the new breed of singers and musicians who would burst out in a few years were still working the "basket houses" of McDougal Street, playing for whatever tips the customers threw into a basket that was passed around several times per set. The better-known artists from previous years were not going to play those rooms, but the cabarets and jazz venues were no longer booking folk music except on rare occasions. What remained were concerts and college gigs, which Josh in some ways preferred but which were one-nighters rather than the multimonth club residencies of the past. In January 1958 he drew 900 people to Toronto's Eaton Hall, and they called him back for multiple encores. But although such shows paid well, they were not coming regularly enough to provide a good living.

For Josh, as for Pete Seeger and other established folk artists, the campus gigs were what kept body and soul together. Between jobs his managers would take to the road on their own, lining up the next string of dates. "I remember renting a car, Lenny and I, and going upstate, stopping at colleges and booking him," Erlichman says. "All the schools knew him; they just felt he was beyond their means. They'd say. 'We don't have enough money to buy him.'

" 'Well, what do you have?'

" 'Well, we've only got $1,000.'

"I'd pretend to go over my route book: 'Well, $1,000 could buy you a Tuesday night.' "

The northeastern college circuit had become Josh's new stamping ground. "We'd be up in New England, Williams College and every college that you would ever think of — every white college," says Bill Lee, a jazz bass player who had first come in to play with Josh at the Gate of Horn in Chicago and toured with him regularly for the next few years. "We'd be up there in the wintertime, and after we'd finish the concert, Josh was gonna go play in the student room, because he'd want the girls to get feeling hot and everything, and he's gonna sing 'Jelly, Jelly,' and the fellows could go have a good time with the girls. He's gonna stimulate everybody. We went all over there, and I seen places I didn't even know existed or could exist, all through New England."

Josh had played colleges before but never to this extent, and much of his new beat was terra incognita to him. He had been used to working cities — Detroit, Chicago, San Francisco — so from a New York point of view he was going into the hinterlands. The lone telegram that Carol happened to save gives an idea of his bewilderment: MRS WHITE — JUST RECEIVED WIRE WHAT SATURDAY WHERE IS DARTMOUTH COLLEGE WILL ANSWER WHEN WE RECEIVE ANSWER LOVE JOSH

That telegram was sent on November 3, 1958. Two weeks later the Kingston Trio's recording of "Tom Dooley" hit number one on the *Billboard* pop chart. The folk boom had begun.

# 18

# FOLK
# REVIVAL
■ ■ ■ ■ ■ ■ ■ ■ ■ ■ ■ ■ ■ ■ ■ ■ ■ ■ ■ ■ ■ ■

The "Great Folk Scare," as the folksinger and humorist Utah Phillips has dubbed it, was a strange and fertile period in American music. The six years following the Kingston Trio's first hit brought the folk world a wave of mainstream attention and commercial success that alternately delighted and horrified the longtime acolytes and cognoscenti. As in any pop music boom, stars were born, soared, and died in record time: the Highwaymen, for example, put "Michael, Row the Boat Ashore" at the top of the charts for two weeks in July 1961, then had four more records in the top one hundred, the last—the theme song from *The Bird Man of Alcatraz*—exactly one year later.

To many of the new stars, and even more to the impresarios who managed and recorded them, folk music represented none of the purity and social importance that had attracted people such as Alan Lomax or Pete Seeger to the field; it was simply the latest fad. Bob Shane recalls that the Kingston Trio started out as a white calypso band and added whatever other songs caught their fancy. "We were just entertainers," he says. "We did all sorts of material, but they wanted to call us something, so they called us folksingers. And when a guy hands you a big check and says, 'You're a folksinger,' you say 'You bet your ass I am—I'll be anything you want me to be.' And that's basically what happened.

People realized you could take guitars and banjos and take old folk-songs and throw it at the people and they'd buy it."

Indeed, for a few years it seemed to be just about that simple. The modus operandi for folk stardom was to put together three or four squeaky-clean college types and hand them a stock collection of the latest folk favorites, plus one or two less familiar songs that might hit as singles. The original pattern for these groups was the Weavers, and many slavishly imitated their guitar and banjo backing style and the pairing of two or three male voices with a pretty female singer. The Weavers' suit-and-tie stage wear was, in general, replaced by more casual attire, but shirts and slacks would still be carefully coordinated, and neatness definitely counted. When Peter, Paul and Mary came along, they almost failed to get a record contract because of the men's beards. Even the Kingston Trio, coming out of the bohemian San Francisco scene, was viewed as a bit racy — clean cut but not virginal — by many teenagers of the Eisenhower era, and groups such as the Tarriers were considered daring because they mixed white and black performers. On the whole, though, folk music was marketed as a healthy, middle-class alternative to the greasy dangers of rock 'n' roll.

Indeed, the folk revival can be seen as a brief hiatus in the rock revolution. It is no coincidence that the Kingston Trio's success in 1958 set off an explosion, whereas the Tarriers' hits two years earlier had not. In 1958, Elvis went into the army, and Jerry Lee Lewis dropped from sight after marrying his thirteen-year-old cousin; in 1959, Buddy Holly died in a plane crash, Little Richard gave up his pop career to enter the ministry, and Chuck Berry was convicted of a Mann Act violation. With Fabian and Frankie Avalon as the standardbearers of rock 'n' roll, and black music abandoning pop teenage sounds for the deeper seas of soul, the way was clear for something else to hit on the white youth market. The folk boom would last until the Beatles arrived to point a new direction and usher in rock's second empire.

Histories of the folk revival, with the benefit of hindsight, tend to focus on Bob Dylan and other New York- and Boston-based performers, whose work overlapped with the later rock world and forever affected popular music. This makes perfect sense but ignores what the mass of folk fans were buying at the time. During most of the folk boom, the 1950s cabaret stars, though no longer particularly relevant in artistic terms, were still on top of the commercial heap, along with the perky collegiate singers. Eric Darling, who had replaced Pete Seeger in the

Weavers, led the Rooftop Singers to number one on the charts with "Walk Right In." In the younger generation the New Christy Minstrels charted several records, and it was their lead singer Barry McGuire's 1965 hit, "Eve of Destruction," rather than Dylan, that took protest music to middle America. Then, there was a fraternity quartet from the University of Washington, the Brothers Four, who racked up a long string of hits, and of course Peter, Paul and Mary's smoothly upbeat versions of Seeger and Dylan material.

For Josh, as for many performers of his generation, the revival was a somewhat anomalous experience. On the one hand, it brought plenty of work, new clubs, television exposure, and a flood of young listeners. He had been one of the original folk popularizers, blazing a trail for people like the Kingston Trio, whose musical approach clearly owed a heavy debt to him and Burl Ives. Bob Shane says that it was by watching Josh and listening to his advice that he learned how to present himself on stage, how to control an audience and make them listen to the songs; Peter Yarrow of Peter, Paul and Mary declares a similar debt. The new folk fans may not have made this connection explicitly, but they reacted with gratifying fervor to the same sexy, commanding persona that had captivated the New York cabaret audiences two decades earlier.

On the other hand, Josh and his peers lacked the perky youthfulness that was one of the folk boom's strongest selling points. He and Theodore Bikel would be mentioned in pretty much every article on folk music but more often as predecessors to the new stars than as stars in their own right. This would have been annoying enough by itself but was even more aggravating when one considered how painfully amateurish many of the new groups sounded. Where the Kingston Trio could at least manage some tight harmonies and sprightly banjo licks, a lot of the new acts were kids who had heard a Trio record, bought their first guitars, gotten together a few friends, and within months were in the recording studio, supported by a powerful record company and a producer trying to catch a ride on the hootenanny merry-go-round.

Josh was supportive of any young player who came his way but bemused by the caliber of talent that shared the stage with him at college clubs and on the network variety shows. "Sometimes I'm afraid that the fad is killing folk," he told one interviewer. "Folk singing is story telling; you've got to live your story and believe it, feel what you're doing up there. It's getting so that anyone in blue jeans who can twang a little on the banjo thinks he's a folk singer."

Any misgivings, though, were more than balanced by the fact that there was a huge new audience ready to hear his music. After years in the wilderness, Josh was suddenly getting bookings at nightclubs and college campuses across the country, and the press was showing up again to cover his appearances. He re-signed with Elektra (which had dropped him when his asking price rose but now was flush with folk revival dollars) and recorded four more albums. All were essentially revisitings of earlier material, with a few new tunes thrown in, but the young crowd hearing him for the first time reacted much as their parents had.

Josh even found himself back at the scene of his greatest success. Cafe Society was gone, but a new club, One Sheridan Square, opened in the same basement room in September 1959, and Josh was booked as its first headliner. Kelsey Marechal, who reopened the room in partnership with Martin Lorin, says that Josh just seemed like a logical choice. "We knew his work and admired it, and our press agent was Ivan Black, who had been the press agent for Cafe Society Downtown, so I don't remember whose idea it was, but we knew that Josh had been one of the original people at Cafe Society and it had been rather important to him and vice versa. And it worked well. I think he came in for four weeks, six weeks, something like that. His agent, Marty Erlichman, thought that it was going to be mostly the old people coming in, and Josh, of course, wanted young people as well, and we got both. Marty resisted my suggestion that we have the Clancy Brothers and Tommy Makem, who nobody outside of folk music had ever heard of, and we invited Josh to come down to meet them, and he liked their work and immediately told Marty that they were going to be on the bill with him, and Marty ended up managing the Clancys."

Josh had already met the Clancys socially. Liam, the youngest brother by some ten years, remembers that his brothers threw a party when he first arrived in New York, and Josh was there. "I was rather shocked, actually," Clancy remembers, laughing. "Because I was just a pup, coming from Ireland, and here was my great hero and he didn't seem to have any interest in sounds or music or anything like that. He was only interested in this woman who turned out to be a notorious, expensive call girl who was making headlines in America at the time. She spent the night on Josh's lap — or at least most of it. At one stage of the night she set her eye on me. I was twenty, and here was this very, very worldly, charming, beautiful prostitute, and she called me aside and said, 'You have the most *wonderful* innocence.' Yes. And then she went back to Josh's lap."

Clancy's memory aside, Josh continued to do most of his partying with guitar in hand. His social life was full of romantic liaisons but also of music, and he was unfailingly supportive of any young player or singer who sought him out. "Josh was the sweetest, most open and most gentle person," Len Rosenfeld remembered. "And he was totally giving to the new generation of singers."

Indeed, there were few things that seem to have given Josh more pleasure than acting as a father figure for young musicians. Katie Lee remembers him, back in the 1950s, taking an afternoon to help her find a guitar. "I had this big huge Martin guitar at that time, and Josh came in to listen to me. And he says, 'Part of the problem you're having is you're fighting that damn guitar. Why don't we go this week sometime and pick out another guitar for you.'

"I said, 'Groovy, let's go. Cool.'

"So he came by and picked me up, and we went all over town, to all the guitar shops. He would point to one and take it, and then in five seconds it was strung. That was a little trick he had, to do it so fast. He had people standing around watching in all the places that we went. He'd put this guitar together and get the tone out of it that he wanted, or didn't get it. Finally, we were about desperate, ready to give up, and we went into Lyons Music Store.

"He said, 'We'll go in here, baby and see what's happening.' So he pulled out three or four guitars, and he sees one clear up by the ceiling, hanging up, and he asked the man to go get it, and in three seconds or so it's strung, and he gives it two or three bangs and pulls on it and says, 'This is it,' and he hands it to me.

"I said 'Wow, that's nice.'

"And he said, 'Sing.'

"I said, 'Here?'

"He said, 'Sing some notes with it.'

"I didn't know why I was doing this, but I did it and it sounded just great, and he said, 'Yup that's it.' "

Josh went on to give Lee playing tips, telling her to go into a dark closet to practice so that she would get in the habit of not watching her fingers, and she also remembers him comforting her after she had been insulted by a drunken customer. He would be equally generous with Peter, Paul and Mary, the Kingston Trio, Don McLean, and anyone else who asked him. To him, it made little difference if the questioner was a rising young star or simply a kid who wanted to strum a few chords at home. A *Chicago Tribune* piece said that he was being called "the grand-daddy of folk," and described the way he greeted the mob of young fans who turned up to hear him at a local coffeehouse:

> He answered questions carefully, explained techniques, and gave two quick lessons. . . .
>
> "Here, try this," he said to one college musician.
>
> "Me? Play your guitar? Mine's right outside," the boy answered anxiously.
>
> Josh shook his head, tapped the guitar, and watched with a faintly pensive look while the boy played. "Should be an A7th there," he said once—and later, "Good, that's good."
>
> The door kept opening and more people edged in. Some lined up along the walls and stayed, some got their autographs and left quietly. The casual ones lit cigarets and lounged in chairs, asking questions.

Along with the lessons and advice, Josh also offered some words of caution:

> "These kids have been spoiled some by hootenannys. You notice they start clapping right away, without listening. Listening is everything. You've got to have big ears for music.
>
> "But they're appreciative, and they're eager. I'm turning more now to college concerts because you can reach them at that age. It's important to reach them. We have a lot of fun, too."

Josh liked being around young people, and he tried to keep in touch with what was happening in the musical world. Back in England in 1960, he provided a full-length article for *Melody Maker*, commenting on blues and folk but also on the more current sounds that would soon fuel the "British invasion." After suggesting that Leadbelly, had he remained alive, "could have been one of today's top rockers," and delivering a brief lecture on blues singing, he moved on to Ray Charles and Elvis Presley:

> [Charles is] tops among the young blues men I've heard. He's mixing spirituals with blues though, and many people don't like that.
>
> I think he makes a mistake when he takes a beloved spiritual and

turns it into a sex song. That's sacrilege, and a man with Charles's talent could write his own blues and leave the spirituals alone.

You talk about blues artists and you have to mention Presley. I think Elvis has something.

He's listened carefully to Negro blues men and sanctified singers, swallowed all of that music and combined it with hillbilly sound. I guess you have to admire him for that.

I can enjoy Elvis, but I can't watch him. Those movements that he and a lot of rock 'n' rollers go through with guitars they can't play very well — are real phony. A singer like Elvis doesn't need that stuff.

This criticism was typical of Josh's outlook on performing. Though critics were more and more frequently condemning his work as slick and showy, he felt that his performances grew out of his experience, and "phony" was his ultimate term of condemnation. To him, whatever stage business he used was simply a way of reaching the audience and of helping him tell the stories in his songs. Listening to other people, he would speak well of any performers he considered true to themselves, whether or not their music was to his taste, and take others to task for forcing or overdramatizing their material.

Some people think you must make a person have an orgasm on every word. If sex is in there, it's going to come out whether you try for it or not. Don't practice for it. And I won't call names, but that's what some of these people are doing.

Now Pete Seeger . . . Pete has a lot of balls. Pete is a gutsy man — unpretentious. I mean, a spade's a spade, and what he feels he does. I buy that. He's not trying to plan for this to happen or that to happen. Pete sings a song — tells a story. But when Seeger feels that a song isn't in his field, he doesn't bother with it — which is a beautiful thing.

Woody Guthrie and I came up together. Let's face it. He's got his bag, and it's a great bag he's in. Dylan has a hell of a bag. He writes some beautiful things . . . that I believe in. I'd rather hear someone else do his songs than to hear him do them, I tell you this, but I wish there were more Dylans around . . . writing. I mean this, really. He writes a hell of a song. He thinks, which is important. But, as of yet, I haven't heard him perform the things he's written. I think he doesn't do them justice, actually.

Josh's views on Dylan were typical of a rift that had formed in the folk scene, one that would further isolate him and most of the other early stars. He was from a world of professional entertainers, people who saw their craft as performing for an audience. To him, as to most artists of his generation, being professional meant dressing well, having your show well organized, and delivering carefully rehearsed material in a polished, expert manner.

In the 1950s, though, a new aesthetic had arrived. In the jazz world, Miles Davis not only failed to grin and joke but made a point of turning his back on the audience, forcing it to deal with the music and only the music rather than enjoying some sort of pop show. In folk circles, along with and in vicious opposition to the clean-cut college groups, there was a new wave of what Dave Van Ronk — one of the leaders — now refers to as *neo-ethnics:* musicians who patterned themselves on their fantasy of the rural primitives the Lomaxes had recorded for the Library of Congress. Among this group the very idea of entertaining an audience was anathema. Folk music was something that existed outside the commercial world, and if it had to be played onstage, every care was taken to avoid anything that smacked of show biz. As Van Ronk puts it, looking back with wry amusement, "If you weren't staring into the sound-hole of your instrument, we thought you should at least have the decency and self-respect to stare at your shoes."

On one level this attitude could not have been more absurdly distanced from its putative source. Whereas the neo-ethnics came onstage in loggers' shirts and blue jeans, the singers the Lomaxes had recorded, when they were occasionally brought up to the city to give concerts, always wore their best clothes. Those who had had professional careers in the rural South actually presented a problem for the new arbiters of taste, as they were entertainers from the tops of their neatly slicked hair to the tips of their boots. Lonnie Johnson and Lightnin' Hopkins had to be told to use acoustic rather than electric guitars; T-Bone Walker had to be told to sit still rather than play guitar behind his head and do the splits; hillbilly entertainers had to be discouraged from showing off a century's worth of minstrel routines and singing their versions of Tin Pan Alley pop numbers. "It's always the mistake that people make," Pete Seeger says. "What was old-fashioned was more 'genuine' than something new-fashioned. In other words, Doc Hopkins and his Buckle Busters were more genuine [than current country stars], because they weren't electric. But they were as commercial as they come for 1928, 1935."

To the new arbiters of folk purity, Woody Guthrie was a god, whereas Burl Ives and Oscar Brand were pop-oriented junk. Leadbelly, safely dead and unable to show up in a natty suit singing "Dancing with Tears in My Eyes," was a god, whereas Josh had sold his soul for Cafe Society dollars. (Seeger was in a class by himself, regarded as a bit too much of a showman, but a hero for political reasons and a sincere supporter of the older, rural stylists.)

"Josh was too slick for us," Van Ronk says. "Occasionally, somebody would exhume one of his recordings from the '30s and have a good word to say about that, but that was as much to prove a point as because they actually liked them. The perception was that Josh had adapted too completely to nightclub work. And we were right. Josh had smoothed all the rough edges off his act, and he was essentially a cabaret singer. And we were not interested in that at all."

Van Ronk adds that his own opinion was somewhat more nuanced. "I personally always liked him. I mean, I didn't like him when he sang 'Molly Malone' — at that point I'd, discreetly if possible but undiscreetly if not, make for the door — but I thought his blues stuff was first rate, always. Any time he wanted to do 'Outskirts of Town' or something like that, I was his. And I loved the way he played the guitar. Also, I met him a few times, and he was always very, very nice to me. So I had no animus for him."

Others took a harsher view. The *Little Sandy Review,* a small but influential publication that set itself up as the guardian of folk taste, savaged Josh whenever his name came up. It referred to him snidely as "that redoubtable folknik favorite who *is* the blues to every folk fan under 15," and wrote in a review of two later Elektra albums, "There are no real surprises . . . Just the incessant (aphrodisiac to his followers) a-yumph of his guitar, and the arrogant blandness of his voice."

As for the new wave of blues fans, they ignored Josh completely. In part this was a genuine aesthetic judgment. Josh's music was smooth and clean, quite unlike the sound of Charley Patton, Reverend Gary Davis, or the other early, rural singers who had become the new models. It must be added, though, that there was a good deal of romanticism and more than a little condescension in the prevailing view. The artists being "discovered" by the white blues aficionados, along with being fine musicians, were mysterious figures whose lives came wrapped in legend. Blind Blake, for example, was as slick a player and as bland a singer as Josh, but he was blind and obscure; no one even knew when or where he had died. Mississippi John Hurt, one of the most charming and tasteful performers ever to record but hardly a deep bluesman, was a Mississippi sharecropper recently arisen from the primeval Delta. Even Lonnie Johnson, who had hit the pop charts as late as 1949, and who preferred to use an electric guitar and play jazz standards rather than his old blues numbers, had at least had the good grace to be down on his luck, a janitor unremembered by any but a handful of hard-core blues record collectors.

Josh, meanwhile, had committed the unpardonable sin of remaining a successful entertainer. When his race-records peers had gone back to day jobs or singing on street corners, he had gone to Cafe Society. Anyone who listened seriously to his records could not help but consider him one of the most talented and distinctive guitar players in the field, but to the urban, white audience he had made himself too common. On a blues scene where it was a matter of prestige to be familiar with the most obscure 78s of the 1920s, Josh's work was beyond the pale. Worse, in an era when blues was greeted by middle-class kids as an earthy antidote to the whitebread conformity of the previous generation, Josh was the blues singer their parents had known and loved.

The irony in all of this was that Josh had done more than almost any other popular performer to nurture the aesthetic that now condemned him. From the beginning, he had spoken of the "whiskey voices" of the southern chain-gang prisoners and the primitive power of Lemon Jefferson's late-night blues, praising their folk honesty over the pop-blues of the R & B charts. Now, when Alan Lomax brought a genuine group of chain-gang veterans to the Newport Folk Festival and Jefferson's records were reissued on widely available LPs, Josh's music sounded pale by comparison. He would condemn Belafonte's attempts at chain-gang songs, backed with trained choruses and string orchestras, as sounding fake and forced, but to people familiar with the Lomax prison recordings, his own treatment of the songs could be placed in roughly the same category — or at best regarded as a halfway mark between Belafonte and the real thing. To the purists, he was the founding master of a fake-folk trend.

There was some truth to this view, but it ignored a vital point. Unlike the younger singers, Josh had grown up in the world that the revivalists were trying to revive. He knew what a real work gang sounded like, or a street-corner gospel shouter, and the changes he had made in the music were quite deliberate. The debate over "authenticity" was one he had been hearing since his days with Leadbelly, and his response to those who accused him of "refining" the material was not denial but explanation: "If you can't be understood, you're damn near lost," he said, in the notes to his *Chain Gang* LP. "I've tried to make the songs clear; and I feel if I and some others hadn't done that and helped people understand what the stories say, we wouldn't have as much interest in folk music as we do now." He added that if he did not sing with the gruff power of the oldtimers, that was because the need for that power did not exist in the concert halls and coffeehouses: "You don't have to shout. Sure they did in the open in the South; but now you can get into the intimacy of what this music says. It ought to be as if I were just talking to you."

For most of the folk audience, Josh's approach remained far more accessible than that of the deep Delta bluesmen, and the purists were a minority, grumbling on the sidelines. Popularizers, from Bikel and Josh to Belafonte, the Kingston Trio, Joan Baez, and Peter, Paul and Mary, were the ones selling records, appearing on television, playing packed concert halls, and showing up on the cover of *Time* magazine. Josh was even asked to write an article giving advice to teenagers in the pop pages of *Seventeen*. Indeed, for a man who had been recording since the 1920s, his following among young fans was impressive. When *Billboard* took a poll of musical tastes on college campuses in 1963–64, the zenith of the folk revival, Josh was ranked third among male folksingers, behind Belafonte and Seeger and just ahead of Bob Dylan.

It was Dylan's success that changed everything. Dylan's triumph, when he went electric and put "Like a Rolling Stone" on the charts in 1965 (two months after the Byrds took his "Mr. Tambourine Man" to number one), spelled not only the beginning of the end of the folk revival but the total eclipse of the cabaret style. Folk-rock, as the new music was called, had arrived a year earlier — when the Animals put Josh's old standard, "House of the Rising Sun" on top of the American charts for three weeks — and it would become the sound of a generation. Electricity aside, Dylan differed from previous folk stars in two seemingly contradictory ways: he was both a traditionalist neo-ethnic and an innovative songwriter. It was the former characteristic that had, at first, seemed to limit his show-business potential. Just as Woody

Guthrie had been a minority taste made palatable for a mass audience by Burl Ives, and Leadbelly by Josh, Dylan at first looked to be the brilliant but raw artist who would provide material for Peter, Paul and Mary. When they put "Blowin' in the Wind" and "Don't Think Twice, It's All Right" in the top ten in 1963, the conventional wisdom was that his voice was too abrasive and unmusical ever to reach mainstream listeners. Along with Van Ronk and the New Lost City Ramblers, he had immersed himself in the deepest, roughest examples of southern rural music, and he made no attempt to prettify his delivery. On the contrary, he nurtured a country twang with the same assiduousness that Josh had employed three decades earlier to gain the urbane speech patterns of New York. Once Dylan hit, smooth singing was out, the mark of everything false and commercial.

The earthy ethnicity of Dylan's singing was juxtaposed with lyrics that, more and more, drew on the least folk-oriented of modern poetic styles. His borrowings from modern literary movements, from the beat poets, the French symbolists, and surrealism, had an immediate appeal for listeners and fellow songwriters who were far more familiar with college texts and "little magazines" than Oklahoma dust storms, and they swarmed along the trail he blazed. Those who remained caught up in rural idioms were, virtually overnight, relegated from hard-core to old-fashioned. After "Like a Rolling Stone," folk music — in the sense of singing and playing old songs — was all but dead as a mass movement. The cabaret singers were doubly damned; their smooth sets of traditional material were both too folkie and not folkie enough.

Josh was one of the few older artists to speak out in support of folk-rock. Unlike most of his peers, he had been keeping up with advances in R & B, jazz, and gospel, and although his own shows had hardly changed over the years, he had found much to applaud in the newer trends. Drawn into a discussion about the electrification of the folk scene, he could describe it as liberating: "What's happened with folk-rock wouldn't have happened years ago because it would have been sacrilege," he told a group of young Canadian singers. "They wouldn't accept anything from me other than folk songs then. But I'm doing more than that in my shows now."

It is interesting to think about what Josh might have done, given an electric band. His attempts at R & B had been creditable, if hardly earthshaking, and Len Rosenfeld would insist that he was a much stronger singer than anyone knew. In relaxed moments, singing along with the car radio, Rosenfeld said, "Josh could out–Ray Charles Ray Charles." As it happened, though, his appreciation of folk-rock did not reflect any fundamental change in his music, and the time for sophisticated folksingers was over. His blues work might stand the test of time, but his versions of "On Top of Old Smoky" and "Molly Malone" were sounding more archaic every day.

There was yet another area that threatened to leave Josh behind. As in the 1940s, the rise of folk music in the 1960s was intimately connected with a rise of the American left. Although both the Kingston Trio, at one extreme, and the *Little Sandy Review*, at the other, tended to be studiedly apolitical, by the mid-1960s there were few people who did not associate folk music with the civil rights and antiwar movements. On this front Josh's position was decidedly ambiguous. As a prominent black performer he continued to talk and sing about racial issues, but his HUAC testimony was bitterly remembered by many people on the left. This doomed him, along with Ives, to exclusion from two of the trend-setting venues of the folk boom: the pages of *Sing Out!* and the stages of the Newport Folk Festivals. The first Newport festival, in 1959, had featured an array of cabaret stalwarts and Elektra recording artists, but Josh was not among them. The next year was more of the same, plus a few more traditional performers, but still no Josh. After a brief hiatus the festival returned in 1963 with pretty much everyone in folk music except Ives and White. Josh finally made his Newport debut in 1965, the year Dylan went electric and threw the crowd into a turmoil, but by then the folk wave was receding. Adding insult to injury, the review in *Sing Out!* cited 1965 as the year "the traditional singers came storming out of the background . . . pushing such old festival warhorses as Theo Bikel, Joan Baez, Peter, Paul and Mary, Josh White, Ronnie Gilbert, and others back into the unheroic shadows."

Of course, the red scare was not simply a memory of the left. While Josh was denied space at Newport, Seeger was banned from the far more influential forum of network television. Producers of the *Hootenanny* program absurdly explained that he was too amateurish, and a group of folk musicians organized a boycott of the show in response — there are still people who remember exactly which singers did and did not choose to appear. Seeger, though, was at least being banned because of his current beliefs and actions; Josh was condemned for his behavior in a polarized time more than a decade earlier, generally by critics who would never have to face the sort of pressures to which he had bowed.

Although he was not considered a protest singer, and indeed was openly scorned by many people on the left, Josh continued to speak and sing in support of his beliefs. His largest audience of the 1960s was the crowd gathered on the Capitol Mall on August 28, 1963, for the March on Washington for Jobs and Freedom (at which Martin Luther King Jr. delivered his epochal "I Have a Dream" speech). Josh may have been there in part because the march had been organized by his old sideman Bayard Rustin, but his participation was not entirely atypical. He always spoke admiringly of King, whom he called "the black Gandhi," and of the other protestors down south. The *New York Times* reported him as present at a Greenwood, Mississippi, concert in support of the southern voter registration drive. He went to Washington for another rally after the civil rights leader James Meredith was shot. He even teamed up with the blacklisted harmonica player Larry Adler for an Africa Defense and Aid Fund benefit at the Village Gate. Still, these appearances were the exceptions rather than the rule, and he never did more than show up and sing his songs. Since other artists were not only singing but marching, joining arms with King in Selma or Montgomery, Josh's absence was cause for some comment. Interviewers regularly asked him whether he was going down south and, if not, why not.

His answer was always more or less the same. "I admire Dr. King and the passive resistance movement," he would say. "But I don't like to be hurt and if somebody jumps me, that business about turn the cheek isn't for me. I'd be a bad egg in the group marching down South. I was asked to go down to Selma with Dr. King. I couldn't go down there. I was in Detroit and Cleveland doing concerts to help raise funds. But I couldn't march because if they had jumped me, with whatever I could find, we would have had a battle together."

In a sense, this response was in keeping with Josh's image as a tough, manly figure, and it also reflected a feeling that was not uncommon among African Americans in the North, a position that might be summed up as "Things are bad enough where I am; why the hell would I go to Mississippi?" Josh was facing racism all the time as he traveled through what was still a largely segregated country, and he did not share the white folk stars' need to make a physical demonstration of his goodwill. That said, Josh's statements were also an easy way to duck the issue without seeming to back down. He had strong feelings about civil rights, but after his experience in the 1950s he was not about to get mixed up with any political organizations, no matter how much he favored their causes. Even if he had wavered, Carol was prepared to fight that battle to the death. She had always felt that he was too easy, too willing to play free benefit concerts, and then she had seen his career and, with it, her secure family life shattered by the results. For her, it was a simple case of once burned, twice careful.

The folk revival brought many rewards, but Josh could never feel entirely part of it. He had plenty of work, but his music no longer had much relevance to what was happening around him. And yet, when he got out in front of an audience, it could seem as if nothing had changed. College students of the 1960s talk about his shows in the same awed tones that their parents' generation uses to describe his appearances at Cafe Society.

"That man was magic on the stage," Bill Lee remembers. "There'd be a thousand people in the audience, and each one felt just like, 'There's nobody in this audience listening to this song but me.' That man personalized a song so much — I'd go on the stage with him, and I heard him sing these songs over and over again, but every time he sang a song you would think that it was the first time he ever sang it. I have never witnessed anything like that in my life. I have been with Billie Holiday, with Billy Eckstine, I've been around Carmen McRae, I've heard Nat 'King' Cole in person. I can name them going and coming, but I have never in my life witnessed anybody that could take a song and personalize it so meaningfully, to himself and to the listener."

# 19

## HOUSE
## OF THE
## RISING SUN
## 1958-1963
■ ■ ■ ■ ■ ■ ■ ■ ■ ■ ■ ■ ■ ■ ■ ■ ■ ■ ■ ■ ■

As the folk revival became a major force in the entertainment world, Josh returned to the public eye, and his career once again becomes relatively easy to trace. He was recording regularly, and his live appearances were covered by a press eager to involve itself in the latest craze. After resigning with Elektra in 1958 he recorded *Chain Gang Songs.* The album revamped the old Carolinians' arrangements, this time putting more emphasis on recapturing the feel of a work gang and less on the original album's sweet harmonies. It became his best seller after *Josh at Midnight,* and the label followed up with three more albums: *Spirituals and Blues* in 1960, *The House I Live In* in 1961, and finally *Empty Bed Blues* in 1962. All but the last had liner notes by the jazz critic Nat Hentoff, who sought to place Josh in the context of the revival: "Long before the singing of folk songs became an urban avocation and a growing segment of show business in all its forms, Josh White was telling his burningly candid and insistently hopeful stories to strikingly diversified audiences. As the field itself had widened, Josh has remained a major figure here and abroad because he retains the ardor and strength of someone who has lived the songs he performs."

The albums were workmanlike but added little to Josh's legacy. The songs were virtually all old material and had gained nothing with the years. Indeed, Jac Holzman says that the reason Josh left Elektra after the fourth album was that he simply was no longer capable of working at the level of his earlier recordings. "The psoriasis on his nails really took its toll, his voice wasn't what it was, and we couldn't really continue making records because he just wasn't able to play and sing to the standard that I thought he should be performing at."

There is some truth to Holzman's assessment, but the real problem was that Josh had already run through all his basic material and had no particular interest in expanding his repertoire. Technically, he was still quite capable. He would go on to make records for another couple of years, and his playing remained fine, the attack crisp and the tone as beautiful as ever. His voice was less supple, the high range not as high as before and some of the vocal tricks no longer coming off, but it remained warm and direct, and the delivery was every bit as effective as it had been at the beginning of his Elektra run. Josh had always said that he was a storyteller rather than a singer, and he still knew how to put across a lyric as well as anyone in show business.

As the revival heated up, he again found himself playing New York nightclub residencies. After opening One Sheridan Square in September 1959, he appeared for three weeks at the Village Gate at the beginning of 1960, then returned to One Sheridan Square in the fall. He went on from there to a posher club, the Round Table, for most of January, on a bill with jazzmen Herbie Mann and Cootie Williams — a lineup more reminiscent of his 1940s bookings than most of the dates he was playing.

According to Bill Lee, the Round Table gig recalled old times in less pleasant ways as well: "The Round Table was on the East Side, midtown New York. At that time, the East Side was white. Nothing but white businessmen were at those places, 'cause they were the only ones who could afford to be sitting up in there. Well, Josh and I were onstage, and during these days they had little hard sugar cubes for your coffee. So it seemed to me there must have been four hundred to five hundred white men started throwing them at us. Most of them were zooming by Josh's head. He continued playing. Josh had his foot propped up on a chair in his usual way, singing like mad, when one of them hit him right on the forehead. He stopped and put his guitar down, came off the stage, walked to where he felt that one came from, in the back of the audience, and told the motherfucker who threw it to 'admit it right now and I'll wipe up this fucking floor with your coward funky ass.' You could have heard a rat piss on lint cotton. Josh walked all through that crowd until he got tired of trying to hear one word. He talked about everybody's mama to get one person to 'fess up, and nobody did. We came off that stage, and for the rest of that engagement we had no trouble."

Along with the New York dates, Josh was appearing at colleges and festivals across the country and making annual, month-long visits to San Francisco and Chicago. In March 1960 his Chicago visit included an appearance on a new, short-lived television show called *Playboy's Penthouse.* Surviving videotape gives an idea of the offhand ease with which he could capture the attention of a sophisticated nightclub audience: in a penthouse high above the city, Hugh Hefner is hosting an array of well-dressed guests. Various performers are singled out to do their shtick—including a young Bob Newhart—but none seems as relaxed as Josh. He appears in uncharacteristically formal evening dress, but during the second song, "Nobody Knows You When You're Down and Out," he decides to get comfortable. Over the course of the first verse, without ever pausing in his performance, he manages to remove his watch and tie and to unbutton his shirt collar. Then he swings into "Jelly Jelly." As Hefner nods in time, he teases the lyric, then brings his left hand up over the guitar neck and fires off a set of electrifying bass slides, played with the side of his thumb, before sinuously wrapping his hand around the neck for a sexy finish. To end the show, he gets the whole room singing along with him on the hoedown "Cindy."

In addition to his American tours, Josh was traveling overseas, going not only to England and Scandinavia but on to Israel and Spain in the summer of 1959, back to England and Spain the following spring, and to Scandinavia and Israel that summer, in what would become something of an annual pattern. In 1961 his English visit included the taping of thirteen twelve-and-a-half-minute programs for the Granada television network, in which he ranged through his repertoire, from two programs on work songs to three each on spirituals, blues, and the John Henry story, the musical bits interspersed with spoken commentary. That April he also recorded his first live album at London's Royal Festival Hall, before a capacity crowd of 4,000 people. It was largely devoted to songs he had been singing for well over a decade, though he had added one new item to his repertoire, a piece of syrupy sentiment called "Scarlet Ribbons," which had been making the rounds of the pop-folk scene. He introduced it with a comment aimed directly at the folk purists: "Some really died-in-the-wool folk critics won't accept these kinds of songs, and I think they're wrong, because if you stop acknowledging the young folksingers and writers, where will folk sort of end up?"

On record, at least, Josh's performances were as strong as they had been a decade earlier. He played with enthusiasm and precision, accompanied by his regular English bassman, Jack Fallon (and with a frustrated Josh Jr., who had not gotten a working visa, lending moral support from the audience). His song introductions have relaxed humor and the sly sexiness his fans had come to expect. "There's a very special request from all of the males in the house tonight, that I received backstage. They want me to sing a song to the females in the house tonight. I'd better explain it first: This is a song about a boy and a girl. In this song, the boy wants to kiss the girl and he wants to hug her, and he wants [pause] . . . but he's patient." The crowd laughs, and he goes on: "Max Jones [the English jazz writer] tells me, 'When a boy and a girl meet, if something doesn't happen,' he says, 'shame on 'em.' Well, the song's entitled, 'You Know, Baby, What I Want from You [pause] . . . period.' "

The record ends with "Strange Fruit," though on stage Josh had, as usual, followed up with "The House I Live In." As noted in his HUAC testimony, Josh had always refused to perform "Strange Fruit" when he was on tour outside the United States; he felt that America's racial problems were something to be dealt with at home and preferred to act as an ambassador rather than a critic when he went abroad. In the 1960s, though, he took to singing it wherever he went, in part because it was constantly requested, but also because he had decided that it could have implications beyond national borders. "Lynching and race hatred have been something dirty in our house, but you don't make a show about that to other people," he told a Canadian reporter. "But now this thing is spreading. You have this terrible situation in South Africa, and you've had race riots in England, in Notting Hill. So I decided to sing 'Strange Fruit.' It doesn't change things in South Africa — they don't let my records in there, and they certainly wouldn't let me in — but it does make a protest, and that's what you need."

Though much of the left continued to regard him as a sellout, Josh's outspokenness on racial issues was not lost on the mainstream liberals in his audience. Among them, as in the past, were some very prominent figures, and in 1960 Josh even had another fan elected president. Soon thereafter Judith White (then twelve) recalls answering the phone to hear a thoroughly confusing announcement: "I picked up the phone and said 'Hello,' and they said, 'This is the White House.'

"I said, 'Yeah, right. This the White house.'

" 'No, this really is the White House.'

"I said, 'Yeah, I know.'

"Then somebody heard me and they took the phone from me, thank goodness."

John F. Kennedy had been listening to Josh since his college days, and he was undoubtedly aware of Josh's Roosevelt connection as well. The White family was invited to his inauguration, and Josh later performed on a television show, *Dinner with the President,* a folk showcase hosted by JFK and organized as a fund raiser for the Anti-Defamation League of the B'nai Brith. Josh appeared along with Odetta, Judy Collins, the Clancy Brothers and Tommy Makem, and several lesser-known singers. He performed "John Henry," "Hard Times Blues," and "Free and Equal Blues," standing on a set designed to resemble a southern cabin. Patrick Clancy remembers that as they were waiting backstage, the president came in, and, as the other singers shyly drew back, not sure how to behave, Josh strode forward and greeted him as if he were an old friend.

Everything seemed to be going well, but there was a dark cloud on the horizon. In June 1961, Josh set out for Chicago. For once, Carol had decided to accompany him. The kids were old enough to get along for a while without her, and she felt like getting out of New York and finally seeing some of the places and meeting some of the friends she had been hearing about for years.

"That was very rare for me," she remembers. "I was never a traveler. He always wanted me to go with him, but I was not that kind. If I could travel during the day and go home to my own bed at night, you had me as a traveler. Other than that, no. But friends of ours had been begging, 'Please have Carol come. Bring her with you.' So, finally, the children decided I should go with him on a little vacation.

"We stopped in Michigan because Donny [Josh Jr.] was appearing there. We were staying with a doctor, a dentist, who was a friend of Josh's, and Josh was not feeling good at the club, so I said, 'Josh, just go on home and get some rest.' We went back to the house, and during the night I got up for some reason, and when I looked at Josh he was square; he had swollen up all the way down. It was frightening, and I woke up the doctor. We were supposed to leave that following day to go to Chicago, but the doctor decided Josh shouldn't leave. They got another doctor and they gave him whatever — I think that it was maybe a medication that had swollen him up. So, he said, 'Maybe by Wednesday you'll feel better.' And we stayed over and finally left there early Saturday morning, because we got into Chicago around noon on the Saturday before Father's Day.

"Josh had this friend of his there [Wardell Murphy], who he called his brother, that had an automobile place, so Josh dropped me off at his house. Josh came back about six o'clock and when he came in he began to complain about his stomach hurting. I didn't know what to do, so I called the doctor in Michigan and he said, 'I'm going to give you the name of a doctor friend of mine in Chicago, Dr. Kaplan. I'll call him and then when you call him you tell him that I told you to call.' That's what I did, and he said to me, 'Bring him to Michael Reese Hospital, and I'll meet you in the lobby.'

"I was really so frightened. This fellow that he called his brother and another fellow took us in their car, and Josh then began to have pain from his arm. I didn't even want to think of a heart attack, but all the way there they were saying, 'heart attack.' When we got there I looked for the doctor, and he was right there, and he took him in the emergency room and examined him. He was the nicest man, with a wonderful manner, and I'm sure Josh had said, 'My wife is just in. She knows no one and you have to be careful. Treat her very gentle.' Because I would have panicked. So he called me aside and he said, 'I'm not going to say it is a heart attack, but just to be sure I'm going to keep him and take him upstairs to do some further studies.'

"They had a place for me to sit, and we stayed a long time; this was like eight-thirty at night, and the doctor was still there at two in the morning. And then he finally came to me. He said, 'I don't want you to get that worried. It's going to sound worse than it is.' And then he told me Josh had had a heart attack."

This time, there was no question as to whether Josh was exaggerating his health problems. He would spend the next month and a half in the hospital. Carol stayed in Chicago and, rather surprisingly, enjoyed herself. "I had the best time. Studs Terkel, [Irv] Kupcinet, the newspaperman, and Hugh Hefner, they took me out and just showed me the best time. They were wonderful. So I really didn't have time to worry. You know, God gives you time to reassess and reevaluate what is important and what is not important, and the fact that he didn't have [the sort of attack] where he was unconscious or any of that stuff—there were a lot of things to be grateful for."

According to Carol, Josh was having a pretty good time himself, at least considering the circumstances. "He never stayed anywhere without having his guitar. I wanted to beat him sometimes. By the time I'd get to the hospital he'd have four hundred nurses on his bed and he'd be singing to all of them. His ego would not allow him to stop performing. There were many times I walked into the hospital in Chicago and got very angry, because the doctor wanted him to rest and I'd walk up there and he'd have maybe six nurses sitting on his bed. And if the nurses weren't there, the doctors were there. And he loved it. It helped him get through. Because in the early years in life, he didn't have that petting and spoiling, so he really enjoyed the attention. And, knowing that he was feeling better, it gave me that ease to relax and enjoy myself."

From his hospital room, Josh moved after a few weeks to a special recuperative section, then to an apartment. Carol had Judith, her youngest daughter, come out and join them as soon as school was over and, in retrospect at least, treated the Chicago stay as a vacation. She does not seem to have concerned herself with how the bills were getting paid, and apparently Josh's friends had that part of the situation under control. "There were so many friends of ours," she says. "Like the doctor, and we had this big-time lawyer that just loved Josh, and everything was fine. No one suffered for one thing, and we were there the whole summer."

In early September they headed back to New York. The doctor had told Josh not to drive, so he allowed his Chicago friends to handle the first leg of the journey. As soon as they were out on the open road, though, Josh got back behind the wheel. There was nothing he enjoyed better than driving, and Carol felt that despite the doctor's advice, it acted as a sort of therapy for him.

Once home, Josh got right back to work. On September 23, he gave a Town Hall concert that was recorded and released on the Mercury label. He was accompanied by Josh Jr. and Beverly, Bill Lee on bass, and a small combo of piano, drums, conga drum, and a flute and tenor saxophone player named Jerome Richardson. The record shows the looseness with which Josh could treat some aspects of his performances. He clearly had not rehearsed with Richardson, who simply noodles around trying to follow the changes and not get in the way. When his kids join him for a final "Green Grass Grows All Around," however, the informality is what makes the song work, giving the feeling of an impromptu family sing-along. Josh sounds glad to be back in the world, but rather than dominating the record, he uses it to showcase Josh Jr. and Beverly, who sing two solo numbers each, taking up almost half the album.

Josh had always imagined his children not only as guest artists on his shows but as performers in their own right, and his heart attack seems to have spurred him to push this idea even more strongly. Mercury was amenable, and in the spring of 1962 the whole crew drove down to Nashville for a "Josh White Family" recording session produced by Quincy Jones. The session included eleven titles, three from Beverly and two each from Josh Jr., Judy, Fern, and a friend of Fern's named Lonzine Cannon. Josh himself did not sing, though, and after some consideration Mercury chose not to issue the album. In the end, although the three younger girls occasionally appeared as the Josh White Singers, and Judy had a brief recording career in the mid-1960s, Josh Jr. was the only one who actually made a go of it as a performer.

As for Josh, as soon as he felt up to it he was back at work, both on the road and in the studio. The weekend after the Town Hall concert he was playing Toronto, and the next two months included tours of the West and South. A recording session with chorus and orchestra produced two 45-rpm singles comprising three gospel numbers and a version of "Bonbons, Chocolate, and Chewing Gum." For the Christmas season he was back in Chicago, where he did so well that a full-page ad in *Variety* reprinted a letter to him from the Gate of Horn's Alan Ribback: "In five years of operation we've seen nothing like it. You took every attendance record, even during a blizzard."

In March 1962, Josh was in the hospital again, in New York, but this stay was relatively short, and by May he was off on a two-month tour of Europe. Back in the States he was featured at the Seattle World's Fair in June, his concert there drawing some 5,000 people. The spring and summer also brought three more Mercury sessions, two made up of old standards and one including such unlikely material as "Danny Boy" and "September Song," though none of these sides were deemed strong enough to release. Josh toured through the Midwest and down to North Carolina, then made it to Chicago again for the holidays — and another one-week hospital stay, reported to be simply a checkup because he was "rocky from reaction to a flu shot." Typically, he was on the road immediately after leaving the hospital, driving nonstop to Philadelphia to publicize an upcoming gig and visit three fans from Temple University who had had a car accident, then heading straight back to Chicago, where he took up his usual residency at the Gate of Horn.

In Chicago, Josh went into the studio for the first session of what would prove to be his final album project. The resulting pair of records were, at last, something different, if not exactly something new. Produced by Alan Ribback for Mercury, and titled *In the Beginning* and *In the Beginning, Volume Two,* they took Josh back to his roots. He relearned a couple of forgotten songs from his first records, such as Funny Papa Smith's "Howling Wolf," and came up with quite a few blues and gospel standards that he had not previously recorded. He made no attempt to recapture his old playing or singing style, and at least one song, "Goin' Down Slow," was actually a blues hit from the 1940s, but the session was still a welcome departure from a repertoire that had been revisited far too many times. He was accompanied by a small combo including the Chicago harmonica master Sonny Boy Williamson, and the records were the most satisfying he had made in years.

Robert Shelton, the folk music critic for the *New York Times,* had been hired to write a brief biography of Josh for the forthcoming *Josh White Song Book.* He was present at the Chicago session, and his account provides a snapshot of the proceedings:

> At the corner of Rush and Walton, five musicians, a few technicians and a straggle of watchers assembled in Studio A of the Universal Recording Company. . . . Josh White appeared to be all health, vigor and self-assurance. At forty-nine, he retained his nimble athlete's body. A mustard-colored shirt open at the collar revealed a sensual neck and throat that had made so many women think twice. Sleek olive trousers ran down to a pair of custom-made shoes. Gracefully, he strode the studio floor joking with his accompanists.
>
> A swirl of cigarette smoke moved around his head. He coughed to clear his throat, then took another deep drag. He fingered the talisman of St. Christopher that hung at his neck. Exploring, he touched the guitar strings. His lighted cigarette was parked straight up behind his right ear. . . . He tried a half-voice run-through, just singing

to himself. Josh White is the total actor, a showman in his sleep. He threw his head back and laughed uproariously. He closed his eyes, pursed his lips, pushed the words through. . . .

It was rough and painful to sing that night. "The doctor had told me to cancel the session and go to bed, alone. Hell, they've been telling me to rest since I was born. Seems I'm always fighting doctors, lawyers, A&R men, whites and Negroes. Maybe it's just me I've been fighting. It's like the Moor in 'Othello' after he killed Desdemona. The Moor says, 'I've done some good and they know it.' But I say I've done some good and I know it. . . ."

The bottle of Cutty Sark was finished and so was the recording session . . . Josh drew tight the belt of his green leather topcoat. "Sonny," he said to the whimsical old harmonica man, "I've learned a lot from you tonight." Sonny smiled and invited him to his little rhythm and blues club on West Lake Street. Josh said he'd try to make it later. . . .

Josh and his troupe walked three blocks to the Gate of Horn, a temple of night life. He entered the dimly lighted club with a swagger and smile for everyone. The bartenders waved as if it were some triumphal return. With both hands extended at once, he shook hands with two musicians. "Hey, mother, how the hell are ya?" he asked one of them. They asked how the session went, and he replied in mock concern, "Oy, Vey!" Josh ordered a favorite drink, a White Spider—two shots of vodka with a dash of peppermint schnapps. Tourists watched the party with ogle-eyes.

There would be two more sessions in New York, and then the albums were completed. They were well received by reviewers, and there were plans to follow up with an album to be titled "The Roosevelt Years," but somehow that idea never came to fruition. Josh would make one abortive attempt to produce a pop single, and at some point in the next years he also cut three of his folk standards for the tiny Mirwood label, but essentially, his recording career was over.

# 20

## GOIN' DOWN SLOW
### 1963-1969
- - - - - - - - - - - - - - - - - - - - - -

On the whole, 1963 was a good year for Josh. It included the two most prominent television appearances of his career, the *Dinner with the President* broadcast and his performance at the March on Washington, as well as two spots on *Hootenanny*, in March and September. He was recording for a major label and, along with the club and college dates, was playing larger concerts in such places as the Santa Monica Civic Auditorium and the Queen Elizabeth Theatre in Vancouver. His audience spanned two generations, making him one of the biggest live draws on the folk scene. With success came more ambitious ideas: in an interview during his annual European tour that summer, he spoke of plans to open a club in Santa Monica called the Josh White Room. Like the Italian *Porgy and Bess,* however, that scheme seems never to have been mentioned again.

Josh had never ceased to comport himself as a star, and he reveled in the wave of attention. "He had such charisma about him," says Chuck Ramsey, his road manager for the mid-1960s. "We would walk into the room at the Sherman House in Chicago, like around six-thirty or seven, and have dinner at a ringside table before the actual dinner show. There would be other people in there also, and he would just walk down the stairs and a hush would fall over the room and people would look at him. People that had their backs to him somehow would know he was in the room. He was that much bigger than life. I've never seen anything like it.

"There were always groups of people around him. Everywhere we went, there were hangers-on that met us like at the town limits and grabbed on for the week or day or whatever it was, these endless people. Somebody would invite you back to their house or their bar or their whatever after the show, to get to know Josh better etc., etc., etc., so that group of fans began to know each other, and the next time he was in town, there they'd be. Then there was always the town or regional female that we met at the airport or the town limit or the hotel, who was with us for the entire tour."

Ramsey had signed on as Rosenfeld's assistant after booking Josh for a gig at Wittenburg University in Springfield, Ohio. Originally, the date was scheduled for January 1964, and Ramsey laughs as he recalls the mishaps that followed. "What I didn't know was that every Christmas Josh played the Gate of Horn in Chicago and then instantly went in the Michael Reese Hospital to recover. My engagement happened to have been during his Michael Reese thing, so it was canceled. That's how I got to know Len Rosenfeld, was working on rescheduling this concert. When we negotiated the deal, we took all of the out-of-pocket expenses [from the canceled concert] out, even with the 'act of God' clause, and Josh was all upset because Len should have known better than to book him during that time period, since anybody that knew him knew that he finished at the Gate of Horn and went into the Michael Reese." By the time the date was rebooked and successfully played, Ramsey had become well acquainted with both Josh and Rosenfeld, and he soon took on the job of being Josh's road manager.

Despite the hospital stays (his January illness had forced him to cancel not only Ramsey's date but also a third *Hootenanny* appearance), the good times continued through 1964, and Josh ended the year at the Village Gate, celebrating his thirty-fifth anniversary as a professional musician. A reporter who came backstage found Patrick Clancy of the Clancy Brothers massaging his bare back and shoulders while Josh Jr. brought him drinks. Josh was complaining about his fingers, and spoke of having had three heart attacks (there is no record of the second and third, but it may be that relatively mild ones were the reasons for hospital stays that are otherwise unexplained). Otherwise, he seemed cheerful as he donned a gray silk sport shirt and prepared to go onstage following opening sets by Buffy Ste. Marie and John Hammond.

Ramsey still has the logbooks for Josh's tours from 1965 through 1967, and they trace a zigzag path back and forth across the United States, and on to Europe and Australia. There are weeks where there is a different gig every night, then two-week residencies in Chicago, New York, or Los Angeles. As Ramsey points out, though, there are also months with only a couple of dates, and for a touring musician those blank spaces soon begin to look huge. As Len Rosenfeld put it, "Entertainers—particularly when they are out of town, or if they have had a barren day or week, in a world where their only inventory is that they are working—can't 'mark down' what they have to offer. Your only inventory is time, and if it's not being used there's a great tendency to become concerned about what's happening to your career."

Ramsey says that even during weeks that look profitable on paper, Josh never had any money to spare. Over the years, this fact led to a good deal of ill feeling. Carol believed that Rosenfeld was cheating Josh, taking more than his share of the money and finagling tricky deals. None of Rosenfeld's associates or other clients believe this, but the truth was hardly an improvement: Rosenfeld was not a crook, but neither was he a particularly good manager for an artist like Josh. The nature of the folk business is such that it does not attract hotshot, go-getting businessmen, and the few who did get into the field, like Marty Erlichman, soon moved on to greener pastures (Ehrlichman to manage a young unknown named Barbra Streisand). Rosenfeld meant well and managed to shepherd his artists through decent, midlevel careers, but no one was getting rich, himself included. Josh, who would remain the biggest name in Rosenfeld's stable, presented special problems because his health was shaky and his expenses were high.

"The income never met the spending," Ramsey says. "Let's say that he made $3,000 for a week at a club. At that time, a hotel room was about twenty-five bucks a night, and there would be three rooms, for Josh, me, and the bass player. Then, he was paying the bass player, and many times we had to fly the bass player in, and in those days we flew the bass in the passenger compartment of the airplane, strapped to a seat at full fare. Then there were three squares a day for each of us, plus a unique consumption of alcohol."

To make matters worse, the food and drink bills would frequently be for a good many more than three people. "On the road, Josh picked up every tab. We could be at a dinner and drinking event for thirty people, and all of a sudden he would [make a signal] and my hand would go the

Diner's Club card. I could sign 'Josh White' just as well as he could, so I would pay for the entire thing. He was grandstanding. Or it could be an issue where, in Chicago, Wardell [Murphy] fixed his car for him, so we'd all go down to some place and buy leather overcoats at five hundred bucks apiece."

In Mary Chase's day, she had collected all the income, paid the White family's bills, and given Josh an allowance for his day-to-day needs. Rosenfeld and Ramsey left Josh to take care of his own financial affairs, and he handled them in a way that was lackadaisical to the point of anarchy. When he had money, everyone around him had money. When he did not, he would hope for a similar generosity in return and received it often enough to keep his affairs afloat. As a result, the higher income of the 1960s did not make for any lasting wealth.

The road also continued to have special drawbacks for a black performer. In the clubs or behind the wheel of his Lincoln Continental, Josh was in his element, but at every stop between towns he could find himself facing the same old problems. The 1960s were a time of great advances, but at the counter of a small-town diner it was still the 1940s. Bill Lee recalls that when they drove out to California, Josh advised him to eat only eggs, sunny-side up, to avoid getting something nasty put into his food. A Texas fan remembers packing a lunch for Josh and Rosenfeld after they stayed with her in San Antonio, as there would be no place where both of them could eat until they hit the next big city.

"Going down south, you'd call ahead for a reservation," Josh Jr. says. "You know you're gonna be at X point by a certain time, so you'd reserve a room; then you get to Ma and Pa's Motel, and when they see you, it's 'I'm sorry, that room's been rented.' When Holiday Inn came out, they did not have that practice, and Holiday Inn used to be our home away from home because we knew that they could not discriminate. Except for Holiday Inn, it was take a chance.

"When we went down to Nashville to record, there were five or six of us in the car, and not too far from Nashville my sister Judy got sick. We're near a gas station, it wasn't a major Shell or Mobil, but it was a gas station, and so we pulled up. There were some white people in the little office and maybe a couple of kids, eleven, twelvish, and we sat there for a while. They just looked at us and no one came out. They finally sent a young kid out. My father said, 'I've got a sick daughter. Could we just use your bathroom? I'll even buy gas. We don't need the gas, but I'll buy the gas.' They would not let us use the bathroom. Now, everybody in the car except my father was livid, but the old man maintained his composure, and we went on."

Josh knew enough to pick his battles; he had no interest in getting into a scuffle in a small-town gas station, but when he saw a way to influence the world around him he would try to do it. As always, he considered his songs his most potent weapon, but he could also make more concrete suggestions. Josh Jr. recalls, for example, a trip to Chapel Hill, North Carolina, to play at the university there. "The kids loved him, of course, and he enjoyed talking to kids. Sermonizing, but not sermonizing. This particular time, they wanted to take us to a place that they always hung out in — it was a big deal for them, to take Josh White to a place where they hung out every day. Then we got there, and the proprietor wouldn't serve us. The kids were gonna trash the joint, and my old man said, 'No. Just don't give him your business anymore. Just don't go in there.' And I think the joint closed. He loved to do things like that, to show that the way to win the war is not always by fisticuffs. You have to be smart about it."

Another time in the mid-1960s, while playing in Baltimore, Josh stepped out to have a drink at a local tavern and was refused service. The next morning he complained to the Maryland Commission on Racial Problems and Relations, which made an official investigation of the tavern owner, and he also spoke to local reporters. The result was an agreement by the owner to avoid discrimination in the future. To test the genuineness of the deal, Josh went back the following night and had his drink.

"As sure as I live and breathe I had to go back," he told a reporter from the *Baltimore Afro-American*. "I've been in this mess long before the NAACP, CORE, SNCC, and many of the other groups now doing such a good job. You see, I remember when colored people had to pay to walk the streets in Greenville, South Carolina, and ever since then I swore I would be treated like a human being. . . . I might have gotten in trouble, but I just had to go back."

Josh protested where he could see a chance to win. Where he could not, he got back in his Lincoln and rolled on to the next job. All in all, it was not the ideal life for a man with a heart condition. Between the traveling, the stress, the alcohol, and Josh's diet — which continued to be heavy on the eggs, steak, and pork chops — his condition deteriorated through the 1960s, with periods of recovery interrupted by ever more frequent relapses. In 1965 the *New York Times* reported that he was in a hospital in Stockholm with heart trouble, and some of the gaps in Ramsey's road logs are undoubtedly health-related.

Still, Josh kept going, and the people who saw him on the road rarely noticed the problems. In Sweden, in particular, he was still lionized, making long annual tours there throughout the 1960s, usually with one or two of his kids in tow. One of his closest Swedish friends was Bengt Ohlsson, whom he would dub his "road manager" and who named his first son after Josh. Another was Lasse Sarri, a Swedish television producer who had first met him in London in 1959 and who did a show with Josh, Josh Jr., and Beverly in 1963, following Josh's regular nine-day residency at the Grona Lund Tivoli, an outdoor amusement park in Stockholm. Sarri traveled with Josh through twenty performances over the next three weeks and recalls both his charm and the complex family dynamic. Apparently, Josh and his kids were hitting a particularly difficult time, and for a while Josh Jr. actually went to stay in Sarri's apartment while Sarri took his hotel room. Nonetheless, Sarri recalls that they showed a rare willingness to confront their differences rather than bury them. "They met as equals, with great respect for each other, and did not give up until they found a way to deal with their weaknesses in order to solve the problem," he says. "It was a loving and democratic way of working as a family." Josh Jr., thinking back, is less impressed with the level of democracy in the relationship, and it was one of the last times he and his father worked together. Nonetheless, he and Beverly remember the Swedish visits fondly, as does Judith, who replaced her older siblings as Josh's companion for tours there in 1967 and 1968.

The children were not children anymore, and as they grew up, Josh and Carol's home life was also changing in other ways. In 1965 they left the Harlem apartment where they had lived for twenty years and moved out to Rosedale, Queens, where he would be nearer the airport. They bought a compact, two-story house in what was then still a largely white neighborhood. As Carol remembers, that caused a few immediate problems, but the transition was fairly smooth. "At first, there was my girlfriend on the corner and another lady around the corner that had already moved in. So it was 'The blacks are coming!' It made me very angry, to the point that it took me a couple of days to figure if I wanted to come live there. But after that first while, we all got to be real good friends." It is not clear that Josh ever really felt at home in his new neighborhood, but it was a victory to own his own house at last, and his friends continued to come over for card games and conversation.

The house soon saw some unusual visitors as well. In 1966 a Connecticut-based aircraft manufacturer named Charlie Kaman had conceived the idea of building a guitar with a fiberglass back, which he named the Ovation. Armed with a prototype, Kaman went to see one of his favorite guitarists, Charlie Byrd, in Washington, D.C. Byrd explained that although he liked the guitar, he played nylon rather than steel strings, and he sent Kaman to see Josh, who was appearing across town. According to Kaman's son Bill, Josh's reaction was, "This guitar has got the biggest motherfucking balls I ever heard."

Soon, Ovation engineers were showing up in Rosedale, measuring Josh's guitar, asking his advice, and spreading diagrams and plans on the dining room table. They built a guitar to his specifications and issued it as the Josh White model, with Josh as the company's first endorser. "The Josh White model is a precise replica of the steel string classic designed and built to the exacting requirements and preferences of Mr. White," the advertisements read. "Josh is one of guitardom's immortals, respected as instrumentalist and performer. As such, we went to great lengths to respond to his demands for a superlative guitar to match his emphatic skills. The styling is impeccable and dynamic enough to complement his image as a performer. It is the ideal model for the guitarist who, like Josh, prefers the width of a classical neck, but the report of steel strings."

Josh also began making regular trips up to the Ovation plant to get special fingernails made. His psoriasis had gotten so bad that he would come offstage with his fingers bleeding, and at times he had to get novocaine injected into his fingertips before he could perform. There was nothing he could do about his left hand, but for his right the Ovation technicians would build him nails. Bill Kaman remembers Josh coming out to the factory every month or so. "We had to make a real slow mix of the material, and it would take about an hour to cure. Normally, you mix up the resin and the fiberglass and it cures in about five minutes, but it gives off an awful lot of heat. Since it was on his fingers, we had to slow it way, way down. In the early days, they'd make the nails and he'd sit around and play for them and drink. Toward the end, he'd be eating a tub of yogurt and would say, 'That's all I can do now.'" An Ovation guitar history adds that the special mixture they used to attach the nails would later be marketed as Super Glue.

While Josh continued to make the rounds of clubs and concerts, the other members of his family were also setting about their business. Josh

Jr. had gone solo in 1961 — as with his Cafe Society debut at three, he says this was a decision of Josh's managers rather than his own choice — and was building a respectable career as a singer and performer. He had records and fans and a repertoire that reflected his more youthful tastes. He wrote some of his own material and sang songs by his contemporaries and pop numbers such as "They Call the Wind Maria." His stage manner was friendly and funny in a way that owed as much to his friend Jackie Washington, the toast of Harvard Square, as it did to his father.

Still, the name on the marquee was Josh White, and the comparisons, unfair and unwelcome as they might be, were inescapable. "When I became a solo performer, people would capitalize off the fact that I was his son. It might happen, if it was a joint my old man had not played because they couldn't afford him, but they could afford me, there would be big letters outside. 'JOSH WHITE,' and then a tiny 'jr.' Which was not fair to the people and was not fair to me. So we had to put in my contract that the 'J' in 'Jr.' was to be in 100 percent type and the 'r' to be no less than 60 percent, so they could not do that."

In 1967, yet another White took her shot at show business: Judith teamed up with Miriam Makeba's daughter to form the duo Judy and Bongi; they recorded a single, "What Should a Young Girl Do?" which got some limited airplay. She also joined Josh at New York's Bitter End, earning rave reviews from audience, critics, and, of course, her proud father, who never hesitated to brag on his children. "Before long, I want to see her on her own," he told a reporter. "She can do any-thing — dance, a Broadway show — anything. First of all she's got this [he pointed to his ear]. She's got the voice and she's got phrasing. Don't worry, I won't let Lovebug [his name for her] get a fat head, but the truth is that all she needs is a break, and she can make it." That break never quite came, but Judy continued to sing, and even teamed up for a time with Fern and Beverly as the Josh White Singers.

One young fan who was present at that Bitter End gig was Don McLean, already beginning to make his own name as a folksinger. For him, the night was magical: "Josh walked in the door with his daughter, hand in hand, fingers entwined, and he looked sharp. He had that jet black, charismatic look to him that he had when he was on fire. And he hit that stage, and I want to tell you, he was using some kind of a classical guitar that he had modified for steel strings. And this fucking thing sounded amazing. And he had his bass player, and he just freight-trained through the set. It was his usual set that he always did, but somehow it was just gleaming, it was polished. The lighting, and his look, it was just fabulous. And his hand would just do these wonderful movements over the top of the guitar."

McLean got a chance to work with his hero the following year at the Cellar Door in Washington, D.C. "I was the opening act, and I did nine sets with him," he remembers. "He was one of my idols, so I sat there every night and watched him sing. Sometimes he would feel very poorly. He'd say, 'I have pains coming down my arm and I have to go to the hospital.' And he'd perform his set, and it would be a little wobbly. Then sometimes he would feel better, and he'd be immediately like his old self, and that set would be stinging, fiery. But he always swaggered in every night, looked good, and had that energy level.

"I would say his career had begun to slip again by then, because attendance wasn't that good in that little nightclub. But he had his alligator shoes and his Lincoln Continental, and he had a whole mess of women everywhere. They would call up and just jam the switchboard. And then it was over, and his brother Bill drove him home."

Josh continued to perform into 1969, but he was definitely slowing down. He was home more than ever, and Carol had a telephone installed by his favorite chair in the living room so he could answer it without having to get up. "He would get in that corner, and he'd get a book, and he'd read and he would stay there for days," she remembers fondly.

For Carol, Josh's illnesses and enforced vacations were to some extent a mixed evil. She hated to see him getting sicker and losing work, but she liked to have him home. Their relationship had been complicated by all of Josh's running around, his public persona, and his constant need to be the sexy devil, but it had endured for thirty-five years. Outsiders were often surprised to see how Josh changed when he was with Carol. Chuck Ramsey, for instance, remembers that when she came to stay with Josh in Chicago, at the Sherman House, "that was the one time I saw him just being the husband, and it was a side of him I had never seen before. He wasn't performing for anybody, he was just a normal guy, sitting there with glasses on [which he used for reading in later years], woolly socks and floppy slippers. We would have breakfast together in the room and dinner together before the first show, and it was the only time I ever saw him where he was just completely relaxed. He'd be reading the newspaper in the morning, and when I got up there in the evening he'd be sitting around talking about what we were going to do for the show this evening and so on—just a really smooth, quiet kind of a guy. I never saw him that way before and never saw it after."

Josh never forgot where his home was, or who made it work. Despite his dalliances, Carol stresses, when he was really needed Josh always came through. She recalls that in 1967, when her sister died, Josh drove down from Canada in a blizzard to be at her side. Now, Josh was home more and more often, spending time with her and getting to know his grandchildren. Bunny's son Craig remembers him getting up to fix them breakfast, just as he had done for his own children. He still toured, but the gaps between jobs were longer, and his New York stays involved more quiet time in the house and fewer parties.

By this time, Carol worried when he was out on the road, and not about the women he might be meeting. In Florida he had to go into the hospital again, then "he came home, and he was better for a while, but it was just kind of a slow downhill," she remembers. "And he never wanted me to have to worry about anything. He had always taken care of us. Everybody said, 'With Josh sick, what is Carol going to do? She never had to worry about anything, so how is she going to make it?' "

To the surprise of everyone, and over Josh's objections, Carol went out and got a job, the first she had had since the 1930s. "I worked for a duplicating place, when they first started making [cassette] tapes," she said. "Josh was not happy about it. He almost died when I told him I was going to work. But once I started, I would get up every morning and have a bath, and he would make my coffee and pour me some juice and bring it to me."

Even with Carol working, though, the financial situation was tough. Friends remember Josh calling to borrow small sums of money, and Oscar Brand recalled going with him "to sell his 'original' guitar so he could pay some current bills for the family. . . . The amount he sold it for was but a fraction of what it would have been if he advertised the sale, but he didn't want anyone to know of his debts—especially his family." Similarly, Chuck Ramsey remembers seeing an accumulation of pawn tickets pinned up on the wall of the basement room where Josh kept his records and scrapbooks. He adds that this was nothing new but had long been Josh's way of coming up with immediate cash: "That was going on for years. Every so often we would have to go get a Martin out of the pawn shop on the way to someplace."

By 1968, Josh was working only occasionally. In the spring of 1969 he made his last visit to the West Coast. He did not find a booking in San Francisco, appearing instead at a club in Los Gatos, and while he was there, his heart started acting up again. He checked into a nearby hospital, but this time things were worse than usual. "I would speak to his doctor, then I'd speak to Josh, and I noticed that he really didn't seem to be doing well," Carol remembers. "At that time, my sister's husband was in the hospital dying of cancer here; I was working in the city; and I had a sister that was sick at the same time. I would leave here in the morning at six and go to work, then I would leave there, go uptown to see how my sister was, go see my brother-in-law, then I'd rush home in order to call the doctors in California so I could find out how Josh was. And one day, he was unable to speak clearly and he was stammering, and they said it was because of the medication.

"Well, that was it. Donny was out working and traveling, and he came home and I said 'Go get your dad.' I could not deal with it anymore. So Donny went and got him, and he came home on Father's Day. We were here at the airport, and I want to tell you there was no question in my mind when I saw Josh that he was sick. You see, when I first met Josh he was very thin, and when he stepped off that plane he had gotten so small he looked like young Josh. He didn't look bad, but I was not used to seeing him like that anymore, and it was very frightening. After a couple of days, though, I got used to it and I kind of liked him little again."

With Josh home, the next step was to decide what to do about his condition. He was able to get around but had clearly deteriorated, and his local doctor, Bernard Levine, who had been treating his psoriasis and bursitis, recommended a heart specialist. The specialist examined him and decided that the best hope would be surgery to replace a defective valve. So, in August, Josh checked into North Shore University Hospital in Manhasset, Long Island.

Serious as the situation was, he remained in good spirits. As always, he had his guitar with him and, as usual, a large complement of nurses. What Carol particularly remembers, though, was the young man who was his roommate. "He was the only son of these Jewish people, and his parents assumed that he had taken some kind of drug, but they did not know and he would not tell them. But he would talk to Josh. Josh got along with everybody; he could make a *nail* talk. So the mother asked me, 'Do you think that Josh could find out, so that we will know what we need to do for him?' I said, 'Well, if anybody can get it out of him, Josh can.' Sure enough, Josh found out that he had been taking some kind of drug that messed him up, and they were able to help him."

She says that Josh was also up to his old tricks. "He was really terrible. I went up there one day, and there was a girl there, and she was sitting on her cousin's bed, which was right by Josh's bed. They were laughing and talking, and Josh put his hand on her knee. And I leaned over and said, 'Josh, you're never gonna give up, right, buddy? Put your hand on her leg one more time, brother, and your party is over.' We laughed so hard about that, I said, 'You're still flirting, you bum. You're laying here sick, and you've got the nerve to flirt.' "

Finally, it was time for the surgery. Josh Jr. flew in the day before, and the whole family gathered in the hospital room; Josh was optimistic and happy to see them. At the end of the visit the surgeon came in and told Carol that the operation would start at six in the morning and last until around eleven, and that she should get plenty of sleep and not try to come in before then.

Frankly, Carol needed the rest. To compound her other worries, there had been a huge storm, and the whole area around her house was flooded. "I had water in my basement, water in the back yard. Frogs doing the ballet in the water. It was a crazy thing. So this white girlfriend of mine, she said, 'Don't drive to the hospital; I will come and get you.' She came over that morning, and we went out to the hospital. Donny had to fly out to Buffalo that same morning, and I had left the girls home. I thought, 'Let me go see how the land lays.'

"I went upstairs, and I asked had anybody been looking for me, and they said no. So I sat there. After some time, Fern came, and Judith had gotten there. Donny called from Buffalo, and I said, 'I don't know anything to tell you yet, but if you call back later I'll be able to tell you.' He said, 'OK, Mom, I will.' And then almost immediately after that the doctor comes out and says, 'Mrs. White, do you want to come with me?' And we go through this door, and this area here is intensive care, beyond that are the doctors' offices, and then in that same area is where the operating room is. And he said, 'I really don't know how to tell you this, but we lost him.'

"I said, 'I really don't know what you're telling me. You told me to bring him here. You gave me the hope. I know you're not God, but you gave me the hope that . . .'

"And he stood there and he cried. I was so angry at that time I couldn't even cry.

"He said to me, 'Can I give you anything?'

"I said, 'You can't give me Josh back; you can't give me anything.'

"I didn't want him to touch me. And then I took the kids by the shoulder and decided to walk out. By the time I got myself together with other friends that were there and we got downstairs, Beverly and Bunny were rushing to come in, and when I told them that Daddy had passed, it was disastrous. I really held myself together very well—I always felt like I had to do that for them—but the minute I turned that corner and saw this house it was over. It was *over.*"

Carol remembers arranging for Josh's body first to be laid out at a funeral home on 52d Street, for the people in the entertainment business who might not be able to come to the formal funeral. Then she moved him up to Epworth United Methodist Church in the Bronx, her church, where they had first met and had been married. The funeral was held on September 10, and the police had to cordon off two blocks. The television cameras came, and the reporters. Gospel singers led the congregation in hymns and performed solos, and Josh Jr. read a eulogy.

The body remained in the church overnight. Josh had requested cremation, but Carol could not stand the idea, so the next morning the coffin was transported to Cypress Hills cemetery in Brooklyn. The policeman in charge startled Carol by asking her permission to give Josh's body a full escort to the Triborough Bridge. "I thought, 'Josh is not the president. Come on.' But they escorted us to the Triborough Bridge, up to where you pay the toll. Then they got out, and as we went through they saluted."

At the cemetery, Fern sang "It Is Well with My Soul" as the casket was lowered. Carol had one final consolation: "I buried him exactly like you'd see him onstage," she says proudly. "He was in a green velvet shirt opened to the chest, and the pants were another shade of green, and green alligator shoes. He was as handsome in death as he was on the stage, and I'm happy for that because I would not want his feelings to be hurt that he looked bad. I wanted everyone to remember him just the way he looked up there."

# EPILOGUE

▪ ▪ ▪ ▪ ▪ ▪ ▪ ▪ ▪ ▪ ▪ ▪ ▪ ▪ ▪ ▪ ▪ ▪ ▪ ▪ ▪ ▪

Josh would be remembered fondly by his family, friends, and
fans, but for twenty-five years after his death he was all
but forgotten in the larger world. By 1969 his style was already considered rather archaic; the folk music boom was
just about over, and those singers who wanted to remain
commercial were playing contemporary material and using
bands. His death was noted with obituaries in the major
newspapers and some tender remembrances by old friends.
Don McLean penned a long-overdue appreciation in *Sing
Out!* and Jac Holzman went back into the Elektra vaults to
compile a two-record album, *The Best of Josh White,* issued in
1971. By that time, though, it was a rara avis in the catalogue, appearing between the Doors' *Morrison Hotel* and
Judy Collins's *Whales and Nightingales.*

Josh's music had influenced many of the later folk and
folk-rock performers, but that influence was often at second
or third hand, and even the artists themselves were not always aware of the fact. Most of his records went out of print,
and the music histories tended to mention him only in passing, if at all. In part, this was because music marketers and
historians have usually arranged their work by genre, and
they have never known quite where to file him. Was he a folk
or a blues singer? Or should he be considered a mainstream
entertainer like Harry Belafonte? His failure to fit into a

neat box was part of what made his work unique but also makes it hard for people to figure out how and where he belongs in the music world.

Indeed, one of the problems in assessing Josh's legacy is that his strengths and weaknesses were so often the same. His showmanship and the imagination with which he reshaped his musical influences made him the only early blues star capable of reaching outside that field but earned him the contempt of a generation of later blues fans. He helped to create and popularize the modern concepts of "folk" and "blues" music but was not "folk" or "blues" enough for the audience he had developed. His politics made him a star but cost him his stardom. His flamboyant lifestyle made him larger than life but helped bring about his early death.

If evaluated more justly, Josh's contradictions might have been seen as strengths. To him, "folk" was not a stylistic straitjacket but a category that could encompass virtually anything that moved him. What mattered to him in a song was that he could believe in it and communicate what he found in it to his listeners. It was the breadth of his vision that made him a successful performer over more than four decades, moving from southern street corners to huge concert halls halfway around the world.

There was more to Josh's success than the music, though, and more than musical reasons for his subsequent eclipse. There was also the politics, and, probably more important in the long run, there were all the contradictions of race. Josh proclaimed himself black and proud twenty-five years before James Brown, but his audience was overwhelmingly white. During his life he was always straddling what for most people was an impassable boundary. Until his very last years, his home remained in Harlem, and his closest friends — at least the male ones — were black, but he moved comfortably in white society and made his whole later career there. He would have loved to have the wide, interracial acceptance of a Nat 'King' Cole, but paradoxically, his commitment to older black styles alienated him from the African American audience of his time. Today, his race ensures that his CDs will end up in the blues bins at record stores, even though the blues audience was never his strongest constituency.

Blues continues to be marketed with the mythology of Delta juke joints, noisy roadhouses, and the stereotyped themes that Richard Wright summed up back in 1941 as "love, razors, dice, and death." Its history has little room for a sophisticated performer who made most of his living playing at fashionable clubs and concert halls for a wealthy, white clientele. Meanwhile, folk music has become segregated to a greater degree than ever before, with only two or three black artists managing to be included at all. As for pop, the idea that a black man singing traditional songs accompanied by his own acoustic guitar could have ever been a pop star seems crazy to most modern listeners.

Outside the music world, Josh has been almost completely forgotten. His few appearances on Broadway and in films were important as entrees, as symbols of a black artist breaking unfamiliar ground, but neither the plays nor the movies were very good, and his contributions were soon eclipsed by those of Belafonte, Poitier, and the generation of performers who followed. Books on black entertainers rarely mention him, much less give him his due as a pioneer: the smart, cool man of the future.

Of course, some people have remembered and applauded his work. First among them is Josh Jr., who, along with pursuing his own career, has done his best to keep his father's name before the public. In 1983 he toured briefly in a one-man show based on Josh's life, and in 1986 he earned a Grammy nomination for an instrumental tribute album of Josh's trademark material. In the last two years he has also done an instructional video and a book of Josh's guitar arrangements, and his latest album is titled *In Tribute to Josh White: House of the Rising Son*. (Josh's other children made lives outside of music, though Judith still sings with a gospel group in Atlanta.)

In recent years there have even been hints of a Josh White revival. As the first generation of blues and folk historians, many of whom resented Josh's overarching popularity, have given way to younger writers, his work is being gradually rediscovered. Whereas in 1994 none of his recordings were available on compact discs, there are now over a dozen on the market, and more are forthcoming. Document Records, a specialist label for blues collectors, released three CDs containing his complete race 78s; these met with enough success that the label broke its usual rule of sticking to prewar material and went on to produce three more, extending through his work of the mid-1940s. The Sony/Columbia "Roots 'n' Blues" series, best known for its Robert Johnson box, released a sample of the race material as well, and Smithsonian Folkways weighed in with an overview of Josh's Asch recordings. Meanwhile, Audio CD and Tradition Records released several of his 1950s sessions.

In 1998 came an honor that would have made Josh particularly proud: the U.S. postal service included him in its "Legends of American Music" series. A painting of him, guitar in hand, appears on a sheet of "Folk Musicians" stamps, alongside Woody Guthrie, Leadbelly, and Sonny Terry.

So maybe it is Josh's time once again. If so, the fact would not have been entirely surprising to him. He liked to make self-deprecating statements, to describe himself as having no voice or as more of a storyteller than a musician, but he was also very proud of his work and of what he had made of his life. He was well aware that he could be less than heroic but also believed that he had earned the applause and the love he received from so many people. And I think he would be pleased that thirty years after his death, someone should care to write this book.

# NOTES

CHAPTER ONE

Page 2. "As long as grandpere lived"    All uncited quotations are from interviews conducted by the author between 1994 and 1998.

Page 3. "We couldn't do anything at home . . . too much stinks"    This quotation is from the first of three interviews conducted with Josh c. 1963 by Robert Shelton, for Robert Shelton, with Walter Raim, *The Josh White Song Book* (Chicago: Quadrangle Books, 1963). Quotations from interviews 1 and 2 are drawn from a transcript, apparently made for Shelton's use, of the tape-recorded interviews. His book often condenses these originals and sometimes adds a sentence here or there, either from further conversations, through editorial choice, or by using the original tape to correct transcript mistakes. Since only the third tape seems to have survived, it is impossible to check the accuracy of transcription of the other two, but since their transcripts are more complete than the quotations in Shelton's book, I have treated them as a primary source; for interview 3 I have corrected the transcript from the original tape. In minor cases I have accepted without comment Shelton's insertion or deletion of a word or two from the quotations, but none of these differences is in matters of substance.

Page 4. "The first indication . . . families of Greenville"    Josh White Christmas broadcast, 1955, produced by Charles Chilton for the BBC, courtesy of Charles Chilton.

Page 5. "Whenever the Constitution"    Quoted in Robert Burke Everett, *Race Relations in South Carolina, 1900–1932* (Ann Arbor, Mich.: University Microfilms, 1970), pp. 9, 191.

Page 5. "black brutes"    Quoted in Everett, *Race Relations,* p. 187.

Page 5. "In South Carolina they hung colored people"    Quoted in Bruce Bastin, *Red River Blues: The Blues Tradition in the Southeast* (Urbana: University of Illinois Press, 1986), p. 171.

Pages 6–7. "My daddy was a learned man . . . fixing his tie"    The story of Josh's father's beating, incarceration, and death are from Shelton interview 1.

Page 7. *Father's heart condition*    Georgina Campbell, "Study in White and Blues," *Negro Digest,* November 1945.

Page 8. "We got a different kind of feeling"    Studs Terkel radio interview with Josh White, c. 1964, courtesy of Katie Lee.

Page 10. "I was coming home from school" Studs Terkel radio interview with Josh White and Katie Lee, 1955 (to which the sentence about the bushels of corn is added from a similar telling of the story in Shelton interview 1), courtesy of Katie Lee.

CHAPTER TWO

Page 12. "To a kid" Quoted in Avery S. Denham, "Preacher in Song," *Collier's,* November 16, 1946, p. 44.

Pages 12–13. "In those days on highways . . . the direction from which we came" Shelton interview 1. (For the sake of clarity, I have taken the liberty of switching the words "torture" and "mutilation" in this quotation, which either Josh or the transcriber seems to have mixed up.)

Pages 13–14. "As I went into the jail . . . beating the tambourine" Shelton interview 1.

Page 14. "I never had the childhood" Shelton interview 1.

Page 14. "While we were in a city" Shelton interview 1.

Pages 15–16. "All blind people" Quoted in Max Jones, "Josh White Looks Back, Part 2," *Blues Unlimited,* September 1968, p. 16.

Page 15. "It's hot" Shelton interview 1.

Page 15. "Wherever we stayed at night" Denham, "Preacher in Song," p. 72.

Page 15. "Why didn't I run away" Denham, "Preacher in Song," p. 44. (The employer mentioned in this quotation was Joe Taggart, but there was clearly some confusion, as Josh always maintained in other interviews that his first employer was Arnold, followed some years later by Taggart. Either Josh was mixed up this time, or he was simplifying a previously confused story in the interest of producing a cohesive narrative, or the interviewer messed it up. Whatever caused the switching of names, though, the general picture remains the same.)

Page 15. "People seemed to come out of the earth" Denham, "Preacher in Song," p. 72.

Page 16. "Dan Patch II, a pacer" Shelton interview 1.

Page 16. "It was so cold" Shelton interview 1.

Page 17. "We called it canvassing" Terkel radio interview, 1955.

Page 17. "It was a life" Denham, "Preacher in Song," p. 44.

Page 18. "Arnold had a powerful voice" Shelton interview 1.

Page 18. "He played about four chords" Terkel radio interview, c. 1964.

Page 18. "even better than Blind Blake" Jones, "Josh White Looks Back, Part 2," p. 16.

Page 20. *learning the guitar all wrong* Paul Oliver, *Blues Off the Record* (New York: Da Capo Press, 1984).

Page 20. *sebastopol tuning*   I use the term "sebastopol" rather than "open D" tuning throughout this book, because among Josh's gifts was a superb pitch sense that allowed him to retune his guitar with unusual speed. As a result, few of these songs are in the absolute key of D; he would simply tune to suit his vocal range, often changing by as much as three full tones from one song to the next, and sinking as low as Bb.

For those interested in the history of the term, "Sebastopol" was a beginner's guitar piece set in this open D tuning, a partner to the ubiquitous "Spanish Fandango," which gave its name to the open G ("Spanish") tuning. Both date from at least the 1840s, though blues historians commonly but mistakenly link sebastopol to a later piece, "The Siege of Sebastopol," a piano work written in the 1890s to commemorate a battle of the Crimean War. It is also common to treat this nomenclature (which sometimes uses the mispronunciation "vestapol") as insider jargon of the blues world, but both "Spanish" and "sebastopol" were used as names for G and D tuning by white, middle-class parlor guitarists, since the two songs were often the first "open" pieces a novice player would be taught. The terms appear without explanation, though placed in quotation marks, in guitar magazines of the 1890s.

Page 21. "He would sit all night long . . . and that was powerful"   Jones, "Josh White Looks Back, Part 2," p. 16.

Page 21. *Josh's early playing*   Some experts have claimed to hear similarities to Jefferson's playing in Josh's work, but these are far less marked than in the playing of hundreds of other guitarists. Jefferson was a huge star, and his licks became part of the basic language of blues. As far as direct transmission goes, however, Josh's blues records do not include one tune chorded in the key of C, which was Jefferson's favorite. (Josh did record one song in C, "Baby, Won't You Doodle-Do-Do," but since it was chorded in barred F chord shapes, without any C shapes, it does not change the argument about his relationship to Jefferson.) As chord shapes are generally the first thing one picks up from watching another player, it is extremely unlikely that a student of his would not have at least occasionally used that key. Josh's early blues recordings find him virtually trapped in the key of A, with an occasional excursion into E (when not playing in sebastopol tuning), as was typical of many Carolina blues players. The left-hand positions for E and A are quite different from those for C, G, and F. Jefferson was a virtuoso and made some very popular recordings in E and a few in A, but C was his favorite key (with G also fairly common), and virtually all the guitarists who took him for their model followed his lead in this matter.

Page 21. *Carl Martin and Josh*   Some experts have suggested that Josh may have known and even studied with Martin. There is no direct evidence for this, but he clearly was aware of Martin's work. In 1935 he recorded Martin's "Badly Mistreated Man," and if he did not learn it directly from the source, he certainly picked it up speedily, recording it only a month and a half after Martin cut his original in Chicago.

Page 21. "I managed to get on those recordings" Jones, "Josh White Looks Back, Part 2," p. 15.

Page 23. "*Scandalous and a Shame*" Transcribed from Blind Joe Taggart and Joshua White, "Scandalous and a Shame," Paramount 1270, 1928, reissued on *Blind Joe Taggart: Complete Recorded Works in Chronological Order, Vol. 1,* Document Records DOCD5153, Vienna, Austria, 1993.

Page 24. "Josh loathed the idea" Quoted in Shelton, *Song Book,* p. 20 (as of 1994, Shelton could not remember this man's name or why he chose not to be identified).

Page 24. *Charlie Spand and Carver Boys* Josh's presence on the Spand date is probable but not certain, but there is ample evidence for his appearance with the Carvers: the Paramount recording log lists him as a performer on the session, and he spontaneously recalled the record more than thirty years later.

Page 25. *Vocals on Taggart's records* Josh is not listed on these records, but the aural evidence leaves little doubt that the second voice is his.

CHAPTER THREE

Page 27. "The nurses took a liking to me" Shelton, *Song Book,* p. 20

Page 28. *Thomas A. Dorsey and changed blues style* Harris, Michael W., *The Rise of Gospel Blues* (New York: Oxford University Press, 1992).

Page 29. "Josh was very weak" Quoted in Shelton, *Song Book,* p. 21.

Page 29. "She prayed over it" Nan Winton BBC radio interview with Josh White, transmitted August 17, 1963; available in BBC archives.

Page 30. "*Greenville Sheik*" Transcribed from Josh White, "Greenville Sheik," ARC 6-05-63, reissued on *Josh White: Complete Blues Singer 1932–1936,* Columbia Legacy CK67001, New York, 1996. This record was recorded on April 11, 1932, but not released until 1936, as Josh's final release for ARC.

Pages 32–33. *Slidelike vibrato* B. B. King, who brought a similarly vibrato-marked approach to electric lead playing, has said that he developed his style in an attempt to imitate the sound of a slide guitar.

Page 33. *Influence on Blind Boy Fuller and Buddy Moss* Bastin, *Red River Blues,* p. 169. (The guitarist's name was Willie Trice.)

Page 33. *Song learned from Joe Walker* Shelton, *Song Book,* p. 56. The ARC recording cards list W. R. Calaway as both author and publisher for all the songs recorded at the August 1933 session, but since these include two traditional religious songs recorded years earlier by Blind Willie Johnson, it is clearly a matter of a producer cashing in by signing his name after the fact, rather than a legitimate claim of authorship.

Page 33. *Sales of religious records*  Sales figures for race records are largely a matter of speculation, but the popularity of these sides is further attested by their relative lack of rarity on the later collector's market for blues 78s.

Page 35. *Langston Hughes on Harlem Renaissance*  Quoted in Nat Brandt, *Harlem at War: The Black Experience in WWII* (Syracuse, N.Y.: Syracuse University Press, 1996), p. 32.

Page 35. *WPA study*  Brandt, *Harlem at War.* p. 40.

Page 36. "Usually admission was fifteen cents"  Roi Ottley, *New World A-Coming* (Boston: Houghton Mifflin, 1943), p. 63.

Page 36. *Salary for early radio show*  Campbell, "Study in White and Blues."

Page 36. "He'd entertain us after dinner"  Quoted in Dorothy Schainman Siegel, *The Glory Road: The Story of Josh White* (New York: Harcourt Brace Jovanovich, 1982), pp. 14, 50.

Page 39. *Josh in Greenville jail*  Shelton, *Song Book,* p. 22.

Pages 40–41. *Recording with Carr and Blackwell*  Williams published both of the original songs that Josh recorded at the August session, and the following day he recorded two sides of his own at the beginning of another Carr and Blackwell session, at which Carr recorded several Williams compositions, some coauthored by W. R. Calaway. More Williams and Calaway compositions were cut at the December session, which raises the possibility that Williams, rather than taking over from Calaway, had formed some sort of working arrangement with him. (It should be noted that their shared author credit by no means proves that they were writing songs together. It was not unusual for a producer or publisher to stick his name on someone else's song and collect the composer royalties.) There is strong evidence that Josh had met Carr and Blackwell at least two weeks before the August session: on the first of August he cut a nice version of "I Believe I'll Make a Change," which Carr himself would not record until August 16. Josh's ARC log lists the composer as unknown, whereas Carr's record gives the writers as Sparks and Sparks; this suggests that Carr got it from the authors, whereas Josh got it secondhand. As additional evidence, Josh muffs some words and forgets the punning tag line that rhymes with the song's title phrase: "Gonna turn off this gas stove, I'm bound for a brand new range."

Page 41. *Recording under different names*  This explanation is not only logical but supported by Josh's recollections as given in Marjorie E. Greene, "Josh White Starts Them Listening," *Opportunity* 22, no. 3 (1944), p. 113, and Josh's listing in the 1944 *Current Biography,* p. 735.

Page 41. *Recording "Black Gal"*  "Black Gal" (or "Black Gal What Makes Your Head So Hard?"), recorded in April 1934 by the Texas bluesman Joe Pullum, was a big enough hit to spawn three sequels by Pullum and a cover by Carr and Blackwell, recorded on August 16—two days after their session backing Josh. Josh cut his version the following February.

Page 44. "Bad Nigger Makes Good Minstrel"    "Bad Nigger Makes Good Minstrel," *Life,* April 19, 1937, p. 39.

Page 45. *Progressive and populist circles*    Through the 1930s and 1940s, "progressive" was used in liberal and left-wing circles as more or less a code word meaning Communist, or at least Communist-associated. In general, I have preserved this usage when "Communist" would be too precise for a group that included many non-Party members but that was the general tendency of its political allegiances.

Page 45. *Bob Miller and Aunt Molly Jackson*    Ronald D. Cohen and Dave Samuelson, notes for *Songs for Political Action,* Bear Family Records, 1996, pp. 58, 59. (The 212-page booklet, accompanying a ten-CD set, is the best available work on folk music and the American left, and I have used it as a principal source of information on recordings of the period.)

CHAPTER FOUR

Page 46. "I'm funny"    John W. Riley, "Singer Josh White Tells How He Beat Adversity," *Boston Globe,* March 17, 1952.

Pages 46–47. "That's not really the way"    Richard Southern to the author, June 23, 1998.

Page 47. "I made them sew it up"    Riley, "Singer Josh White."

Page 47. "felt as if"    Siegel, *Glory Road,* p. 52.

Page 47. "I was a stevedore"    Winton radio interview, 1963.

Page 48. "They fired me . . . from the union"    Shelton interview 2.

Page 48. "perhaps the most modern"    Ottley, *New World A-Coming,* p. 180.

Page 49. "Carol worked in walk-up flats"    Shelton interview 2.

Page 50. *Role of Blind Lemon*    This is according to de Paur. In Shelton interview 2, Josh said that originally the baritone Kenneth Spencer was signed to play John Henry, but though he had the voice, he lacked the physique, so Robeson replaced him.

Pages 51–52. "Mrs. Bradford asked me"    Shelton interview 2.

Page 52. *Singing Christian and Pinewood Tom same person*    Shelton, *Song Book,* p. 23.

Page 52. "I wish I could find"    Riley, "Singer Josh White."

Page 52. *De Paur's drawn-out story*    Siegel, *Glory Road,* p. 58.

Page 53. "I told Bradford . . . Paul didn't do it"    Shelton interview 2.

Page 54. *"John Henry" reviews*    Brooks Atkinson, "The Play," *New York Times,* January 11, 1940; "John Henry," *Variety,* January 17, 1940; Martin McCall, "Paul Robeson Stars in New Play, 'John Henry,'" *Daily Worker,* New York, January 12, 1940, p. 7; Dan Burley, "Music Overwhelms Po' 'John Henry,'" *New York Amsterdam News,* January 20, 1940.

## CHAPTER FIVE

Page 58. "We did a number of things" Quoted in Charles Wolfe and Kip Lornell, *The Life and Legend of Leadbelly* (New York: HarperCollins, 1992), p. 213.

Page 59. "We started at 2:00 A.M." Olof G. Nilsson, "Josh Intime: Samtal med en folkmusikens ambassador," *Orkester Journalen* (Sweden), September 1951 (translated by Israel Young).

Page 60. "I massaged that hand" Quoted in Riley, "Singer Josh White."

Page 62. *Gellert collection* Lawrence Gellert, *Me and My Captain (Chain Gangs): Negro Songs of Protest from the Collection of Lawrence Gellert* (New York: Hours Press, 1939).

Page 62. *Gellert's lawsuit* Whether or not this suit actually came to court, Columbia recognized Gellert's claim: although the original recording cards for the *Chain Gang* album list all the songs as traditional, arranged and copyrighted by Josh and DePaur, Gellert's name has been added to the copyright line in a slightly different typeface.

Page 62. "I've been beaten twice" Private tape recorded by Katie Lee at her home, Los Angeles, 1954.

Page 62. *Ownership of folksongs* Many of the songs in Gellert's books are unique to them, and other folklorists have suggested that some may actually be his own compositions. If so, the irony is even deeper, as he would have been suing to protect his right to his own original work while protesting all the while that he was simply an intermediary who had brought the songs to light from an anonymous folk tradition.

Page 62. "They had whiskey voices" Terkel radio interview, c. 1964.

Page 63. "[higher-ups] were terribly upset" Quoted in Siegel, p. 62.

Pages 63–64. "vastly exciting" Howard Taubman, "Records: Chain Gang," *New York Times*, August 18, 1940.

Page 64. "*Trouble*" Josh White and Leonard de Paur, arrangers, "Trouble," transcribed from Josh White and his Carolinians, *Chain Gang*, Columbia Records set C-22.

Page 64. "My Uncle Sonny . . . song about Uncle Sonny" Terkel radio interview, c. 1964.

Page 65. "one of the finest albums" Davis, Frank Marshall, "Rating the Records," *New York Amsterdam News*, August 17, 1940, p. 16.

Page 65. "breaking things up nightly" "He's Newest Rage Downtown," *New York Amsterdam News*, December 7, 1940, p. 20.

Page 65. *Cafe Society and Rosetta Tharpe* *New York Post*, November 23 and December 13, 1940.

Page 65. "really big break" Winton radio interview, 1963.

Page 66. *Lomax and sharecropper* Alan Lomax, *The Land Where the Blues Began* (New York: Pantheon Books, 1993), p. xi.

Page 67. "a jewel of a performer"    Quoted in Siegel, *Glory Road,* p. 66.

Page 68. "conditioned in the South"    Siegel, *Glory Road,* p. 65.

Page 69. "enormous break with every tradition . . . authority of the event"
Ralph Rinzler, interview with Alan Lomax, 1982, from Lomax files.

Page 69. *Library of Congress concert*  Library of Congress discs 6092–95,
"Negro folk music in the Emancipation Celebration," Coolidge Auditorium, December 20, 1940.

Page 70. "galaxy of distinguished artists"    *Washington Post,* January 20, 1941,
pp. 1, 2.

Page 70. *Constitution Hall appearance*  Washington *Daily News,* January 20,
1941, p. 19; and *Baltimore Afro-American,* January 25, 1941.

CHAPTER SIX

Page 72. *Scottsboro Boys*  Leadbelly's song was recorded first in 1938 and
again in 1940. The Scottsboro Boys had been arrested in Alabama in
1931 — accused of raping two women who had been riding the same
freight train — and quickly sentenced to death. Outside the white South
the case was almost universally derided as a racist frame-up, and retrials —
with defense lawyers supplied by the Communist Party — dragged on
through 1937, when four were released. The other five remained in jail
into the 1940s, one until 1950.

Page 73. *Communist Party membership*  It is difficult to come up with any very
good numbers for Communist Party membership. Howard Zinn, in his
*People's History of the United States* (New York: Harper & Row, 1980), p. 420,
estimates that top membership was around 100,000 but higher and lower
figures have been given. Either way, this number does not mean much, as
people were steadily joining and leaving. The hard core of long-term
members was certainly far smaller, the mass of "progressive" sympathizers
far bigger.

Page 74. "They have forgotten"    Rinzler interview with Lomax, 1982.

Page 76. *Party's effect on blacks' self-perception*  Ottley, *New World A-Coming,*
p. 243.

Page 78. *Excusing Hitler-Stalin pact*  By way of context, my grandfather, a
Jewish refugee who had fled Nazi Austria in 1938, felt that Stalin knew
what he was doing and had signed the nonaggression pact in a legitimate
attempt to protect Russia from the Nazi threat.

Pages 78–79. Songs for John Doe *album*  Cohen and Samuelson, notes to
*Songs for Political Action,* pp. 84–85.

Page 79. *Almanac label for controversial album*  Cohen and Samuelson, notes to
*Songs for Political Action,* pp. 77–78.

Page 79. "Not unless you want to ignore"    Pete Seeger with Peter Blood,

*Where Have All the Flowers Gone: A Singer's Stories, Songs, Seeds, Robberies* (Bethlehem, PA: 1993), p. 22.

Page 79. *Album sold in Communist bookstores*   Cohen and Samuelson, notes to *Songs for Political Action*, p. 78.

Page 80. *William Waring Cuney's lyrics*   William Waring Cuney, *Storefront Church*, Heritage Series, vol. 23 (London: Paul Brennan, 1973), p. 14.

Page 81. *"Hard Times Blues"*   Josh White and Waring Cuney, "Hard Times Blues," transcribed from *Southern Exposure*, Keynote Recordings Album 107, New York, 1941.

Page 82. "the 'Spirituals' of the city . . . distance once reigned."   Richard Wright, "Notes on Jim Crow Blues," liner notes to *Southern Exposure*.

Page 83. Fortune *magazine poll*   Michael Denning, *The Cultural Front: The Laboring of American Culture in the Twentieth Century,* (New York: Verso, 1997), p. 4.

Page 83. *Communist Party membership*   Maurice Isserman, *Which Side Were You On? The American Communist Party during the Second World War* (Middletown, Conn.: Wesleyan University Press, 1982), p. 149.

Page 83. "used to play for all the communist dances"   Dizzy Gillespie with Al Fraser, *To Be or Not . . . to Bop: Memoirs* (Garden City, N.Y.: Doubleday, 1979), p. 80.

Pages 83–84. "I don't know whether they're going in"   Quoted in Margaret Walker, *Richard Wright: Daemonic Genius* (New York: Warner Books: 1988), p. 178.

Page 84. "fraught with danger to efficiency"   Quoted in Brandt, *Harlem at War,* p. 69.

Page 84. "confuse the issue of prompt preparedness"   Brandt, *Harlem at War,* p. 70.

Page 85. "We kept driving around . . . to say about Uncle Sam"   Shelton interview 3.

Pages 85–86. *"Uncle Sam Says"*   Josh White and Waring Cuney, "Uncle Sam Says," transcribed from *Southern Exposure*.

Pages 86–87. "One tourist ranch in Taxco"   Bert Robbins, "Blasting Jim-Crow with Song," *Daily Worker,* September 25, 1941, p. 7.

Page 87. "paid homage to Mr. White"   "Guitar Party Big Success," *New York Amsterdam Star-News,* August 30, 1941.

Page 87. "he had just come back from Mexico"   Ben Wilkes, "Tribute to Josh White," *New Masses,* September 9, 1941.

Page 87. "no record library should be without"   Marvel Cooke, " 'Southern Exposure' Discs on 'Best' Recording List," *New York Amsterdam Star-News,* September 27, 1941.

Page 88. *Report of honorary degree*   This presentation is reported in numerous sources, but the Fisk University archivist can find no confirmation. My guess would be that Josh received an award of some kind rather than an honorary degree, but this is pure speculation.

Pages 88–89. "He said he wanted to see what I looked like . . . the kind of guy he was"   Shelton interview 3.

CHAPTER SEVEN

Page 91. "for a nightclub audience"   Quoted in Siegel, *Glory Road*, p. 67.

Page 91. "I turned on the work-lamp"   Max Gordon, *Live at the Village Vanguard* (New York: St. Martin's Press, 1980), pp. 43–53.

Page 92. "got all it takes . . . any level but their best is wrong"   Woody Guthrie to Max Gordon, in Gordon, *Village Vanguard*, pp. 45–53.

Page 93. "the most formal human being"   Asch, Moses, interviewed by Israel Young, in *Sing Out!* 26, no. 1 (1977): 6.

Page 93. "immaculately attired"   Gordon, *Village Vanguard*, p. 45.

Page 93. *"Mr. Lee" and "Mr. Pete"*   Doris Willens, *Lonesome Traveler: The Life of Lee Hays* (New York: Norton, 1988).

Page 93. "He was a fine artist"   Quoted in Bob Dawbarn, "No—Religion and Bunnies Don't Mix!" *Melody Maker,* August 24, 1963, p. 8.

Page 95. "worse than any audition"   Libby Holman, "Footlights: Libby Holman Sings the Blues about Blues That Aren't Blue," *Philadelphia Record,* August 20, 1944.

Page 96. "prepared to forget"   Quoted in Jon Bradshaw, *Dreams That Money Can Buy: The Tragic Life of Libby Holman* (New York: William Morrow, 1985), p. 216.

Page 96. "It took me around twelve months"   Shelton interview 3, p. 1 (the surviving tape does not include the quotations that appear on the first page of the transcript, so for these the transcript has been used as a primary source).

Page 97. "I'm so happy I've found a place . . . sounds simple but isn't"   Marjory Adams, "Libby Holman Presenting Own Americana of Songs," *Boston Daily Globe,* February 17, 1942, p. 19.

Page 97. "she'll sing a tin pan alley 'blues' "   John A. Hamilton, "Time Out for Diners and Dancers," *Boston Daily Globe,* February 20, 1942, p. 23.

Page 97. "My brother was at Fort Devens . . . put up a German swastika"   Shelton interview 3, p. 1. (Josh remembered that Libby was joined by Bobby Short, but this is clearly an error, for Short was only fifteen at the time and says he never even heard of the incident.)

Page 97. "not trying to copy the Negroes"   Earl Wilson, "Libby Holman to Sing with Negro Guitarist," *New York Post,* February 16, 1942, p. 5.

Page 98. *Recording ban*   Sometimes referred to as the "Petrillo ban," after the AF of M's president, James C. Petrillo, this was a strike against the record companies, demanding that some sort of royalty arrangement be worked out to provide recompense for the use of records rather than live music on radio and in places of public entertainment. It lasted two years, until the major labels agreed to pay the union a royalty, and during this time virtually no commercial recordings were made in the United States. The result is some dramatic gaps in the historical record, as those two years were key, for example, to the growth of the bebop movement in jazz.

Page 99. "so full I could barely squeeze in" Dale Harrison, *Grand Forks* (N.D.) *Evening Herald,* November 13, 1942.

Page 99. "on the way to becoming" Earl Wilson, "It Happened Last Night," *New York Post,* April 16, 1943, p. 7.

Page 99. "There are moments" "Tables for Two: Rebirth of the Blues," *New Yorker,* November 14, 1942, p. 54.

Page 99. "I sing them better" Wilson, "It Happened Last Night."

CHAPTER EIGHT

Page 104. "the guitar-strumming colored singer" *Variety,* August 1, 1943.

Pages 104–5. "famed as a singer of traditional spirituals" Dorothy Norman, "A Troubadour Sings of Tolerance," *New York Post,* July 21, 1944.

Page 105. Variety *review* *Variety,* August 1, 1943.

Page 105. *Author of "Little Man"* Arnold Blom, "Heard and Overheard," *PM,* May 25, 1944, p. 21, refers to "Little Man" as "Josh's own composition"; Greene, "Josh White Starts Them Listening," p. 113, says that "he writes or helps write" most of his militant songs. In later interviews, when he spoke about the songs on *Southern Exposure,* all of which were credited to him and Waring Cuney, with Cuney presumably the main lyricist, Josh never bothered to mention that he had had a coauthor.

Page 106. "When I say I wrote it" Quoted in Siegel, *Glory Road,* p. 24.

Page 106. "They found Dorie Miller" Greene, "Josh White Starts Them Listening."

Page 107. "it sounded pretty foolish" Roy Wilkins, *Autobiography,* cited in Brandt, *Harlem at War,* p. 93.

Pages 107–8. *"Freedom Road"* Langston Hughes and Emerson Harper, "Freedom Road," transcribed from Josh White recording, Asch 349-3B, reissued on Josh White, *Free and Equal Blues,* Smithsonian/Folkways 40081, Washington, D.C., 1998.

Page 108. "White Folks Do Some Funny Things" *New World A-Coming,* no. 7, "White Folks Do Some Funny Things," April 16, 1944 (script and tape in Schomburg Library, New York).

Page 108. "Music at War" *New World A-Coming,* no. 19, "Music at War," October 29, 1944 (script and tape in Schomburg Library).

Page 109. "Josh had his little prejudice 'tests'" Shelton, *Song Book,* p. 27.

Page 110. "long and amicable sojourn . . . worked to his advantage"   "Trouble Stalks Heyward and White," *New York Amsterdam News*, September 30, 1944.

Page 110. "on several occasions"   Doug Yeager, notes of interview with Mary Lou Williams.

Page 110. "to sit at the next table"   Siegel, *Glory Road*, pp. 80–82.

Page 111. "we talked and finally came downstairs"   *Melody Maker* (London), August 8, 1959, p. 5, cited in John Chilton, *Billie's Blues: Billie Holiday's Story 1933–1959* (New York: Stein & Day, 1975), pp. 103–4.

Page 111. "that song should be sung"   Quoted in Shelton, *Song Book*, p. 27.

Page 111. "I'm no speech maker"   Quoted in Greene, "Josh White Starts Them Listening," pp. 112, 115.

Pages 111–12. "If I reach one person . . . things to come"   Nat Low, "Talking It Over with Josh White," *Daily Worker*, May 1, 1945.

Page 112. "The sound of his guitar"   Eartha Kitt, *Alone with Me* (Chicago: Henry Regnery, 1976), p. 94.

Page 112. "Josh was a wonderfully sexy man"   Lena Horne and Richard Schickel, *Lena* (Garden City, N.Y.: Doubleday, 1965), p. 116.

Page 112. "He played sex to the hilt"   Doug Yeager, notes of interview with Barney Josephson.

Page 112. "When they saw that neck"   Quoted in Whitney Balliett, *Barney, Bradley, and Max: Sixteen Portraits in Jazz* (New York: Oxford University Press, 1989), p. 48. (Balliett's profile of Barney Josephson also provided much general information on Cafe Society.)

Page 113. "I told Barney . . . greatest goddam nightclub in the world"   Shelton, *Song Book*, p. 26.

Page 114. *Sammy Benskin story*   Quoted in Siegel, *Glory Road*, pp. 77–78.

Page 114. "as stern in his audience demands"   *Cue*, June 2, 1945, p. 8.

Page 117. "You could call Josh White . . . also sings easy"   Langston Hughes, notes to *Songs by Josh White*, Asch album 348, c. 1944.

Page 119. "most of his tune singing"   *Billboard* (apparently, though the clipping is not clear), November 4, 1944.

Page 119. "an old Irish sea song"   Luther A. Townsley, "Early American Blues Paint Race's Epic Economic Struggles Says Critic," *Kansas City Missouri Call*, December 15, 1944.

Page 120. *"One Meat Ball" history*   Betty Moorsteen, and Eleanor Morehead, "The Saga of the Meatball," *PM*, March 16, 1945, p. 13.

Page 120. "the three girls do no better"   *Down Beat* (Chicago), January 15, 1945.

Page 120. "Listening to Josh White"   "Tables for Two," *New Yorker*, January 20, 1945.

Page 121. *Chicago newspaper reviews*   Bulliet, C. J., *Chicago Daily News*, December 4, 1944; Claudia Cassidy, "Libby Holman and Josh White Sing Blues, and How They Sing!" *Chicago Daily Tribune,* December 4, 1944, p. 13; Al Monroe, "Josh White and Libby Holman Please Throng," *Chicago Defender,* December 9, 1944, p. 7.

Page 122. "The idea of a Negro and white artist"   Low, "Talking It Over."

Page 122. "the strongest thing that we did"   Shelton interview 3.

Page 122. *Strain in relationship*   Bradshaw, *Libby Holman* p. 241

Page 123. Blue Holiday *reviews*   All reviews found in *New York Theatre Critics' Reviews* (New York: Critics' Theatre Reviews, 1945), pp. 216–18.

Page 124. "a singer doesn't have to worry"   *Cue,* June 2, 1945, p. 8.

Page 124. *Plans for national and European tour*   *Newark Star-Ledger,* July 1, 1946.


CHAPTER NINE

Page 125. *Cafe Society salary*   Note by George Hoefer in Rutgers University Jazz Archive, New Brunswick, N.J.

Page 128. "To this day, Mama has never heard me"   Siegel, *Glory Road,* p. 43, quoted from an interview on Cynthia Gooding's radio show.

Page 132. "One night I suddenly heard"   Quoted in Helen McNamara, "Josh White Is Proud of His Children," *Toronto Telegram,* January 9, 1959.

Page 133. "the express stipulation"   Blom, "Heard and Overheard," p. 21.

Page 134. "My parents never told me"   Shelton interview 1.


CHAPTER TEN

Page 138. *Sonny Terry*   Max Jones, "Josh White Looks Back, Part 1," *Blues Unlimited,* July 1968.

Page 139. *Concert at Detroit Art Institute*   *Detroit News,* April 6 and 8, 1946.

Page 139. *Week at Earle Theater, Philadelphia*   Richard Dier, "Josh White: Foremost Singer of Folk Songs," *Baltimore Afro-American,* January 25, 1947, p. 1.

Page 139. *Newcastle concert story*   "Josh White Hits Hard on 16,000 Mile Singing Tour," *Baltimore Afro-American,* January 25, 1947, p. 7.

Page 140. *Josh at People's Songs' founding*   Peter D. Goldsmith, *Making People's Music: Moe Asch and Folkways Records* (Washington, D.C.: 1998), Smithsonian Institution Press, p. 174.

Page 141. "Kids are no dummies"   "Josh White Hits Hard," p. 7.

Page 141. "except for a few lucky townspeople"   *Fargo* (N.D.) *Forum,* November 19, 1946.

Page 141. "nearest approach that we have"   Denham, "Preacher in Song," p. 44.

Page 142. "main attraction, Josh White"   *Mademoiselle,* December 1946.

Page 143. "Medium tall, with a slow, mischievous smile . . . high-bracket income."   Denham, "Preacher in Song," pp. 44, 72–73.

Page 143. "People who have heard of me"   Chet Skreen, "Mr. Blues Comes to Town," *Tacoma Times,* November 25, 1946.

Page 143. "love, razors, dice and death"   "Look Who's Coming, the Great Josh White, Folksinger," *Denver Post,* December 5, 1946.

Page 144. *Odometer reading: 16,923 miles*   "Josh White Hits Hard," p. 7.

Page 144. "The career of Josh White"   People's Songs bulletin, New York, January 1947, p. 2.

Pages 144–45. "Music is my weapon . . . helluva potent weapon"   Ann Seymour, "Josh White Says: Music Is a Mighty Sword against Discrimination," *Daily Worker,* January 15, 1947, p. 11.

Page 146. *Truman pronouncements*   Zinn, *People's History,* pp. 417, 420, is the source for both quotations.

Pages 146–47. *Leon Josephson trial*   Walter Goodman, *The Committee: The Extraordinary Career of the House Committee on Un-American Activities* (New York: Farrar, Straus & Giroux, 1968), pp. 191–93.

Page 147. "My life turned inside out"   Quoted in Balliett, *Barney, Bradley, and Max,* pp. 52–53.

Page 147. "Kilgallen would write . . . blacklisted if they appeared in my clubs"   Quoted in "Barney Josephson. . . . How He Changed America for Good," *New Common Good,* November 1984, p. 13. An example of the press that Cafe Society was receiving is in Westbrook Pegler's column called "Debunking Some 'Loveable' Nightclub Characters" *New York Journal-American,* February 11, 1948: "Josephson is a brother of Leon Josephson, one of the most sinister Communists in the United States. His Cafes Society have been hangouts for Communists and their fellow travelers for years. Barney himself, although he is not identified as a Party member, nevertheless has been so seriously implicated in the works and affairs of known Communists that there is no excuse for any New York byline reporter to purport to give him the character treatment in a column or book, and totally ignore his political personality."

Page 148. "Entertainer at the Washington meeting"   Goodman, *The Committee,* p. 201.

Page 148. "Mary would talk with Howard Rushmore"   Shelton interview 3.

Page 150. "it might do you more harm"   Letter in the Alan Lomax files, dated November 17, 1947.

Page 150. "at dinner Mrs. Roosevelt would be right there"   Script for an Alan Lomax–produced concert recalling folk music in the Roosevelt White House, in the Lomax files.

Page 150. "its message is to polio victims"   "Cafe Society Downtown (Followup)," *Variety,* February 26, 1947.

Page 150. "one of the most mawkish"   *PM,* September 23, 1947.

Page 151. "slightly stylized," "very mannered"   *New Yorker,* February 23,

1946, p. 4, and John Martin, "Josh White Joins Draper and Adler," *New York Times*, December 26, 1947.

CHAPTER ELEVEN

Page 154. "No waiters, no dishes"   Leonard Harris, "No Sad Notes for Josh White, 35 Years a Star," *New York World-Telegram and Sun*, November 13, 1964.

Page 154. "ten most handsome Negro men"   "Cover Girl Moune de Rivel Picks the Ten Most Handsome American Negro Men," *Our World*, March 1947.

Page 156. "just out of Zanesville . . . told them to go to hell"   Paul Denis, "Why Josh White Needed a 'Middle Man,' " *Daily Compass*, July 21, 1949, p. 1.

Page 158. *Extramarital affairs*   For example, his FBI file (received through a Freedom of Information Act request), includes the report of a divorce case in which he was named as a corespondent.

Page 161. *Los Angeles party*   Home recording, 1954, courtesy of Katie Lee.

CHAPTER TWELVE

Page 163. "The landlord's wife"   Lee Newton, " 'A Long Way from Home,' a Long Way from Truth," *Daily Worker*, February 10, 1948.

Page 163. "The performance as a whole"   Brooks Atkinson, "At the Theatre," *New York Times*, February 9, 1948.

Page 164. "I'd like to do things like Dooley Wilson"   Quoted in "The Walking Hills," *Ebony*, October 1948, pp. 64–66.

Page 164. Ebony *magazine piece*   "The Walking Hills," pp. 64–66.

Page 165. "I don't talk in dialect . . ."   New York Post, May 16, 1949, p. 27.

Page 166. "When I started there . . . escaping all the time."   "White Audiences Like His Songs Better than Negroes," *Ebony*, October 1948, p. 66.

Page 167. "In only a few spots"   "Concert by Josh White," *Christian Science Monitor*, Boston, November 6, 1948.

Page 168. "My head is bloodied"   "Barney Josephson . . . How He Changed America for Good," p. 13.

Page 168. "false material statement"   Josh White FBI file, report of January 19, 1955, p. 2.

Page 169. "I got to thinking"   Quoted in Vernon Rice, "Curtain Cues," *New York Post*, December 12, 1949, p. 40.

Page 169. *Reviews of "How Long till Summer"*   All reviews are taken from *New York Theatre Critics' Reviews*, Theatre Critics' Reviews, New York, 1949, pp. 182–84, except the *New Yorker*'s, which is from the issue of January 7, 1950, pp. 44–45.

Page 170. *Racial barriers in television*   "Television," *Ebony*, June 1950, p. 22.

Page 170. *Painting for Urban League benefit auction*   *Ebony*, March 1950, p. 45.

Page 171. "At first I did not think . . . necessary contribution to make"   Eleanor Roosevelt, "Some of My Best Friends Are Negro," *Ebony*, February 1953, pp. 17–26.

Page 171. "She thought I was the one American"   Shelton interview 3.

Page 171. "That should help him"   Eleanor Roosevelt to David Gurewitsch, June 4, 1950, in Joseph P. Lash, *A World of Love: Eleanor Roosevelt and Her Friends, 1943–1962* (Garden City, N.Y.: Doubleday, 1984), p. 321.

Page 171. "There was King Gustav"   Shelton interview 3. Josh mistakenly placed this party in Copenhagen, but Gustav was a Swedish king, and it is clearly the one specified in Mrs. Roosevelt's column as occurring in Stockholm.

Page 171. *"My Day" column*   Cited in *Counterattack*, New York, July 28, 1950. (I have been unable to locate Mrs. Roosevelt's original column among the "My Day" pieces on her trip, but have no reason to doubt its existence.)

Page 172. "Josh White is drinking"   Eleanor Roosevelt to David Gurewitsch, June 10, 1950, in Lash p. 322.

Page 172. *Josh's arrival in Paris*   "Josh White, Le Troubadour Noir," *Jazz Hot*, October 1950, pp. 12, 13.

Pages 173–74. "On Monday night I saw the impossible . . . academic schooling on their instruments"   Dennis Preston, "I Sing the Songs of the People," *Melody Maker*, July 15, 1950.

Page 174. "before the excellent Josh arrived"   *Jazz Journal*, September 1950, p. 11.

Page 175. "To a great singer"   Max Jones, and Sinclair Traill, eds., "Collectors' Corner," *Melody Maker*, July 29, 1950, p. 9.

Page 175. *Recording with Steve Race*   Steve Race, *Musician at Large: An Autobiography* (London: Eyre Methuen, 1979).

Page 175. "I have met so many wonderful people"   Alan Stevens, and Harry Giltrap, "Alan Stevens and Harry Giltrap Meet Josh White," *Jazz Review*, n.d.

Page 176. "The atmosphere was informal"   *Melody Maker*, August 19, 1950, p. 9.

CHAPTER THIRTEEN

Page 178. "They do nothing . . . publication is not false"   Testimony of Hazel Scott Powell, September 22, 1950, in House Committee on Un-American Activities, *Hearings* (Washington, D.C.: Government Printing Office, 1950), pp. 3617–18.

Page 178. *"Red Channels" entry on Josh*   *Red Channels: The Report of Communist Influence in Radio and Television* (New York: American Business Consultants, 1950), pp. 157–58.

Page 179. "In one of her 'My Day' columns . . . entertainers in foreign countries"  *Counterattack,* July 28, 1950.

Page 180. "I got a telephone call . . . left London the next afternoon"  Shelton interview 3.

Pages 180–83. *Customs and FBI interrogations*  The story of Josh's arrival and interrogation is from Shelton interview 3.

Page 183. "I told them I didn't come to attack Robeson"  Shelton, *Song Book,* p. 31. (This interchange seems to have been told to Shelton at another time, as it is not on the interview tape or in the transcript.)

Page 184. *Josh's published HUAC testimony*  White, Josh, "I Was a Sucker for the Communists," *Negro Digest,* December 1950, pp. 26–31.

Pages 186–87. "I began to see what harm"  Florabel Muir, "Reporting," *Los Angeles Mirror,* October 5, 1950, p. 6.

Page 187. "The threats and intimidations of the Klan"  Charlotte Pomerantz, ed., *A Quarter-Century of Un-Americana* (New York: Marzani & Munsell, 1963), p. 47.

Page 187. *HUAC's treatment of black witnesses*  Victor S. Navasky, *Naming Names* (New York: Viking Press, 1980), pp. 186–87.

Page 188. "I've been asked to express my views"  House Committee on Un-American Activities, *Hearings Regarding Communist Infiltration of Minority Groups—Part 1, 81st Cong., 1st sess.* (Washington, D.C.: Government Printing Office, 1949), pp. 481–82.

Page 188. "on the backs of the white workers"  Quoted in Martin Bauml Duberman, *Paul Robeson* (New York: Knopf, 1988), pp. 341–42.

Page 189. *Josh disagreeing with Robeson*  In at least one interview, published by the conservative columnist Florabel Muir in the *Los Angeles Mirror,* October 5, 1950, Josh took a stronger line on Robeson: "When I was a beginner just getting the breaks I looked up to Paul Robeson and thought he was some sort of a god. Now I know he must be sick or something to fall so completely for that subversive stuff. It would be more understandable if he had folks living in Russia and was afraid for them but the way it is I can't understand his motives."

Pages 189–92. *Josh's HUAC testimony*  *Hearings regarding Communist Infiltration of Minority Groups—Part 3 (Testimony of "Josh White")* (Washington, D.C.: Government Printing Office, 1950), pp. 2835–41.

Page 192. *Newspaper reports of Josh's testimony*  "Josh White Insists He Is Not 'Red,' " *Amsterdam News,* September 9, 1950, p. 3; *Washington Times Herald,* September 1, 1950, p. 1; *New York Daily Mirror,* September 2, 1950, p. 4.

Page 193. "They've got me in a vise"  Duberman, *Paul Robeson,* p. 391.

Page 193. "people said I went to Washington and called names"  Shelton, *Song Book,* p. 38.

Page 194. *Eartha Kitt's charge*  Eartha Kitt, *I'm Still Here: Confessions of a Sex Kitten* (New York: Barricade Books, 1991), pp. 76–77 (she gives Josephson the transparent alias "Barnaby Conrad").

Page 194. "police the airwaves . . . judge the facts for themselves."  *Counterattack,* no. 172, September 13, 1950, pp. 1–3.

CHAPTER FOURTEEN

Page 197. "earned the contempt of all"  John Pittman, "Time of the Toad," *Daily Worker,* New York, September 12, 1950, p. 6.

Pages 199–203. *FBI interviews*  All information on Josh's interaction with the FBI is drawn from his FBI file.

Pages 203–4. *Jac Holzman memo*  Jac Holzman, "Memorandum: Josh White — National Republican Club," March 8, 1956, from Len Rosenfeld's files.

Pages 205–6. *Len Rosenfeld–Ed Sullivan correspondence*  Correspondence between Len Rosenfeld and Ed Sullivan, from Rosenfeld's files, is now in the possession of the White family.

Page 206. "This is our new, non-political Josh White"  "The New 'Safe' Josh White," *Daily Worker,* June 14, 1951, p. 6.

Page 207. *Josh's omission from* Sing Out!  "Jerry the Mule" is printed in *Sing Out!* 4, no. 3 (1954). Every issue of the magazine was searched in an attempt to find mention of Josh, but nothing turned up until his obituary except once when he was included in a list of "old . . . warhorses" at the 1965 Newport Folk Festival. It is possible that a still more thorough search would find another such brief mention of him, but considering his stature on the folk scene, that would in no way invalidate the observation that he was pointedly ignored and banished from its pages.

Page 208. "I spent many, many hours with him"  "Josh White Dies at 61; Blues and Ballads Star," *Washington Evening Star,* September 6, 1969, p. A-15.

CHAPTER FIFTEEN

Page 214. "I want to come back to Britain"  "A Letter from Josh White," *Melody Maker,* April 14, 1951.

Page 214. "still a knowing interpreter"  "Josh White Offers Folksong Program," *New York Times,* June 11, 1951.

Page 215. "If anyone had told me"  Josh White to Rene Dannen, letters from Paris and Italy, n.d. (I have taken the liberty of adding a period here and there, as Josh was in the habit of signifying new sentences just by capitalizing the first letter of the first word, without other punctuation. Other than that, I have left all spelling and punctuation as it was in the originals.)

Page 216. "Baby I am so sorry"  Josh White to Rene Dannen, n.p., n.d.

Page 217. "Altho I dident miss a show as yet"  Josh White to Rene Dannen, Stockholm, August 21, 1951.

Page 217. "He uses amplifiers"  Nilsson, "Josh Intime." This is a bit mysterious, as there is no record of Oscar Moore singing, and his brother's name was Johnny, not Buddy. There was a singer named Buddy Moore, who recorded blues with the Sterling Malone Quintet, or Josh might have been thinking of Charles Brown, the superb singer with Johnny Moore's group, or one of the other singers who followed him there.

Page 218. *First solo tour to Sweden*  "Meet Josh White and Daughter," undated clipping from unnamed newspaper, Sheffield, England, courtesy of White family.

Page 218. *British press response to Beverly*  Charles Chilton's clippings, including *Star,* October 1, 1951, *Manchester Evening Chronicle,* October 2, 1951; *Daily Express,* October 3, 1951; *Sheffield Star,* October 4, 1951.

Page 218. *Beverly among popular child entertainers*  "Kid Entertainers: New Crop of Child Stars Delight Audiences," *Ebony,* September 1950.

Page 219. "a bedroom strewn with wires"  "The Girl the BBC Brought Over Catches Up with Her Sums," *Daily Express,* October 3, 1951.

Page 220. "If anybody ever told you"  BBC Home Service broadcast, January 14, 1955.

Page 220. *British audiences*  Not all British listeners knew quite what to make of him. An undated clipping in Chilton's collection reviewing a concert at Westminster's Central Hall quotes two paragraphs from a review of the same concert in the London *Daily Telegraph:* "Josh White, a Carolina Negro, who accompanied himself on the banjo, sant to a large audience last night. . . . By comparison with Mr. Paul Robeson, Mr. White is primitive; and a loud-speaker added nothing to the meagre pleasure afforded by the banjo. But there could be no doubt of the racy authenticity of the singer's native art."

Page 221. "He cain't sing the blues"  Humphrey Lyttelton, *Best of Jazz: Basin Street to Harlem* (London: Penguin, 1980), pp. 72–73.

Pages 222–23. *Eartha Kitt, Orson Welles, and Josh*  Kitt's reminiscences are drawn from her second and third autobiographies: *Alone with Me,* pp. 154–55, 164–65; and *I'm Still Here,* pp. 76–78, 84–85.

Page 224. "I am allowed to do only"  Unidentified clipping from an English newspaper, 1951.

Page 224. "I explained that I would never have consented"  "London Concert Dispute Josh White Flays the 'Minstrel Routine,'" *Melody Maker,* December 1, 1951.

Page 226. "Right now I am some goddam place in Italy"  Josh White to Rene Dannen from Italy, n.d.

## CHAPTER SIXTEEN

Page 228. "again making new box office history"   *Variety,* August 6, 1952, p. 56.

Page 229. "I arrived safe"   Josh White to Rene Dannen, New York, January 1, 1952.

Page 230. "They have been trying to get her out"   Josh White to Rene Dannen, New York, June 3, 1952.

Page 233. *Playing Black Orchid, Chicago*   Arnold Shaw, *Belafonte: An Unauthorized Biography* (Philadelphia: Chilton, 1960), p. 115.

Page 233. *Broken ankle, studying Italian*   "Josh White Breaks Ankle In Chicago Accident," page 53 of an unidentified pocket-sized magazine, apparently published in Chicago and aimed at an African American audience, courtesy of Rene Dannen Gordon.

Page 235. "Belafonte has a lot of s.a."   Quoted in Shaw, *Belafonte,* p. 115.

Page 235. *Black friends of Eleanor Roosevelt*   Roosevelt, "Some of My Best Friends," pp. 17–26.

Page 235. *Dealing with hecklers*   "How to Handle Hecklers," *Ebony,* September 1953, p. 106.

Page 235. *Articles about Josh's kids*   Freda DeKnight, "Date with a Dish: Super Sundaes," *Ebony,* August 1954, p. 76; "School for Child Entertainers," *Ebony,* August 1953, pp. 62–65.

## CHAPTER SEVENTEEN

Page 240. "We certainly had no budget"   Jac Holzman, notes to *The Best of Josh White,* Elektra 75008.

Page 240. *No American record for seven years*   It is possible that there was one previous U.S. recording in the 1950s. Len Rosenfeld's files include correspondence relating to a session that Josh was scheduled to do for CES Recordings of Livingston, New Jersey, on March 26, 1954. Since he was apparently appearing at Ciro's in L.A. on March 27, that session may not have happened. But later correspondence suggests that CES did end up with a recording which it released as Livingston #1085 and licensed to London Records. There is further reference, in a letter from 1959, to this material as having been licensed to Period Records in the United States. As the notes to the Period album, which was supposedly recorded in 1956, refer to running through the session in one night because Josh was flying out to L.A. the next day, it is tempting to guess that this is that album, and that it was recorded before Josh signed with Elektra. There is no proof either way; no one with clearer knowledge has so far come forward; nor have I been able to locate anyone who has heard of CES or Livingston.

Pages 244–45. "Baby I wish I could tell you"   Josh White to Mrs. Josh White, November 22, 1955.

Page 244. Sam Gary Sings *record*  It is not clear which of these was the original issuing label. Laurence seems to have been American, and the liner notes seem to have been written for the U.S. market, but the recording dates place Josh in London.

Page 245. "He was a master . . . nor would he pass one"  Ivor Mairants, *My Fifty Fretting Years* (London: Ashley Mark, 1980).

Pages 245–46. "I want to commend Ivor Mairants"  Josh White and Ivor Mairants, *The Josh White Guitar Method* (London: Bossey & Hawkes, 1956), p. 3.

Page 246. "I found things so bad"  Josh White to Rene Dannen, February 28, 1956.

Page 247. "I havent work as of yet"  Josh White to Rene Dannen, March 21, 1956.

Page 247. "You know what its like"  Josh White to Rene Dannen, June 17, 1956.

Page 247. *Josh and women with money*  Chuck Ramsey, Josh's road manager in the 1960s, was so shocked by this suggestion of mercenary love affairs that I took the precaution of checking with Josh Jr. as to whether it seemed probable that his father would have behaved this way. His response was laconic: "A man's gotta do what a man's gotta do."

Pages 248–49. "The recording techniques . . . taking this just as seriously as we"  Notes to *Josh White Comes A-Visiting*, backed with *Big Bill Broonzy Sings*, Period LP 1209, 1956 (but see note 2 for doubts about the date).

Page 251. "he was singing in a club just round the corner"  Unsigned, but reportedly Alexis Korner, *Josh White Sings: Music of the New World* (a pamphlet from the Granada TV network in England, 1961), p. 28.

Page 252. "right now my fingers are like boils . . . it wouldent do me much good ok?"  Josh White to Rene Dannen, Summer 1957.

Page 254. "an unrelenting voice of conscience"  "Josh White, His Guitar and His Ballads, *Christian Science Monitor,* Boston, October 21, 1957.

Page 256. *Concert in Eaton Hall, Toronto*  Helen McNamara, "It Was Just White Magic," *Toronto Telegram,* January 30, 1958.

CHAPTER EIGHTEEN

Page 260. "Sometimes I'm afraid"  Mary Maher, "Josh White Hero to Folk Song Fans," *Chicago Tribune,* February 12, 1965.

Pages 262–63. "He answered questions . . . 'a lot of fun, too' "  Maher, "Josh White Hero."

Pages 263–64. "Charles is tops . . . doesn't need that stuff"  Josh White, "Sex-Song Sacrilege," *Melody Maker,* April 9, 1960.

Page 264. "Some people think . . . doesn't do them justice, actually"  Quoted in Chris Van Ness, "Josh White Retrospective," *Los Angeles Free Press,* September 18, 1970 (an interview conducted in 1964).

Page 266. "that redoubtable folknik favorite" Unsigned, *Little Sandy Review,* no. 19, p. 30; and Barry Hansen, *Little Sandy Review,* no. 16, p. 8, both undated.

Page 268. "If you can't be understood" Quoted in Nat Hentoff, notes to *Chain Gang Songs, Spirituals and Blues,* Elektra LP 158, 1958.

Page 268. *Advice to teenagers* Josh White, "Josh White Talks to Teens," *Seventeen,* April 1965.

Page 268. Billboard *poll* Ronald Cohen, "Rainbow Quest: Folk Music and American Society, 1940–1970" (manuscript).

Page 269. "What's happened with folk-rock" Quoted in Marvin Schiff, "Josh White and Friends Talk Folk," *Toronto Globe and Mail,* November 12, 1966.

Page 270. "the traditional singers came storming out" Paul Nelson, "What's Happening," *Sing Out!* November 1965.

Page 271. Supporting southern voter registration drive Robert Shelton, " 'Freedom Songs' Sweep North," *New York Times,* July 6, 1963.

Page 271. "I admire Dr. King" Quoted in Schiff, "Josh White and Friends Talk Folk."

CHAPTER NINETEEN

Page 273. "Long before the singing of folk songs" Nat Hentoff, notes to *The House I Live In,* Elektra LP 203, 1961.

Page 276. "There's a very special request" *Josh White — Live!* ABC-Paramount LP 407, 1961.

Page 276. "Lynching and race hatred" Quoted in Alan Anderson, "Negro Folk Singer Welcomes Toronto's Protest on Africa," *Toronto Telegram,* April 27, 1960.

Page 277. "Dinner with the President" broadcast *Dinner with the President,* CBS-TV, January 31, 1963, in the Museum of Television and Radio, New York.

Pages 279–80. *Town Hall concert recorded live* *Josh White at Town Hall,* Mercury LP 20672, 1961.

Page 280. "In five years of operation" *Variety,* January 17, 1962.

Page 280. *Concert at Seattle World's Fair* *Vancouver Sun,* May 28, 1963.

Page 281. "rocky from reaction" *Chicago Evening Bulletin,* December 6, 1962.

Pages 281–82. "At the corner of Rush and Walton . . . watched the party with ogle-eyes" Shelton, *Song Book,* pp. 10–13.

CHAPTER TWENTY

Page 284. *Village Gate appearance* Leonard Harris, "No Sad Notes for Josh White, 35 Years a Star," *New York World-Telegram and Sun,* November 13, 1964.

Page 285. "Entertainers can't 'mark down' "   Quoted by Dorothy Siegel on a sheet sent to Rosenfeld for his approval before publication of her *Glory Road,* but not included in the published book.

Page 287. "As sure as I live and breathe"   *Baltimore Afro-American,* December 22, 1964. Further information came from *Baltimore Sun,* December 18, 1964.

Page 288. "They met as equals"   Lasse Sarri, interviewed for the author by Israel Young, December, 1998.

Page 289. *The Ovation guitar*   Walter Carter, *The History of the Ovation Guitar:* Hal Leonard, 1996, p. 42.

Page 290. "Before long, I want to see her on her own"   Al Cohn, "A Josh-and-Judy Show Packs a Gentle Wallop," clipping from unnamed New York paper, June 23, 1967, in White family collection.

Page 292. "to sell his 'original' guitar"   Author's conversation with Doug Yeager, confirmed by Oscar Brand.

Page 293. *Last visit to West Coast*   Ralph Gleason, "Born Too Early, Died Too Soon," *San Francisco Examiner & Chronicle,* September 14, 1969, p. 34.

# BIBLIOGRAPHY

Anderson, Jervis. *This Was Harlem: A Cultural Portrait, 1900–1950.* New York: Farrar, Straus & Giroux, 1988.

Baggelaar, Kristin, and Donald Milton. *Folk Music: More Than a Song.* New York: Thomas Y. Crowell, 1976.

Balliett, Whitney. *Barney, Bradley, and Max: Sixteen Portraits in Jazz.* New York: Oxford University Press, 1989.

Bastin, Bruce. *Red River Blues: The Blues Tradition in the Southeast.* Urbana: University of Illinois Press, 1986.

Bradford, Roark. *John Henry: A Play.* New York: Harper, 1985.

Bradshaw, Jon. *Dreams That Money Can Buy: The Tragic Life of Libby Holman.* New York: William Morrow, 1985.

Brandt, Nat. *Harlem at War: The Black Experience in WWII.* Syracuse, N.Y.: Syracuse University Press, 1996.

Carter, Walter. *The History of the Ovation Guitar.* Hal Leonard, 1996.

Charters, Samuel B. *The Country Blues.* London: Michael Joseph, 1960.

Chilton, John. *Billie's Blues: Billie Holiday's Story, 1933–1959.* New York: Stein & Day, 1975.

Cogley, John. *Report on Blacklisting II: Radio-Television.* Fund for the Republic, New York: 1956.

Cohen, Ronald D., and Dave Samuelson. *Songs for Political Action: Folkmusic, Topical Songs, and the American Left.* Hambergen, Germany: Bear Family Records, 1996.

Crossman, Richard, ed. *The God That Failed: A Confession.* New York: Harper, 1949.

Cuney, William Waring. *Storefront Church.* Heritage Series, vol. 23. London: Paul Brennan, 1973.

Denning, Michael. *The Cultural Front: The Laboring of American Culture in the Twentieth Century.* New York: Verso, 1997.

Devlin, George A. *South Carolina and Black Migration, 1865–1940: In Search of the Promised Land.* New York: Garland, 1989.

Dixon, Robert, and John Godrich. *Blues and Gospel Records, 1902–1943.* Chigwell, Essex: Storyville, 1982.

———. *Recording the Blues.* New York: Stein & Day, 1970.

Duberman, Martin Bauml. *Paul Robeson.* New York: Knopf, 1988.

Everett, Robert Burke. *Race Relations in South Carolina, 1900–1932.* Ann Arbor, Mich.: University Microfilms, 1970.

Gavin, James. *Intimate Nights: The Golden Age of New York Cabaret.* New York: Grove Weidenfeld, 1991.

Gellert, Lawrence. *Me and My Captain (Chain Gangs): Negro Songs of Protest from the Collection of Lawrence Gellert.* New York: Hours Press, 1939.

Goldsmith, Peter D. *Making People's Music: Moe Asch and Folkways Records.* Washington, D.C.: Smithsonian Institution Press, 1998.

Goodman, Walter. *The Committee: The Extraordinary Career of the House Committee on Un-American Activities.* New York: Farrar, Straus & Giroux, 1968.

Gordon, Max. *Live at the Village Vanguard.* New York: St. Martin's Press, 1980.

Gornick, Vivian. *The Romance of American Communism.* New York: Basic Books, 1977.

Horne, Lena, and Richard Schickel. *Lena.* Garden City, N.Y.: Doubleday, 1965.

Isserman, Maurice. *Which Side Were You On? The American Communist Party during the Second World War.* Middletown, Conn.: Wesleyan University Press, 1982.

Kanfer, Stefan. *A Journal of the Plague Years.* New York: Atheneum, 1973.

Kitt, Eartha. *Alone with Me.* Chicago: Henry Regnery, 1976.

———. *I'm Still Here: Confessions of a Sex Kitten.* New York: Barricade Books, 1991.

Klein, Joe. *Woody Guthrie: A Life.* New York: Knopf, 1980.

Lash, Joseph P. *A World of Love: Eleanor Roosevelt and Her Friends, 1943–1962.* Garden City, N.Y.: Doubleday, 1984.

Lomax, John A. *Adventures of a Ballad Hunter.* New York: Harper, 1971.

Lynn Farnol Group, Inc. *The ASCAP Biographical Dictionary of Composers, Authors, and Publishers.* New York: American Society of Composers, Authors, and Publishers, 1966.

McCarthy, Albert, ed. *Jazzbook 1947.* London: Editions Poetry London, 1947.

Mairants, Ivor. *My Fifty Fretting Years.* London: Ashley Mark, 1980.

Naison, Mark. *Communists in Harlem during the Depression.* Urbana: University of Illinois Press, 1983.

Navasky, Victor S. *Naming Names.* New York: Viking Press, 1980.

Nichols, Charles H., ed. *Arna Bontemps–Langston Hughes Letters, 1925–1967.* New York: Paragon House, 1990.

Oliver, Paul. *Blues Off the Record.* New York: Da Capo Press, 1984.

———. *Songsters and Saints: Vocal Traditions on Race Records.* Cambridge: Cambridge University Press, 1984.

Ottley, Roi. *New World A-Coming.* Boston: Houghton Mifflin, 1943.

Perry, Hamilton Darby. *Libby Holman: Body and Soul.* Boston: Little, Brown, 1983.

Pomerantz, Charlotte, ed. *A Quarter-Century of Un-Americana.* New York: Marzani & Munsell, 1963.

Race, Steve. *Musician at Large: An Autobiography.* London: Eyre Methuen, 1979.

*Red Channels: The Report of Communist Influence in Radio and Television.* New York: American Business Consultants, 1950.

Rust, Brian. *Jazz Records, 1897–1942.* Chigwell, Essex: Storyville, 1970.

Rust, Brian, with Allen G. Debus. *The Complete Entertainment Discography: From the Mid-1890s to 1942.* New Rochelle, N.Y.: Arlington House, 1973.

Seeger, Pete, with Peter Blood. *Where Have All the Flowers Gone: A Singer's Stories, Songs, Seeds, Robberies.* Bethlehem, Pa.: Sing Out, 1993.

Shaw, Arnold. *Belafonte: An Unauthorized Biography.* Philadelphia: Chilton, 1960.

Shelton, Robert, with Walter Raim. *The Josh White Song Book.* Chicago: Quadrangle Books, 1963.

Siegel, Dorothy Schainman. *The Glory Road: The Story of Josh White.* New York: Harcourt Brace Jovanovich, 1982.

Southern, Eileen. *The Music of Black Americans.* New York: Norton, 1971.

Walker, Margaret. *Richard Wright: Daemonic Genius.* New York: Warner Books, 1988.

White, Josh, and Ivor Mairants. *The Josh White Guitar Method.* London: Boosey & Hawkes, 1956.

Willens, Doris. *Lonesome Traveler: The Life of Lee Hays.* New York: Norton, 1988.

Wolfe, Charles, and Kip Lornell. *The Life and Legend of Leadbelly.* New York: HarperCollins, 1992.

Wright, Richard. *American Hunger.* New York: Harper & Row, 1977.

# INDEX

Columbia Concert Management, 120, 124

Communist Party, 54; and African Americans, 76–77, 81–84; and folk music, 73–74, 186; and Josh, 83, 181–83, 186–87, 189–91, 200–201; and postwar change, 145–46

Cuney, Waring, 79–80, 87–88, 311

Cutler, Jean, 48, 50–51

Dallas, Karl, 221

Dannen, Rene, 214–19, 223, 225, 229, 246, 252–53

Davis, Benjamin, 143, 179, 200–201

Davis, Reverend Gary, 5, 19, 21, 34, 266

Dee, Ruby, 163

De Paur, Leonard, 49–52, 54–56, 61–65, 68, 88

Dixon, Dean, 139

Dorsey, Thomas A. ("Georgia Tom"), 28, 44

Draper, Paul, 162

Dunham, Katherine, 122

Dyer-Bennett, Richard, 63, 103–4, 151, 206

Dylan, Bob, 259–60, 264–65, 268–70

Eldridge, Roy, 166–67, 234

Erlichman, Marty, 255–56, 261, 285

Fallon, Jack, 276

Federal Bureau of Investigation (FBI): interviews with Josh, 181–83, 199–203; blackmail rumor, 185–86

Fitzgerald, Ella, 139

Folk music: and the left, 72–74, 234; 1940s revival, 57; 1950s/1960s revival, 256, 258–60, 265–70

Francis, Panama, 249

Fuller, Blind Boy, 32–33

Fuller, Perry, 2, 9, 11, 27

Fuller, Sam, 2

Gabler, Milt, 153

Gary, Sam, 60, 76, 79, 83, 87, 98, 155, 161, 218–20, 225, 229, 232, 244, 249

Gary, Sue, 229, 232

Gaskin, Leonard, 249

Gateway Singers, The, 251

Gellert, Lawrence, 62, 64, 307

Gillespie, Dizzy, 83

Glazer, Tom, 116

Golden Gate Quartet, The, 57, 65–66, 68–70, 74, 86, 221

Gooding, Cynthia, 159, 242

Gordon, Max, 91–93, 102, 228

Greenhill, Manny, 135, 207, 254

Grossman, Albert, 155, 255–56

Grossman, Stefan, 246

Gruber, Harry "Jay", 237, 240, 254–55

Guthrie, Woody, 57, 64, 66, 74–76, 140, 149, 264, 266, 269, 299; on Josh and Leadbelly, 92–93

Hall, Edmond, 90, 123

Hammond, John, 58, 61, 63, 65, 75–76, 79, 103

Handy, William Christopher, 17, 87–88

Harlem, 35–36, 48, 94, 108, 131, 165–67

Hartnett, Vincent, 177, 184

Hawes, Bess Lomax, 67, 94

Hays, Lee, 75–76, 87, 93, 140, 196–97

Hefner, Hugh, 275, 278

Hendricks, Jon, 39

Hentoff, Nat, 273

59; *Chain Gang,* 62–65, 118, 121, 142; *Southern Exposure,* 79–82, 86–89, 118, 143; *Songs by Josh White,* 117; Italian album, 227; *The Story of John Henry,* 241, 243; *Josh at Midnight,* 241–43, 247, 273; *Josh Sings Ballads and Blues,* 241, 243; English album (*Josh White's Blues*), 244–45; Period album (*Josh White Comes A-Visitin'*), 248–49, 320; *The Josh White Stories,* 249–50; *Chain Gang Songs,* 268, 273; *Spirituals and Blues,* 273; *The House I Live In,* 273; *Empty Bed Blues,* 236, 273; *Josh White Live,* 275–76; *At Town Hall,* 279–80; *In the Beginning,* 281–82; *The Best of Josh White,* 296

recording sessions: with Joe Taggart, 22–23, 25; as accompanist, 24–25; early 78s, 29–34; "cover songs," 31; gospel 78s, 33–34; with Leroy Carr 41; with Buddy Moss, 43–44; first comeback 57–59; with Carolinians 61–65; with Almanac Singers, 78–79; with Libby Holman, 97–98; with Union Boys, 116; in England, 175, 212; with Sam Gary, 244; with White family; 280; unissued sessions, 280–82

record labels: Paramount, 20, 22, 33; Gennett, 20; Herwin, 22; ARC (American Record Corporation, including Banner, Melotone, Oriole, Perfect, Romeo), 28–33; Vocalion, 33; Blue Note 57–59; Musicraft, 58–59; Columbia, 61, 63, 65; Harmony, 65; Keynote, 79, 118; Conqueror, 90; V-discs, 116,

119–20; Asch, 116–19; Decca, 118, 123, 153–55; English Decca, 175, 245; Apollo, 154; Vogue, 172; Melodisc, 175; London, 175, 249, 320; Elektra, 240–43, 247–50, 261, 266, 273–74, 296; Marble Arch, 244; Mercury, 244, 279–82; Emarcy, 244; Period, 248–49, 320; ABC-Paramount, 249–50; Mirwood, 282; Livingston, 320

religion, 3, 8–9

repertoire 27, 32, 98, 117–18, 235, 241–43

residences, 47, 48, 53, 288

sex life: womanizing, 156, 158–61, 215–17, 231; rumored romances, 122, 159; sex appeal, 112–13, 158–61

songs: "Ballad of the Boll Weevil," 219–20; "Careless Love," 20, 80; "Dorie Miller," 106–7; "Freedom Road," 107–8, 149, 191; "Greenville Sheik," 30; "Hard Times Blues," 80–81, 118, 277; "The House I Live In," 109, 139, 147, 166, 191, 276; "Jelly Jelly," 165–66, 275; "John Henry," 241, 275, 277; "Little Brother Blues," 30; "The Man Who Couldn't Walk Around," 150, 152; "Miss Otis Regrets," 118; "On Top of Old Smoky," 98, 212, 270; "One Meat Ball," 118–21, 123, 132, 139–41; "The Riddle Song," 105, 115–16, 118, 140, 164, 242; "Scandalous and a Shame," 22–23; "Scarlet Ribbons," 276; "Strange Fruit," 110–12, 118, 121, 139–41, 144, 147, 149, 166, 191, 202,

White, Josh (*continued*)
276; "Trouble," 64, 118,
"Uncle Sam Says," 84–86, 108
songwriting, 30, 62–64, 79–80,
105–8, 311
television, 170; *Hootenanny*, 270,
283–84; *Playboy's Penthouse*, 275;
Granada Television, 275; *Dinner
with the President*, 277, 283
tours: with Libby Holman, 120–
22; with Josephine Premice,
138–44; Australia, 285; Canada, 233; England, 172–76,
210–16, 218–21, 224, 225,
243–46, 263, 275–76; Europe,
280, 285; France, 172, 175,
222–25; Hawaii, 252; Israel,
275; Italy, 226–27; Mexico, 86;
Scandinavia, 171–72, 179, 217,
275, 288; Spain, 275; United
States, 155–56, 162, 280, 285
vocal style, 31–32, 123, 136, 151–
52, 268, 274
White, Josh Jr., 113, 115, 126–27,
157, 164, 206, 233, 277, 284,
286–88, 294–95; birth, 68, 89;
musical debut, 132–33; performing with Josh, 155, 167, 191, 235,
279–80; acting, 168–70; relation-
ship with Josh, 235–37, 288; solo
career, 289–90, 298
White, Judith, 162, 279–80, 288,
290, 294
Williams, Clarence, 40–41, 305
Williams, Cootie, 274
Williams, Mary Lou, 103–4, 110,
122
Williams, Mayo, 23, 28
Williamson, Sonny Boy, 281–82
Wilson, Orlandus, 68, 86
Wilson, Stan, 251–52
Wilson, Teddy, 87
Wolfe, Jacques, 50–51
Wood, John Stephens, 187, 195
Woodward, Isaac, 182
World War II, 82, 84
Wright, Richard, 81–83, 88; notes to
*Southern Exposure*, 81–82, 143

Zaret, Hy, and Lou Singer, 118–20

ELIJAH WALD went off to Europe as a traveling minstrel at age eighteen, and spent most of the next dozen years wandering the world with his guitar, as well as touring the United States and recording two albums, *Songster, Fingerpicker, Shirtmaker* and *Street Corner Cowboy.* In the 1980s, he began writing for *The Boston Globe,* becoming the newspaper's "world music" critic, as well as writing on American and international music for various magazines. He assisted Ruth Hubbard in writing *Exploding the Gene Myth* (Beacon Press, 1993, 1997), acted as writer and music consultant for the PBS series *River of Song: Music Along the Mississippi,* and wrote the accompanying book (St. Martin's Press, 1998). He is currently completing a book on the contemporary Mexican corrido.